728.81 £2-

Norman Castles
in Britain

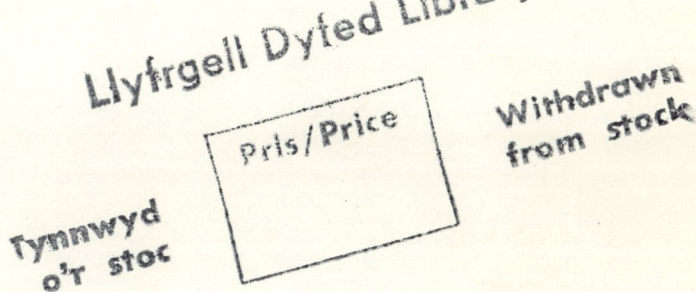

for Ann

Dover Castle

Norman Castles in Britain

D. F. Renn

SECOND EDITION
64 photographs and 278 drawings

John Baker
Humanities Press

© 1968, 1973
D. F. RENN

First published in Great Britain in 1968 by
JOHN BAKER PUBLISHERS LTD
4, 5 & 6 Soho Square
London W1V 6AD

First published in the U.S.A. in 1968 by
HUMANITIES PRESS INC.
303 Park Avenue South
New York, N.Y.

Second edition published 1973

UK ISBN: 0 212 97002 X
USA ISBN 0 391 00276 7

CARMARTHENSHIRE COUNTY COUNCIL

COUNTY LIBRARY

CLASS...... 728·81

Acc. No. 583,718

Printed in Great Britain by offset lithography
by Billing & Sons Limited, Guildford and London

CONTENTS

		page	
	Preface		vii
1	Fortification in England and Normandy before 1066		1
2	The parts of a Norman castle		9
3	The building of Norman castles		12
4	Sources of evidence for castle-building		21
5	The castles of the Conqueror, 1066–86		27
6	The completion of the Conquest, 1086–1138		34
7	The castles of the Anarchy, 1136–54		46
8	Rectangular and polygonal keeps in the reign of Henry II, 1154–89		54
9	Castle halls and experiments in fortification, 1160–1216		63
10	The rise and fall of the Norman castle		70
	Glossary		76
	Alphabetical Gazetteer		83
	Gazetteer: Addenda for the Second Edition		352
	County Guide to Castles		358

Preface

In 1945 I searched the downs above Folkestone in vain for the 'Norman Fort' shown on the one-inch map. Later on, when I realized that not all castles were built of stone, I was led to inquire into the evidence for their date and function. This involved the visiting — and revisiting — of nearly all the castles in the British Isles which might be Norman, together with the abstracting of the published evidence, both archaeological and documentary. The major part of this book is a *corpus* of this evidence; it would be considerably larger if it included all those earthworks of the *motte* and bailey type whose sites are unexcavated and whose history is unknown. Excavation proves the Norman origin of one or more sites each year and this is usually recorded in *Medieval Archaeology*, the journal of the Society for Medieval Archaeology. No work can claim to be definitive, but to the best of my knowledge and belief I have included all discoveries up to the time of publication.

Although several general works on castles have been published, only one substantial study of Norman castles has been made. Mrs. E. S. Armitage's *The Early Norman Castles of the British Isles* (London, 1912) effectively ended the controversy on *mottes* in favour of a Norman (rather than a Saxon) origin. Concerned as it was with early earthworks, it did not cover the whole of the Norman period; English castles in particular were only dealt with if of eleventh-century origin. The architectural evidence was dealt with very briefly and without illustration. In the fifty years since this work appeared more evidence has been excavated in the field and in the library, but, although royal castles have been extensively documented in *The History of the King's Works* (London, 1963), and many individual castles studied separately, no general survey

PREFACE

of Norman military architecture has been made. The present reappraisal has enabled a more logical chronology of Norman castle building to be developed and firmer dates to be given to artistic and military features of Romanesque architecture. It cannot be the last word; the Royal Archaeological Institute began in 1967 a research programme into the origin of the medieval castle which may modify certain of the statements made in the early chapters.

I am most grateful to the Trustees of *Antiquity* and the Councils of the Society for Medieval Archaeology and the British and Cambrian Archaeological Associations for permission to use material that first appeared in their journals. My thanks are due to those landowners who gave me permission to visit their castles and to those archaeologists who have told me of their discoveries. The facilities of the library of the Society of Antiquaries of London and the help of its librarian, John Hopkins, have been invaluable.

For this second edition a number of corrections and additions have been made, many being due to Mr. D. J. C. King.

ACKNOWLEDGEMENTS

I wish to express my thanks to a number of organizations who own the copyright of the plates and who kindly allowed them to be reproduced in this book. They are as follows: the Department of the Environment for permission to include Plates IV, V, VII, VIII, IX, XIII, XIV, XVI (Farnham), XVII (Goodrich), XVIII, XX, XXI, XXXII, XXXV (Oxford), XXVI, XXVII, XLIII and XLVI; the National Monuments Record for plates II (Barnard Castle), III, X, XII, XVI (Durham), XIX (*right*), XXIV, XXV, XXVI, XXVII (Middleham), XXVIII, XXX, XXXIII, XXXIV, XXXV (Pembroke), XXXVIII, XXXIX, XL (*above*), XLI, XLII, XLVI, XLVII and XLVIII, Crown Copyright is reserved; the Ulster Tourist Board and J. Allan Cash for Plates VI and XXIII; to Bord Fáilte Eireann for Plates XXIX and XLV and to Philipson Studios for Plate XXXI.

Plates I, II, (Bishop's Waltham), XI, XVII (Framlingham), XIX (*left*), XXII, XXVII (Lydford), and XL (*below*) are my own copyright.

D. F. RENN

PLANS

The earthwork castle plans have been chosen to illustrate the layouts adopted by the Normans: necessarily only a selection can be printed here. On the other hand, plans of nearly all substantial buildings are given. The main exceptions are those sites currently being excavated, where a plan would be rapidly out of date owing to fresh discoveries. Standing Norman walls are shown in solid black, foundations and earlier walls in outline. Later walls, doorways and other openings have been omitted. Damaged walling is indicated by ragged ends. The various floor plans are numbered, commencing with the lowest above any solid basement. Where two numbers are given for one plan, that in brackets is generally similar to the plan of the other and so has not been drawn separately. An open circle denotes the well, and contemporary churches and chapels are marked †. Slopes are indicated by hachures — 'tadpoles' with their tails running down the slope, the heads being squared off if the slope is largely natural.

The sketch plans of earthworks are nearly all reproduced at a scale of 200 ft to the inch (1/2400) and those of buildings at 32 ft to the inch (1/384). A few large but simple plans are reproduced at one-half of these scales, 400 ft to the inch (1/4800) and 64 ft to the inch (1/768). Drawn scales are only given for these latter, referring to all the plans on that page. As far as space and scale allow, they are arranged in alphabetical order.

1	Traces of Wooden Castles: Abinger (after Brian Hope-Taylor in *Archaeological Journal* CVII), Farnham, Leicester and Rayleigh	Page 85
2	Acre	87
3	Adare, Aldingbourne, Allington, Appleby, Ascot d'Oilly (after E. M. Jope in *Antiquaries' Journal* XXXIX) and Athlone	91
4	Aldford, Anstey and Ashley	95
5	Bamburgh and Barnard	99
6	Arundel, Barwick in Elmet, Bishopton and Bramber	101
7	Barnstaple, Basing, and Brinklow	103
8	Benington, Berkeley, and Berkhamsted (keep)	106
9	Berkhamsted and Bletchingley	108
10	Bowes, Brandon, Bridgnorth and Bristol (after K. Marshall in *Transactions of the Bristol and Gloucestershire Archaeological Society* LXX)	114

PLANS

11	Bronllys and Brough	Page 119
12	Brougham and Bungay	123
13	Burwell, Cardiff and Carisbrooke	125
14	Caldicot and Canterbury	129
15	Carlingford and Carlisle	133
16	Carrickfergus (keep) and Cary (after T. H. Francis in *Proceedings of the Somersetshire Archaeological and Natural History Society* XXXVI)	137
17	Chepstow, Chilham and Christchurch	141
18	Buckenham, Clare and Elmley	145
19	Caus	147
20	Chartley, Clun, Coity and Dingestow	149
21	Clitheroe, Clun (keep), Craigie and Cubbie Roo's	150
22	Colchester 1	152
23	Colchester 2	153
24	Conisbrough (keep), Corfe (hall)	156
25	Corfe (keep), Dolbadarn and Dolwyddelan	158
26	Carrickfergus and Devizes (after E. H. Stone, *Devizes Castle*)	165
27	Conisbrough, Corfe and Durham	167
28	Dover 1 and 2	170
29	Dover 3 and 4	171
30	Duffield, Dundrum, Elmley (keep) (after H. S. Braun), Ewloe and Exeter (gatehouse)	175
31	Eardisley, Egremont, Exeter	181
32	Dinefwr and Eynsford	186
33	Farnham, Godard's and Helmsley	188
34	Framlingham	192
35	Goodrich, Grosmont, Guildford and Kenfig	198
36	Hedingham and Leicester	203
37	Hanslope, Kenilworth and Knepp	209
38	Kenilworth (keep) and Kirkwall	213
39	Kidwelly, Kilpeck and Meppershall	217
40	Lancaster and Ludlow	221
41	Launceston, Lewes and Longtown	224
42	Inchiquin, Longtown (keep), Lydford and Lyonshall	234
43	Lincoln, Marlborough and Nether Stowey	236
44	Lydney (after D. A. Casey, *Antiquaries' Journal* XI) and Morgraig (after J. W. Rodger, *Transactions of the Cardiff Naturalists' Society* XXXVIII)	237
45	Maynooth, Merdon, Monmouth and Newark	241
46	Middleham	244
47	Midhurst, Mileham and Mitford	246
48	Nenagh and Newcastle upon Tyne	256

PLANS

49	Norham and Norwich	*Page*	260
50	Norwich (continued)		261
51	Oakham, Odiham (keep), Okehampton and Orford		264
52	Odiham, Ogmore and Oxford		266
53	Old Sarum and Ongar		268
54	Newcastle Bridgend, Old Sarum (keep) and Prudhoe		269
55	Pembroke, Pendragon and Peveril (keep)		274
56	Peveril, Pickering, Plympton and Rayleigh		277
57	Pevensey and Rushen		278
58	Portchester and Richmond		282
59	Portchester (keep)		284
60	Richmond (hall and keep)		286
61	Pleshey, Sauvey and Windsor		287
62	Restormel and Rothesay		292
63	Rising and Saltwood		296
64	Rising (keep) and Scarborough (keep)		297
65	Rochester and Stokesay		300
66	Rochester (continued), Sutton Valence (after G. K. Horner) and Tintagel		301
67	Scarborough, Sherborne and Thetford		309
68	Sherborne (keep), Tamworth and Taunton		320
69	Tomen y Mur and Tonbridge		325
70	Sween and White Tower of London		327
71	Tickhill (after R. Young, reproduced in *The History of the King's Works* Vol. I), by permission of the Controller of Her Majesty's Stationery Office. White Tower of London (continued) and Tretower		328
72	White Tower of London (concluded) and Trim (keep)		329
73	Tomen y Faedre, Tomen y Rhodwydd, Totnes, Tower of London and Trematon		331
74	Trim, Warkworth, Weeting and Wiston		334
75	Walden, Wareham, Warkworth (gatehouse), Wattlesborough and West Malling		343
76	Waytemore and White Castle		346

MAPS

A	Castles in Northern France before 1066	*Page*	6
B	Castles built between 1066 and 1071		13
C	Castles built by 1086		15
D	General map of *mottes*		16
E	Castles of the Anarchy around Cambridge (see p. 50)		53
F	The demilitarized zone around Leicester (see p. 51)		53

PLATES

BETWEEN PAGES 98–9

I The shell-keep on the *motte* at Arundel
II Barnard Castle (*above*) and Bishop's Waltham (*below*)
III The stone-cased *motte* at Berkeley
IV The keep at Brough
V The keep at Brougham
VI The keep at Carrickfergus
VII The early hall at Chepstow
VIII The hall at Christchurch
IX The keep at Colchester
X The cylindrical keep at Conisbrough
XI Corfe Castle
XII The ruined and altered keep at Coity (*above*) and the keep at Dolwyddelan (*below*)
XIII The Avranches tower at Dover
XIV Part of the entrance staircase of the keep at Dover
XV The two chapels in the keep at Dover
XVI The hall doorway at Durham (*left*) and the entrance to the shell-keep at Farnham (*right*)

BETWEEN PAGES 178–9

XVII The wall of the first hall at Framlingham (*above*) and the keep at Goodrich (*below*)
XVIII Guildford keep
XIX The keep at Hedingham (*right*) and the entrance doorway (*left*)
XX The keep at Kenilworth
XXI Lunn's Tower of the curtain wall at Kenilworth
XXII The round keep at Longtown
XXIII The great gatehouse at Ludlow with its entrance blocked thus converting it into a keep
XXIV Part of the blind wall-arcade of the entrance passage inside the keep at Ludlow (*above*) and the round nave of the Norman chapel (*below*)

PLATES

XXV	A close-up of the west doorway of the chapel at Ludlow (*left*) and the diapered soffit of the chancel arch (*right*)
XXVI	Six capitals from the blind arcade within the nave of Ludlow castle chapel
XXVII	The late keep at Lydford (*above*) and the rectangular keep at Middleham (*below*)
XXVIII	The hall at Monmouth (*above*) and the gatehouse at Newark (*below*)
XXIX	The round keep at Nenagh
XXX	The remarkable gateway at Newcastle Bridgend (*left*) and the ornamental arches of the chapel in the keep at Newcastle upon Tyne (*right*)
XXXI	The entrance and postern doorways to the keep at Newcastle upon Tyne
XXXII	Restored ornamental details of the keep at Norwich

BETWEEN PAGES 274–5

XXXIII	The elaborately sculptured arcades of the hall at Oakham
XXXIV	The three large turrets of the polygonal keep at Orford (*left*) and twin window openings (*right*)
XXXV	A contrast in keeps: the plain stepped tower at Oxford (*left*) and the domed round tower at Pembroke, with its two-light window over the door (*right*)
XXXVI	The keep at Portchester
XXXVII	The original gateway at Richmond which was converted into a tower with a separate upper entrance
XXXVIII	Richmond Castle from the south
XXXIX	The highly decorated exterior of Castle Rising (*above*) and the entrance stairs and middle doorway (*below*)
XL	The keep at Rochester with its forebuilding (*above*) and the arcaded cross-wall (*below*)
XLI	The surviving half of the keep at Scarborough and its early curtain walls (*above*) and the gatehouse at Sherborne (*below*)
XLII	The timber gallery at Stokesay
XLIII	Castle Sween with its central round-headed entrance
XLIV	The White Tower of London
XLV	Trim Castle from the air
XLVI	The Norman hall and later round tower at Tretower (*above*) and the keep at Usk (*below*)
XLVII	St. Leonard's Tower, West Malling
XLVIII	The Round Tower at Windsor

CHAPTER I

Fortification in England and Normandy before 1066

To provide the setting for a survey of Norman castles in Britain, a little must be said of the development of fortification before the Norman Conquest. Man has had to defend himself against other creatures (including his fellow man) ever since he first made enemies. The simplest protection round his hut — or group of huts — was a fence of wood or stone, whichever material lay nearest to hand. If he dug a ditch and piled the spoil up as a bank, the fence itself could be made difficult to approach. Considerable earthworks of irregular plan were erected in prehistoric Britain, but the coming of the Romans introduced a system of military engineering of standard design. The standard Roman fortress was rectangular (often with rounded corners), within which the buildings to be defended were laid out in a regular pattern. The defences would be ditched around, with earth and timber or masonry walls; the buildings defended might range from an entire city, like London or Colchester, to a small watch-tower like that on the cliff within Scarborough castle. The idea survived the collapse of the Roman empire; what did vanish was the comprehensive military system behind it, in which each fortress had its appointed task and every tiny fortlet was a link in the chain.

Thus, when Scandinavian expansion gave rise to Viking raids on coastal market-towns, curvilinear versions of Roman forts were built at Dorestadt and Hamburg at the turn of the ninth century. Charlemagne sought to protect his empire's coasts by defending the mouths of the rivers, but, after his death in A.D. 811, the collapse of central authority allowed the Vikings to penetrate the Loire and Seine valleys as far as Paris. Anglo-Saxon England was equally powerless to put up an effective resistance, and in A.D. 865 the raiders were confidently overwintering in England within simple bank and ditch defences to protect themselves and their ships. However, when Alfred and a small company built a fort in Athelney in A.D. 878 and inflicted the defeat of Edington on the invaders, major Viking raids were then switched to France. The breathing-space was used for the creation in southern England of a series of fortified towns with permanent garrisons, supported by men and money from the districts they were designed to protect.

These *burhs* lay beside the rivers that were the Viking entry routes, copying the Carolingian system of the beginning of the century, for the forts of Charlemagne were not solely coastal; late Carolingian pottery has been found under the ringbank at Hilden near Dusseldorf. A half-built fort near the mouth of the Lympne was stormed by the Vikings in A.D. 892, and the Danish fort on the Lea was blockaded by two forts built by Alfred in A.D. 895, one on either side of the river. Most of the *burhs* were the work of Edward the Elder and Aethelflaed, lady of the Mercians, in the period A.D. 910–23. Sometimes a second *burh* was built on the opposite bank of a river to the first, as at Bedford, Buckingham, Hertford, and Stamford; at Nottingham the *burh* was linked to an abandoned Danish fort by a bridge. Details of the defences vary; at Eddisbury and Witham prehistoric hill-forts were strengthened by clearing out the silted ditches and increasing the height of the bank; at London and Colchester the Roman town walls were repaired and perhaps a bastion or two added. Excavation at Cricklade, Lydford, and Wareham has revealed ditches and stone-faced ramparts, and Edward the Elder is said to have enclosed Towcester with a stone wall.

Like their predecessors, these fortifications were communal ones for collective defence. Where and when the 'private' castle first appeared in Europe is debatable, since the idea is difficult to define rigorously. The distinction between the defence of a small community and that of a lord and his personal staff probably went unrecognized at first. Contemporary writers use the Latin *castellum* and the Saxon *castel* indiscriminately for all sorts of defences and even for unfortified towns. Circular enclosures of bank and ditch were built in many places, particularly Flanders and Westphalia, in the ninth and early tenth centuries. Several have been excavated;

the usual approach was by a causeway across the ditch to an entrance cut through the bank, revetted and defended by a timber tower over the passageway. The buildings within might be neatly sited against the bank, or just put up higgledy-piggledy as need arose.

Since any fortification offered a possible threat to authority, the legal theory grew up that such fortresses were the king's and only held on licence by loyal vassals. Charles the Bald allowed the construction of 'castles, forts and hedgeworks' in A.D. 862; although their destruction was ordered in A.D. 864, reconstruction was permitted in A.D. 869. The thesis was strongly upheld in Normandy, where the eleventh-century Customs of the Duchy forbade the erection of castles without licence, and in turn in England where a formal royal 'licence to crenellate' became a necessity from the beginning of the thirteenth century (if not before) for each fortress built, except by the king's direct command.

In A.D. 911, Charles the Simple gave Rollo and his *nortmanni* the region around Rouen, between the Epte, the Orne and the sea. Although restrained by the powerful duchy of Maine beyond the Avre to the south, the 'Normans' had pushed their other frontiers to the Bresle and Vire valleys within a generation. At about this time we begin to hear of individual towers, unconnected with churches, first in northern France and soon afterward in Anjou. After A.D. 975 the Counts of Anjou built many castles in the middle Loire region.

Some at least of the castles were of stone, and the two-storey hall on a hillock in the park of the Château de Langeais is accepted as the work of Fulk Nerra about A.D. 992. Parts of the keeps at Beaugency and Montrichard need not be much later. The origin of the defensive stone tower is still obscure, but may be sought in the Byzantine empire — there is a keep at Saône (Sayhun) near Antioch dating from A.D. 976, while early ninth-century stone halls can be traced in Charlemagne's palace at Aachen and in a group of hall-churches near Oviedo.

Excavations in the Low Countries and the Rhineland have shown examples of low dwelling-mounds raised by stages into high *mottes*, but the date of this development cannot yet be closely defined. Later examples are Irish raths raised into *mottes* by the Normans in the twelfth and thirteenth centuries. Compared with masonry, earthwork is relatively quick and easy both to build and to destroy, and it is dangerous to assign dates to an earthwork without knowledge of the entire history of a site.

Four ring-works in Denmark exhibit a rigorously geometrical layout; three date from the late tenth century, but the fourth and largest may have been built some fifty years later. In each case an accurately circular area, surrounded by a perimeter track, was divided into quadrants by two main roadways passing through gaps in the stone-faced bank and ditch, with a timber tower at each entrance. At Trelleborg, the first to be fully excavated, each quadrant contained four similar barrack blocks, arranged round a square. Such a highly mathematical design suggests a limited and precise function; naval barracks for the Viking fleet seems probable. During the Viking siege of London in 1016, the Danes built earthworks 'so that no one could get in or out'.

From the time of William the Conqueror's inheritance of Normandy in 1035, castles played an important part in the warfare on the southern borders of his duchy. When Geoffrey Martel, count of Anjou from 1044, began pushing northward, castles were built in Maine. The first castles were in those frontier districts where loyalties were likely to be divided, and the counts and dukes both endeavoured to put their own *vicomtes* in charge of them. During William's minority, the castle of Tillières was dismantled after a successful siege on his behalf; later his steward, William fitz Osbern, was to fortify Breteuil against a rebuilt Tillières. After his triumph at Val ès Dunes, William ordered the destruction of all unlicensed castles, and the remaining opposition centred on the castle of Brionne, which held out until 1050 despite his siege-towers. Again in 1052 we find William, based on the castle of St Aubin, using a wooden tower to besiege Arques.

The Customs of the Duchy of Normandy (1091) forbade the erection of castles without licence, specifying that no ditches were to be dug so deep that the earth could not be thrown out without staging, and that neither high palisades nor *propugnaculis et alatoriis* (bastions and galleries?) were to be made. No defences of any sort were to be made on rocks or islands (presumably because of their natural strength) and the duke could take possession of any castle, even if licensed, whenever he considered it desirable. So, despite a marriage alliance with Flanders, and the recent deaths of the king of France and the count of Anjou which had put him in an extremely strong position, William still found it necessary to control the castles of his duchy. Map A shows some of the castles of Normandy, shortly before the invasion of England.

In England, continued Viking pressure led to alliance with Normandy. Disputes arising from the use of Norman harbours by Viking pirates were settled for a time by a treaty of 991. Aetheldred married the duke of Normandy's sister, and was forced to flee to his brother-in-law before Cnut's accession in 1018. Thus Edward the Confessor was brought up at the Norman court, and some Normans accompanied him on his return to England in 1042. The 'new burgh' (Hastings?), Steyning, Rye, and Winchelsea were given to Fécamp Abbey, and Edward's brother-in-law Ralf later became Earl of Hereford, ruling a military province on the uneasy frontier with the Welsh.

Under the (corrected) date of September 1051, the Anglo-Saxon Chronicle records that 'the foreigners had built *aene castel* in Herefordshire in Earl Swein's territory and inflicted all the injuries and insults they possibly could upon the king's men in that region'. That the foreigners were Normans is made clear by later references to the Frenchmen who were 'in the castle' or 'from the castle'; one manuscript of the Chronicle used *Normannis* instead of 'foreigners'. Duke William visited Edward that winter, but most of the Normans were expelled when Earl Godwin returned from exile in the following autumn (1052):

> 'When archbishop Robert and the Frenchmen learnt this, they took their horses and some went west to Pentecost's castle, some north to Robert's castle . . .'

and Florence of Worcester supplements the *Chronicle* here by mentioning the surrender of castles by *Osbernus vero cognomento Pentecost et socius ejus Hugo*.

Where were these castles, and what were they like? It is a reasonable guess that the first castle in Herefordshire was in Hereford

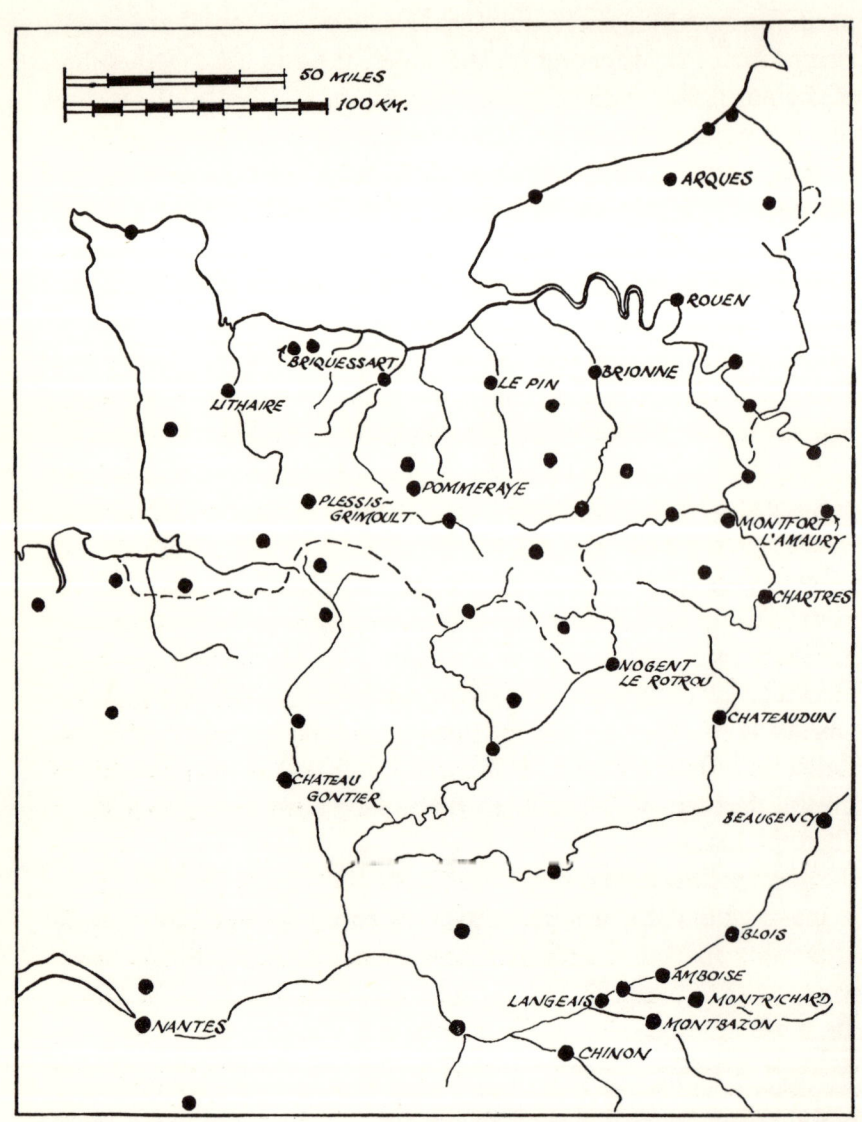

Map A

itself. The city was fortified by Earl Harold in 1055 after the Welsh rising and the castle certainly existed by 1067, but what, if anything, of the remaining earthwork dates from 1051 it is impossible to say. Since it is not clear where all the Frenchmen were when they heard of their enemy's triumphant return in 1052, we cannot be certain whence they fled. Pentecost's castle could be that later called Ewyas Harold, since its tenant in 1086 also held manors that his nephew Osbern had held in 1051-2. Ewyas was rebuilt by William fitz Osbern before 1071, so that any pre-Conquest work may have been swept away. Robert's castle has been identified as Canfield or Clavering in Essex, since these manors were held by Robert fitz Wymarc, who came over from Normandy with Edward in 1042. It cannot be Rayleigh, since Robert's son built that castle on land which had not belonged to his father. The context of the reference might indicate that the refuge was the Archbishop Robert's castle. Both Robert and Hugh are common names, so certainty here is impossible. The Hugh's Castle on the border between Carmarthenshire and Glamorgan seems an unlikely spot for a refuge, given the turbulence of the Welsh under Gruffyd ap Llewelyn. In 1055 Earl Harold took the English militia to the Black Mountains, camping beyond the Golden Valley in a show of strength, but only a combined operation along the coastal strip of Wales from north and south finally conquered Gruffyd in 1062-3.

As part of his celebrated oath to Duke William, Harold is said (by William of Poitiers) to have promised to build and provision a castle at Dover and wherever else he wished. Until recently, the ring-work around the Roman lighthouse and late Saxon church in Dover castle was identified as the result of this promise since, after the battle of Hastings, William stayed at Dover adding to the defences there. But excavation has now shown that the main construction was not earlier than the late twelfth century, although there were traces of an earlier bank and ditch which might belong to 1064-5, or equally, of course, to late 1066. In short, we cannot point to any certain pre-Conquest castle in England today.

NORMAN CASTLES IN BRITAIN

BIBLIOGRAPHICAL NOTE

The Dorestadt fort is described by J. H. Holwerda in *Dorestad en Onze vroegste middele euwen* (Leiden, 1929) and the Hamburg defences by R. Schindler in *Alt-Hamburg*.

Ringworks generally are surveyed by R. von Uslar, *Studien zu frühgeschichtlichen Befestigungen zwischen Nordsee und Alpen* (Cologne, 1964) and the Danish forts by J. Brondsted in *Danmarks Oldtid* III and *The Vikings*. The most recent discussion of the forts of the Burghal Hidage is by D. H. Hill in *Archaeological Journal* CXXVII, and of the contemporary earthworks of the Low Countries by W. C. Braat in *Opus Musivum*. The customs of Normandy were studied by C. H. Haskins in *The English Historical Review*, XXIII and the pre-Conquest evidence for castles in England by J. H. Round in *Feudal England*. The documentary evidence for castles built in Normandy before 1150 is surveyed by J. Yver in the *Bulletin de la Société des Antiquaires de Normandie*, 53.

CHAPTER 2

The Parts of a Norman Castle

The design of any building should answer the purpose for which it is intended. At first, the Norman castle was designed as a base from which a small body of mounted soldiers under a single leader could range over an area, and to which they could retire if attacked. The base would contain a hall, well, and kitchen, sleeping quarters and stables, storerooms and workshops for the smith and armourer, and perhaps a chapel, all surrounded by a ditch outside a bank. The entrance would be by a bridge across the ditch to a gap in the bank, which would be further strengthened by a high timber fence. This constituted the bailey. In time it was found necessary to have a watch-tower to overlook the whole bailey, both to control its operation and as safeguard against treachery within the gate. For added height and safety the tower was raised on a mound, ditched around, often on one side of the bailey. The earliest appearance of the true mound, or *motte*, is disputed; low mounds around the bases of Roman towers have been found in Europe, but the high *motte* appears in the late eleventh century in England. The *motte*-top had its own fence and gate, and was reached either by a flying bridge or a gangway against the slope. The size of a *motte* and bailey castle was largely dictated by the needs of the garrison it held and the nature of the site available. Often the whole site was within bowshot of the *motte*.

Such a *motte* and bailey castle was cheap and quick to construct, but a castle of permanent importance needed more permanent buildings and defences, when it became a centre of government (however localized) and the residence (from time to time) of persons of importance in the feudal world. Timber in contact with the soil rots quickly, and buildings would be raised on stone sleeper walls, either timber-framed or rebuilt entirely in stone as circumstances allowed.

The first structure to be built in stone was often the tower; because of the instability of an artificial mound, it would usually be built on the natural level. The principal tower is usually called the keep or *donjon* to differentiate it from other lesser towers which might be built of the defensive perimeter wall. Such a keep provided the lord of the castle with an inner castle within a castle; a place of privacy and safety for himself, a prison for his captives and a strongroom for his treasure and documents. It often held out after the rest of the castle had been overrun by an attacking force. Almost fireproof, the keep could only be destroyed by undermining or captured by starvation, pestilence or treachery.

A keep would consist of three or four main rooms with smaller rooms contrived in the thickness of the walls. Usually the rooms would be stacked vertically, so increasing the height at the expense of convenience, since the various floors would be linked only by a ladder or a spiral staircase. More rarely the rooms would be arranged side by side, with fewer floor levels. The usual arrangement was for the lowest floor to form a storage basement, often with a well independent of that in the castle bailey. Above this would be the entrance floor, reached by an outside staircase of stone or timber, with a gap in it crossed by a movable bridge. The entrance door — or series of doors — would be strengthened with timber bars sliding into recesses in the wall and portscullis — iron-shod grilles that could be dropped to form an immovable screen in front of the door.

Since everybody — and everything — had to go in and out at this one door, a form of lobby was frequently built to provide a 'landing' — and also ancillary accommodation; often the upper part of this *forebuilding* formed the chapel. This or the next floor of the tower formed the hall for public business, and that above the private suite of the owner, or his resident agent, the constable. The walls were carried up above the roofs to protect them against missiles, and a wall-walk behind the parapet provided for the watching of the castle below. To overlook the base of the wall wooden galleries might be hung out in front of the parapet on brackets. A parapet on the inner side of a wall is called a parados; a crenel is a gap in a parapet, the solid part being the merlon. Recesses in the walls and roof-space provided tiny private rooms, cupboards and latrines; the medieval

THE PARTS OF A NORMAN CASTLE

term *garderobe* means a cupboard but is often used as a euphemism for a latrine. Fireplaces and windows are often found in the upper floors of a keep, but narrow slits are common near ground level for protection. Some of these slits (but not all) could have been used by archers defending the keep.

Sometimes instead of an ordinary keep the palisade round the *motte*-top was built in stone to protect the buildings within; this is termed a shell-keep. The palisades of the bailey might be replaced by a curtain wall designed as a protection against high-trajectory stone-throwing engines such as the trebuchet (in which the projectile is slung on the longer arm of a pivoted beam, hauled down against a heavy counterpoise weight and then suddenly released) or mangonel (where the projectile arm is turned against a fixed stop by a twisted skein of cords). Small towers might be built at intervals along the curtain to overlook the face of the wall. These might have movable bridges too, so isolating each section of curtain from the next in case of their being captured. Because of its continual use and its exposed position to an attacker, the gatehouse was often rebuilt in stone long before the curtain wall flanking it. The entrance gates might have advance defences called barbicans in front of them.

The design of a Norman castle was often elaborated with other enclosures, with gardens, fishponds and deerparks. The day of the *motte* and bailey is not yet over: in *The Times* for 29 November 1962 appeared photographs of strategic hamlets in Vietnam, their concrete shell-keeps on *mottes* surrounded by forests of sharpened stakes.

CHAPTER 3

The Building of Norman Castles

After the coronation of William the Conqueror as king of England, castles were built at a number of places to deter attempts at local rebellion (Map B). For this purpose they were usually sited overlooking towns, on the highest available ground and often adjoining a river which provided both a moat and an avenue of escape. William himself selected the site for Exeter castle, although he left the organization of its building to others. The provision of an adequate water supply was essential and this often explains why an otherwise poor site was chosen. Wholesale clearance of the existing buildings took place: at York, one of the seven shires into which the city was divided was entirely 'wasted' for castle-works; at Lincoln one hundred and sixty-six houses had stood on the site of the castle (and lesser numbers elsewhere) and excavation has revealed the basements of Saxon huts under the castles at Northampton and Oxford. But as conditions became more settled the legal niceties were observed and the sites for castles were obtained by purchase or exchange of land (as at Corfe and Canterbury) and even minor encroachments on the property of others was recompensed, as at Gloucester and Worcester.

Each major Norman landowner had a castle as his principal seat, which he held technically on behalf of the king. When the Conqueror died, there was a fairly even distribution of castles over England south of a line from Chester to Lincoln (Map C). The denser distribution on the Welsh border reflects the disturbed state of the frontier, and the number on the east and south-east coasts the continuing threat of invasion from across the North Sea. The few castles stretching northward from Lincoln to Newcastle upon Tyne provided some backing for expeditions into Scotland.

Distribution maps at later dates might be drawn, and the addi-

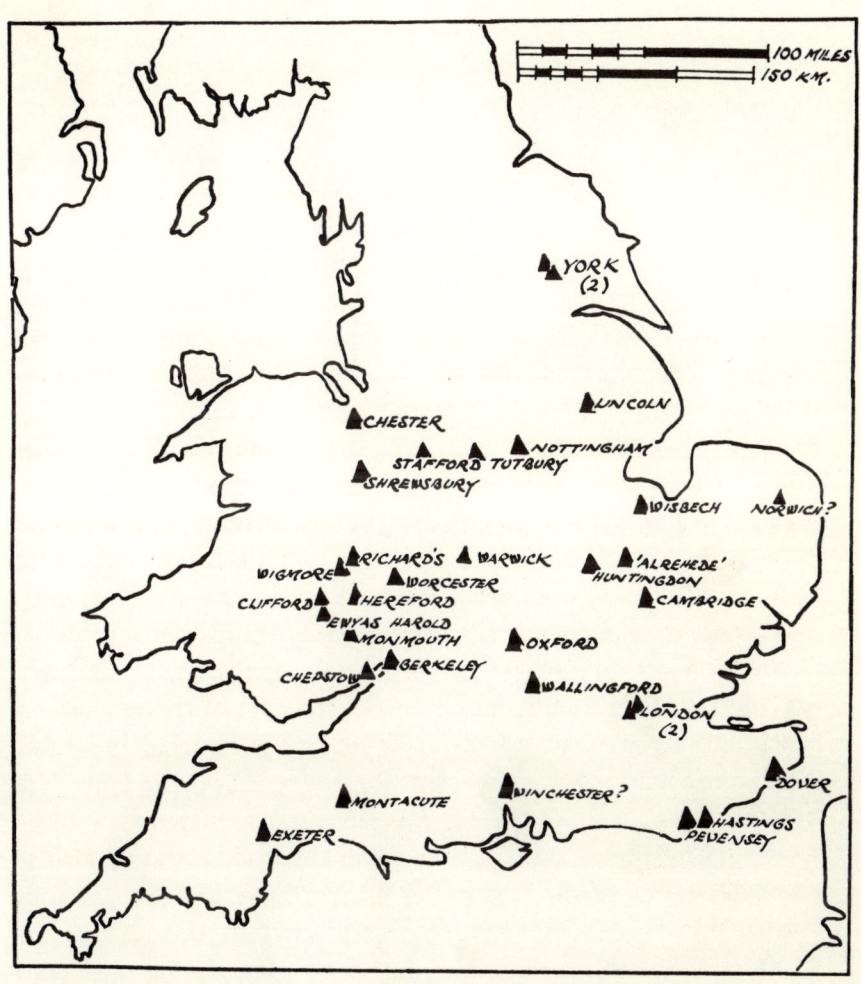

Map B

tional castles would represent the effect of particular rebellions or threats of war at particular times. While not all *mottes* are necessarily Norman, the overall distribution (Map D) is interesting in showing the concentration on the Welsh border and south-west Wales, reflecting the Norman penetration of the lowlands around the Cambrian Mountains, continuously disputed by the Welsh. Castles in this area were often captured, burnt or recaptured year after year.

We cannot speak of an overall strategical plan in castle siting; castles were built as need arose or opportunity offered; to guard a pass or river crossing, to control a road or overawe a town, to protect a gang of adventurers trying to carve out a landholding for themselves in debated country or to provide a Norman earl with a suitable headquarters to govern his lands. Needs and resources dictated the sort of castle that was put up — a *motte* and bailey with rough timberwork, put up in a matter of months (the chroniclers' records of days must be taken with a pinch of salt) or an architectural masterpiece in stone, with every comfort and defensive feature possible, which would take as many years as the other took months.

No contemporary writer has described how a *motte* and bailey was laid out. Shallow gulleys have been found underlying Norman banks, but not enough was exposed to determine whether or not these were marking-out trenches for the earthworks. Once the simple idea of such a castle was grasped, the actual layout could be varied to suit the site and the labour available and to provide for the particular needs of the lord and his men. Ditches were dug to a V-shaped profile, unless they were water-holding, since it was impossible to dig much below water level and a few feet of water (and mud) are sufficient obstacle. In any case the sides of the ditch were made as steep as possible. The banks might have timber faces to render them unclimbable. The *motte* would be made by throwing the earth inward as the surrounding ditch was dug, and levelling off the upcast with reinforcing layers of rock or beaten earth from time to time, exactly as is shown in the building of Hastings castle in the Bayeux Tapestry. The foundation of the watch-tower might be incorporated in the mound as it rose, and the *motte* finished with an outer crust of clay, which might prevent uneven settlement or slipping of the face of the slope. The feet of timber posts were usually

Map C

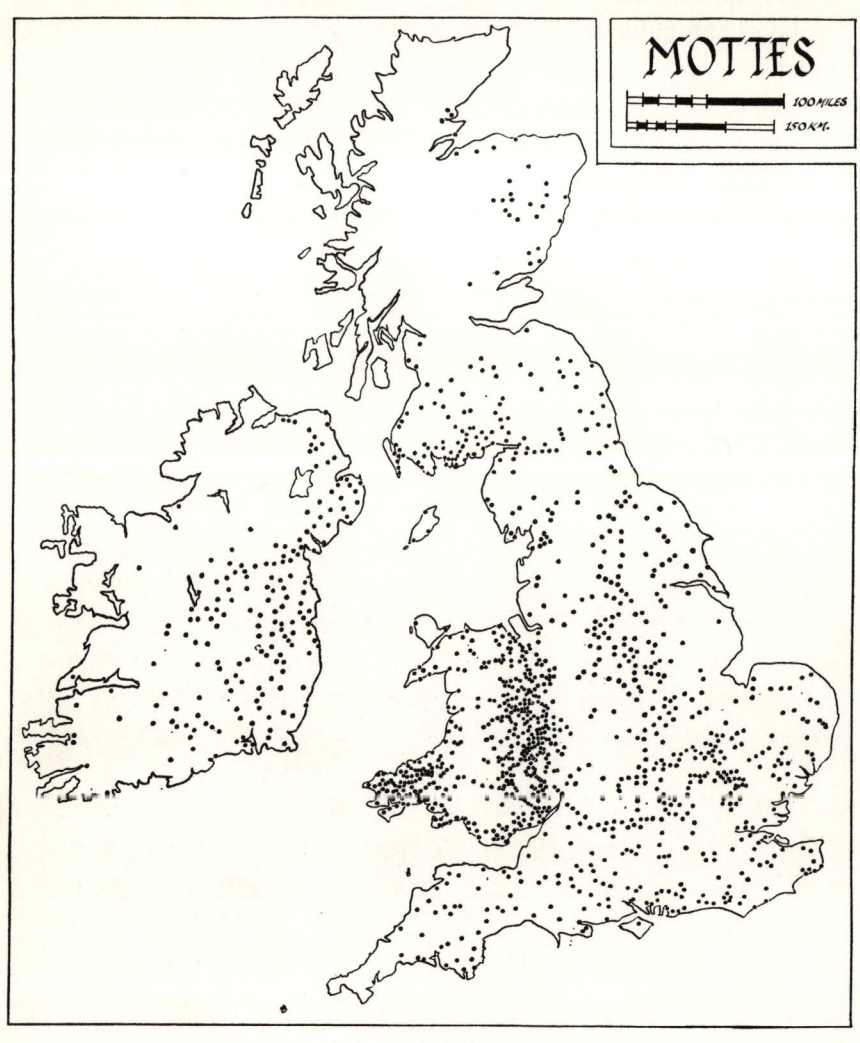

Map D

buried by digging a hole rather larger than the post and packing stones round it when in position.

One of the obligations of Saxon times had been work on communal defences and the provision of a garrison. The Normans diverted this obligation into castle-work by their tenants. A particular task allotted to a particular holding when a castle was built became a traditional duty, if it was not later commuted for a money payment. A *motte* and bailey could be built using the labour and materials immediately to hand; a stone castle was another matter and a great deal of organization was required. While the lord — or the king — would know what he required in terms of space, he needed an architect, or military engineer, who could translate that need into terms of buildings and defences, and could plan their construction. Specialists in the art of castle building came from various parts of feudal society, and few of them seem to have been trained masons. A defensive feature found useful in one castle would be copied or improved upon in another. But here and there we find an anachronism, a castle ahead of its time, embodying some principle of military engineering that went unrecognized until it was rediscovered years later and used extensively thereafter. We do not know the names of many of these military engineers, and their castles are their anonymous monuments.

The records of the Crown have been preserved more carefully than those of many lesser landholders, and this fact and the extensive royal requirements in castle-building mean that much of our surviving data relates to royal works. But the greater landowners doubtless organized castle-building in much the same way as the Crown. A royal castle would be ordered by the king's writ addressed to the sheriff of the county as the king's agent, with other writs to other sheriffs for help in providing labour, transport and materials, by a system of conscription; the king's work must come first. The actual work might be supervised by the castle constable-to-be or an official representative of the king.

Major quarries were owned by the king or by a monastery. The whole quarry might be hired for the period of a major building operation, or an agreement made for the supply of a given quantity of stone. The stone would be extracted by driving iron wedges into the bed, and the rough lumps sawn or split to the desired size (a common Norman size is about a foot cube), and dressed to a fair face (Norman masonry is often tooled diagonally across the 'grain' of the stone). Because of the cost of transport, it was usual to use the nearest available quarry, or even to mine stone on the site if it were usable. Water transport was cheaper than cartage and much Norman work in south-east England is in Caen stone, a cream limestone imported from Normandy. The major quarrying centres of Barnack, Maidstone and Quarr were near navigable rivers, by which the stone was moved considerable distances. For timber supplies, a whole wood or forest might be bought outright, or an agreed amount of timber purchased, felled and used at once: it was seldom allowed to season before use. Sand and lime for mortar would be dug and burnt, lead (from Derby or Mendip) cast and iron worked as near the site as possible. Building materials were often used a second time, and the large thin red Roman bricks can be seen in many Saxon and Norman buildings. But it does seem from recent excavation that the Saxons and Normans did sometimes make bricks of their own.

On the site itself, heavy materials would be moved on sledges and lighter loads on two-man stretchers, or in baskets and wheelbarrows. Wherever possible, walls were founded on solid rock (quarried flat for the purpose). Otherwise deep trenches were dug, wider than the intended walls, and filled with rammed stone rubble, or oaken stakes driven into the subsoil by a crude pile-driver consisting of a weight slung over a pulley. Sometimes the foundations of an earlier building were used again, the new walls being founded on a timber raft above them.

Norman walls usually consist of ashlar (stone wrought to a smooth face of regular shape) on the outside, with a core of rubble (rough unworked stones), or even builders' rubbish, mortar being poured in to bind it together. Wood or metal ties might be inserted to help 'frame' the walls. Occasionally the whole wall would be of rubble, supported between wooden shuttering until the mortar had set. As the walls rose, wooden scaffolding was erected against them; the holes left by the removal of the cross-ties can often still be seen. Materials were raised into position by a pulley-crane operated by

THE BUILDING OF NORMAN CASTLES

hand or a treadmill; medieval crane-wheels still remain in the towers of Canterbury, Peterborough and Salisbury cathedrals. Builders' hand tools have not altered greatly since Roman times, although often the edge of the tool only was of iron or steel. A contemporary writer, William fitz Stephen, has left a vivid picture of work on the Tower of London 'with so many smiths, carpenters and other workmen working so vehemently with bustle and noise that a man could hardly hear the one next to him speak' (*Materials for the History of Thomas Becket* III, pp. 19–20).

Building work often stopped between Michaelmas and Easter, but urgent work like castle-building might be pushed on through the winter, and even night work by candle-light is on record. Unfinished walls would be thatched over to protect them against frost. On completion, they were coated with plaster or whitewash (to act as a stone preservative) and painted: a common Norman finish was thin lines imitating the joints in the stonework. The White Tower of London owes its name to the frequent whitewashing it received in the Middle Ages.

The main beams of floors and roofs were either based on recesses in the walls themselves, or on projecting stone brackets, called corbels. Roofs were usually high-pitched (to judge from the marks on the walls, since no Norman castle roof remains in Britain) and were covered with thatch, wooden shingles, clay tiles, stone slates or lead. Lead waterspouts, drainpipes and waterpipes were also used in Norman castles. Door and window arches were often built around a temporary wooden infilling or centring. Doors were hung on butt hinges (rather like old farm gates) and fastened with drawbars sliding into holes in the sides of the doorway, and locks (the spring lock had been known since Roman times). A two-leaved door would have a central 'flail' bar pivoted in the centre, like the modern button-catch. Window glass was known in the twelfth century, having been excavated in the Oxfordshire castles of Ascot d'Oilly and Deddington.

How was all this paid for? The sheriff at his annual audit could set off the income from royal estates and other crown revenues against his expenditure on royal castles (for which he had to have witnesses), but often additional taxation or direct grants from the king's treasury were necessary. Only the annual total expenditure is recorded for each English royal castle, and few details are given. However, at Château-Gaillard (Eure) the cost of Richard I's crash programme of 1196–8 may be analysed in further detail from the Rolls of the Norman Exchequer (edited by T. Stapleton, London 1830, Vol. I, also printed in Sir Maurice Powicke's *The Loss of Normandy*, Manchester 1925):

(converted to £ sterling)

	Materials and Extraction	Transport	Finishing	Total
Cartage and labourers	—	1,010	2,432	3,442
Stone	2,030	425	650	3,105
Timber	1,005	251	838	2,094
Sand, lime, and plaster	395	—	1,002	1,397
Metal (including cords and cables)		160	113	273
Miners	—	—	445	445
Warders and porters	—	—	136	136
	5,276		5,616	10,892

So half the cost was spent on getting materials (including carriage, amounting to half the cost of materials) and half on finishing them and erecting them on the site. Over one fifth of the total cost went on pay to the 'hodmen with baskets, bags, hand-barrows and tubs, carriers of water in barrels and watchmen'.

CHAPTER 4

Sources of evidence for castle-building

A castle may be defined as a defensible structure held on behalf of one man, be he king or rebel, by his supporters, rather than by the inhabitants of a region collectively. Like most definitions, this distinction blurs on occasion: castles were often sited to control a town, and it was only commonsense to integrate the defences of the two. The erection of a castle was sometimes accompanied by the planting of a new town or suburb, as at Carlisle and Pembroke. Many castles never proceeded beyond rough timber palisading; their architecture was rudimentary, and 'Romanesque' is far too grand a title for them.

The Norman dynasty ended with the death of Stephen in 1154, but there was no corresponding change in architectural development until the gradual transition to the Early English style at the end of the twelfth century. 1200 did not mark a sharp break either, but after the crisis measures of John's reign, that of Henry III was long and relatively tranquil, and saw little new castle-building. Repairs and improvements were the order of the day, and 1216 marks a pause in the development of military architecture in Britain, thus fittingly closing our survey.

How do we know that a castle is Norman? Building accounts are a primary source, and the Pipe Rolls provide evidence for royal works. In response to a royal writ, the sheriff or other local officer (such as the Constable) rendered account of his expenditure for the year ending at Michaelmas. Usually only a single total figure is recorded for 'the works of the castle' and rarely are particular structures, or the nature of the work specified. Obviously it took time to assess the cost of individual items, and the account for a given year will not accurately measure the work done in those twelve months. Materials might be ordered in bulk for future use. Even the final total was probably not the true amount involved: local taxes might be levied, and goods and customary services in kind go unrecorded. Bearing these limitations in mind, there are six examples of royal castles built entirely in the course of a few years whose expenses we can analyse season by season. Three were polygonal keeps: Chilham was the smallest in size and cost, being founded on an existing building, while Odiham probably had a gatehouse as well, and reflects the rising prices of thirty years later. Orford was contemporary with Chilham and was the most elaborate of the three, with a towered curtain wall surrounding the keep. The three rectangular keeps may have had expenditure on curtain walls included in the accounts also.

Orford		Chilham		Odiham		Scarborough		Newcastle-upon-Tyne		Horston	
	£		£		£		£		£		£
1165–6	663	1170–1	100	1206–7	39	1157–8	4	1167–8	121	1199–1200	299
1166–7	323	1171–2	154	1207–8	288	1158–9	134			1200–1	246
1167–8	120	1172–3	167	1208–9	387	1159–60	91	1171–2	185	1201–2	140
1168–9	135			1209–10	300	1160–61	107	1172–3	254	1202–3	23
1169–70	75	1174–5	7	1210–11	(456)	1161–2	90	1173–4	12		
1170–1	30			1211–12	72	1162–3	77	1174–5	188		
1171–2	8					1163–4	86	1175–6	145		
1172–3	58			1213–14	14			1176–7	142		
								1177–8	97		

At Orford nearly half the total expenditure was in the first year, and expenditure tails off rapidly thereafter. The same feature is apparent at Horston, where the strengthening of an existing castle may have cut down costs of ditches and foundations which would otherwise have been incurred at the start. Bearing in mind that the amounts for the first and last financial years do not represent a full season's work, the expenditure on the other castles is reasonably uniform year by year. This suggests that often there was no stockpiling of materials in advance of requirements. Orford was a special case, rushed up to support Royal authority in Suffolk — it had a constable and stores by 1167. Similarly, the timber keep at York, burnt down in 1190, was replaced for £219 of which £190 was spent within the year.

The *Pipe Rolls* of the English Exchequer are practically complete from 1155 onward and the solitary roll for the 31st year of Henry I,

SOURCES OF EVIDENCE FOR CASTLE-BUILDING

the second, third, and fourth years of Henry II and the first year of Richard I have been published by the Record Commission. The remainder of those of Henry II, Richard I and John have now been published by the Pipe Roll Society, apart from the lost rolls of the first year of Henry II (extracts survive in the *Red Book of the Exchequer*) and the fifteenth year of John. Each publication is indexed, and so page references have not been cited in the gazetteer. The major expenditure on castles has been extracted and reviewed by R. Allen Brown in *The English Historical Review* LXX.

'Domesday Book' references to castles are incidental, since castles were sources of expenditure rather than income, and the lack of any mention of a site is no proof that it was not fortified by 1086. The castle references are collected in Sir Henry Ellis' *Introduction to Domesday* I (pp. 214–40).

The monastic chroniclers vary both in the amount and accuracy of their information. In most cases the reference is to the existence or destruction of a castle (rather than to its erection) in a given ecclesiastical year. The *Historia Ecclesiastica* of Ordericus Vitalis (ed. A. le Prévost, Paris 1838–55), the *Chronicon ex Chronicis* of Florence of Worcester (ed. B. Thorpe, London 1848) and that of William of Poitiers (in *Scriptores Rerum Gestarum Willielmis Conquestoris*, ed. J. A. Giles, London 1845) and the Irish *Annals* have been published separately. The *Chronicles and Memorials of Great Britain and Ireland* (the 'Rolls Series') editions of the others have been used in this survey, except where better versions have been produced subsequently, viz.:

Anglo Saxon Chronicle (ed. G. N. Garmonsway (Dent), 1954).
Brut y Tywysogion (University of Wales, History and Law series, Vols. 11 and 16).
Gesta Stephani and William of Malmesbury, *Historia Novella* (both ed. G. R. Potter (Nelson) 1950).
Liber Eliensis (ed. E. O. Blake, Royal Historical Society Camden Series 3, XCII).

Monastic charter evidence is cited from the various editions of Sir William Dugdale's *Monasticon Anglicanum*. Scots and Irish references are largely derived from the first volumes of the *Calendar of Documents of Scotland* and *of Ireland*, edited by J. Bain and H. S. Sweetman respectively for the Record Commission. A transcript of one Irish Pipe Roll (14 John) has been published (*Ulster Journal of Archaeology*, third series, Vol. 4 Supplement).

The dating of architectural features according to their style is subject to a margin of error. The detailed analysis of certain major ecclesiastical building, linking structural features with documents (such as that by Professor Willis at Canterbury and Dr Bilson at Durham), have established certain criteria and for lesser churches there is an excellent survey by Thomas Rickman (*An attempt to discriminate the styles of architecture in England*, usually called *Gothic Architecture*). Several of Rickman's points are worth repeating here:

(1) The first fine-jointed ashlar is attributed to the episcopate of Roger of Salisbury, 1115–39 by William of Malmesbury (*Gestis Regum* II, p. 484; see also *Monasticon* I, p. 253) but occurs previously in special circumstances as in the Saxon church of Bradford on Avon.

(2) Round and flat arches occur at all periods, but there is a general tendency for ornament to become more delicate with time.

(3) The carving of details may take place long after building. It may be pointed out that the three dated dedicatory inscriptions in twelfth century churches cited and illustrated by Rickman are all suspect. That at Castor (1124) is in raised lettering except the vital XXIIII which is engraved; the inscription in the Temple, London (1185) is from a destroyed doorway and that at Clee (1192) is inserted into an earlier pillar.

(4) The foundation date of a monastery is only the date *after* which building work began on the basic minimum necessary for worship and shelter. This is not so true of castle-building, when heavy expenses were soon incurred in compensating dispossessed landowners, digging foundations and defensive ditches, quarrying stone and cutting timber and transporting it to the site. This difference arises from the concept of a castle as a (relatively) short-term need, rather than an everlasting one. Many castles were of course later rebuilt or extensively altered.

SOURCES OF EVIDENCE FOR CASTLE-BUILDING

The later editions of Rickman's work had many historical additions by J. H. Parker, two of whose comments should be remembered:

'There are people who are old-fashioned and those who are new-fashioned at all periods.'
'For all practical purposes, if we can arrive within 20 years of the actual date by the architectural character only, that is as much as can be expected.'

Archaeological evidence, in the sense of objects excavated, is subject to an even wider date-bracket at present. Soil movements caused by human or natural agency make solitary finds suspect. A single coin is not real evidence, and a hoard only gives the date after which it was deposited, although the regular recoinage in the reigns from Eadgar to Stephen do make a closer approximation possible. So far only two sites (Llantrithyd and Rayleigh) have produced a coin group. The dating of medieval pottery was discussed at a conference of the Council for British Archaeology in 1962 (see also J. G. Hurst in *Medieval Archaeology* VI/VII) and the general lack of fixed points in chronology agreed. Approximate dating has led to loose terminology; material attributed to the twelfth century, for instance, might be up to half a century before or later, i.e. 1050–1250.

Scientific dating tests, such as the fluorine or C^{14} content of bone and timber respectively or the direction of the remanent magnetism of a kiln are of limited use, since the measurements do not lead to a unique date, but only a range of dates. Tree-ring analysis may be able to provide dates for surviving timber, but very often the survivals are earth and stone alone. Future work on the identification and analysis of stone and mortar may enable us to separate the work of different seasons; a change in masonry style, size or type can sometimes be detected by eye. There is some evidence that the optimum height per season for church tower-building (John Harvey, *The Gothic World*, London, 1950, p. 17) was 10 to 12 ft and this is supported by the seasons of work on castle keeps (judged by the expenditure of at least £100 per annum).

	Seasons of work[1]	Height in feet[2]	Average height per season[3]
Scarborough	10	90	10
Orford	7	65	11
Newcastle upon Tyne	8	80	11
Chilham	3	35	12
Bowes	5	50	10
Dover	9	80	10
Odiham	5	50	12

1. From Pipe Roll expenditure.
2. Approximately to base of parapet.
3. Allowing one season for foundations except at Chilham and Bowes which were built directly upon earlier masonry.

Used with caution, this can provide an index for dating features at different levels. Bearing these limitations of evidence in mind, we can commence a chronological survey of the Norman castles.

CHAPTER 5

The Castles of the Conqueror, 1066–86

Ordericus Vitalis blamed the defeat of the English on the fact that castles had not been adopted by them.[1] So, if we follow the Conqueror's actions after his landing, we should be able to deduce something of contemporary *Norman* fortification.

'He landed at Pevensey, where he built a castle with a very strong rampart (*statim firmissimo vallo castrum condidit*).'
'He seized and fortified first Pevensey and then Hastings (*prima munitione Penevensellum altera Hastingas occupavere*), intending that these should serve as a stronghold for themselves and a refuge for their ships.'

So wrote William of Jumièges and William of Poitiers soon after 1070;[2] a century later Wace stated that the duke brought over a wooden fort and had it erected immediately after the landing.[3] No other writer mentions this; although William certainly had used wooden towers in besieging castles,[4] Wace may have been thinking of twelfth-century Angevin practice; such prefabricated forts were employed by Henry II in the conquest of Ireland and by Richard I in the Mediterranean.[5]

At Pevensey, the south-east side of the Roman fort wall has been destroyed by landslip; if this had occurred before 1066, the 'very strong rampart' may have been erected to close the gap. Alternatively, the rough masonry at the sides of the early thirteenth century inner gatehouse suggest that it was built into an existing bank nearly thirty feet wide with a ditch (only half the width of the present one) beyond it. The earthwork may either have enclosed the same square area as the present inner bailey, or have run across the north-east part of the Roman enclosure to form an oval ring-work. Again, the ditch forming a D-shaped barbican outside the west gate contained early Norman pottery. One or the other of these earthworks is probably that of September 1066, since the Norman repairs and additions to the stonework of the walls and gates must have taken longer than the few days before the move to Hastings.[6]

'As soon as his men were fit for service, they constructed a castle at the town of Hastings' says the Anglo-Saxon Chronicle[7] and the Bayeux Tapestry shows a horizontally-striped mound on which is a structure with flanking posts, looking like an old-fashioned metal bedstead. Figures in front are picking, digging and shovelling soil, and above is the inscription

IVSSIT: VT FODERETVR : CASTELLVM : AT. HESTENGACEASTRA

Since the Tapestry is held to have been embroidered in time for the consecration of Bayeux cathedral in 1077,[8] it has been frequently cited as contemporary evidence for the erection of the *motte* at Hastings, although fifty years ago the Hon. F. H. Baring advanced topographical reasons for the site of the first castle having been further west.[9] The present site has been largely destroyed, but the scale of the ditches suggests an Early Iron Age hill-fort, and the shapeless mound at the angle has been much dug over, but excavation has revealed the sequence – if not the close dating – of the earthworks.

After the battle, the army moved along the coast to Dover, where William spent eight days adding what fortifications were lacking to the *castrum*. Even if Harold had honoured his alleged promise to build a castle for William,[10] the *castrum* was either the Early Iron Age fort still surrounding the later castle on the cliff-top or the Roman fort in the narrow valley below. William still needed to keep contact with his ships, and we cannot be certain of his works, in view of the wholesale alterations to both sites ever since.

Canterbury made a politic surrender, and William spent a time at the *Fractam Turrim* while he and his men recovered from an epidemic (malarial dysentery?). Whether the Dane John (*donjon*) at Canterbury was used as a *motte* is unknown: the hill seems to have been a Roman burial mound and its present shape dates from 1790.[11] The *Fractam Turrim* seems unlikely to have been at Canterbury or Dover, unless the Roman *pharos* at the latter was meant, since either would have been identified by name. Could it have been Richborough, where a huge tower-like structure may still have stood on the Roman foundation visible today? Nearby Sandwich was then a naval haven in frequent use, and in 1069 its garrison beat off a Danish landing. Little is known about the royal castle there, except that its site lay to the south-east of the town.[12]

William headed for London: baulked at Southwark, he made a wide detour and eventually crossed the Thames at Wallingford. The castle there was certainly in existence by 1071 and cuts off a quadrant of the town enclosure. Various earthworks in the Chilterns have been suggested as campaign forts on William's progress to Berkhamsted, and the *motte*-and-bailey there *might* have been built while the surrender of London was being arranged.[13] Detachments were sent to erect fortifications in the city, and William waited at Barking until these were complete. Recent excavations have shown that the first earthwork on the site of the Tower of London ran closely north and west of the keep to enclose the acute south-east angle of the Roman city wall.[14]

So far the castles described have been campaign-forts, designed to defend a large body of men for a short time. When William returned to Normandy in 1067 castle-building went on under the vice-gerents William fitz Osbern and Odo of Bayeux.[15] Fitz Osbern was killed in February 1071 so that the castles attributed to him in Domesday Book must have been built between 1067 and 1070: these are Berkeley, Chepstow, Monmouth, Clifford, *Guenta* and Wigmore, and the rebuilding of Ewyas Harold. At the first three named sites, there are remains of long narrow halls lit by narrow loops between pilaster buttresses which may well be of fitz Osbern's time. (Plates VII, XXVIII, Figs. 17, 45). The most complete, that at Chepstow, has crude Romanesque carving round the entrance door, an internal blind arcade of rounded-headed arches and tapering circular holes in the gable-end. In layout these halls invite comparison with those at Langeais (Indre et Loir) of A.D. 992 and Ste. Suzanne (Mayenne) of pre-1081.[16] The other castles have been altered by later hands; even the reference to the *re*building of Ewyas Harold does not enable us to differentiate fitz Osbern's work. Professor Barlow has argued recently that *Guenta* should be interpreted as Winchester (where there are traces of a long hall) rather than Norwich, and the vice-gerents held a Dover/Winchester axis.[17] We do not hear of Odo as a builder of specific castles, but it is worth noting that both Hampshire and Kent (the centres of power of fitz Osbern and Odo respectively) are full of ringworks; the only large conical *motte* in either county is at Tonbridge. This spread of ringworks around the early centres of Norman power lends support to Mr Davison's theory that *mottes* did not come over with the Conquest but a few years later.[18]

Although Dover was held successfully against a rising, William found it necessary to build further castles upon his return late in 1067. After putting down a rising at Exeter he chose a site for a castle leaving others to build and garrison it. The rectangular gatehouse of plain Romanesque style may well be of this date (Fig. 30). The pair of Saxon triangular-headed windows framed in stone strips rest on a central Norman capital, but the three successive plain round-headed arches of the two bays below are reminiscent of those of La Pommeraye (Calvados). To subdue the Northern earls Morcar and Edwin, castles were built at Warwick, Nottingham, York, Lincoln, Huntingdon and Cambridge in the spring of 1068. Apart from Nottingham, these follow a consistent pattern of a *motte* at one corner of a square enclosure; the opposing castle at Northallerton may be the simple ring-work of the older type. A Danish invasion fleet landed in Yorkshire in 1069 and York castle was burnt by its garrison, but was soon rebuilt and reinforced by another across the river. The fortresses at Montacute and Shrewsbury were besieged, and castles were built at Chester, Stafford and Worcester (cutting off part of the abbey cemetery) to control the Welsh border after the defeat of Edric the Wild. In 1070 the Danish forces burnt Peterborough and went to Ely in support of a local rising under Hereward. After blocking the Aldreth causeway into the fens with a fort, William took the Isle of Ely and compelled the men of the neighbouring shires (Bedford, Buckingham and Cambridge) to build a castle on the abbey lands. Turold, abbot of Peterborough, led a mercenary force in support and built a castle beside his own abbey. William added to the defences of the Fenland by having a castle built at Wisbech in 1072. Hereward's traditional prison was Buckingham castle – certainly Wallingford castle was used as a prison in 1071. At Bramber the tall fragment of a square gate tower of two bays and the plain rubble curtain wall may well go back to the earliest reference of 1073; the large *motte* occupies a lonely place in the centre of the site.

It is uncertain whether the *motte* at Oxford or the tall plain tower of rubble masonry (Plate XXXV, Fig. 52) beside it was built first: the castle was erected in 1071 and the chapel in 1074, but the latter has been moved at least once and the tower is 20° out of orientation. The gatehouse and bridge lay between the *motte* and the tower, and the latter probably served as keep, church tower and town belfry like that at Vendôme (Loir et Cher). There is a similar problem at Earl's Barton, where the Anglo-Saxon church tower appears to stand on part of the *motte* ditch. But the *motte* there appears to be an addition to the earthwork bank across the ridge, and without excavation we cannot be certain that the *motte* ditch underlies the tower; even then the exact date of the tower is unknown. It seems unlikely that a mason would deliberately build on disturbed ground, and the church may have been incorporated in the defences as a precaution, being a ready-made stronghold in itself. Examples of the use of churches as castles can be quoted from the period of the Anarchy;[19] an earlier example may be the incorporation of St Martin's church at Thetford into the Red Castle ring-work, perhaps at the time of the East Anglian risings which ended in the surrender of Norwich castle in 1075. The *motte* at Norwich was heightened and extended, perhaps to take the ornate keep,[20] and the same operation took place at Durham, partly burying the early Romanesque chapel with its grotesque capitals (Fig. 27) which probably dates from the castle's foundation in 1072.

Excavation has also revealed evidence of how some *mottes* were built up. York castle was raised over a crouched burial in the natural marl-covered clay in three deep strata of clay and stones, a compacted layer between looser ones, the uppermost being coated with clay when the height was increased. Two platforms of oak timbers were found near the original summit-level, the lower supported on forked stakes 7 to 9 in. diameter and 8 ft long, and the upper covered in clay and burnt wood (the result of the Norman evacuation of 1069 or the anti-Jewish riots of 1190?). The 5 ft of sand and $9\frac{1}{2}$ ft of gravel above the chalk at Norwich may be natural, but the turfline above is covered with 11 ft of loam and then thin layers of chalk, loam, and chalk again. At Oxford the natural gravel was honey-combed with late Saxon pits, over which a level layer of dirty gravel was spread and other layers piled up within the ditch to form a mound, with a coating of blue clay to the sloping side of *motte* and ditch to prevent slipping. Cambridge castle seems to have been thrown up over a Saxon graveyard, and Domesday Book records that twenty-seven houses had been destroyed to make room for the castle. Comparable numbers are thirty-two at Canterbury (including exchanges) and twenty at Huntingdon. The five *hagae* at Stamford, eight at Wallingford, and four at Warwick may represent a lower density of occupation. At Exeter forty-eight houses had been destroyed 'since King William came to England' while at Shrewsbury fifty were uninhabited and fifty-one covered by the site of the castle; at Norwich the respective numbers were one hundred and ninety, and ninety-eight, plus fifteen *burgenses*, quite comparable with the one hundred and sixty-six destroyed for the castle at Lincoln.

Of the other castles mentioned in Domesday Book, the *motte* at Carisbrooke was thrown up over drystone walling of uncertain date (also found at Stamford) and was composed of chalk strata based on a layer of single stones (chiefly flint), 16 in. of loose chalk alternating with a 6 in. rammed layer. Tipped and rammed chalk layers have been found at Old Sarum. The *motte* at Penwortham was thrown up over a circular wooden building with a cobbled floor, well above which another floor had been laid and the *motte* raised a a further 7 ft. A stone foundation 30 × 20 × 10 ft was found in the *motte* at Caerleon, while at Waytemore the shell-wall round the *motte*-top partly over-rides two quadrilateral sunk chambers. Early drawings show terraces at Waytemore and Lincoln, suggesting a stratified construction;[21] the two *mottes* of Lewes castle are said to be composed of roughly squared chalk blocks. At Rayleigh, excavations in the bailey near the *motte*-ditch revealed part of a 9 ft wide gangway of re-used oak planks, flanked by oak posts tapering from 18 in. square scantling at the base to a height of over 8 ft, exactly as can be seen in the Bayeux Tapestry representation of the castles of Dinan and Dol (Fig. 1).

THE CASTLES OF THE CONQUEROR, 1066-86

Besides castles, Domesday Book mentions two *domus defensabilis*, both in Herefordshire: that at Eardisley is a quadrilateral moated site with rounded corners, one occupied by a mound (without a separate ditch) and guarded on the outside by a steep bank in plan like a manuscript R. Apart from the mound the plan is repeated at Clavering which has been suggested as a pre-1066 castle.[22] To illustrate the spread of castles, two maps (B and C) show the sites, known to have been built by 1071 and by 1086, five and twenty years after the Conquest respectively.

REFERENCES

[1] *Historia Ecclesiastica* (ed. A. le Prévost, Paris 1838-55) II, p. 184.

[2] *Gesta Normannorum Ducum* (ed. J. Marx, Rouen, 1914) I, vii, ch. 34; *Scriptores Rerum Gestarum Willielmis Conquestoris* (ed. J. A. Giles, London 1845) p. 127.

[3] Roman de Rou (ed. Sir A. Malet, London 1860) pp. 66-7.

[4] p. 4.

[5] p. 58.

[6] References to individual castles are assembled in the Gazetteer pp. 83-352.

[7] (Ed. G. N. Garmonsway, London 1953) p. 199.

[8] (Ed. Sir F. M. Stenton *et al.* London 1965).

[9] *Sussex Archaeological Collections* LVII, pp. 119-35; *Geographical Journal* 56, p. 107.

[10] *William of Poitiers*, pp. 104, 139-40, 212.

[11] Mrs D. Gardiner, *Canterbury Castle and Dane John Manor* (Canterbury 1948).

[12] *Ordericus Vitalis* II, p. 191; W. Boys, *A History of Sandwich* (London 1773).

[13] *Transactions of the London and Middlesex Archaeological Society* VII, pp. 602-9.

[14] *William of Poitiers*, p. 147; *Medieval Archaeology* VIII, pp. 255-6. See also BAYNARDS (London) and MONTFICHET in the Gazetteer.

[15] *Anglo-Saxon Chronicle*, p. 200.

[16] *Congrès Archéologique de France* 105, pp. 378-85; 119, pp. 265-9.

[17] *Antiquaries' Journal* XLIV, pp. 217-9. William fitz Osbern's *aula* is mentioned by *Ordericus Vitalis* II, p. 166.

[18] *Isle of Wight County Press*, 13th November 1965.

[19] p. 49.

[20] p. 259. The fractures of the keep walls (see drawings by Francis Stone in Norwich Castle Museum) suggest the slipping of an extension north and east of the original *motte*.

[21] B.M. Add. MS. 6753, 6768; Bucks' sketchbook reproduced in J. W. F. Hill, *Medieval Lincoln*.

[22] *Victoria County History of Essex* I, p. 345.

CHAPTER 6

The Completion of the Conquest, 1086-1138

Gundulf, Bishop of Rochester 1077-1108, was described as competent and skilful at building in stone and was the principal overseer and surveyor of the building of the White Tower of London.[1] The roughly square keep (Plate XLIV, Figs. 70-72) has a projecting apse and round stair-turret at the eastern angles, with four pilaster buttresses to each wall beside those at the angles. The windows have been altered (except two two-light windows high in the south wall) and the entrance doorway converted into a window. The capitals in the apsidal chapel have tau-crosses and fluting, apart from one with angle volutes and a necking row of upright leaves. The top storey is an addition marked by changes in the mortar and masonry and in the window openings.

Colchester castle was in existence by 1086[2] and the keep there has similarities with the White Tower, but also significant differences. The similarities are confined to the double-flued fireplaces and latrines and to the apsidal chapel, although this has no ambulatory but cross-apses and an oratory. It is built round the vaults of a Roman temple with heavy turrets to strengthen the corners, the north-west one being recessed for a small landing before a plain round-arched entrance to the upper floor. There is a similar landing below the plinth on the south side, where the doorway appears to have replaced a smaller opening. It has deep roll-mouldings with billet ornament, the outer order of cushion capitals having a necking row of upright leaves. About 20 ft up, the Barnack stone quoins give way to tile, and a row of tiles on edge runs almost entirely round the keep, together with traces of temporary battlements. Above this level the pattern of the putlog holes for the building scaffolding changes (Plate IX, Figs. 22, 23).

The threat of an invasion of England by Cnut of Denmark

existed between 1081 and 1087. If the breaks in construction mark the imminent invasion of 1086–7, or the famine of the same year, the foundation of the White Tower can be put back to about 1079 by our 10-ft per annum rule[3] so that 1078 (the date given by Stow) may be accepted. Similarly backdating, Colchester may have been started in 1083, when William was building certain castles and laying waste the east coast as a 'scorched earth' policy.

It is just possible that Gundulf saw the Byzantine citadel at Saône (Sayhun) during his visit to the Holy Land: its dimensions are close to those of the White Tower, and its heavy buttresses resemble those of Colchester. These keeps represent a brilliant compression of the Carolingian palace, with its great hall, apsidal church and other buildings, into a single building. Dr Allen Brown has suggested that *la Vieille Tour* at Rouen (A.D. 942–96) may have been the lost precursor of Colchester and London;[4] it is worth noting the similarity of the *turris Rainerii* of Rouen and the 'little castle that was Ravengers' at London.[5] Gundulf's Tower on the north side of Rochester Cathedral and St Leonard's Tower at West Malling (Plate XLVII, Fig. 75) might be considered either as military or ecclesiastical structures. They have parallels in Lombardy (Parma cathedral; Sta. Maria Maggiore, Tuscania) and their functions may have been as complex as St George's Tower at Oxford.[6] Gundulf certainly agreed with William II to build a stone castle at Rochester between 1087–9 and part of the curtain wall there is probably his work, with simple round-headed openings like those in St Leonard's Tower.

At Corfe (possibly the *Castellum Warham* of Domesday Book), there is a herring-bone-coursed revetment wall round the hill-top with a long buttressed hall of similar masonry further west; three round-headed loops are blocked by a later wall (Fig. 24).

At Ludlow and Richmond (Figs. 40, 58) the late eleventh-century curtain walls have projecting towers. Those at Richmond are square; one is barrel-vaulted at two levels, the lower lit by round double-splayed openings flanking a central loop. Two towers placed together protect the exposed end of the hall (Fig. 60), which had an external wooden gallery above the cliff. The main hall entrance is roll-moulded with a Corinthian capital surviving and this level has two-light windows with central shafts. The original doorway through the curtain has shafts and volute capitals, like one found at Westminster Hall;[7] it now gives access to the ground floor of the later keep. The herringbone-coursed curtain was built around timber frames and on a framed foundation of softwood piles. The similar curtain walls of Lincoln (Fig. 43) were also built on frames. Richmond was begun before 1089 and Lincoln walls were erected before 1113. At Ludlow (Fig. 40) the northern pair of the four rectangular towers have their angles chamfered off; the T-shaped gatehouse projected inward, with wall arcading (like the vaulted tower at Richmond) and a narrow passage by-passing the main door. A wall stair led to the room over the passage; the first building phase is attributed to *circa* 1085-95. Herringbone-coursed masonry was used by Saxon and Norman alike;[8] it forms a very convenient bond for walls ascending a slope (as at Tamworth and Exeter castles), is ornamental in appearance (Benington and Guildford keeps, Plate XVIII), and its use as plain curtain walling at Egremont and Peveril, besides Corfe and Richmond, shows a wide geographic distribution.

The reign of William Rufus saw an expansion of Norman influence into Scotland and Wales in greater depth than the Conqueror had secured. The planting of a colony and castle at Carlisle in 1092 and the successful sieges of Bamburgh and Tynemouth in 1095 find their echo in Edinburgh (1093), Edgar's stone castle at Invergowrie before 1107, and the castle begun in Lothian before 1106. The penetration of the coastal plain of South Wales as far as Pembroke in 1093-4 was secured by the planting of castles at Cardiff, Carmarthen and Cardigan, and others were built on the Welsh March in 1097.[9] Sometimes the castle was accompanied by a planted *bourg*, but there does not appear to have been any regular plan for these new towns. At Rhuddlan (1075) it was a quadrilateral ditched enclosure beside the river, with the *motte* and bailey castle in the centre of one side, at Abergavenny, Carlisle and Pembroke the settlement flanked the ridge of the promontory whose apex was the castle. The penetration of North Wales proved more difficult — the Normans reached Anglesey by 1094 and built castles at Aber Lleiniog, Bangor and Caernarvon, but were defeated in a

THE COMPLETION OF THE CONQUEST, 1086-1138

chance encounter with Magnus Barelegs and his fleet in 1098. Magnus based himself on Man and caused castles to be built there of timber from Galloway[10] and made himself master of the Western Isles 'around which a boat could be steered' including Kintyre (so the story goes) by having his ship pulled across the Tarbet isthmus.

Cumbria can be approached from the south by way of the Lune valley or over Stainmore. The rectangular keep at Lancaster (Fig. 40) is traditionally attributed to Roger of Poitou (1092-1102) and has some resemblance to the Poitevin keep of Chauvigny (Vienne). The narrow neck of the Stainmore pass is blocked by two Roman forts, one on each side of the col. At Bowes there are traces of another building under the rectangular keep of 1170-4 (Fig. 10) while at Brough the basement of a keep of herringbone-coursed masonry has been found sandwiched between a Roman turret and the existing tower (Fig. 11). The keep at Carlisle has traces of early features (Fig. 15) – the general squat impression, straight wall stair and perhaps a ground floor entrance. If not the work of Henry I after 1122, it may be that of David (1136-53), although its stylistic dating could be as early as William II.[11]

Bamburgh keep is usually attributed to 1164-70 on the strength of a small entry in the Pipe Rolls and the fines imposed on those not assisting in the work,[12] but there was a royal mason here by 1130 and the keep still has several early features, notably the ground floor entrance without a forebuilding, the internal apsidal chapel and a straight wall-stair and passages leading to a domed fireplace (Fig. 5). Bamburgh was impregnable at the time of Mowbray's rebellion in 1095 and the keep was an obvious need if the Normans were not to be caught between two fires; the Viking invasion threat was not over, and the Scots had forayed as far south as the Tyne in 1079 and to Durham in 1091.

Canterbury castle existed by 1086 but is not mentioned during the 1088 rebellion in Kent, so that the keep could hardly have been defensible by then. Like Bamburgh, it has wall-stairs and a domed fireplace with two pilaster buttresses on the long walls (Fig. 14). One corner turret is recessed (as at Colchester) for an entrance landing. £103 was spent on the keep in 1172-5, but this is far too little time and money for a completely new building. A small polygonal keep at Chilham nearby cost £429 in 1170-3 (Fig. 17). Again, archbishop Corbeuil would hardly have built a keep at Rochester after 1126 unless his cathedral city had such a defence already, and the martyrdom of Becket would have made a new show of royal authority politically unwise after 1170. The pottery found under the keep and in association with its earlier floor can be dated to soon after 1070.[13] The keep at Domfront (Orne) is closely similar in size and detail to Canterbury, and may have been built by Robert of Bellême, lord of Domfront 1082-92. The collapse of the rebellion had left a dangerous situation in Kent, with a vacant archbishopric and invasion expected at the ports near Canterbury.[14] Robert of Bellême was reconciled with William II in 1088, and he may have built Canterbury as a copy of the lost Domfront in the nine seasons 1089-97 (sufficient for 80 ft of original height) before he began work at Gisors (Eure). The latter was largely rebuilt in the twelfth century, but an early tower foundation remains under the keep beside the shell-wall with its pilaster buttresses at the angles, rather like that at Tamworth (Fig. 68). Robert of Bellême was noted as a military engineer; there is a striking similarity in the roll-moulded doorways of the castles with which he was associated — first Gisors and in 1102 Arundel, Tickhill, Bridgnorth and Shrewsbury where his rebellion ended.[15] Alternatively, both Canterbury and Domfront may belong to the early years of Henry I; the archbishopric was again vacant 1109-14 and Robert of Bellême was partly reconciled with Henry between 1106-12. Domfront was Henry's only holding in Normandy after the Treaty of Alton (1101) and was the invasion base of 1105-6; it became less important after the Treaty of Gisors (1113) had given Henry both Brittany and Maine. Both Bamburgh and Canterbury possess elaborately-moulded plinths, perhaps of the repairs about 1170.

At Eynsford the flint rubble curtain wall was perfectly plain, without even the narrow parapet crenels common about 1100. It was egg-shaped in plan, and surrounded the stone base of a timber tower (Fig. 32). The *motte* at Totnes was built around the quadrilateral foundation for a small tower, probably before 1103 (Fig. 73). In the first half of the twelfth century, a stone hall was built across the site of the Eynsford tower, the upper floor being approached through a small lobby — hardly a forebuilding — a design later copied in the Norwich Music House. A two-bay gatehouse was added to the inside of the heightened curtain wall, a scaled-down version of those at Bramber and Lewes. Fragments of similar gatehouses remain in the Kentish castles of Binbury and Godard's.

The keep at Canterbury has a remarkable parallel beside Loch Sween in Kintyre (Plate XLIII, Fig. 70),[16] complete to its parapets but with one side rebuilt. Its date is uncertain but it is possible that Magnus's empire-building — including south Kintyre — after 1098 may have led to its erection to guard the mouth of the extensive deepwater fiord. Fragments of a buttressed keep have been found in Inchconnell castle near Loch Awe. Robert of Burgundy was involved in a Loch Leven dispute soon after 1124[17] so the Normans had penetrated thus far already. At Kirkwall in Orkney, part of a long Romanesque hall survives, with details like the neighbouring cathedral begun in 1137 (Fig. 38). Again the tower basement with its pilaster buttresses at Norham may be part of the castle built in 1121 (Fig. 49) and Romanesque mouldings found at Morpeth may belong to the castle of 1095 or 1138. Stone castles were built in the north almost as soon as in the south.

A change in the route of cross-Channel traffic came about soon after the accession of Henry I; the route between Purbeck and the Cotentin (Henry's oldest possession) now provided the shortest safe crossing between England and Normandy.[18] The early history of the Purbeck castles of Corfe and Wareham is complicated by confusion in the records. The square keep at Wareham was built on a flat plinth of mixed rubble (some of it from the Cherbourg peninsular, probably brought over as ballast), with polychrome ashlar dressings — white Purbeck and brown Holme sandstone — to the deep buttresses. A sealed deposit on the clay basement floor contained pottery imported from Normandy — a loose baluster-shaft suggests two-light windows. Robert, Duke of Normandy was a prisoner at Wareham after 1106 and was described as *in arce regia* in 1119; Robert of Bellême was imprisoned here from 1113 and was still in Dorset in 1129–30.[19] Wareham, while defending the landing and roadhead, lacked a view of the Channel and approaching ships. This was provided at Corfe, first with a ringwall and hall, and later with a tall tower of local ashlar (Plate XI, Figs. 24, 25). A flight of steps rose to a large open landing before the entrance doorway; a blind arcade ran round the upper part of the walls. A latrine block was added to one side: the toothed-in arches can be seen above the passage floored by the earlier ringwall. A small doorway above has shafted jambs and a recessed roll-moulding round a plain tympanum, the capital having a tau-cross and cabled necking; these can be paralleled elsewhere in the late eleventh century,[20] but the possibility of survival or re-use exists.

The castle of Gloucester was extended between 1086 and 1101, and the great tower begun by 1108-9; a medieval sketch indicates that it was three storeys high, with high angle turrets. A wall of *opus gallicum* (yellow sandstone cubes) found at Bristol may be part of the castle of 1088, but the large corner turret nearby is perhaps part of the keep attributed to Robert of Gloucester, who married the heiress of Robert fitz Hamon in 1109: the tower was the prison of Robert of Normandy in 1126. This fragment (Fig. 10) compares closely with the corner turrets of Kenilworth, built after 1122. The latter keep has a high chamfered plinth round the (now) clay-filled basement, and heavy corner turrets, one recessed before a square-headed doorway with a plain tympanum like that at Corfe. The forebuilding is an addition out of alignment with the main keep and providing a difficult approach, (Plate XX, Fig. 38). A double-splayed window (and the high stepped plinth) provide a link with Portchester, but the angle turrets there are mere buttresses; the keep has been heightened and the adjoining courtyard surrounded with ranges of Norman buildings and a trapezoidal tower at the opposite angle (Plate XXXVI, Figs. 58, 59). The landing of Robert of Normandy in 1101 must have caused Henry I to consider the fortification of Portsmouth Harbour; there is circumstantial evidence for work in 1133-5. Similarly the failure of the castles built in Sussex to contain the invasion[21] may have led to the overhaul of Pevensey in 1114. That squarish keep existed by 1130, and the basement was clay-filled like Kenilworth; the solid buttresses may be later additions (Fig. 57).

Little structural remains exist of the South Wales castles mentioned about 1115; some doubtful foundation courses of the Llandovery *twr* and a single capital at Kidwelly. The reference to *novo castello* (in apposition to Coity) in a document of 1090–1106 may refer to Ogmore rather than Newcastle Bridgend. No traces of a previous castle were found at Bridgend before the existing late twelfth-century masonry, whereas the narrow loops, rubble quoins and tau-crosses on the chimney-breast capitals (with smoke vents like Portchester) of Ogmore (Fig. 52) suggest an early twelfth-century date. Gwilim o Lundein fled from his castle in 1116 and Maurice Londres is later found in possession of Ogmore.[22] The polygonal curtain is reminiscent of that round the ringwork of Coity (Fig. 20) whose much-altered keep (Plate XII) retains a plain sloping plinth. Polygonal shell-walls of smaller radius were built in the 1120s and 1130s round the *motte*-tops of Burton-in-Lonsdale, Carisbrooke, Durham, Kilpeck, Lincoln, Wiston, and perhaps Lewes. The curious detached building across the Ogmore ringwork from the keep has a vaulted passage to its basement, and might be the base of a timber tower like that excavated at South Mymms, there dated 1142–4.

The White Ship disaster of 1120 created a disputed succession and it is significant that we first hear of major castle-works by private individuals after this date.

Gervase of Canterbury tells us that Henry I gave Rochester castle to Archbishop Corbeuil (1123–38) in the twenty-sixth year of his reign with permission to build an *egregiam turrim*. This grand square tower, 120 ft high to the angle turrets, was approached by a staircase ramp through a sentry-box turret and over a movable bridge to a forebuilding covering the entrance. Chevron ornament is everywhere: on the double shafts to the doorways and around the arches to doors and fireplaces. The crosswall is pierced by an arcade of roll-moulded arches on round columns with scalloped capitals, and the twin angle stairs are linked by wall passages at the upper level. The tower is complete to the high angle turrets, but has lost most of its window dressings. Our 10-ft per annum rule would fit the tower exactly into the thirteen-year ownership of William Corbeuil; it was certainly complete enough by 1141 to be Robert of Gloucester's prison (Plate XL, Figs. 65, 66).

The keep at Hedingham is a three-quarter scale copy of Rochester, but in fine ashlar instead of rubble. The smaller size meant that fewer windows and only one staircase were necessary, and the arcade was replaced by a single-span arch (with scalloped capitals to the responds). The chevron ornament is flush (not out-turned as at Rochester), with more window detail and billet-ornament to the capitals. Here the forebuilding is definitely an addition: the ashlar of the main keep continues behind the rubble base of the stairs, and the toothed-in arch at the foot of the staircase can be traced. If the traces of a break in construction about 70 ft up (where some internal facing is rubblework and not ashlar) are due to the outbreak of open war in 1138, or to the castellan's death in 1141, the foundation date suggested by our rule is 1130–3; Aubrey de Vere, lord of the manor, was made Great Chamberlain in 1133. If the break is imaginary, then the date of foundation may be put back further, since ashlar in such quantity and quality could hardly have been obtained — and transported — during the Anarchy (Plate XIX, Fig. 36). Indeed, we cannot be certain whether Rochester pre-dates Hedingham or vice versa.

By contrast to all these tall towers of the reign of Henry I, two chunky citadels in Norfolk follow the tradition of the Tower of London. Norwich keep has five pilaster buttresses on each face and is lavishly ornamented with tiers of blind arcading pierced by small windows (Plate XXXII, Figs. 49, 50). The entrance door, with sculptured capitals and jumbled voussoirs was approached by a stair carried on arches. The interior was divided by a cross-wall, the northern floor being carried on a row of columns. A domed chimney occupies one angle, with a skewed chapel apse (with sculptured capitals) in that opposite, and stairs to a wall-gallery in the others. Norwich was a centre of the 1087 revolt, and the keep has certain resemblances to Bamburgh and Canterbury so that it might have been begun about 1094 like the cathedral and palace. However all these buildings going up together would have strained local resources even in this rich district; the cathedral was only partly built on Losinga's death in 1119. The break in construction until 1132 may have been used to impress masons into building or finishing the keep; the decoration and sculptured capitals are very similar to those of Castor church (1124?).

THE COMPLETION OF THE CONQUEST, 1086–1138

A developed version of Norwich was built at Falaise (Orne) probably between 1105–23, with an integrated forebuilding-block and decoration confined to shafts in the angles of the pilaster buttresses. At Castle Rising the forebuilding was an integral part of the design; the triple-cusped windows can be seen in the upper Loire valley — farther south they are dated 1120–5 at the town house of Archambaud at St Antonin (Tarn et Garonne). The elaborate external ornament can be paralleled in major ecclesiastical buildings of the early twelfth century, particularly Southwell. The arcading resembles that at Castle Acre priory, the axe-carving that of Ely and the circular windows of Norwich cathedral and the abbey gatehouse of Bury St Edmunds (Plates XXXIX, Fig. 64). The traditional attribution to William d'Albini (1110?–1176) is probably correct: descended from the Bigods of Norwich, he married the widow of Henry I (the builder of Falaise) soon after 1135. The keep may have been a wedding present of a familiar design, built by masons thrown out of work by the Anarchy and marking William's interest in the Fenland while Earl of Lincoln (1139–40). After their creation as Earls of Sussex, the family's interest moved southward.

The ornamental glories of these two citadels do not obscure the fact that they were somewhat archaic and out of the main stream of development in fortification. This is particularly noticeable within; rooms were contrived by cutting off the angles, the openings were cut for lighting rather than for fields of fire and at Rising a gallery had to be hacked through the walls. The *motte* at Norwich seems to have been extended to take the keep, and signs of unequal settlement could be seen in its walls. In many ways these keeps were less efficient than Colchester and the White Tower of fifty years before, which were updated with forebuildings. The future lay with the high tower and the fortified curtain wall.

Bishop le Poer began a castle in 1118 on land seized from Malmesbury abbey, and the main tower is mentioned in 1153. Devizes castle, burnt down in 1113, was rebuilt by 1121; after its capture in 1140 some of the defenders held out in a very high tower. Neither tower has survived, although the foundations of a large aisled hall and buttressed curtain remain at Devizes (Fig. 26). At Old Sarum, the purchase of a cellar door for the tower in 1129–30 suggest that the tower was fairly advanced, even if not finished. The plan of the tower to the north east of the quadrangle of buildings within the ring-work resembles the turrets at Bristol and Kenilworth, and may have been a latrine-block only, like that attached to the Devizes hall (Fig. 54). Some remains of a vaulted chapel remain, at the south-east of the quadrangle, and an important find nearby was the elaborate decorated chimney cowl with radial smoke-vents. Contemporary (but restored) examples can be seen on the north porch of Southwell cathedral. Much of the masonry of the quadrangle is in polychrome masonry which seems to have enjoyed a vogue from about 1090 to 1140. An independent keep on a different alignment beyond the quadrangle completely altered the arrangements. Its integral latrine-block and lack of buttresses might imply a much later date,[23] but the profile of the plinth resembles that at Kenilworth, Portchester, Taunton and Wolvesey and it need not be later than le Poer's fall in 1139.

At Sherborne the tower was integrated with the courtyard buildings, a wall passage linking it with a latrine block. Scalloped capitals, out-turned chevron ornament and an intersecting-arch wall arcade support a date around 1130–40. Some details of a chapel survive, with a column with scalloped capital re-used in an extension to the keep (Figs. 67, 68). The whole was surrounded by a rectangular outer curtain wall with simple square towers at the canted-off angles, two forming gatehouses. At Newark the limited licence of 1133 seems to have been fully exploited, since by 1135 the Bishop of Lincoln had secured the release of one-third of his knights to guard the new castle. The gatehouse (with elaborately-decorated windows like the Rising forebuilding) is fitted rather awkwardly into an inturned angle of the enclosing wall, like Carisbrooke (Plate XXVIII, Fig. 45), and the tall tower at the opposite angle is of slight projection. The earthworks of the bishop's other castle at Sleaford also suggest an open plan, a survival of the Carolingian palace layout. A strong tower (embedded in the later bishop's palace) at Norwich stands at the end of the range running north from the cathedral, and at Minster two parallel wings were added to an early hall, one with a strong tower at the junction. Defensible church towers were built in various exposed parts of England, but their primary purpose was ecclesiastical not military; the ambiguous towers at West Malling and Rochester cathedral have been discussed already.

REFERENCES

[1] *Textus Roffensis* (ed. T. Hearne, London 1720) pp. 145–8, 212; J. Stow, *A Survey of London* (London 1598) quoting Edward de Hadenham, *The Register Book of the Acts of the Bishops of Rochester*. It is interesting to compare Bennon, Bishop of Osnabruck (1054–79) '. . . architectus praecipuus caementarii operis . . .' (Mortet, *Textes Relatifs* . . . I, p. 70).

[2] *Cart. Mon. S. Johannis de Colecestria* (ed. S. A. Moore, London 1897) I, p. 27.

[3] p. 25.

[4] *The Bayeux Tapestry* (Second edition, ed. F. M. Stenton, 1965) p. 81.

[5] P. Mortet and P. Deschamps *Receuil de textes relatifs à l'histoire de l'architecture*; J. H. Round *Geoffrey de Mandeville* (London 1892) pp. 89, 141.

[6] p. 31.

[7] *Archaeologia* XXVII, p. 7.

[8] H. M. and J. Taylor *Anglo-Saxon Architecture* (Cambridge 1965) and in the *Journal of the British Archaeological Association*, third series XXVII, pp. 4–13.

[9] *Anglo-Saxon Chronicle*, p. 233.

[10] *Chronicle of Man* I, pp. 56–8.

[11] *Notes and Queries*. Eighth series VIII, pp. 321–3 surveys the documentary evidence and concludes that a date after 1139 is most likely.

[12] *Archaeologia Aeliana*, new series, XIV, pp. 235–6.

[13] *Archaeologia Cantiana* LXVIII, pp. 129–32. I am most grateful to Professor S. S. Frere for showing me the records of the excavation of the keep.

[14] Anselm *Epistolae* III no. 35.

[15] *Ordericus Vitalis* III, p. 300; IV, pp. 21, 169–73.

[16] Built by the *predecessors* of Dougal McSwine (*fl.* 1220) *Scottish History Review* third series, 9, p. 207.

[17] Lawrie, *Early Scottish Charters* (Glasgow 1905) No. LXXX; *Bulletin of the Institute of Historical Research* XXIX, p. 2.

[18] Compare the pottery trade: *Antiquaries' Journal* XXXI, pp. 180–7.

[19] *Dictionary of National Biography* and le vicomte de Motey, *Robert II de Bellême* (Paris 1923).

[20] Canterbury (cathedral crypt). Colchester (keep). London (White Tower).

[21] *Florence of Worcester* II, p. 48; *Chronicles of the reigns of Stephen* . . . IV, pp. 2–3.

[22] *Brut y Tywysogion* p. 126; *Liber Landavensis* (ed. J. G. Evans, Oxford 1893) p. 37.

[23] This alters my previous opinion (*Journal of the British Archaeological Association*, third series XXXIII, p. 17) in the light of arguments put forward by Mr H. M. Colvin in *The History of the King's Works* (London 1963) II, p. 825.

CHAPTER 7

The Castles of the Anarchy, 1136-54

In 1136, Baldwin de Redvers seized Exeter castle 'raised on a very high mound, with unassailable walls and Caesarian towers of hewn limestone', probably the curtain wall and tower still surviving. Stephen captured an outwork 'raised on a high mound to defend the castle'; this could have been the Danes Castle (now destroyed) a possible relic of the 1069 siege of the city. When the Exeter springs dried up, de Redvers flitted to his castle in *Wiht* (almost certainly Carisbrooke) 'built of strong and ornamental stone' but the well there failed. The 'ornamental stone' can hardly be the rough drystone walling underlying the banks and more probably related to the curtain wall with its open-backed square towers and perhaps also the angular shell-keep on the *motte* (Fig. 13). In 1137-8, Miles de Beauchamp had to be starved out of Bedford castle, 'fortified with a strong and unshakeable keep'.[1]

The castles of Bishops Waltham, Downton, Farnham, Merdon, Taunton, and Wolvesey are said to have been built for Henry de Blois in 1138.[2] Bishops Waltham and Wolvesey are being excavated; both had a square gatehouse with a central passage leading into a courtyard surrounded by buildings including a long hall beside a square tower. Although the 'house built like a palace with a very strong keep' at Wolvesey was so described in 1141, the castle was later rebuilt. The square tower has ashlar buttresses and a sloping rubble plinth; fragments of shafts are used as a bonding-course to the upper walling. The solid tower at the other end of the hall is of similar construction but the angles are slightly chamfered and the plinth stepped. A fragment of scale ornament here can be paralleled in a pier near St Lawrence's church, said to be part of the Conqueror's palace which was ruined in the 1141 siege and probably supplied much of the rebuilding material for the castle. Merdon has a square tower with a guardroom on one side of the entrance passage alone, and part of a courtyard wall (Fig. 45); we do not hear of this castle after de Blois's temporary disgrace in 1155–8. At Taunton there are the remains of a barrel-vaulted rubble hall with ashlar pilaster buttresses and a chamfered plinth continued along the curtain wall. Part of a large rectangular keep has been excavated, with many chamfered offsets (Fig. 68). These courtyard and keep castles may be compared with Sarum and Sherborne of about the same time.

At Farnham, the well-shaft was continued upward in a hollow rubble block of masonry, against which a mound of marl had been packed. At the mound top the block was widened with a flange of masonry to form the base of a square tower of which nothing remains (Fig. 33). Christchurch castle was captured in 1147–8; the square keep there (with chamfered-off angles) goes down into the *motte* as do the (later?) towers at Kenfig and Lydford (Plates XXVII, Figs. 35, 42). The keep-remains above ground at Christchurch do not show any Norman features, however. The Farnham *motte* was later revetted with a buttressed shell-wall (Plate XVI, Fig. 33). The design can be seen elsewhere; at Acre the rectangular keep within the shell had much thicker walls on two sides than those opposite them, perhaps to support an unequal load (Fig. 2) while the chamfered plinth of the rectangular keep at Aldingbourne was buried in a clay mound which was revetted with a buttressed wall (Fig. 3). It seems senseless to bury such decoration immediately; at Wareham (Fig. 75) the gravel mound may be later than the keep against which it is piled since the gravel merges with badly-built rubble above the ashlar quoins it covers. Wareham disappears from history as a castle after 1143, although strongly fortified in 1141. The base of the keep at Bungay was similarly buried in a gravel mound, but it is uncertain whether the loose ashlar plinth stones found were originally above or below its level (Fig. 12). The gravel and mortar spread at Ascot d'Oilly (1129–42) suggested that the mound was raised at the same time – and speed – as the keep. This was confirmed by the petrology of the stone chippings found stratified in parallel with the masonry.[3] The plain square keep has a slight buttress projection (Fig. 3) near one angle like that of Mileham

(Fig. 47), an undated keep also buried in its mound. At Cary (1138–47) the petrological evidence is not so clear; a layer of stone chips was found in the bank at a level with the top of the surviving ashlar of the keep with a deposit of masonry debris in the ditch beyond. The keep was roughly square 75 ft each way but no two walls parallel (other than the cross-wall). An oblong pit in one wall with a chamfered projection probably marked the entrance (Fig. 16).

Charters were granted in 1141 for markets to be held in the castles of Beaudesert and (Saffron) Walden. Walden was surrendered in 1143 and destroyed in 1157–8, but rubble fragments remain of a square keep with a forebuilding similar in plan to Hedingham and Rochester but with a central pier to support the floor (Fig. 75). At Benington, the keep is smaller than Walden and retains part of a chamfered plinth round the ashlar pilaster buttresses (Fig. 8). The owners of Benington and Walden were both at Stephen's Easter Court of 1136, and were dead or disgraced by 1142/3, which may provide a terminal date for the building of these two keeps. At Guildford, the square keep overlies the shell-wall round the *motte*-top and is built partly down its slope, with patterned coursed rubble *abcbcba* between the ashlar buttresses. The entrance doorway is placed centrally with a buttress above it like that at Sween, but at first-floor level (Plate XVIII, Fig. 35). A small sum was paid for the king's works at Guildford in 1129–30 and an early charter of Stephen was dated from the town,[4] which may indicate that the castle was then in existence. The rectangular keep at Clun is built down the slope of the *motte*, round the top of which is a shell-wall. This castle is mentioned in a charter of 1140–50 (Figs. 20, 21).

Siege-castles were frequently built during the civil war that lasted for much of Stephen's reign. We hear of them in 1138–9 at Arundel, Dunster, Ludlow and possibly Corfe; another was to have been built before Harptree had that castle not been taken by a feint attack. When Wallingford was strengthened against him in 1139, Stephen built two counter-forts, one of which was destroyed in 1140 but others were built in 1145 and 1152. His attack on Ely was based on a refortified Aldreth and another work by the river. At Christmas 1140, the Earl of Chester seized the keep at Lincoln and Stephen turned St. Mary's church into a siege-castle. Eighty workmen were killed in 1144 while building another siege-work opposite the west gate. Lincoln was surrendered by the Earl in 1146 in exchange for his freedom, but even then he was allowed to fortify a tower there until he received Tickhill castle in exchange, and was permitted to build Newcastle under Lyme.[5] A siege-work was built opposite Oxford castle in 1140 and against Faringdon in 1145; the capture of the latter castle by assault was reckoned to be the turning-point of the war. The Bishop of Salisbury had a siege-castle built opposite Downton and two facing *Lidelea*; others at Cary and Coventry were levelled in the same year, 1147.

At such a time, ecclesiastical property was misused; a stone church was a ready-made fortification and churchyards were recognized places of defence. One of the 1139 siege-works at Wallingford was in – or near – a church; in 1141 Stephen fortified St Mary's Lincoln and Matilda built a castle on the church tower at Bampton (Oxon.).[6] Another beside Cirencester Abbey was promptly levelled. Wilton nunnery was converted into a fort, and an attempt to fortify Wherwell was only frustrated by setting fire to the abbey. In the siege of Hereford (1140), the cathedral cemetery was the site of a siege-work and arrows and catapults were fired from the cathedral tower itself. The monks were ejected from Bridlington and Coventry priories and Ramsey abbey, and their sites fortified. Ring-works were erected around the churches of Merrington and St Martin, Thetford, and on the cemetery at Eaton Socon; the castles at Cuckney and Hailes also seem to have been very close to the church. In 1147 the Pope was moved to complain of Hugh de Bolebec's illegal castleworks and the general statement of the Anglo-Saxon Chronicle (1137):

> 'And they filled the whole land with these castles. They sorely burdened the unhappy people of the country with forced labour on the castles. And when the castles were made they filled them with devils and wicked men.'[7]

is understandable, but not all operations were one-sided. The removal of Folkestone priory *extra balliam* in 1137 was probably a clearance, of convenience to both sides, and the handing over of the *castella diruenda* of (Old?) Buckenham to the Austin Canons (about

1146) a diplomatic way of sterilizing an abandoned site. The same motive may have inspired the transfer of Oversley to Alcester Priory and Skipsea to Meaux before 1154.

At New Buckenham, the ring-work partly buries a square gatehouse (as at Castle Rising) and the basement of a very large round keep, which has a cross-wall to carry an upper floor. There may have been another such keep at Stansted Montfichet and an earthwork of similar plan and scale has been found recently at Biggleswade.[8] The Buckenham keep may have been built by William d'Aubigni to defend the *caput* of his honour during the disturbances of the Anarchy, and also the strengthening of Rising. Tamworth castle is first mentioned in 1138, and the shell-wall with its internal tower and wall-stair may be as early as this, as may the similar Round Tower at Windsor (Figs. 18, 68, 61).

After his disgrace in 1143, the renegade Earl of Essex seized and fortified Ramsey Abbey, despite a personal act of bravery by the abbot-elect, who set fire to the invader's tents and the outer gate they had erected. The Isle of Ely was overrun, and fortresses were put up at Benwick, Fordham and Wood Walton. Stephen built a series of castles to contain the rebellion; that at Burwell is certain, the unfinished rectangular 'island' being fortified with a square gatehouse and part of a curtain wall (Fig. 13) before the attack by the Earl which led to his death and the abandonment of the unfinished castle. Others of similar plan (Caxton, Lidgate, Rampton; perhaps Eaton Socon, and Weeting) may date from this operation: we hear of the Bury St Edmunds knights being withdrawn to do castleguard in the town of Bury between 1139 and 1146[9] and these places form a screen (at 10-mile intervals) for Cambridge and the region south-east of it (Map E). The returning abbot was forced to buy out twenty-four castellans controlling the Ramsey abbey lands, and the compact group of earthwork castles on the high ground south of the Icknield Way and west of Saffron Walden may include many of their works. Those of Anstey, Therfield and Wymondley had village enclosures attached. A stone foundation, perhaps for a small timber tower, has been excavated on the *motte* at Anstey, while the castle at Therfield does not seem to have been finished.[10] Castles sometimes had very short lives: that at Selby was captured within a week of the commencement of building and we hear no more of it. Ipswich and Newbury castles are only mentioned during a siege and the earthworks of Meppershall and Wycombe may also be dated by charters dated there *in obsidione*. The castle of Reading was built in 1150 and destroyed in 1153 and short lives were common for castles on the Welsh March.

Apart from frontal assault or surrender, castles changed hands in a variety of ways. Thorngate was pledged to Stephen, who sold the pledge to the Bishop of Lincoln. Dymock was lent to Braose by the Earl of Hereford. Harptree was captured by a feint attack elsewhere and infiltration was practised when Robert fitz Herbert scaled the walls of Devizes and Henry fitz Tracy threw lighted torches in through the loopholes of William fitz Odo's tower (perhaps Nether Stowey, or Torrington). The Earl of Chester on a friendly visit to Lincoln seized arms and expelled his host, and Downton also was lost by trickery. Stephen had to eject his own caretaker from Walden by force in 1145, and the 1153 agreement to demolish Malmesbury was broken when the neutral appointed went over to Stephen.

Despite the disturbed state of affairs, the most powerful men still found it necessary to obtain written agreement for their actions, whether between themselves or with the ruler of the moment. Thus the Earl of Essex in 1141–2 first obtained a charter from Matilda to hold the Tower of London 'and the little castle that was Ravenger's' and to strengthen and hold castles where he would, then obtained a charter from Stephen with the significant improvement 'to strengthen and *build* such castles as he would', with a second charter from Matilda referring specifically to a new castle *super Luviam* built by the Earl, and giving him permission to build yet another where he would, and promising to assist his efforts to obtain Stortford castle.[11] The last castle may be South Mymms, on the edge of the Earl's estates, where a stone foundation of a timber tower has been excavated in the *motte*, or possibly Luton.

An isolated charter to fortify a *domus* at Bishopton in 1143 is worth noticing, both on account of the large scale *motte* and bailey that seems to have resulted (Fig. 6) and for its being perhaps the earliest licence to crenellate a house, as opposed to the strengthening of a castle.

A treaty between the Earls of Chester and Leicester (1148–53) is remarkable also. The Earl of Chester granted Mountsorrel castle to the Earl of Leicester to hold of him; Leicester's castles were not to be used as bases for attacks on the Earl of Chester. The earl of Leicester was to destroy Ravenstone castle unless the Earl of Chester allowed it to remain; if the castle was held against one Earl, the other was to assist in its destruction. The castle of Whitwick remained to be fortified. Neither Earl was to build castles between Leicester – Donnington – Coventry – Hinckley – Hartshill, nor at Gotham, Kinoulton or nearer, nor between Kinoulton – Belvoir – Oakham – Rockingham or nearer, except by mutual consent. Both Earls would destroy any castle built by others in this demilitarized zone round Leicester (Map F). Like the Cambridge group a few years previously, these castles were about 10 miles apart.[12]

REFERENCES

[1] *Gesta Stephani*, pp. 22, 29, 31–3.
[2] *Annales Monastici* II, p. 51.
[3] *Antiquaries' Journal* XXXIX, pp. 231–3.
[4] *Pipe Roll* 31, Henry I: P.R.O. *Ancient Deeds* A 5276.
[5] William of Malmesbury *Historia Novella*, p. 48. *Henry of Huntingdon*, p. 277. For a *novo castello super Luviam* see J. H. Round, *Geoffrey de Mandeville* pp. 166–9.
[6] Stenton, *English Society in the Early Middle Ages* (second ed. 1952 pp. 207–8). A timber fort existed on the church tower at Dugny (Meuse) into the nineteenth century (Enlart, *Manuel d'Archéologie francaise* first edition II, p. 551).
[7] *Anglo-Saxon Chronicle*, p. 264.
[8] *Antiquity* XL, pp. 142–3, plate XXIV.
[9] *Annales Monastici* IV, p. 142; Cambridge University Library Mm.19.ff., 98b, 106 printed in D. C. Douglas *Feudal Documents of the Abbey of Bury St. Edmunds*, pp. 83–4, 160–1.
[10] J. H. Round *Geoffrey de Mandeville* (London 1892); *Journal of the British Archaeological Association*, third series, XXVII, pp. 53–91, especially pp. 66–8.
[11] J. H. Round *Geoffrey de Mandeville*, pp. 89, 140–4, 166–9.
[12] B. M. Cott. MS. Nero C.III f.178 cited and discussed by Sir F. M. Stenton in *The first century of English feudalism*, pp. 250–6.

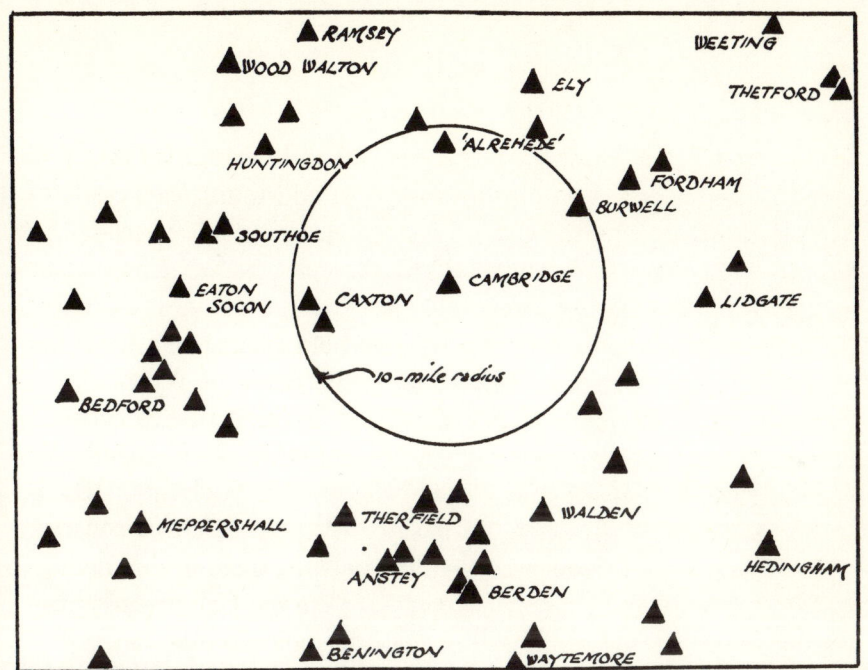

CASTLES OF THE ANARCHY AROUND CAMBRIDGE

Map E

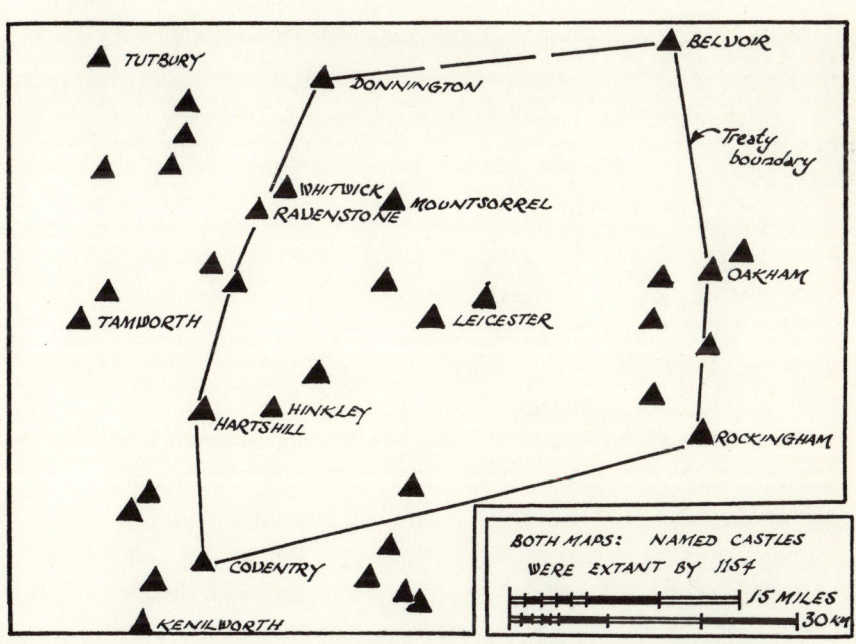

THE DEMILITARIZED ZONE AROUND LEICESTER

Map F

CHAPTER 8

Rectangular and polygonal keeps in the reign of Henry II (1154–89)

The manor of Berkeley was granted to Robert fitz Harding about 1153–6, Henry II pledging himself to fortify a castle there to his requirements. The reasons for the promise are not clear — probably support at a difficult time — but it seems to have been honoured by casing fitz Osbern's *motte* with a masonry wall carried above the *motte*-top, with three (originally four?) semicircular turrets with pilaster strips between. One turret was ornamented as a chapel, beside the entrance doorway, and the interior of the shell was crossed by a wall on an arcade of piers (Plate III, Fig. 8). There is a somewhat similar casing at Farnham, but the turrets are rectangular and a fifth one is longer to form a fighting gallery over the gate (Fig. 33). Farnham was one of Henry de Blois's castles which Henry II had destroyed in 1155. On his accession in the previous year, the new king had found baronial castles outnumbering royal ones by nearly five to one,[1] and set about reducing this majority both by confiscation and destruction.

The surrender of King Malcolm of Scotland and Hugh Bigod, Earl of Norfolk, gave castles to the Crown and permitted the further strengthening of royal authority on the Scots border and in East Anglia. In the north, the castles of Appleby and Brough, surrendered in 1157, have early curtain walls without towers, entered through simple gateways. Their rectangular keeps (mentioned in 1173–4) have slight buttresses and plain entrances, with two-light windows in the upper walls (Plate IV, Figs. 3, 11). Appleby has narrow crenels built up in the walls, and Brough (whose windows, if fewer, were more decorative) was also raised in height. The visible keep at Brough was raised on a timber frame at a slight angle to an earlier keep with a forebuilding, which in turn stood partly on a

Roman turret.² The rectangular keep at Bowes, a few miles away, also appears to stand on earlier foundations; it was begun about 1171 (Fig. 10). At Norham, rebuilt by the Bishop of Durham on Henry's orders after 1153, the earlier hall was raised and integrated with a curtain wall. A somewhat similar plan was adopted at Harbottle, also built on Henry's orders about 1157. A square gatehouse and tower can be traced on the curtain wall, and a rectangular keep on the *motte*. Nearly £400 was spent on the refortification of Wark on Tweed between 1158–61,³ probably including the polygonal shell-wall on the mound. A similar shell surrounded the *motte* at Newcastle upon Tyne (now demolished) which presumably preceded the square keep begun about 1170.⁴ At Warkworth, parts of the curtain wall and a fragment of plinth and doorway incorporated in the later tower on the *motte* may belong to the castle of 1158 (or earlier) (Fig. 74).

At Scarborough, the precipitous rock had been fortified with a curtain wall and tower by the third Count of Aumale (1127–79); the curtain wall contains fragments of early work with narrow pilasters and solid rounded buttresses. The square keep (on which sums were spent from 1158 to 1169) stands overlooking the entrance causeway. Its west wall (destroyed above the chamfered plinth) was thicker than the others, probably because the spiral stair connecting the floors was in the centre of that wall instead of the more usual corner position. Otherwise the keep much resembles Hedingham and Rochester of a generation earlier, with traces of a single-span arch below an arcade in the crosswall, loop-lit basement and two-light windows above, although some of the rear-arches are pointed and the exterior anglenooks of the buttresses filled with engaged shafts (Plate XLI, Fig. 64). The foundations of a keep with similar details have been excavated at Bungay, buried in several feet of fine gravel (Fig. 12). It was faced with sandstone from the Scarborough region,⁵ but its forebuilding was larger than that of Scarborough and a mine gallery had been driven through the adjacent angle of the keep. Hugh Bigod's castle of *Bunie* was captured in 1140, returned and surrendered to the Crown in 1157 with Framlingham; both were repurchased in 1165 and destroyed in 1176. The dating alternatives seem to be:

(i) Bungay built before 1157 and Scarborough by 1155 and the latter only repaired, or reconstructed on the original plan, by Henry II.
(ii) Both built by Henry II — Bungay 1157–65, Scarborough 1158–69.
(iii) Scarborough built by Henry II 1158–69 and Bungay in imitation 1165–76.
(iv) Bungay built before 1157 and Scarborough in imitation after 1158.

Both barons were in possession for upwards of fifteen years during the Anarchy, so that either keep could have been built then. But William of Newburgh makes it clear that Scarborough tower was decayed by 1155[6] and the keep at Bungay contained re-used mouldings[7] so the facing may also have been second-hand material from an earlier building. There is no obvious re-use or break in the masonry at Scarborough. This leaves us with alternatives (ii) and (iii). There is no reference to Crown expenditure on Bungay in the Pipe Rolls, which could dispose of (ii), but local revenues may not have been accounted for centrally for such a work.[8] While the remaining alternative (iii) may be correct, it seems remarkable that Henry II should allow such a work at the same time that he was building Orford to control the Suffolk coast. It is also surprising that Bigod should copy a design at least ten years old when the latest thing in military architecture was being built at Orford. However, since Bigod's other castle at Framlingham, only a few miles from Orford, was also returned, we may not fully appreciate the pressures on Henry II at that time.

Work on Orford castle commenced in the year ending at Michaelmas 1166, when £663 was spent; after this the amounts tail off rapidly and the keep was probably habitable by 1168 when both supplies and a constable are mentioned; the now-vanished curtain wall with rectangular towers may be a year or so later. The keep is cylindrical within and multangular without: between each of the three rectangular turrets were four wall faces, the two central ones having a two-light window at each of two levels. Wall-passages lead to turret-chambers at the same and also mezzanine levels, and the turrets were carried above the former conical roof. The lower part of the stair-turret was extended to form a right-angled prow containing the forebuilding and chapel, the former with joggled arches to its doorways. Many small but delightful architectural details survive (Plate XXXIV, Fig. 51).[9] The inspiration of this new idea the quasi-cylindrical plan, came from abroad. At Søborg in Denmark an octagonal tower was erected about 1120 on two square timber frames overlapped at 45°, while at Svintuna in Sweden remains of a seven-sided tower of 1125 have been found.[10] In France, the cylindrical keep at Houdan (Seine et Oise) had four large hemicylindrical turrets, with a stepped plinth, so that the ground plan was almost square. The interior was square, but the angles were canted off. It is attributed to Comte Aumary d'Evreux (1108–37). At Provins (Seine et Marne) the octagonal plan within and without had hemicylinders against each alternate face, again with a squarish plinth. Turret-chambers are reached by wall-passages from window recesses, as at Orford. The octagonal keep (cylindrical within) built by Henry II at Gisors (Seine Maritime) between 1161–84 was on the foundation of an earlier tower built against a shell-wall with buttresses at the angles. A straight wall-stair led up from the entrance doorway. Again, the octagonal keep (cylindrical within) at Fougères (Ille et Vilaine) may have existed before the castle was demolished by Henry II in 1166.[11]

An octagonal keep was built at Chilham in 1171–74, with a diamond-shaped forebuilding-cum-stair-turret linked to a rectangular curtain wall with shallow angle towers (Fig. 17). The keep was built upon a mound thrown up over a stone hall of two bays; the mound of Groby castle (demolished in 1176) also covered a stone building and that at Bledisloe a timber one. The octagonal keep on the *motte* at Richard's Castle was supplemented by a keep-like tower on the curtain wall of the bailey. The decagonal keep on the *motte* at Oxford may be that referred to in 1173; it must have been built by 1213–14 when it is distinguished from St George's tower (Fig. 52). An eleven-sided tower was built on the *motte* at Tickhill about 1179–82 (Fig. 71).

Towered curtain walls had of course been built before those at Orford — Carisbrooke, Ludlow and Richmond come immediately to mind, and the latter two were in the hands of the Crown in the 1170s. The more immediate inspiration may have been Saltwood, confiscated on the disgrace of Henry de Essex in 1163. The oval ringwall there has open backed turrets and three (originally four?) square towers stitched inside the curtain. They were probably built before 1163 since there is no record of royal expenditure before the demolition of 1175 (Fig. 63). At Portchester the rectangular gatehouses built inside the Roman wall may date from the 1160s; they occupy about half the width of their predecessors. Between 1168 and 1190 the entrance to the earthworks at Dover castle was blocked by a semi-octagonal tower with a vaulted fighting gallery, flanked by curtain walls defended by rectangular towers with open backs; three arrowslits open off each embrasure (Plate XIII). In 1165–71 a courtyard palace was built at Windsor, on similar lines to those of thirty years earlier at Old Sarum and Sherborne. This was incorporated in 1173–9 into a curtain wall round the bailey with open backed square towers (Fig. 61). Similar curtains existed at Bamburgh and Shrewsbury but the dating evidence is slender.

Private castle-building continued: an agreement to build a perch of wall at Welbourne was made in 1158, and we hear of castles in the north at Duffus (1151), Cairston by 1154, Cubbie Roo's by 1158 and at Elgin by 1160. Cairston now has a badly-built curtain wall, but the other Orkney castle (Cubbie Roo's) still retains the basement of a well-built square keep (not quite right-angled) against which a small annex was built later (Fig. 21).[12] The *motte* at Forres near Elgin had a seven-sided shell-wall round the top with angle buttresses.

The invasion of Ireland closely followed the pattern of that of England a century before; the beach-heads were fortified with ringworks (Baginbun, Carrick) and a castle built in the capital, Dublin, on its capture in 1172. The great *motte* and bailey at Downpatrick is either incomplete or quarried into. Henry II was sending prefabricated wooden towers over from Bristol in 1171–2[13] and he maintained control of the adventurers by requiring the cession of their castles periodically. As late as 1186, Hugh de Lacy was murdered by an Irish labourer he was supervising digging the *motte* ditch at Durrow.

RECTANGULAR AND POLYGONAL KEEPS, 1154-89

A very ordinary square keep with double-splayed windows was built at Bridgnorth between 1166 and 1174 (Fig. 10); another at Peveril (1173-6) has reeded capitals to the shafts occupying the buttress-angles (Fig. 55). At Duffield there are the foundations of a square keep nearly as large as the White Tower, with a pier for a second division as well as a cross-wall, together with part of a forebuilding. One wall was thicker than the others (like Scarborough) although the stairs seem to have been in the angles here. The keep seems to have been burnt down, and none of the objects found in the excavations (in particular the carved capitals) need be later than the demolition of the castle in 1175. Henry II had spent £1,800 on Nottingham castle in 1170-5, perhaps including the (now vanished) square tower and shell-wall on the mound which resembled those of Tamworth. Together with expenditure on Bolsover and Peveril in 1173-4, this suggests an attempt to contain Duffield and the Ferrers.

Many castles were demolished after the rebellion of 1173-4 and more were confiscated.[14] One siege-work of the war survives — a *motte* and bailey out of arrow-range of Huntingdon castle. Some remains of masonry survive: at Allington there are the foundations of a buttressed building with a rounded end (perhaps a stair-turret) (Fig. 3) and a few ashlars remain on Castle Hill, Thetford, in contrast to the many built into nearby houses. Some demolitions were less entire, but probably as effective: at Benington one wall only of the keep was removed and about one-third of the perimeter of the Saltwood curtain wall was similarly swept away. One angle of Bungay keep was pierced by a mine gallery, while at Framlingham a hall and chapel remained standing and were incorporated into the later curtain wall. At Groby (and probably at Dunham Massey, Kirby Malzeard, Northallerton, Thirsk and Weston Turville too) the *motte* was partly quarried away to undermine any building on top. The timbers of Mountferrant castle were transferred to Meaux. Those responsible for the demolition of Owston Ferry castle were fined in 1180 for the inadequacy of their destruction.

The gatehouse and oblong keep of Prudhoe (Fig. 54) had probably been built in time to help ward off the Scots' sieges of 1173-4; the gatehouse corbels are interesting and the tiny pilasters of the keep show how atrophied the buttress could become. The keep (with enclosing wall) built at Newcastle upon Tyne between 1168 and 1178 shows an interruption in its masonry and a change of design, when a wall-stair below the gallery was abandoned. This can probably be dated to 1173-4 when little was spent on the castle, due to the invasion of William the Lion, King of Scots. The basement of the keep is vaulted, the central column with its scalloped capital being hollow to take the well-shaft. The walls are riddled with chambers at all levels; most of the windows are mere slits, but there is a fine two-light window to hall and gallery, and the entrance door and lobby are chevron-decorated, as is the vaulted chapel contrived beneath the forebuilding stairs (Plate XXX). The angle opposite to the entrance is chamfered off so that the buttress presents six outward faces to an attacker instead of the usual two (Plate XXXI, Fig. 48).

The second building phase at Dover lasted throughout the 1180s and cost over £6,000. It included the cubical keep, surrounded by a curtain wall defended by fourteen square towers, two gatehouses being formed by building pairs of towers close together (Frontispiece). A somewhat similar curtain studded with *open-backed* towers can be seen at Framlingham (Fig. 34). Since there is no obvious sign of the demolition paid for in 1173-6 to be seen, the walling is presumably later, perhaps even after the castle's repurchase from the Crown in 1189. The triangular joggled arch to the entrance provides a link with Orford, and Framlingham may preserve an echo of that castle's lost curtain wall. The keep at Dover has a sloping plinth and deep buttresses, the angle ones being carried high above the wall-head as turrets. The forebuilding surrounding one angle contains chapels on two levels (Plate XV) each highly ornamented in the style of Conisbrough and Newcastle. One man, Maurice the Engineer, seems to have been in control of the building of both Dover and Newcastle keeps.[15] But with its cross-wall, wall chambers and angle staircases, Dover keep shows little improvement in military architecture over the keeps of fifty years before (Plate XIV, Figs. 28, 29) despite its ingenious plumbing system. Only in its concentric curtain walls did Dover show any evidence of development, and even this was foreshadowed at Orford 25 years earlier.

RECTANGULAR AND POLYGONAL KEEPS, 1154-89

The completion of the outer curtain wall at Dover, with its half-round towers (two placed close together as a gatehouse) had to wait another 17 years for a start to be made and 25 years before completion.

However the multangular idea – and its linking case, the cylindrical – of Buckenham, Orford, Chilham and Tickhill had not died completely. The chapel of Conisbrough castle is first mentioned in 1189 but the castle had a constable by 1178 so that the cylindrical keep there may be only ten years or so later than Orford. It is ashlar faced within and without, with six enormous buttresses projecting like the teeth of a gearwheel, and rising above the conical roof. There is no forebuilding and the stairs rise in the thickness of the wall. There are joggled heads to doors, windows and fireplaces, with quatrefoil windows and carved bosses and ribs in the chapel contrived within one buttress (Plate X, Figs. 24, 27). A smaller version of the keep remains at Mortemer (Seine Maritime), also owned by Hamelin Plantagenet.

It is worth noting the improvements of a decade, of Conisbrough over Orford. The rectangular turrets with their blind corners, where stresses were greatest and visibility least, were swept away and replaced by wedge-shaped buttresses like stout fins. An open space overlooking the drawbridge and steep stairs replaced the bottleneck of a forebuilding. The wall thickening to support a spiral stair was avoided by a return to the wall-staircase, interrupted at each floor and resuming on the other side, so that an attacker had to win each floor in turn instead of taking the stairs in one rush and so controlling the battlements.

The one really weak feature of Conisbrough was its curtain wall with rounded buttresses, which was butted against the keep in an awkward re-entrant angle. This covered a vulnerable point on the perimeter of the defences, allowed the latrines to discharge into the ditch and provided a last chance of escape for the defenders, but at the cost of losing the allround view and control of the castle. Exactly the same feature is present at Château Gaillard (Eure) of 1196-8. Here the buttresses taper vertically into the sloping plinth of the round keep with its angular prow. Attackers approaching the keep entrance were further sheltered by buildings against the curtain.

At Barnard Castle (Plate II, Fig. 5) and Pembridge the 'prow' provided flat abutments for the domestic ranges. At Bonneval, La Roche Guyon and Issoudun the *donjons* stand free, their prows jutting toward the line of approach. Philippe-Auguste's architects did not repeat the mistake of Richard Coeur de Lion.

REFERENCES

[1] R. Allen Brown 'A List of Castles 1154-1216', *English Historical Review* LXXIV, pp. 249-80.

[2] *Transactions of the Cumberland and Westmorland Archaeological Society*, new series XXVII, pp. 224-7.

[3] *Pipe Roll* expenditure from 17, Henry II.

[4] *Pipe Roll* expenditure from 14, Henry II.

[5] *Proceedings of the Suffolk Institute of Archaeology* XXII, p. 210.

[6] *Chronicles of the reigns of* . . . *Henry II* . . . I, p. 104.

[7] *Proceedings of the Suffolk Institute of Archaeology* XXII, pp. 208-10.

[8] As at Orford: *Red Book of the Exchequer* cclxxx, No. 54.

[9] See Dr Allen Brown's invaluable guidebook (M.P.B.W.).

[10] *Aarbøger* 1934 pl. ix opposite p. 264 *Fornvännen* 1933, p. 269, fig. 77.

[11] *Chronicles of the reigns of* . . . *Henry II* . . . IV, p. 209; *Magni Rot. Scacc. Norm.* (ed. Petrie): G. Enlart *Manuel d' Archéologie* II, pp. 504-8; *Bulletin Monumental* 76, pp. 1-16.

[12] J. S. Clouston *Early Norse Castles* (Kirkwall 1931); *Proceedings of the Orkney Antiquarian Society* VII.

[13] *Pipe Roll*; Giraldus Cambrensis, *Opera* V, p. 285.

[14] See reference 1.

[15] *Pipe Rolls* Henry II, 21, pp. 183-4; 28, p. 150; 29, p. 160; 30, p. 144; 31, p. 224; 32, p. 186; 33, p. 205. Similarly Richard of Wolviston appears to have been in charge at both Bowes and Norham and Ralph of Grosmont was also at Dover later. A Ralph Berenger received £30 — nearly three times as much as others — at Château Gaillard.

CHAPTER 9

Castle Halls and experiments in fortification, 1160–1216

Changing needs often led to the rebuilding of a castle's domestic accommodation more frequently than its defences, and so Norman halls are few. Those at Berkeley, Chepstow, Eynsford, Monmouth and Richmond are the main survivors from pre-1160, together with the lower parts of the courtyard-halls of Devizes, Durham (?), Old Sarum, Sherborne, Taunton and Windsor, which have been described already. The later Romanesque examples (say 1160–1216) are about as many. Christchurch castle hall lacks only its timber floors and roof: the basement was lit by loops and the upper floor by barred windows on the river front, with highly-decorated windows in the short walls. The east wall of the hall at Framlingham survives built up into the later curtain with a fireplace at each of two levels venting through cylindrical chimneys, one of which has opposed round-headed smoke-vents (Plate XVII). An altered cellar remains at Newark. Scalloped timber capitals from arcades survive in the altered halls at Farnham and Leicester (Fig. 1) and some traces of Norman work survive in Winchester castle hall. The hall at Grosmont (Fig. 35) has been dated to *circa* 1210 because of the vertical tooling on the ashlar quoins and the loose capitals found within, but the pilaster buttresses and long narrow plan might suggest an earlier origin.

Another hall-block has been excavated at Scarborough (Fig. 67). There are substantial remains of a Romanesque hall at Craigie in Ayrshire (Fig. 21) and possible others at Fincharn and Fraoch Eilean near Loch Awe.

At Durham the first hall basement was filled up and a two-storey hall built above, the lower with an elaborate doorway (Plate XVI) and the upper with an arcade of alternate windows and seats. The

Transitional hall at Oakham had dogtooth ornament to the two-light windows, and crocket capitals to the arcade pillars, with carvings in the spandrels and responds (Plate XXXIII).

Many lesser castles had humble halls of timber on sleeper walls: that at Sulgrave was partly rebuilt in stone with a watch-tower nearby, like the timber group at Lismahon. A similar rebuilding occurred at Huttons Ambo, perhaps copying the hall at Pickering. Multi-aisled timber structures have been found at Llantrithyd (with coins of Henry I) and Penmaen, and a curious group of four conjoined longhouses at Lydford.

Early chapels are equally rare: those at Dover, Hereford[1] and Red Castle probably preceded the building of the castle. Ludlow still has the round nave and foundations of a semi-hexagonal ended chancel, like another excavated at Kenilworth (Figs. 40, 37). Excavations have also revealed a chapel at South Witham and an apsidal timber building at Montgomery.

The southern Welsh March was a remarkable centre of military architectural development in the second half of the twelfth century. The gutted polygonal shell round the *motte* at Tretower appears to date from about 1150-75 (Plate XLVI, Fig. 71). It is right-angled to take an L-shaped hall and solar block, with a segmental projection for the kitchen (whose chimney has rows of vents like Ogmore) and a rectangular gatehouse beyond. The oblong keep at Lydney was at one corner of a diamond-shaped enclosure, with the entrance arch between the keep and a shallow gate-tower (Fig. 44). The inner curtain wall at White Castle was built (1184-6) in short straight lengths round the mound to abut against the square keep, as did that at Coity (Figs. 76, 20). At Bwlch y Ddinas the oblong keep is close within one side of a triangular enclosure, with square towers of slight projection at the angles and the centre of each side. Two square towers bestride the wall at Newcastle Bridgend, one overlooking the elaborate entrance doorway dateable to about 1175-80. This curtain wall is also right-angled for the abutment of domestic ranges within (Plate XXX, Fig. 54). At Morgraig the pentagonal curtain wall has an oblong keep at one angle (opposite the entrance) and oval towers at the other four (Fig. 44) — a similar oval tower projects from the curtain wall at Coity.

The squat cylindrical tower on the *motte* at Longtown had three hemicylindrical buttresses: that carrying the staircase beside the entrance has collapsed. Rounded buttresses flank the gate passage to the bailey, and this stonework probably belongs to the *novum castrum* of 1186-7 (Plate XXII, Figs. 41, 42). Only one-half of the basement of the round keep at Lyonshall survives with its octagonal mantlet wall (Fig. 42), probably one of the two castles of John of Evreux mentioned in 1188. At Skenfrith the cylinder is narrower but taller, the foundations descending to the base of the low mound, and the one hemicylindrical buttress for the staircase is balanced by a corbelled-out oriel window. The keep is surrounded by a quadrilateral curtain wall, with round towers at the angles and a solid D-shaped bastion on the side away from the river. All the masonry probably dates from the ownership by Hubert de Burgh (1201-39), although pottery from the keep basement need not be later than about 1220.[2] The ashlar-cased cylinder on the *motte* at Caldicot castle (first mentioned in 1197) has a large hemicylindrical projection but the stairs are elsewhere (Fig. 14). There is not enough left of the bulge on the round tower at Chartley to determine its function; the castle was repaired in 1191-2, but the tower on the *motte* and the round-towered curtain are usually attributed to about 1220 (Fig. 20). The curious assemblage at Taliorum (Llanhilleth) where a cruciform building with round-headed windows stood beside a very large round tower with a central pier, is undated but may be of our period.

Rounded buttresses can also be seen in the forework added to the keep at Colchester (Fig. 22), perhaps the work paid for in 1192-4, and the square keep at Pevensey, built (by 1130) against a buttress of the Roman fort, had three other such buttresses added (perhaps in 1194-8), in ashlar masonry with a sloping plinth (Fig. 57).

The origin of the round keep is debatable. Whatever the date of New Buckenham it was an experiment (with its cross-wall derived from rectangular keep design) that went unrepeated, and the development of the multangular form at Orford led to the heavily buttressed design of Conisbrough. Three hemicylindrical buttresses clasp the round keeps of Eigenberg and Reichenberg in Germany but they are undated, although Germanic influence increased during and after Richard I's captivity and ransom in 1192-3. The one spectacular royal building work in England during Richard's reign was the expenditure of nearly £3,000 on the wall and ditch round the Tower of London. The Bell Tower at the south-west angle rises from a polygonal base to a cylinder above, and the chamfered plinth of Purbeck marble has been traced eastward so far as the Bloody Tower (Fig. 73). Since the evolution appears to be in the direction of fewer buttresses, the source of inspiration may have been Houdan[3] (with its four buttresses).

At Pembroke, the great round keep concealed its spiral staircase in the wall thickness. Each main floor has a dogtooth-ornamented two-light window with side seats, but the most interesting feature is the dome with two concentric fighting galleries around and upon it (Plate XXXV, Fig. 55). It was probably built by William Marshall after he had married the Clare heiress in 1189. His previous adventurous life would have given him many opportunities to observe similar buildings (e.g. Châteaudun, Eure et Loir) and he had plenty of time to build it because he was not permitted to go to Ireland until 1207.[4] The last vestige of the buttress projection can be seen at Nenagh, a wide shallow pilaster covering the stair beside the entrance. The remaining tower was the largest of five on the original circuit of walls, two being placed together to form a gatehouse. Nenagh is dated 1200-20; since the round keep of Dundrum (possibly 1203-10) has no staircase projection, Nenagh might be of the first rather than the second decade of the thirteenth century (Plate XXIX, Figs. 48, 30).

The northern angle towers of Kenilworth may be part of the works that cost £1,000 in 1210-15. The Swan Tower has a solid square base and an octagonal upper floor, while Lunn's Tower has a circular plinth with four pilasters above it (Plate XXI, Fig. 37).

Simple castles were still being erected — ordinary *mottes* at Rhyader (1177-94) and Dingestow (1182), and the money borrowed to fortify Llanstephan in 1192 seems to have been spent on a simple gatehouse and curtain wall on the ring-work. The new castle at Garn Fadrun (1188) was a wedge-shaped enclosure on the hill-top, with a steep approach track reminiscent of Dinas Powis, a site occupied in the Dark Ages as well as later, like Degannwy and

Dinas Emrys. The tower of York castle was rebuilt after a riot in 1190, but a licence to refortify Wheldrake in 1199 was cancelled and the projected castle at Grimsby (1200) eventually abandoned. In the dark days of Richard I's imprisonment, Kingshaugh was used as a castle, but the seizure and fortification of St Michael's Mount by Henry de Pomeroy was soon terminated.

Apart from the solitary Bishopton licence of 1143,[5] the first licences 'to fortify and crenellate with a wall of stone and lime' appear to be those issued in 1195 (Haddon and Matefelun), followed by no less than nine in the first years (1200–4) of John's reign. One licence covered three sites: Ashley or Stockbridge, Bridgwater and an unnamed place in Devon. The usual type of fortification seems to have been a rectangular moated enclosure round the house (Ashley, Bridgwater, Cottingham, Kirkoswald). The sites of Buttercrambe and Cotherstone have been altered, and *Katherain*, *Hartland* and *Stokes* are unidentified, unless the latter is Stokesay, where there is a pentagonal tower with a projecting square turret and an upper timber gallery (Plate XLII, Fig. 65). Ashley has the foundations of a round tower. The royal hunting-lodges seem to have been similarly ditched around: that in Kinver forest had a brattice over the gate, and Woodstock was garrisoned both in 1199 and 1212.

Little survives to show for the heavy expenditure on castles in John's reign, apart from the outer curtains at Dover and Scarborough and the hallblock beside the keep at Corfe, of two storeys with a range of fine windows. At Norham (1208–12) and Southampton (1204–8) a curtain wall was built on foundation piers excavated into a now-vanished bailey bank. Horston passed into John's hands in 1198 and over £700 was spent on it in 1200–3, possibly including the rectangular keep (Fig. 35) which may have been the tower crenellated in 1205. About the same amount was spent at Hanley in 1207–12, but only an oblong moat remains, like that at Frampton (1213). At Odiham, part of an octagonal tower with angle buttresses survives, built in 1207–12 on the pattern of Gisors some forty years before (Fig. 51). A decagonal keep encases the *motte* at Athlone (Fig. 3) having been rebuilt after collapsing in 1211; another once existed at Castleknock. Sauvey too has a mound in the inner bailey that might cover building works of 1210–11 (Fig. 61). There was a short-lived castle at Tweedmouth in 1208–9, and much of the £1,300 spent on Knaresborough in 1203–12 seems to have gone on ditching. The loss of Normandy led to the fortification of the Channel Islands, brattices being shipped to Guernsey in 1206 and a castle in Jersey being mentioned in 1212. Castle Cornet had a great round tower, but only fragments of early work now survive there and at Mont Orgueil.

Rectangular keeps were still being built — Horston has already been mentioned and there is another at Moreton Corbet and perhaps a third (1214) embedded in the later tower at Mulgrave. At Mitford two sides project to make an arrow-head with the cross-wall of a pentagonal keep (Fig. 47). One end of Ewloe and Helmsley is apsidal, but neither are certainly pre-Henry III (Figs. 30, 33). The idea of adding projecting turrets to the sides — instead of the angles — of a square keep is best seen at Trim (Plate XLV, Figs. 72, 74) where the ornamental features may date the whole building to 1190–1200. Square turrets were added to a plain square tower at Rushen (Fig. 57) whose owner (1187–1228) was John de Courcy's brother-in-law and may have known of developments in Ireland. The keep of Marisco castle on Lundy Island is similar in shape, but was built for Henry III in 1242–3. The great fourteenth-century tower-house at Warkworth may be an aggrandisement of a Norman one, of which a hint remains. Trim keep retains its cross-wall, as do the ordinary rectangular keeps at Adare (Fig. 3), Carrickfergus (Plate VI, Figs. 16, 26) and Maynooth (Fig. 45). Part of the curtain wall and towers of Carrickfergus have been excavated and dated to about 1200; those at Trim, round with open backs like the third phase of Dover, may be about 1220. As late as 1203, however, a *motte* was made by filling the church at Meelick with earth up to the gables. If we over-run our chosen limit for a moment, the excavations at Nafferton (Northumberland) show what a small castle of the time was like. A palisaded clay rampart enclosing a rectangular area was being replaced by a stone wall when work abruptly ceased in 1218.[6]

The siege of Rochester in 1215 included the mining of one angle of the keep, but even then the garrison held out beyond the cross-wall. After their final surrender, the angle was rebuilt three-quarters

CASTLE HALLS, FORTIFICATION, 1160–1216

round and solid, but the junction can only be clearly seen within the keep, where ornamental arches are blocked and wall-passages skewed. At Dover the miners never reached the curtain, let alone the keep. Bedford castle has been demolished, but the old tower was incorporated in the improvements of John's reign. The south front of Warkworth castle was rebuilt around 1200 with a semi-octagonal tower at one angle and a twin-towered gatehouse in the middle, the semi-octagonal towers having hemihexagonal buttresses (Fig. 75). This was probably the first true twin-towered gateway built in Britain since Roman times, since those of the second and third building phases at Dover were really only two wall-towers built close together and other gatehouses were solid bastions rather than towers.

Redevelopment and expansion have destroyed most Norman town fortifications. Simple enclosures of bank and ditch remain in a few places, rectangular at Acre, Longtown, Radnor, Rhuddlan, and Wigmore, and rounded at Abergavenny, Ongar, and Pleshey (Figs. 2, 41, 53, 61). Earlier fortifications were repaired: at Wareham and Wallingford the earthworks were strengthened with a stone wall. Drawings of destroyed gatehouses at Barnstaple and Lincoln indicate Romanesque features, and the round inner arch of the Southampton Bargate may date from the works of 1203. The simple gatehouse at Acre too, with its solid round bastions may be of our period. But Britain can show nothing like Avila's walls of 1099.

REFERENCES

[1] *Transactions of the Woolhope Field Club* 36, pp. 343–57.
[2] *Medieval Archaeology* VI/VII, pp. 144–5, note 61.
[3] p. 57.
[4] *Dictionary of National Biography.*
[5] p. 51.
[6] *Archeologia Aeliana,* fourth series XXXVIII, pp. 129–44; XXXIX, pp. 165–98.

CHAPTER 10

The Rise and Fall of the Norman castle

A salient fact emerges from the study of Norman castles: methods of attack and defence were not static, and demanded a flexibility that the keep was unable to provide. The idea of combining the main accommodation in one defensible building whether a stone keep or palisaded enclosure (incorporating a timber tower) on top of an earthen *motte*, while theoretically brilliant, made for very uncomfortable living conditions. Seldom were the aims of architecture and the needs of military engineering entirely compatible, and most castles exhibit a compromise solution.

A rectangular building is the simplest shape to floor or vault, although during the eleventh century there was a persistent inability to construct true right angles. Pilaster buttresses were skeuomorphs of the trusses of wooden halls, whose purpose was now limited to providing a framing of wall surfaces. The 'dead ground' obscured by the angles covered precisely the places where stresses were greatest. The polygonal or round plan reduced the 'dead ground' and had the practical advantages of needing less masonry — both core and facing — to enclose a given volume of living space, and having no angles to be buttressed. Barrel-vaults existed alongside the ribbed groined vault, and domes came in at the end of the twelfth century, at Conisbrough and Pembroke.

The need to stack rooms on top of each other made for difficulties of communication. Staircases weakened a wall, and special provision had to be made for them. Wall recesses for chimneys, fireplaces, sanitation and storage were made at the expense of strength and stability. Window openings were designed to admit light and air; the only concession to defence was the use of small slits at the bottom of walls. Neither sort were of any use to defending archers — slits gave no view of the ground, and windows gave no cover from attackers' arrows. Even the narrow crenels in the parapet were of limited use, and timber galleries had to be built out to command the foot of the walls, where an earthen mound or sloping plinth gave a ricochet surface and deterred boring or mining. What may be a late copy of such a gallery can still be seen at Stokesay.

The entrance was an obvious point to attack, and defended stairs and movable bridges soon developed into a regular forebuilding, which provided extra accommodation but also produced another traffic bottleneck. A water supply was essential — at Dover there is a piped system in the walls, fed from a well. Everything else had to come and go through the one entrance. It is not unusual to find a back door at a different level from the front to ease this pressure. However awe-inspiring its appearance, a keep could only hold a limited number of people for a limited period of time, in an impregnable but inescapable position. A small party of attackers needed only to sit down and wait until disease, starvation, thirst or demoralization set in among those cooped up inside. In any case a small force was no real threat to an army, and the future of castles lay with the larger enclosure capable of holding a fair-sized garrison, its walls studded with towers from which an enfilading fire could be poured upon attackers.

Such early enclosure walling as survives unaltered is usually extremely plain. The stark curtain at Eynsford, without plinth at the bottom or crenels at the top, produces a feeling of shock at first sight. Elsewhere the narrow crenels were cut in the parapet for observation rather than archery; occasionally an inside parapet (parados) provided rear defence as well. Timber galleries were also used here to command the wall face — the whole south front of Warkworth has scaffold-holes for a continuous gallery. Excavation of the post-holes of timber palisades often show an inner subsidiary line of props to support a wall-walk.

Towers at the angles of the enclosure were built throughout the Norman period, particularly when the curtain wall was built as a whole. Sometimes the towers were internal, as if to stop people getting out rather than in. The idea was probably to protect the towers from direct assault with an enveloping wall, and also to enfilade attackers who had penetrated the curtain. Like the keeps, the wall-towers were usually rectangular until the end of the twelfth century, with occasional experiments (as at Ludlow) in chamfering off the angles to improve the defenders' field of fire and to reduce the danger of mining. The short bow (fired from the hip) of the Bayeux Tapestry was succeeded by the longbow which needed a tall embrasure with a deep stance for drawing. The crossbow (fired from the shoulder like a rifle) needed a broader (but less tall or deep) recess. The true arrowslit hardly appears before about 1190, when it occurs in the storeyed fighting gallery of the Avranches Tower at Dover and in the triple arrowslits opening off each embrasure in the flanking walls, a design also to be found at Carrickfergus and Framlingham. A plunging fire could be directed from the sloping arrowslits at the top of Kenilworth and Pembroke keeps, the latter also being a storeyed fighting-top. Horizontal cross slots were introduced to improve the traverse, particularly of the more awkward crossbow.

The first entrances were mere gaps in the earth bank or simple archways in the stone wall, perhaps with an overhanging timber gallery. If the opening were turned into a passage with flanking walls, more control could be exercised. In turn, the passages could be roofed over in timber, with diaphragm arches across the passage, or vaulted in stone, which overcame the danger of an enemy smoking out the defenders by a bonfire in the gate passage. Occasionally the gateway rose several storeys high, but the idea of the gatehouse-keep does not seem to have been successful at this time. In several instances, the early gate-passage was blocked and a new entrance cut through the curtain wall beside it (Exeter, Ludlow, Richmond, perhaps Bramber). This gave rise to the plan of a tower beside the entrance, guarding its approach. At two of Henry of Blois's castles, the gate-passage passes through a square tower so providing one (in the earlier example at Merdon) or two (at Wolvesey) side rooms for guards. Towards the end of the reign of Henry II, two dissimilar towers flanking the passage were built in the inner Dover curtain and elsewhere and eventually at Warkworth the true twin-towered gate reappeared (since it had been common in Roman fortification).

The sliding portcullis was more economical on floorspace than swinging doors, but it needed counterpoise or windlass space, not just a long hole into which a doorbar could be slid when not in use. Similarly, the turning bridge was uncommon since it required sophisticated machinery to operate it, and the simple drawbridge like a ship's gangway was more usually employed. Sheer weight and size of available timbers, and also the problems of manoeuvring and storing the drawbridge, put limits on the size of the gap that could be temporarily bridged in this way.

The criteria for a good defensive ditch are that it should be too wide to leap across and deep enough to make getting in and out difficult. If it can be made boggy and steep-sided, so much the better. Many early castles had relatively small but efficient earthworks, but in the latter part of the twelfth century very wide ditches were constructed (as at Kenilworth and the Tower of London) to keep attackers further away, and banks and walls were raised in height. Improvements in siege techniques, particularly in mining and projectile engines, were probably responsible.

Excavation and repair have revealed interesting construction features. At Richmond the ground was stripped of topsoil and the walls founded on softwood piles. The walls themselves were built around pole frameworks (as at Bramber) — more substantial timbers laced the keep walls of Bridgnorth and Ludgershall. The keep at Brough was built on a timber raft over its predecessor, and that at Chilham was partly supported similarly. Standards of construction varied — foundations were often insufficient and much fine ashlar work was covered with earth, probably for support, within a short time of erection. Thus the fine plinth of Aldingbourne has crumbled within a few years of its exposure.

Castle building, maintenance and repair were expensive, and many castles went out of use for financial reasons. The castellan of Sowerby had been in debt to the Crown for 10 years by 1186, and Benefield castle was actually seized for debt in 1208. Royal castle building absorbed a considerable proportion of the Crown revenues, and lesser men must have found the costs even harder to bear. Wages alone were not cheap: a knight, ten sergeants, a watchman and a porter cost over £21 for the year to Michaelmas 1130 at Burton in Lonsdale castle[1] then on a 'care and maintenance' basis, while 300 men at arms, archers and *artifices machinarum* were put into Norwich castle after the 1075 revolt.[2] A small garrison could be adequate — three knights and ten sergeants held Odiham in 1216 against the French army.[3] A tenant owed 40 days' service at Weston Turville in time of war and 20 in peacetime[4] but commutation of customary services for money became common in the twelfth century.[5] Castle-guard service could be a complex time-table exercise, as the following table for Dover[6] shows:

Honour	Fees	Soldiers	Weeks
Avranches	21	21	28
Fulbert	15½	15	20
Arsic	18½	18	24
Peverel	15	14	20
Port	12	12	24
Mamignot	25	23	32
Crevequer	5	5	24
Ada fitz William	6	6	24

Often political developments, or the accidents of inheritance, left a castle without a function to fulfil. The accommodation might remain in use, but the defences would be allowed to get out of repair or be demolished for their materials or for the convenience of the other users. Most of the money spent on castles by Henry III was on improvements and maintenance, rather than on new works.

The more one reads of the Normans, the more one is amazed at the way they took control of their destinies. The cool audacity with which they seized opportunities, often against tremendous opposition, may be explained as justifiable self-confidence, or a belief that God was on their side, but it must also owe something to their Viking ancestry. The heroic sagas and the early medieval chronicles have much in common. The Normans assimilated the civilizations they met, altering them only to meet their special needs. In Sicily, Arabic, Latin, and Norman cultures intermingled to their mutual advantage, and the same was true elsewhere. The Normans did not invent cavalry, nor the use of simple fortified bases; what they did was to recognize the link between these military elements and to develop both intensively. Their religious fervour — and their treasure chests — supported the building of churches and monasteries, and this architectural development naturally influenced castles as well. The military architecture of the Normans in various parts of the ancient world thus represents an important part of the impact of that vigorous race upon their contemporaries, and hence part of the civilization of today.

REFERENCES

[1] *Pipe Roll* 31, Henry I, p. 138.
[2] *Lanfranci Opera* (ed. Giles) p. 318.
[3] Roger of Wendover *Flores Historiarum* III, p. 371.
[4] Sir Frank Stenton *The First Century of English Feudalism*, p. 208, appendix 42.
[5] Warren Hollister *Military Organisation in Norman England*.
[6] *Archaeologia Cantiana* XLIX, pp. 96–107.

Glossary

Abacus	Flat stone on top of a capital.
Aisle	Space between arcade and outer wall.
Ambulatory	Aisle around an apse.
Apse	Rounded end. A cross-apse is one at right angles to the main apse.
Arcade	Row of arches. A blind (or wall) arcade is a row of recesses in a wall.
Ashlar	Stone with flat surface, usually of a regular shape.
Bailey	Courtyard and surrounding buildings.
Ballflower	Ornament resembling a flower whose petals enclose a ball.
Baluster	Small column.
Bar hole	Horizontal hole for timber bar used as a door-bolt.
Barrel vault	Plain vault of uniform cross-section.
Bastion	Solid masonry projection.
Battlement	Parapet with indentations (crenellations).
Bay	Space enclosed by arch(es).
Bead	Small hemispheres in a row.
Billet	Small raised rectangle.
Boss	Central stone of vault or arch.
Bourg	Early medieval 'new town'.
Brattice	Either a timber tower or a projecting wooden gallery.
Bressumer	Beam to support a projection.
Burh	Saxon communal fortification.
Buttress	Masonry built against a wall to strengthen it.
Cable	Rope of twisted strands.
Capital	Carved stone at the top of a column or pier.
Carotid	Heart-shaped.
Castellan	Person in charge of a castle.
Chamfer	Surface made by smoothing off the angle between two faces.
Chevron	V-shaped moulding.
Clasping	Encasing the angle.
Clunch	Hard chalk.
Column	Pillar of circular section.
Constable	Official in charge of a castle in the owner's absence.
Coping	Covering stones.
Corbel	Projecting stone. A corbel-table is a row of such projections.
Corinthian	Elaborately foliated capital.
Cornice	Decorative projection along wall-top.
Counterfort	Besiegers' defence-work.

GLOSSARY

Counterscarp	Outer slope of a ditch.
Course	Level layer of stones.
Creasing	ʌ-shaped mark on a wall, marking the pitch of a former roof.
Crenel	Gap in a battlemented parapet. To crenellate is to equip with such a parapet.
Crocket	Curling leaf-shape.
Crosswall	Interior dividing wall.
Curtain	High wall 'hung' between towers.
Cushion	Capital cut from a block by rounding off the lower corners.
Cusp	Curves meeting in a point.
Diaper	Pattern of squares or diamonds.
Diaphragm	Wall running up to the roof-ridge.
Dog-legged	With right-angle bends.
Dogtooth	Diagonal indented pyramid.
Donjon	Keep, or main tower.
Double-splayed	Embrasure whose smallest aperture is in the middle of the wall.
Drawbridge	Movable bridge, strictly one moved horizontally like a gangway.
Dressing	Carved stonework around openings.
Dry-stone	Masonry built without mortar.
Embrasure	Opening in a wall.
Fillet	Narrow flat band.
Fluting	Parallel concave mouldings.
Foliated	Carved with leaves.
Footings	Lower part of a wall, including the foundations.
Forebuilding	Block of rooms in front of the main keep.
Freestone	Fine-grained sandstone or limestone.
Gable	Wall at the end of a roof-ridge.
Gallery	Long narrow room or passage.
Greensand	Green sandstone.
Groined	With sharp edges at the intersection of cross-vaults.
Half-shaft	Roll-moulding flanking an opening.
Hall	Main domestic building.
Herringbone	Laid diagonally in zigzag courses.
Hood	Covering arch. A hood-mould is the projection over an opening to throw off rain-water.
Impost	Wall bracket to support arch.
Jamb	Side of an opening through a wall.
Joggled	Keyed together by overlapping joints.
Joist	Main horizontal timber.
Keep	Main tower.
Lattice	Laths or lines crossing to form a network, with spaces between.
Light	Part of a window, divided from others by mullions and transoms.
Lintel	Horizontal stone bridging an opening.
Loop	Very narrow opening.
Lozenge	Diamond shape.

Mangonel	Siege engine, the projectile arm turning against a fixed stop.
Mantlet	Low outer wall.
Merlon	Solid part of a parapet.
Midwall	Feature not at the end of a wall face.
Mine gallery	Cutting designed to cause a wall to collapse.
Moline	Ends curling outward.
Motte	Earth mound.
Moulding	Decoration of masonry.
Mullion	Vertical division of a window.
Mural	Wall.
Nailhead	Pyramidal moulding.
Necking	Ornament at the top of a column, bottom of the capital.
Nookshaft	Shaft set in the angle of a jamb or pier.
Offset	Ledge marking the narrowing of a wall's thickness.
Oolite	Granular limestone.
Open joint	Wide space between faces of stones.
Oratory	Small cell attached to a chapel.
Order	One of a series of concentric mouldings.
Oriel	Projecting curved window.
Palisade	Timber fence.
Palmette	Looped like a palm-leaf.
Parados	Low wall on inner side of a wider one.
Parapet	Low wall on outer side of a wider one.
Pellet	Circular boss.
Petit appareil	Small cubical stonework.
Pier	Support for an arch, often square in section (unlike a column).
Pilaster	Shallow pier attached to a wall as a buttress.
Pipe Roll	Exchequer accounts, so called because they were rolled up into a long pipe-like bundle.
Pitch	Slope of a roof.
Pitching	Rough cobbling.
Plinth	Projecting base of a wall.
Polychrome	Pattern of colours.
Portcullis	Wood or metal grating dropped vertically in grooves to block a passage.
Postern	Small back door.
Prow	Acute-angled projection.
Puddled	Made waterproof.
Putlog	Horizontal scaffold-beam.
Quatrefoil	Four-lobed.
Quern	Hand-mill stone.
Quirk	V-shaped nick.
Quoin	Stone at the angle of a building.
Rath	Low circular ring-work.
Rear-arch	Arch on the inner side of a wall.
Reeded	Parallel convex mouldings.
Re-entrant	Recessed.

GLOSSARY

Relieving arch	Arch built up in a wall to relieve thrust on another opening.
Respond	Half-pier bonded into a wall to carry an arch.
Return	Receding from line.
Rhombic	Diamond-shaped.
Rib	Raised moulding dividing a vault.
Ring-work	Roughly circular earthwork of bank and ditch.
Roll	Moulding of semicircular section.
Romanesque	Style of architecture from the ninth to the twelfth century.
Roof-ridge	Highest line of a roof.
Rubble	Unsquared stone.
Saltire	Diagonal cross with equal limbs.
Scale	Carving resembling overlapping fish scales.
Scallop	Carved in series of semicircles.
Scappled	Cut to a smooth face.
Scarp	Slope (strictly, the inner slope of a ditch).
Segmental	Less than a semicircle.
Set back/off	Ledge on wall face.
Shaft	Narrow column.
Shell keep	Wall surrounding small area.
Sill	Lower horizontal face of an opening.
Skeuomorph	Imitation in another material (e.g. a plastic flower).
Sleeper	Lowest horizontal timber (or low wall).
Soffit	Underside of an opening.
Spandrel	Area between top of a column or pier and the apex(es) of the arch(es) springing from it.
Splay	Sloping face.
Spring	Level at which the springers (voussoirs) of an arch rise from their supports.
Stepped	Recessed in a series of ledges.
Steyned	Lined (of a well).
Stiff-leaf	Many-lobed flower.
Stringcourse	Continuous horizontal moulding projecting from wall face.
Tau cross	Plain T cross with equal limbs.
Tooth-in	Stones removed (or omitted) to allow another wall to be bonded to it.
Transom	Horizontal division of a window.
Trebuchet	Siege engine in the form of an unequal counterpoised arm.
Trefoil	Three-lobed.
Truss	Timber frame, repeated to form roof.
Tufa	Cellular rock.
Turret	Very small tower.
Tympanum	Space between lintel and arch over doorway.
Unbonded	Not incorporated.
Volute	Spiral scroll at angle of capital.
Voussoir	Wedge-shaped stone forming part of an arch.
Wall-plate	Horizontal roof-timber on wall-top.
Wall-stair	Stair in wall thickness.

Wall-walk	Passage along wall top.
Water-leaf	Plain broad leaf moulding.
Wave	Sinuous moulding.
Weathering	Sloping surface to throw off water.
Wing-wall.	Wall descending slope of motte.

Gazetteer

This section is both gazetteer and index of the castles built in the British Isles before the reign of Henry III. Addenda to the section, prepared for the second edition, will be found on pages 352-357.

In the following descriptions, the name of the castle is italicized if there is doubt about its foundation in the period. Where the map reference quoted is preceded by two letters, it is to the British National Grid; the Irish Grid is distinguished by one letter. The county is specified as an indication of general situation. Descriptions are in chronological order of development as far as possible, beginning at the lowest level of each building. Alterations and additions after 1216 are only described where they obscure earlier features. For brevity, the earthworks are coded according to the classification I proposed in *Antiquity* (XXXIII, pp. 106–12), that is:

Motte: Usually round, but if
oval (top diameters differing by 20% or more) — I;
angular (sides at definite angles to each other) — II; and if
high (vertical height greater than minimum top diameter) — A;
low — B;
ring-work (that is, an embanked area) — C.

Bailey: if plan is:
Circular — a; oval — b; triangular — c; quadrilateral — d; lobed — e; polygonal — f; with appropriate subdivision — a halfmoon being a/2, for instance.

Relationship of motte to bailey: central with own separate
ditch — 1;
internal (within the projected line of the bailey bank) — 2;
peripheral (astride that line) — 3;
external (outside that line) — 4.

Where two numbers are given, the second denotes this relationship.

If an adequate description has been published, this is cited at the end and marked with an asterisk. Naturally these vary in approach and quality, but they usually provide more detail than can be given in a summary catalogue. Frequent abbreviations used are M.P.B.W. for the Ministry of Public Building and Works; R.C.A.M., R.C.H.M. for the county inventories of the Royal Commissions on Ancient Monuments (Wales and Monmouthshire), Historical Monuments (England) and Ancient and Historical Monuments (Scotland), V.C.H. means the *Victoria County History*.

ABER AFAN   SS 768920   Glamorgan

Small *motte* (A) in Cwm Clais, attacked in 1153 (*Brut y Tywysogion*) (*Bulletin of the Board of Celtic Studies* VII, p. 223).*

ABER IA   see DEUDRAIT

ABER LLEINIOG   SH 617793   Anglesey

Motte and Bailey (Bc4), built *c.* 1088–90 by the Earl of Chester and captured by the Welsh in 1094 (*History of Gruffyd ap Cynan*, ed. A. Jones, (Manchester, 1910) pp. 133, 138–9); (R.C.A.M., *Anglesey*, pp. 123–4).*

ABERCORN   NT 083794   West Lothian

Motte (B), said to be the castle of William de Avenel in the middle of the twelfth century (Armitage, *Early Norman Castles of the British Isles*, p. 308).

ABERCOWYN (ABER TAV)   SN 297136   Carmarthenshire

Motte with dished top and bailey (Bb3) mentioned in 1116 (*Brut y Tywysogion*) (R.C.A.M., *Carmarthen*, p. 128).*

ABERDEEN   see page 352

ABERDYFI   SN 687968   Cardiganshire

Motte (IB) at the head of the estuary. Built by the Lord Rhys in 1156 (*Brut y Tywysogion*). The reference to a castle at Abereinon built by the same Rhys in 1168 (*Ann. Camb.*) may be the same site.

ABERGAVENNY   SO 299139   Monmouthshire

Promontory at junction of streams cut off by bank and ditch with an altered mound at the apex (Ac1 ?); a print of 1776 (reproduced in the local guide-book) shows the stump of a square keep with a tall *motte* piled against it, leaving the south face free. The oval enclosure of the town dates probably from 1087–1100, when the church and chapel of the castle were given to a Le Mans abbey, with land for making a *bourg* (Round, *Calendar of Documents preserved in France*, No. 1046).

ABERHONDDU   see BRECON

ABERRHEIDOL   SN 585790   Cardiganshire

Ring-work and bailey (IC3) on the ridge a mile south of the town. Excavations showed that the ring-work was revetted with timber and contained a large pit and post-holes. A causeway across the ditch led to a destroyed gateway, over which a new road surface was laid and the banks stone-revetted when the site was levelled and rebuilt at the end of the twelfth century. Large post-holes might be for gate-posts or even a gate-tower.

Built in 1110 by Gilbert fitz Richard, burnt by the Welsh in 1136 and

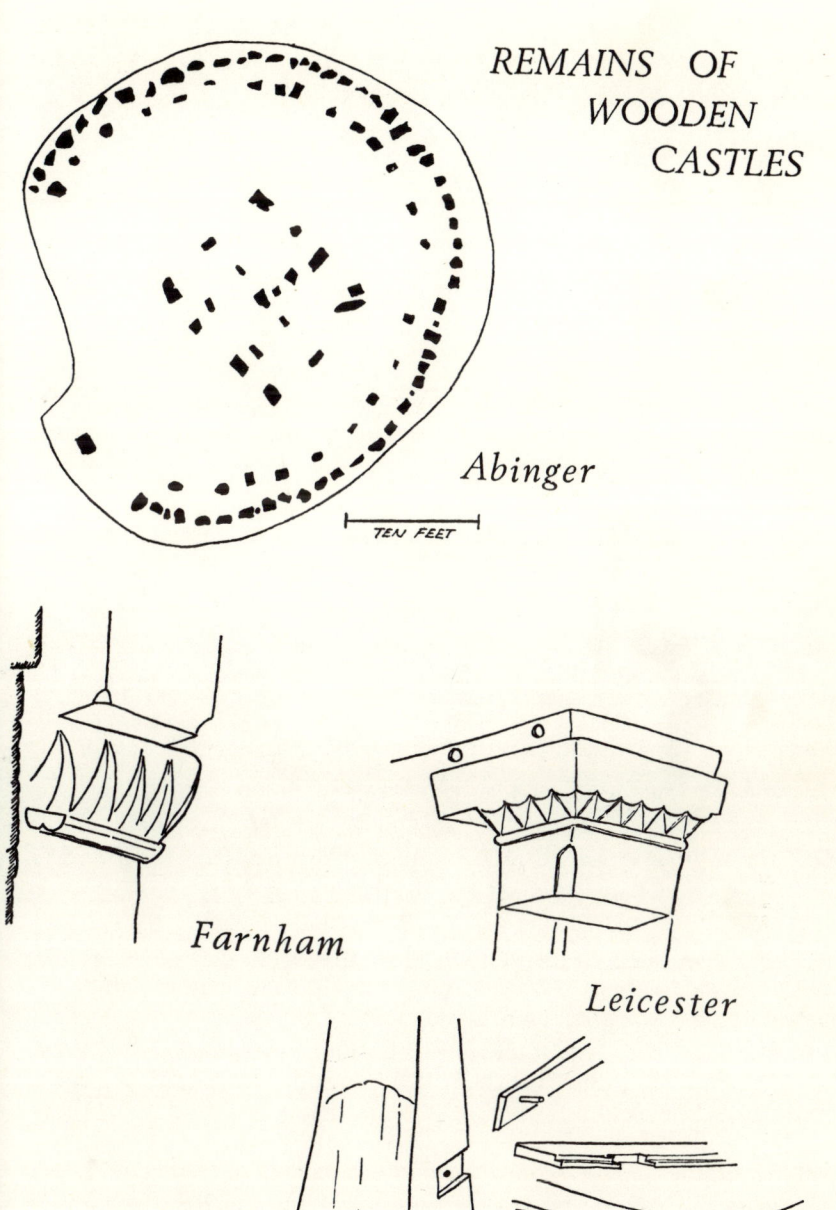

REMAINS OF WOODEN CASTLES

Abinger

TEN FEET

Farnham

Leicester

Rayleigh

again in 1143. It is not clear whether the Aberrheidol castle destroyed in 1164 was the same. Further references to building in 1208 and 1211 (*Brut y Tywysogion*) (*Ceredigion* III, pp. 114–17; *Med. Arch.* VI/VII, pp. 143, 325).

ABERTAWE   see SWANSEA

ABERTEIFI   see CARDIGAN

ABERYSTWYTH   see ABERRHEIDOL

ABINGER   TQ 114460   Surrey

Motte (B) west of church, with possible traces of bailey to south. Excavations in 1949 showed that the *motte*-top had carried a timber tower (some of whose post-holes were recovered) of about 1100, replaced in the twelfth century by another on a different orientation, about 12 ft square. The corner posts had grooves, and those inside suggest the base of steps. There was a timber palisade with struts around the *motte*-top.

The ditch had a flat bottom with a steeper outer slope, interrupted at one point by an original mass of sandstone, scarped so that the ditch is divided into two channels separated from the *motte* and each other by the foundations for a bridge framework.

The dating rests on the interpretation of the pottery found (kept at the Manor House) (*Archaeological Journal* CVII, pp. 15–43).*   (Fig. 1)

ACRE   TF 820152   Norfolk

Mound with revetting octagonal shell wall in flint rubble with ashlar pilasters at the angles, a large U-shaped bailey running down to the water meadows of the river Nar (Bf3) and a square village enclosure to the southwest. The foundations of a rectangular keep 50 ft by 40 ft have been excavated on the mound, the north and west walls being 13 ft thick and the others only 5 ft, with a door in the south wall (Harrod, *Gleanings among the Castles and Convents of Norfolk*, pp. 99–102). Some fragments of bailey curtain survive, together with foundations of buildings within, and an outer gatehouse with solid round towers flanking the pointed arch. *Castelli Nostri de Acra* is mentioned in the (1088) Lewes priory foundation charter (*Monasticon* V, p. 12).   (Fig. 2)

ADARE   R 4546   Limerick

Ring-work with ditch connecting with River Maigue (II Ca/2?) each having a plain square gatehouse. South of the outer gate is a rectangular hall with narrow loops on the river front at ground level and round-headed two-light windows with continuous roll-mouldings to the upper floor. A sleeper-beam of a bridge was found in the river here, and the finds from the clearance of the ring ditch are held to be post-Conquest (*North*

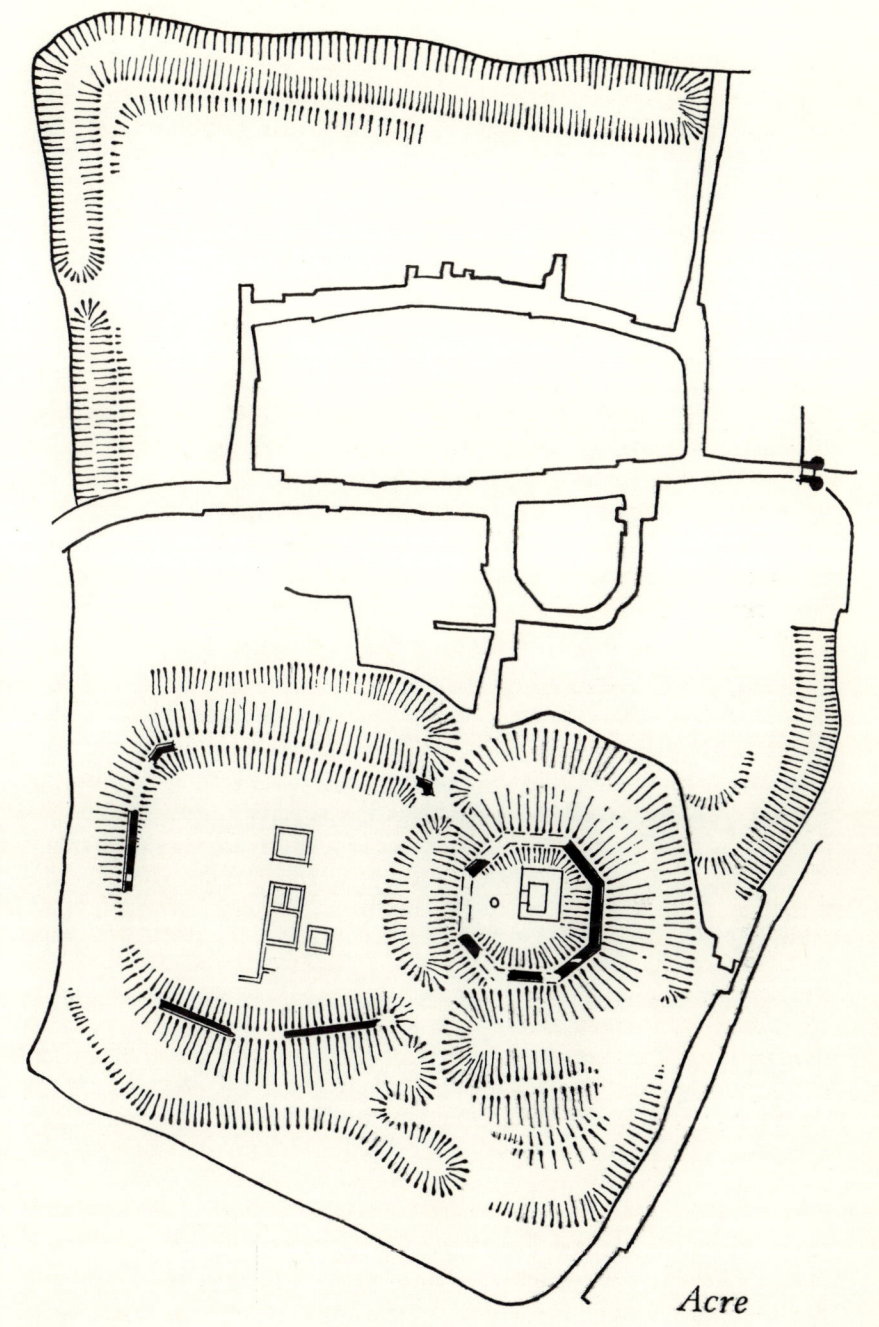

Acre

Munster Archaeological Journal VIII, pp. 193–202). Within the ring-work is a square keep with projecting pilasters at the ends of the east and west walls and a north–south cross-wall, largely destroyed (Dunraven, *Memorials of Adare*).* (Fig. 3)

ALDBOROUGH	SE 407660	Yorkshire

Studforth Hill is a former ringwork (C), probably the *Vetus Burgus* of the *Pipe Rolls* 1205–6 (and *Rot. Chart.* 44).

ALDFORD	SJ 419596	Cheshire

Motte and bailey (Bc3) north of church. Part of the outer face of a collapsed wall round the *motte*-top was excavated in 1959 (*Transactions of the Chester and North Wales Archaeological Society* 47, pp. 35–6).

Richard de Aldeford was succeeded in possession of the castle of Aldford between 10 John and 13 Henry III (i.e. 1209–29) (Ormerod, *History of Cheshire* II, p. 754).	(Fig. 4)

ALDINGBOURNE	SU 923048	Sussex

Square keep of limestone slabs with chamfered ashlar plinth of ten offsets, above which the outer facing is of flints. At the centre and end of each wall is a pilaster buttress of Caen ashlar. A forebuilding was added to the west end of the south wall, of roughly coursed rubble faced inside and out with mortar; the tower itself contained a well. Excavation showed that the tower had been buried in a mound of clay and rock dug from a surrounding ditch and sealing twelfth century pottery; the mound had been partly surrounded with a buttressed stone curtain wall. (*Sussex Archaeological Collections* 107, pp. 141–79).*	(Fig. 3)

ALDINGHAM	see page 352

ALLINGTON	TQ 752579	Kent

Altered *motte* and bailey (Bb4?) on west bank of River Medway. Slight remains of a herringbone-work curtain rubble wall opposite the *motte*, its line continuing to incorporate the western curtain of the later castle. Part of the foundations of a large rectangular building with a western apse and unbonded buttresses have been excavated on the south side of the later courtyard, and the lower part of the round-buttressed gatehouse and adjoining hall are built of reused ashlar with diagonal tooling. The corbels of an earlier roof can be seen above the gate-passage.

The *Pipe Roll* of 1174 records '*in prosternendo castello de Alintone lx.s.*' *Archaeologia Cantiana* XXVIII, pp. 337–62.*	(Fig. 3)

GAZETTEER

ALMONDBURY   SE 152140   Yorkshire

Oval prehistoric hill-fort with bank across minimum diameter, and triangular ring-work with counterscarp bank at south end (IICb2).

A square well-shaft containing bones and dressed stone, and cutting through two layers of pitched stone was partly excavated (*Yorkshire Archaeological Journal* XV, pp. 118–19) and medieval pottery was found in the *motte* (*Bradford Antiquary*, new series I, pp. 396–400), with traces of a shell-wall built in the hollow behind the *murus Gallicus* (*Archaeological Journal* CV, p. 65).

The *castellum de Almanberia* is mentioned in a charter of the reign of Stephen (P.R.O., D.L. 41/1/36 cited by Wightman, *The Lacy Family*, pp. 244–5) and again in the *Pipe Roll* of 1212.

ALNWICK   NU 187137   Northumberland

The castle was rebuilt by Anthony Salvin, but retains traces of its *motte* and bailey origin (Bc1) on a rise between the river Alne and a tributary. The curtain walls and their square towers rest on early foundations, and the inner gatehouse of the clustered *donjon* has round-headed arches, the outer having chevron moulding within a band of alternate nailhead and lozenge; the vaulted passage has chamfered ribs, and the polygonal inner *donjon*-wall may preserve the line of the original shell-wall.

The strong castle of *Alnewic* was mentioned in 1138 (*Chronicles of the reign of Stephen*, III, p. 158) and William the Lion was captured while beseiging it in 1174 (ibid. pp. 332–5) and the castle was ordered to be demolished in 1212 (*Rot. Litt. Pat.* 99; *Rot. Litt. Claus.* I, 343b).

'ALREHEDE'   Cambridgeshire

In the battles for the Isle of Ely in 1069–71 the castle of Alrehede is mentioned (*Liber Eliensis*, pp. 174, 185, 194); it was refortified in 1139 (*B.M. Cotton M.S.* Vesp. A. XIXf. 46d.; *Liber Eliensis*, pp. 314, 315, 328; *Gesta Stephani* p. 66).

Identification is doubtful, but a possible site is Belsar's Hill, Willingham (TL 423703) astride the Aldreth causeway. This large pear-shaped ring-work (Ic) was formerly Belassise (*Rot. Hund.* II, 407, 452) which suggests a post-Conquest origin. A square earthwork further east at Braham (TL 534777) is near the site of the discovery of a number of eleventh-century spears (*Proceedings of the Cambridge Antiquarian Society* xxxi, p. 155; xxxiv, p. 90).

ALSTOE   see BURLEY

ALTON   see page 352

ALVELEY   see page 352

ALVERTON   see NORTHALLERTON

ALYTH   see page 352

ANNAN   NY 199666   Dumfriesshire

Bailey (Cc3?) on east bank of River Annan. Only a curved bank survives of the *motte* — or ring-work — mentioned in a charter of 1124 (*Acts. Parl. Scot.* I, 92; Lawrie, *Early Scottish Charters*, LIV).

ANSTEY   TL 404329   Hertfordshire

Motte and bailey (IBd3) with possible village enclosure immediately north of parish church. Excavations near the eastern edge of the *motte*-top in 1902 revealed flint foundations laid 18 in. deep in solid boulder clay, with plain roofing tiles and fragments of axed clunch 3–6 in. in diameter. The trapezoidal plan (Fig. 4) is based on the dimensions given in the text; no widths were quoted and the re-entrant eastern angle also suggests that the dimensions were internal ones.

The pottery from the excavation was described as having characteristic thumb markings and 'at Nuthampstead to the north and other places similar pottery was always found'. This might suggest parallels with the pottery from the unfinished moated mound in Scales Park, attributed to the late thirteenth century (*Antiquaries' Journal* XXXVI, pp. 138–44), but the only pottery marked 'Anstey Castle' in the Hertford Museum were finds parallel with those from South Mymms castle (q.v.).

Tradition attributes the castle to Eustace, Count of Boulogne, the holder of the manor at Domesday, and certainly the plan has some similarity with his other castles – Ongar, Pleshey (q.v.). In 1218 Nicholas Anstey was given until mid-Lent to throw down the castle so that nothing remained except what was built before the Barons' War (*Close Roll*) (*Transactions of the East Herts. Arch. Soc.* II, pp. 114–18).*   (Fig. 4)

ANTRIM   J 1586   Antrim

Motte (Ad2) mentioned in 1211–12 (*Irish Pipe Roll*).

APPLEBY   NY 685199   Westmorland

Motte and baileys (BCd3?) backed against loop of River Eden. The *motte* is now marked only by the outline of the curtain wall of sandstone coursed rubble surrounding both it and the bailey in a keyhole plan. The entrance to the east has a round-headed arch of two orders with a portcullis groove, between two square buttresses with their outer sides canted.

The keep is in the centre of the *motte* site, of sandstone rubble with ashlar quoins and dressings. There are shallow clasping buttresses at each angle (no plinth is visible), but the cross-wall is a later insertion. The

Adare

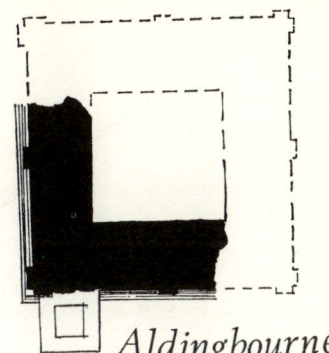
Aldingbourne

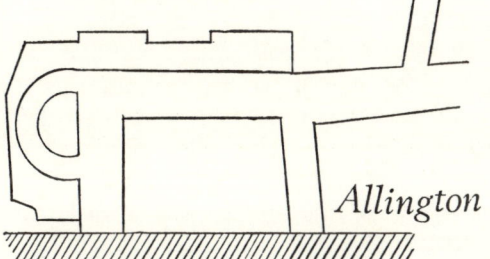
Allington   *Ascot d'Oilly*

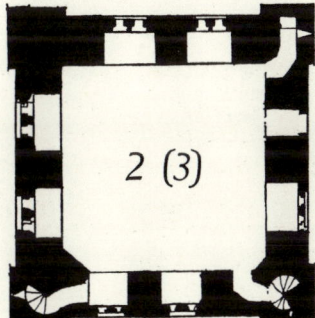
Appleby

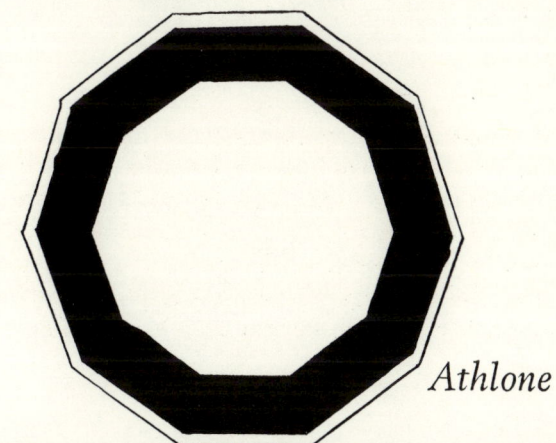
Athlone

ground floor has a round-arched doorway of two square orders at the south end of the east wall, with a sloping loop further north and pairs in the north and south walls. A spiral stair in the south-east angle links all floors, and another, in the south-west angle, the floors above the ground, which have latrines in the north-east angle. These upper floors have pairs of windows on each side, of two square-headed lights under a round-headed outer order, except that the one at the north end of the east wall at first floor level is replaced by a narrow round-headed doorway of two orders (now lowered) with a portcullis slot. These windows are rather low-set and the top stage is blank, apart from the weatherings of the roof with a central east–west valley. There are beam-holes and corbels on the other walls, including an unfinished grinning face on the south side. The bases of narrow crenels can be traced below the present parapet, which seems to have been raised in the thirteenth century, to judge from the moulded shafts and arches at the top of the stairs.

The castle (mentioned in 1129–30) was surrendered to Henry II in 1157 and again in 1173–4 (*Lancashire Pipe Rolls*, p. 390; *Early Yorkshire Charters* I, p. 390, both ed. W. Farrer; *Pipe Roll*). 'Le chastel et la tur' is referred to in the latter year (*Chronicles of the Reign of Henry II*, Vol. III, p. 326) (R.C.H.M. *Westmorland*, pp. 7–12).* (Fig. 3)

A'QI   Limerick

Unidentified site of castle mentioned in 1199 (*Rot. Chartarum* I, 30).

ARCHEN   see ARDKEEN

ARDEE   N 9690   Louth

Motte (Bd4) built by 1192 (Curtis, *Calendar of Ormond Deeds* I, p. 364)

ARDELEA   see EARDISLEY

ARDFINNAN   S 0818   Tipperary

Rebuilt, no certain traces of the castle built in 1185 (Giraldus Cambrensis, *Opera* V, 386; *Annals of Loch Cé*). although the round keep may be of John's reign (*Archaeological Journal* XCIII, p. 199).

ARDGLASS   J 5637   Down

The castle of Jordan de Saukeville where King John stopped on 12 July 1210 may have been on the site of the later castle (*English Historical Review* XXII, p. 445). Tower repaired in 1211–12 (*Irish Pipe Roll*).

ARDKEEN   J 5957   Down

Motte (Bdl) on peninsula in Strangford Lough. Mentioned in 1180 (*Monasticon* II, p. 1019). (*Archaeological Survey of County Down*, pp. 197–8).*

GAZETTEER

ARDMAYLE   S 0547   Tipperary

Motte and bailey (Bd3), attributed to Theobald Walter (d. 1206) (*Calendar of Documents* I, 81, 94, 95) mentioned 1215/6 (*Rot. de Oblatis et Finibus*, 557).

ARDNURCHER   N 2638   Westmeath

Motte and bailey (IIBb3) erected in 1192 (*Annals of Loch Cé*; *Annals of the Four Masters*; *Song of Dermot*; *Calendar of Documents* I, 145). Traces of a round tower and curtain wall existed on the *motte*-top (*Transactions of the Royal Irish Academy* II, part 3, pp. 43–50).

ARDPATRICK   R 2161   Limerick

Site of castle built in 1199 (*Annals of Innisfallen*).

ARDREE   S 6698   Kildare

Motte and bailey (Bd3?) much altered by landscaping for house and churchyard beside river Barrow, built in 1182 (Giraldus Cambrensis *Opera* V, p. 356; *Song of Dermot*; *English Historical Review* XXII, p. 249).

ARDRI   see ARDREE

ARKLOW   T 2353   Wicklow

Castle and town granted by John in 1185–9 (*Curtis, Calendar of Ormond Deeds* I, p. 8)

ARUNDEL   TQ 018073   Sussex

High *motte* between baileys (Ab and d3) above the Arun gap in South Downs. The inner gatehouse is square with plain round-headed arches (with a portcullis-slot), continued as a barrel-vault from a chamfered string-course; it projects inward from a wall which runs up the *motte* to a shell-wall with ashlar pilasters (Caen and Quarr stone) rising from a chamfered plinth, and long narrow crenels to the parapet. There are corbels and fireplaces for an upper internal floor. The blocked entrance has roll-mouldings in the jambs in front of a bar-hole, the arch being ornamented by double chevrons round the whole opening, surrounded by a roll-moulding and an outer border of saltire crosses with pellets in the spaces. An angular projection was added beside this entrance with a vaulted passage beside a square well-tower whose chambered ashlar plinth might be Norman, although the windows above look later.

Among the buildings of the south bailey are two two-light windows in the south-east front of the chapel, with palmette capitals to flanking half-shafts (central double-shaft mullion), and a solid tympanum under a roll-moulding, with a door-head of two round orders with a pilaster buttress on an internal wall. On the east front is a restored doorway with a chevron moulding inside a roll, supported on scalloped capitals with short jamb shafts. Internally one barrel-vaulted cellar has transverse ribs.

The *castrum Harundel* of 'Domesday' (I, 23a) is described like a town, but Florence of Worcester mentions the castle in 1088. The castle passed to the Crown after a siege in 1101, and work here was paid for in 1129–30 and 1176–88 (*Pipe Rolls*), the latter including the planking of the tower.

(Plate I; Fig. 6)

ARUNDEL SIEGE-WORKS   Sussex

Siege-works were built against Arundel in 1102 (*Chronicles of the reigns of . . . Stephen . . .* IV, pp. 82–83) and perhaps in 1138 (*Ordericus Vitalis* XI, 111). These may include the ring-works on Cock Hill, Patching (TQ 089096) and at Warningcamp (TQ 028064) and the square earthwork at Rackham (TQ 050126). Mention should also be made of the large mound The Burgh (TQ 048112) which produced a Norman cooking potsherd with cross stamps (*Sussex Archaeological Collections* LXIII, pp. 1–53; LXXIII, pp. 168–82) and of the ring-work at Lyminster (TQ 030068).

ASCOT DOILLY   SP 304191   Oxfordshire

Slight mound with extensive slight banks and ditches (Bd2?) beside manor-house north of church. Excavation in 1946–7 showed that a square tower of roughly coursed limestone rubble with oolite ashlar quoins had been built on a clay hillock which had been scarped back during the cutting of a surrounding ditch (which contained fragments of timberwork). The ditch was incomplete to the south-west where there was an added abutment against the south end of the west wall of the tower. The mound was raised 3 ft against the outside of the tower up to a slight offset. Inside the walls were plastered down to a gravelly loam floor, sandwiched between mortar layers on to which the upper part of the tower had been demolished. Window glass, nails, arrow-heads, gilt-bronze strip and a horseshoe were found on or near the floor, together with much pottery and deer bones.

The chapel in the castle is mentioned between 1143–62, and again in 1212 (*Cartulary St. Frideswide's*, nos. 1009, 1010, 1019) (*Antiquaries' Journal* XXXIX, pp. 219–73).*   (Fig. 3)

ASCOT EARL   SP 296184   Oxfordshire

Motte and bailey (Ba3), the *motte* producing similar pottery to Ascot Doilly (q.v.) (*Antiquaries' Journal* XXXIX, p. 239).

ASHLEY   SU 385309   Hampshire

Ring-work and bailey (IICc2) south of Ashley church. Loose squared stones, stakes and tiles were to be found on the east side of the enclosure,

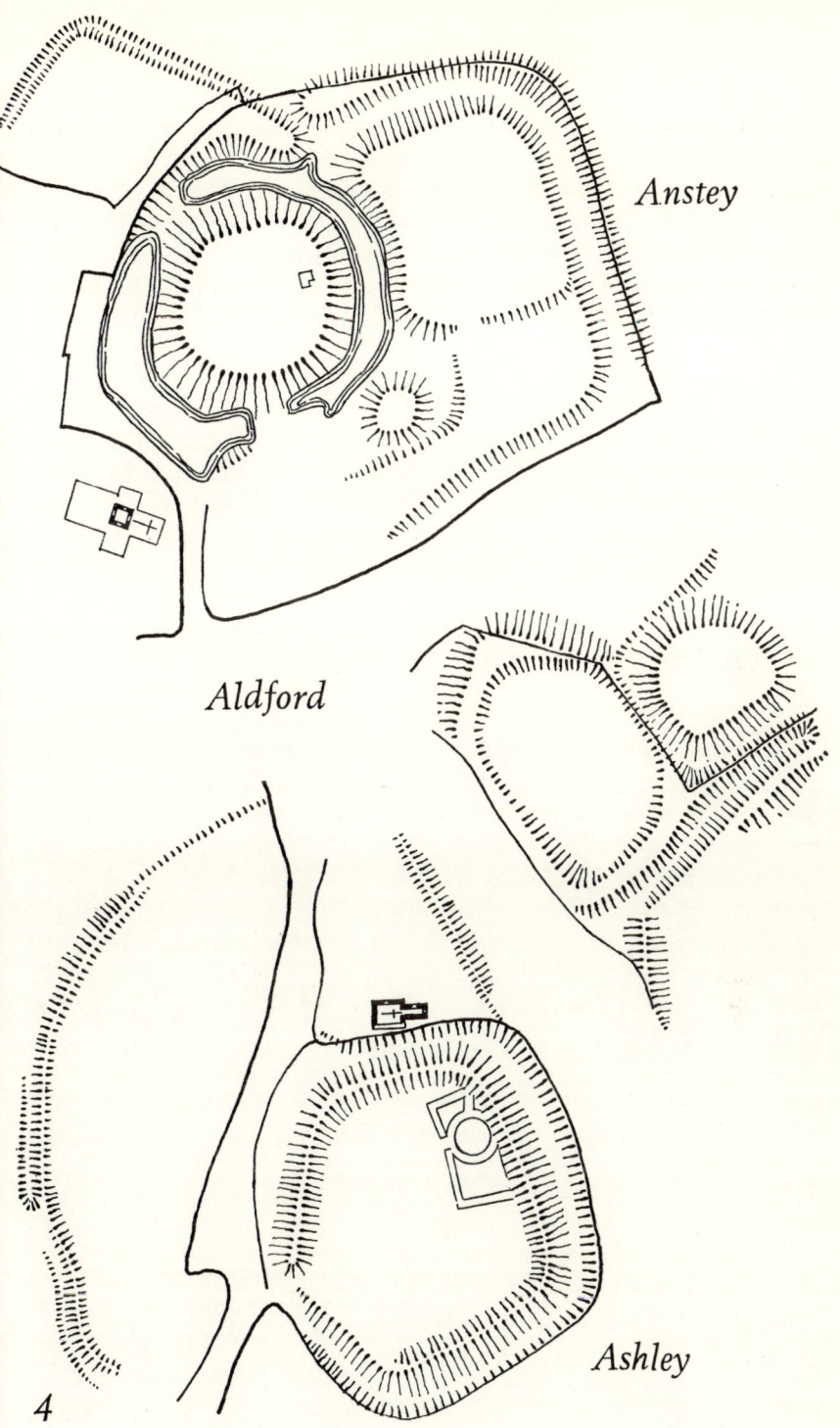

where Williams-Freeman (*Field Archaeology as illustrated by Hampshire*, opp. p. 348) records foundations of an irregularly rectangular building 100 ft long with a round tower (?) 40 ft in diameter toward the northern end. A short pyramidal arrow-head (London Museum *Medieval Catalogue* Type 7) from the ditch is in the Winchester Museum.

William Briwere the elder had licence to fortify a castle in Hampshire either at Ashley or Stockbridge in 1200 (*Rot. Chartarum* I, p. 70). (Fig. 4)

ASHTON KEYNES   SU 049943   Wiltshire

Ring-work and bailey (Ca3) east of village. Excavation showed that the ditch was lined with puddled clay and revetted with brushwood, and the bank contained a drystone wall. The pottery found dated from the early twelfth to the thirteenth century (*Wiltshire Archaeological Magazine* 57, p. 241; *Bulletin Institute of Archaeology* 3, pp. 72–3).

ASKEATON   R 3350   Limerick

Triangular island between River Deel and side-channel, with oval mound in centre (IBc1). The basement of the rectangular hall on the west side has a series of narrow loops cut into pilaster buttresses rising from the sloping plinth. Two loops at the northern end of the wall are double-splayed.

The castle was built in 1199 (*Annals of Innisfallen*) and mentioned in 1203 (*Calendar of Documents* I, p. 92; *Patent* and *Fine Roll* (*Journal of The Royal Society of Antiquaries of Ireland* XXXIV, pp. 117–25; *Architectural and Topographical Record* I, pp. 284–307).*

ASKELON   see CARRIGOGUNNEL

ASSAROE   G 8662   Donegal

Site of castle built in 1212 and destroyed in 1213 (*Annals of Loch Cé*, *Annals of Ulster*) — perhaps the *motte* at Ballyhanna (*Ulster Journal of Archaeology* X, p. 82, n. 46).

ATH GLAISE   see CASTLESKREEN

ATHBOY   N 7265   Meath

Castle mentioned 1211 2 (*Irish Pipe Roll*).

ATHLONE   N 0341   Westmeath

Stone-revetted polygonal mound with base of decagonal keep of coursed rubble. The stone tower of 1210 collapsed in the following year (*Annals of Clonmacnoise*) but was rebuilt in 1215. (*Calendar of Documents* I, 80, 95, 100) in 1211–12 £129 spent (*Irish Pipe Roll*) (*Journal of the Royal Society of Antiquaries of Ireland* XXXVII, pp. 259–73).*   (Fig. 3)

AULDEARN   see page 353

GAZETTEER

AVRETON   see RICHARD'S CASTLE

AYR   NS 333224   Ayrshire

The *novum opidum* between the Doon and the Ayr waters was built in 1197 (*Chronicle of Melrose*, p. 103), probably on the site later occupied by the barracks (*Ayrshire Archaeological and Natural History Society Collections*, second series, II, pp. 5, 81).

BAGINBUN   S 5412   Wexford

Promontory cut off with bank and ditch; smaller inner ring-work with double ditch (IICd3?). Occupied on the landing in 1170 (Giraldus Cambrensis, *Opera* I, 13; *Song of Dermot*) (*Journal of the Royal Society of Antiquaries of Ireland* XXXVIII, pp. 155–60).*

BAKEWELL   SK 221688   Derbyshire

Excavation of the earthwork (Bb3) showed that the *motte* had been added to a rubble rampart in the twelfth century (*Medieval Archaeology* XIV, 175)

BALA   SH 928361   Merioneth

Motte (B), with modern retaining wall, of castle destroyed in 1202. (*Brut y Tywysogion*). Site near lake.

BALIMORE EUSTACE   N 9311   Kildare

Motte (B) of castle mentioned in 1203. (*Calendar of Documents* I, p. 28).

BALLAN MOOR (THE BERRIES) ST 488895   Monmouthshire

Motte with ditched enclosure (Ac3). The place-name suggests the Ballon family of 1086–1106 (Stenton, *The First Century of English Feudalism*, p. 28, n. 2; *Archaeologia Cambrensis* 101, pp. 163–5).

BALLINTRA   G 9068   Donegal

IBb2 site, with a 12ft square stone basement in the mound (Evans, *Prehistoric and Early Christian Ireland*, p. 85).

BALLYBOY   N 2312   Offaly

Site of castle built in 1213 (*Annals of Clonmacnoise*).

BALLYHANNA   see ASSAROE

BALLYKNOCKAN   see LEIGHLIN

BALLYRONEY   J 2240   Down

Motte with flanking baileys and counterscarp bank (Bd4f3) on rise beside River Bann. Excavation of the *motte*-top produced a sword guard, horseshoe, pottery, and silver halfpenny of 1177–99, under a layer of rammed glacial till.

The castle of Magh Cobha is mentioned in 1188 (*Annals of Ulster, Annals of the Four Masters*) and repairs are recorded in the *Irish Pipe Roll* of 1211–12 (*Ulster Journal of Archaeology* XVIII, pp. 95–104).*

BALLYVALLEY   see KILLAHOE

BAMBURGH NU 184350 Northumberland

Very much rebuilt site on prominent basalt rocky hill beside sea. The outer and inner gatehouses have rubble vaulting, slightly pointed, and the inner has a chamfered string-course, repeated in the guardroom beside the passage.

The altered keep is nearly cubical, with a moulded plinth (like that of Canterbury, q.v.), clasping and intermediate pilaster buttresses (two on the north-west and south-east fronts, one on the others). The entrance doorway now is coffin-shaped, with an outer arch of two square orders, on chamfered imposts with shafts having moulded capitals and bases carried upon an extra pilaster. There were three round-headed loops in each wall (except the one, replaced by the entrance door with a wall passage rising to the first floor), reflecting the 3 × 3 division of the interior; the western third was vaulted in three groined bays with a cross-wall and another cutting off the south-west corner bay; the other two-thirds was barrel-vaulted with an arcade on square piers. The western cross-wall becomes secondary above the basement to a southern cross-wall, which cuts off an apsidal chapel with groined-vaulted nave. A spiral stair in the north angle links all the floors. The second floor retains some round-headed windows in the north-west wall and traces of a double-gabled roof, replaced by a flat one to the added top floor which has a wall gallery round three sides complementary to that on the south east wall below.

Foundations of a straight wall with square projecting towers were excavated overlooking the inner gatehouse in 1889, resembling the square tower with spreading plinth (like those at Dover, q.v.) south-east of the keep.

The castle was taken by William II in 1095; (*Ordericus Vitalis* VIII, c. xxi; *Roger of Wendover* II, 46). The gate was repaired in 1129–30 and payments made to Osbert the mason. £4 was spent on the tower in 1163–4, and other payments (and fines for failure) in the 1160s are inadequate for the erection of the keep. Repairs to the gateway and buildings occur in the 1190s and over £100 was spent in 1211–12 (*Pipe Rolls*) (Bateson, *A History of Northumberland* I, pp. 17–72; *Archaeological Journal* XLVI, pp. 93–113).*

(Fig. 5)

BAMBURGH SIEGECASTLE Northumberland

The *novum castellum apud Bebbanburg* built by William II in 1095 is mentioned in a contemporary deed (Lawrie, *Ancient Scottish Charters*, XV).

1 The shell-keep on the *motte* at ARUNDEL, with pilaster buttresses nearly as high as the crenellated parapet. The original round-headed doorway has been blocked and replaced by a Norman gatehouse, on the left.

II *above* BARNARD CASTLE's round keep is of fine ashlar masonry, in contrast to the rubble walling to the left.
below The remains of a hall window at BISHOP'S WALTHAM still shows the fine masonry of the hood-mould, chamfered jambs and the bottom of the central mullion.

III   The *motte* at BERKELEY is entirely cased in stone, with pilaster buttresses and a sloping plinth at the base. A forebuilding has been added in front of the entrance on the right.

IV The keep at BROUGH stands on top of two earlier towers, one being Roman. The other was linked to the early curtain wall of coursed rubble (on the right).

V   The fine details of the masonry of the forebuilding and of the top storey of
BROUGHAM keep show that they are an addition to the Norman tower.

VI At CARRICKFERGUS, the keep is slightly later in date than the curtain walls on the seaward side.

VII The early hall at CHEPSTOW with its doorway with carved lintel and tympanum stands on a cliff above the River Wye.

VIII The hall at CHRISTCHURCH is remarkable for its Norman chimney, and the two-light windows with chevron-ornamented arches over them.

IX Much Roman tile was used in building the keep at COLCHESTER, particularly in the apse. Several of the original slit windows remain in the wall to the right.

x   The cylindrical keep at CONISBROUGH has six wedge-shaped buttresses, with a chamfered plinth.

XI At CORFE an extra block was added to the keep which stood up against an earlier shell-wall (just visible on the right).

XII *above* The ruined and altered keep at COITY.
  below The corbels for a timber gallery throw shadows on the upper part of the keep at DOLWYDDELAN.

XIII The Avranches tower at DOVER has two storeys of loopholed fighting galleries, presenting a formidable defence to the old entrance.

XIV Part of the entrance staircase of the keep at DOVER, between the two chapels of plate XV.

xv The two chapels in the keep at DOVER, decorated with shafts having crocket capitals and chevron and roll mouldings. The upper chapel (*right*) has a ribbed vault supported on corbels.

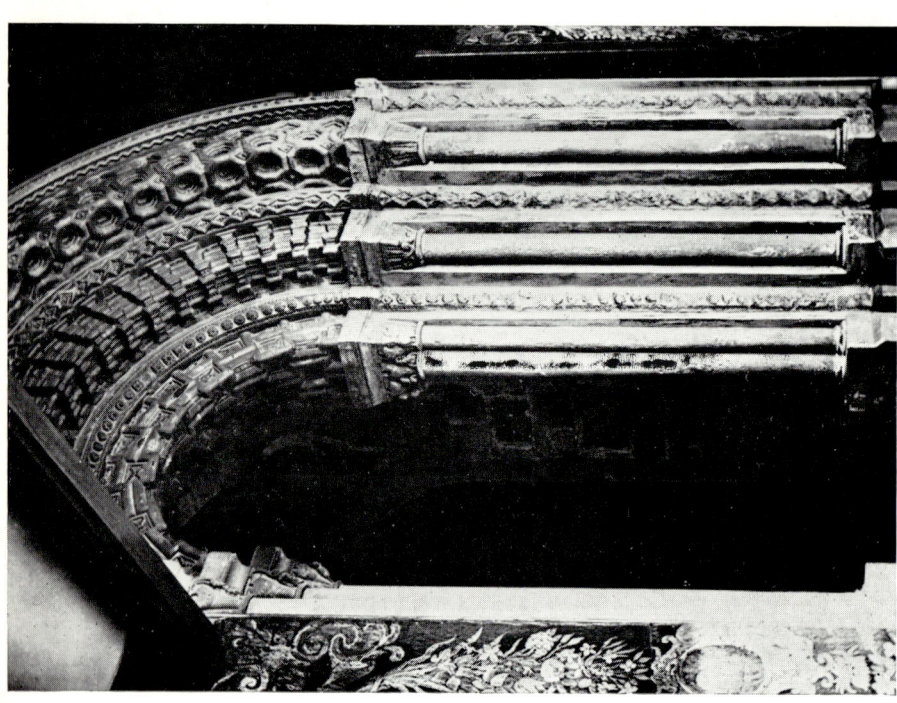

XVI *left* The hall doorway at DURHAM, of three elaborate orders. *right* The entrance to the shell-keep at FARNHAM.

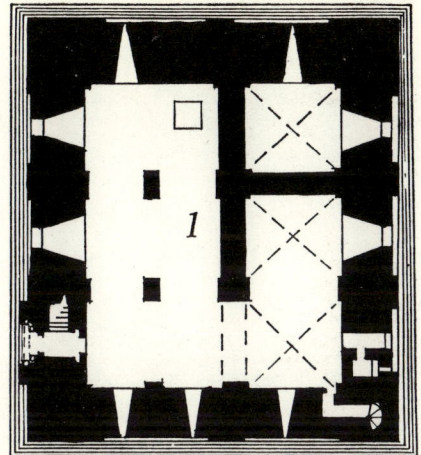
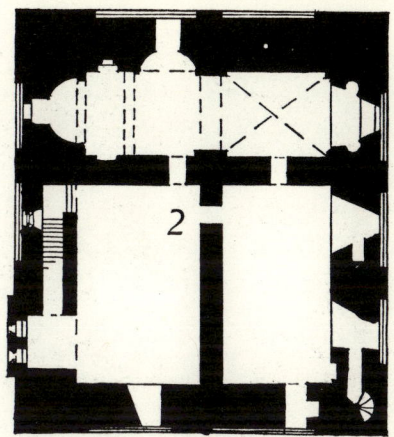

Bamburgh

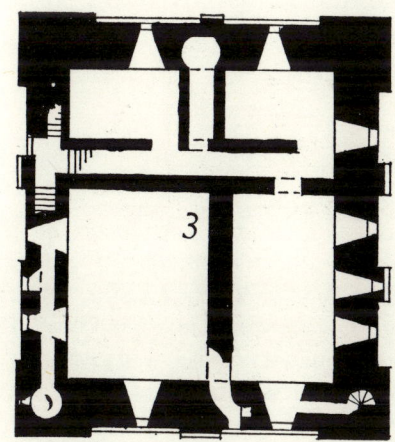
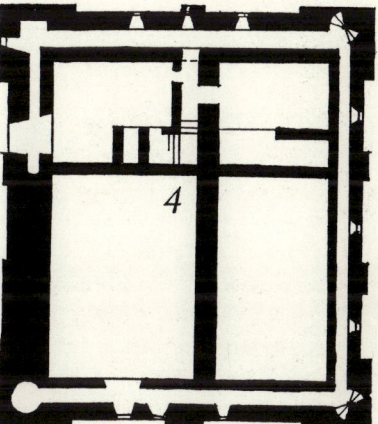

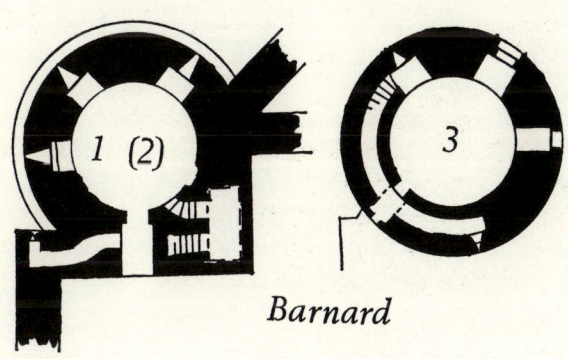

Barnard

| BAMPTON | SS 958226 | Devon |

Motte and bailey (Ad3) with strong east counterscarp bank above river. Perhaps the castle of *Robert de Bathentona* which he held in 1135 and strengthened against Stephen in 1136. (*Gesta Stephani*, pp. 18–20).

| BAMPTON | SP 310031 | Oxfordshire |

A castle was built on the church tower by Matilda in 1142 and taken by Stephen in the same year (*Gesta Stephani*, pp. 91–2).

| BANBURY | SP 454404 | Oxfordshire |

Built-over site beside market place (IIBd2?). Fragment of foundation of keep excavated (*Cake and Cockhorse* I, pp. 6–7). Castle built by Bishop of Lincoln 1136 (*B.M. Cott. MS. Claud*, A.V.) and strengthened in 1201–7 (*Pipe Rolls*) (Potts, *A History of Banbury*, Chapter III).*

| BANGOR | | Caernarvonshire |

The site of the castle built by Hugh, Earl of Chester *c*. 1090–4 (*History of Gruffyd ap Cynan*, p. 133) may be the *motte* (IB) at Aber (SH 656727).

BARDSEY see page 353

| *BARLEY POUND* | SU 797468 | Hampshire |

Oval ring-work with strong enclosure of ditch and bank to the south (ICc2), and rectangular ditched enclosure to the north divided by a slight double bank. Large flints, squared stones and mortar are visible on the ring-bank and that running north from the ring-work.

Excavations in 1920 revealed Norman pottery and a wall 8 ft thick (*Congress of Archaeological Societies Report*, 1921); re-excavation in 1951 revealed a masonry keep (*The Times*, 26 October 1951). See 'Lidelea'.

| BARNARD CASTLE | NZ 049165 | Durham |

Ring-work with large ear-shaped bailey (ICe2) above River Tees. Gateway in north curtain wall is round-headed with two chamfered orders and jambs, the imposts having a bead moulding. At the counterscarp of the inner ditch is a rectangular tower of two storeys, and on the eastern side of the gate the curtain wall has loops with round-headed rear arches. There is a coursed rubble curtain around the crest of the ring-work bank, above a rock-cut ditch. The great round tower is built of sandstone ashlar with a sloping plinth, and rests partly on an earlier structure (seen in the well chamber). The basement has a spirally built rubble dome, three long splayed loops and a fireplace. A spur (giving a square end to adjoining buildings – see joist holes) contains a wall-stair which rises through a cell to the upper round-headed entrance passage with a fireplace and two

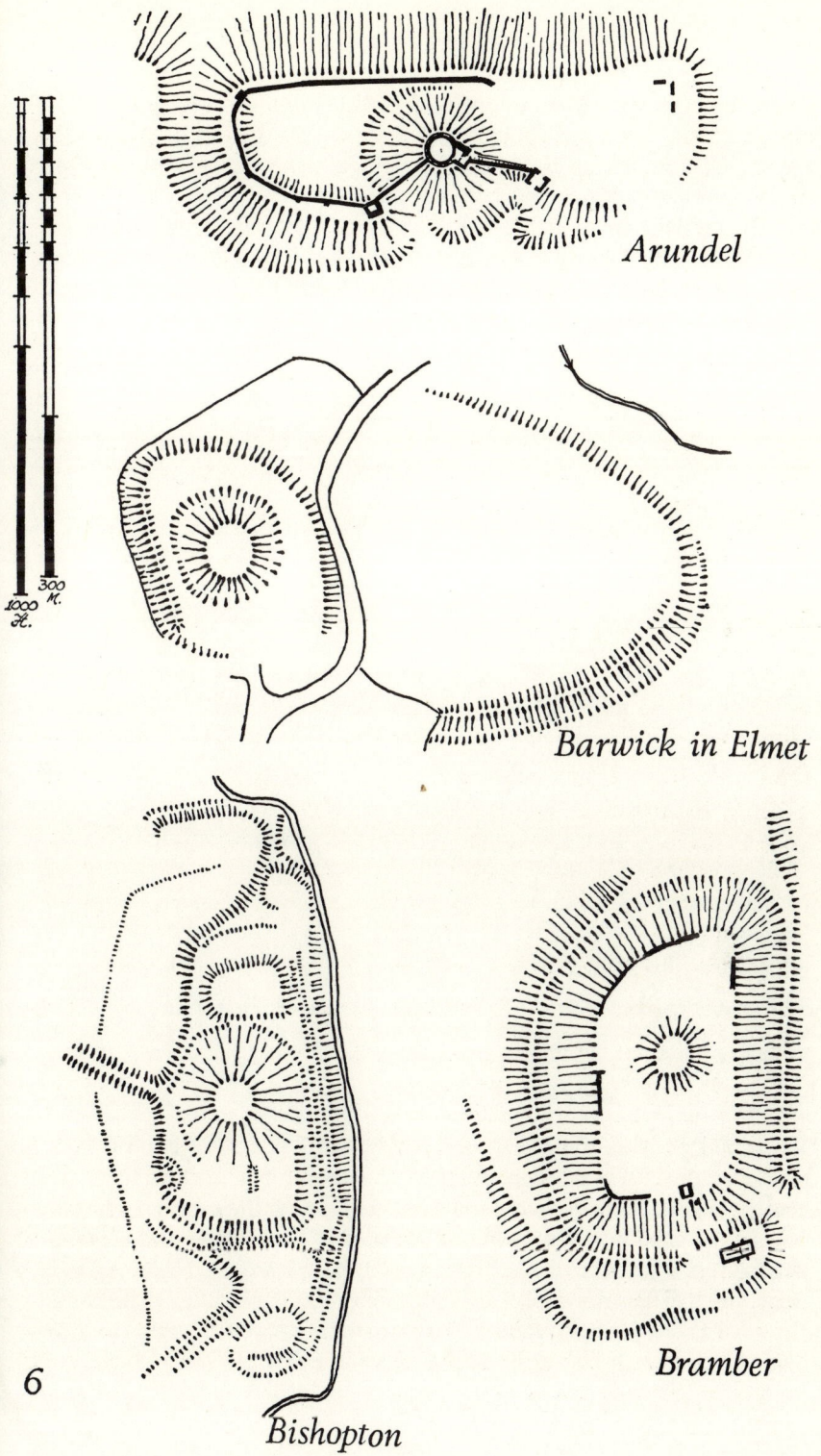

6 Arundel / Barwick in Elmet / Bishopton / Bramber

loops; from the embrasure of one of these a curving wall-stair rises to the altered second floor and parapet; latrines are contrived to discharge into the angle between keep and hall range, largely altered except for a shallow projecting tower added to the curtain wall.

The castle is mentioned by 1133 (*R.R.A.N.* II, 1890) and withstood a siege in 1216 by Alexander of Scotland (*Chronicle of Melrose*, p. 123). An early twelfth century occupation level has been found in the ring-work. (*Medieval Archaeology* VIII, p. 252). (Plate II; Fig. 5)

BARNSTAPLE   SS 556334   Devon

Motte and bailey (Ba3). Excavation in 1927 revealed a clay-set rubble revetment to the *motte*, and part of the keep on the *motte* — a straight length of wall 16 ft thick on the west side, principally limestone rubble set in gravelly mortar, and other fragments suggesting a shell 65 ft across externally with an outer mantlet wall 3 ft 6 in. thick and as far away. The castle is mentioned in a charter of Judael, the 'Domesday' tenant (*Monasticon* V, 197) and was held by him in 1113 (*Hermannus* II, 17, quoted by Round *Feudal England* 1964 ed., p. 369, n. 4) but was weak and powerless in Stephen's reign (*Gesta Stephani*). A charter of the reign of Henry I (Oliver, *Mon. Exon.* 198b) mentions the north and east gates, and descriptions of the north and west gates (destroyed 1842, 1852) suggests Norman work (Wainwright, *Barnstaple Records* ii, 261-2) (*Transactions of the Devon Association* LX, pp. 215-23).* (Fig. 7)

BARROW ON HUMBER   see GOXHILL

BARTON ON HUMBER   see GOXHILL

BARWICK IN ELMET   SE 398375   Yorkshire

Motte in centre of oval bailey (Ab1) with large outer enclosure to the north-east. The *Castellum de Berewicam* was granted with Almondbury to Henry Lacy by Stephen (see Almondbury). Long straight drystone walling 3 ft. thick excavated on *motte*. (*Proceedings of the Thoresby Society* 17, 22). (Fig. 6)

BASING   SU 663526   Hampshire

Large and powerful ring-work and bailey (Cd3) with later earthworks of siege during Civil War. Stone foundations, probably of the late thirteenth century, were excavated in the southern quadrant of the ring and a twelfth-century voussoir was found (*V.C.H. Hampshire* IV, p. 117) and eleventh/twelfth century pottery under the south bank (*Medieval Archaeology* VIII, p.253) with diagonally-tooled ashlar masonry inside a brickwork bastion.

Mention of the old castle of Basing in the mid-twelfth century (*Monasticon* VII, p. 1014) may refer to the altered earthworks (Bd2) at Oliver's battery (SU 667536) (*Archaeologia* LXI, pp. 553-64).* (Fig. 7)

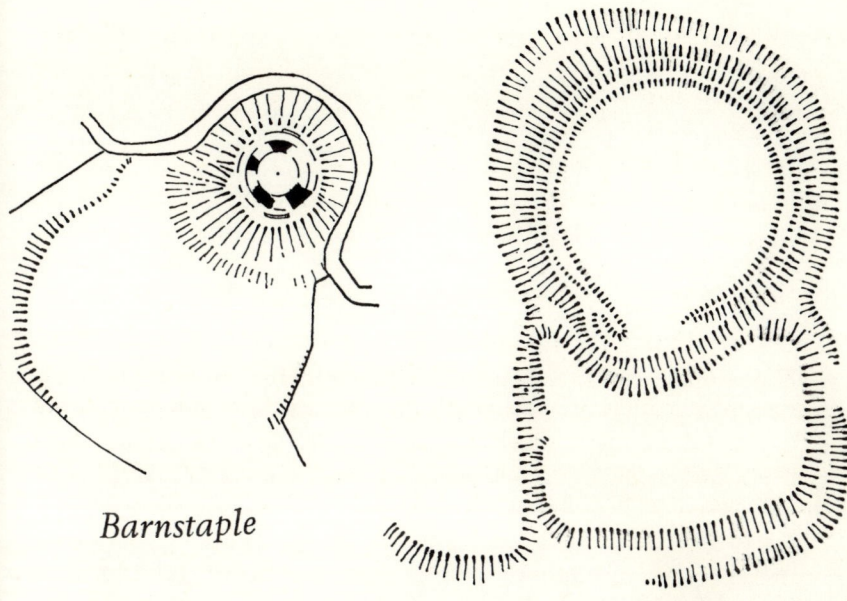

Barnstaple

Basing

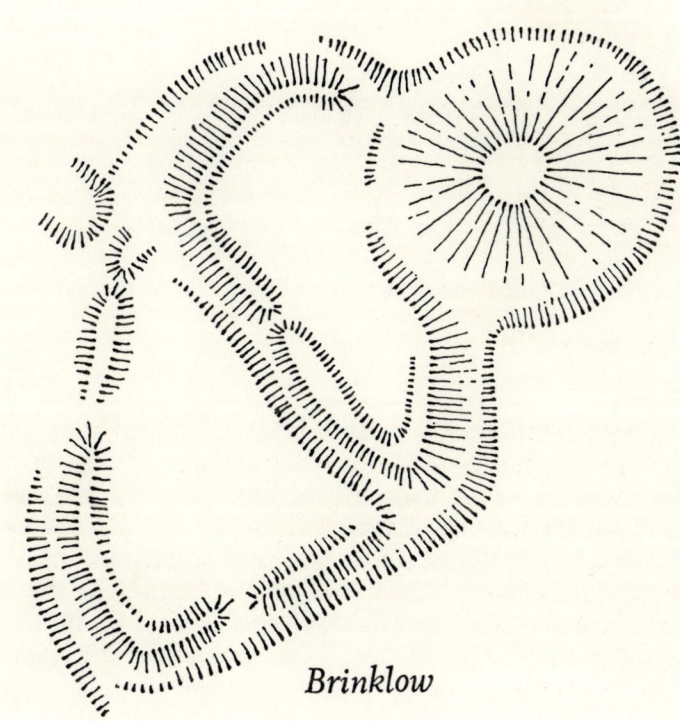

Brinklow

7

| BASINGWERK | SJ 220734 | Flintshire |

Motte and bailey (Bd4?) beside ravine at Coleshill. Excavation in 1954-6 produced a twelfth-century voussoir but no early pottery. Traces of a palisade round the edge of the *motte* ditch and ravine were found, but the site had been largely levelled and rebuilt in the thirteenth century.

Built in 1157 by Henry II (*Annales Cestriae*, p. 21) and captured by the Welsh 1166. *Journal of the Flintshire Hist. Soc* 17, pp.1-15; 18, pp. 13-60.*

BASS OF INVERURIE see INVERURIE

| BAYNARD'S | TQ 319808 | London |

Formerly on the bank of the River Thames south of St Paul's Cathedral. The ditch of the royal castle is mentioned in 1111 (*R.R.A.N. II*, 991), and the name derives from the Baignards who were dispossessed in 1110 (Henry of Huntingdon). Destroyed in 1212 (*Annales Monastici*, III, p. 36).

Ragstone walling with a sloping cement-covered face and a rising underside faced with squared blocks were found in Printing House Lane in 1960 and thick north-south walls in Playhouse Yard a century ago (Merrifield, *The Roman City of London*, pp. 196, 315-16; *Gentleman's Magazine* 1843, I, p. 635; *The Builder* 1855, pp. 221, 269; *J.B.A.A.* 1st series, V, p. 55). A bank against the Roman wall may have been added in the twelfth century. (*Trans. L.M.A.S.* 22.3, pp. 3-8).

BAYNARD'S see COTTINGHAM   Yorkshire

| BEAUDESERT | SP 156662 | Warwickshire |

Oval ring-work (IC) near eastern end of isolated hill; the western end is cut off by a ditch to give three enclosures of about equal area. There are traces of foundations in the ring-work. A charter for a market in the castle was granted in 1141 (Dugdale, *Warwickshire*, p. 798, dated by Round, *Geoffrey de Mandeville*, p. 65, n. 1).

BEAUMONT see MIXBURY

| BEDFORD | TL 053496 | Bedfordshire |

Flattened *motte* with traces of bailey (Af3?) near Ouse Bridge. Castle reputed to have been built by Payn de Beauchamp before 1132 — its strong earthworks, keep and walls are mentioned in 1138 (*Gesta Stephani*, pp. 31-3). Captured in 1215 by Fawkes de Bréauté with John's approval, the castle was greatly strengthened with towers, walls and stone-lined ditches, part of the materials being obtained by demolishing the neighbouring St Paul's Church (*Patent Rolls* 1216-25, p. 29; Coggeshall, *Chron. Ang.*, p. 205). After the siege of 1224, orders were given for the ditches to be filled in and the outer bailey levelled, for the removal of three-quarters of the old tower towards St Paul's Church and for the reduction of the mound and inner bailey walls to one-half their height. (*Rot. Litt. Claus.* 1, 632, 654; *Close Roll* 8, Henry III, pt. 2, m.7d.)

The topography of the site has been dealt with in the *Associated Architectural Societies' Reports and Papers* I, pp. 381–91 and XII, pp. 234–60. A drawing in the Parker Matthew Paris, *Chronica Majora* MS. 16 (Corpus Christi College, Cambridge) shows an embattled wall surrounding a round tower with pilaster buttresses and holes (for wooden brattices?).

BELTURBET   see TURBET

BELVOIR   SK 820347   Leicestershire

Completely rebuilt castle on top of an isolated hill, built by Robert de Todnei by 1088 when the priory was founded *juxta castellum suum* (*Monasticon* III, 288). J. H. Round also argued that the grouping of land around the site in 'Domesday' implied a castle (*English Historical Review* XXII, pp. 508–10).

BENEFIELD   SP 987885   Northamptonshire

A square moat west of the church is the site of the castle seized for debt by John in 1208 (*Rot. Litt. Pat.* 79b, 97b).

BENGEWORTH   see page 353

BENINGTON   TL 297236   Hertfordshire

Motte and bailey (IIBc4) immediately north of parish church. On the east side of the *motte*-top are the remains of a rectangular keep, of flint rubble set in yellow sandy mortar. There is some herringbone coursing in the west part of the north wall, but further on the facing has fallen out and a large panel of masonry (with diagonally tooled quoins) has fallen across the remains of a small annexe to the north-east. It is impossible to tell whether this is bonded into the main keep or not, since the joint is obscured by a semicircular buttress flanking a pseudo-Norman doorway leading to a rough passage through the wall. The west wall ends abruptly in a plain jamb and the south wall is reduced to its footings. There are the remains of pilaster buttresses at each end and the centre of each remaining wall. The best preserved is that at the west end of the north wall, of oolitic limestone diagonally tooled and worked as close jointed ashlar. Above a broad chamfer on the outside face are three courses of clunch set in gritty grey mortar and not bonded into the wall.

Certain similarities to Saffron Walden suggest that the keep may have been begun *c*. 1136; one hundred picks were purchased for its demolition in 1176–7 (*Pipe Roll*) but no other expenditure is recorded, the manor

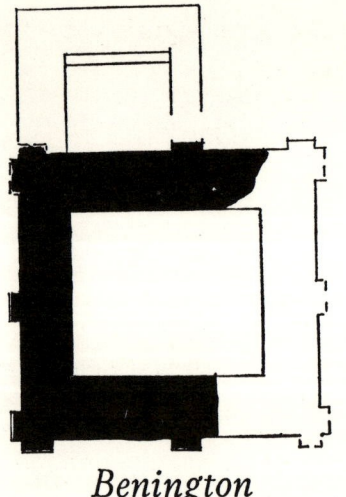
Benington

Berkhamsted

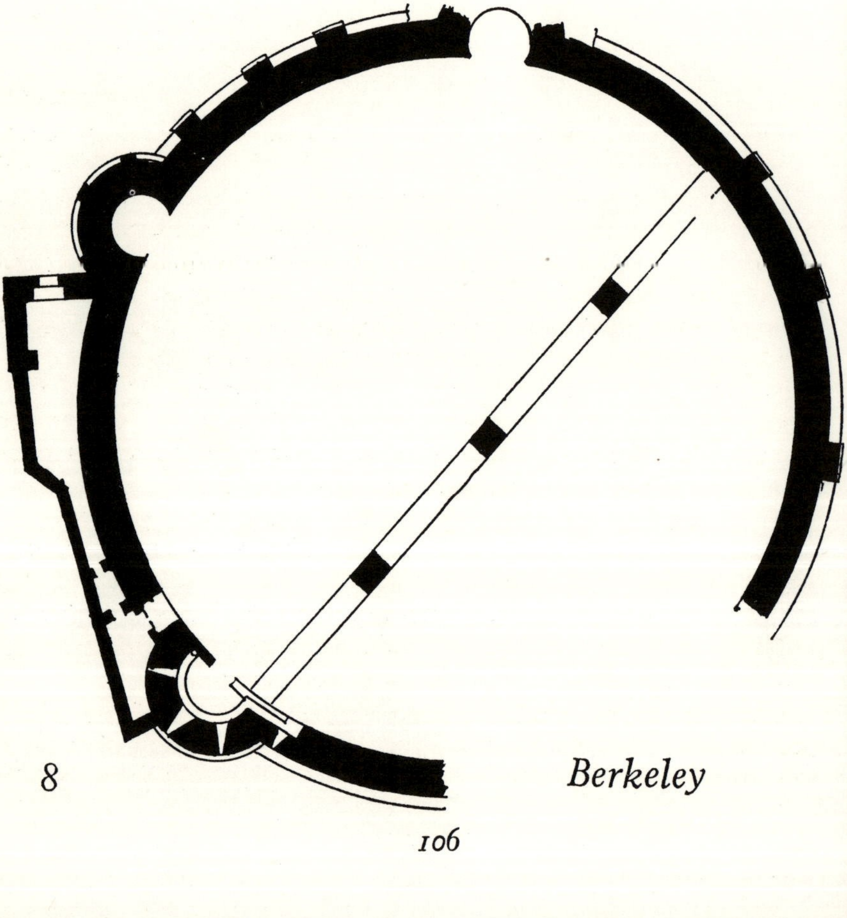

Berkeley

8

remained in the same hands and the castle was strongly garrisoned in 1193 (*Pipe Roll*) during the crisis after the king's capture. Shortly afterward it passed to Robert fitz Walter by marriage and was destroyed on his outlawry in 1212 (*Annales Monastici* III, 35) and there are no further references to the castle after his return in 1213 (*Rot. Litt. Claus.* p. 217) (*Antiquaries' Journal* XLI, pp. 96–7).* (Fig. 8)

BENWICK   see FORDHAM

BERDEN   Essex

Two excavated ring-works (C). The Crump (TL 470289) produced a typical twelfth-century assemblage of cooking pots, figure-of-eight bronze strip, wavy-edged horseshoes and 'fiddle key' nails. The Rookery (TL 467292) (surrounded by a U-shaped ditch) had a twelfth-century pot in the make-up of the bank, and a thirteenth-century pot on the central hearth (*Transactions of the Essex Archaeological Society* 25, pp. 255–62).

BERE FERRERS   SX 458634   Devon

The bottom stage of a keep-like tower remains near the River Tavy, possibly part of the Ferrers manor-house of the time of Henry II (W. G. Hoskins, *New Survey of England: Devon*, p. 332).

BERKELEY   ST 684990   Gloucestershire

Much-altered *motte* and bailey (Bc3?) with outer ditch cutting off natural spur. The ditched mound was encased in a red sandstone rubble wall (with a sloping plinth) carried up higher and traversed by an arcade of four bays on square piers, of which the foundations have been excavated. There are three semicircular turrets; that to the east was an apsidal chapel (wall shafts with cushion capitals supporting ribs); that to the north-east is ornamented with three pilaster-strips, as is the wall on either side of the third turret (largely built up). At a later date a forebuilding was contrived within a tangent wall between the first two turrets. There is a semicircular relieving arch over the entrance, which leads by a part-vaulted staircase to the entrance door (external tympanum and lattice-carved jamb-shafts, out-turned or stepped chevron ornament) adjoining the chapel.

There are traces of the outer wall of the Norman hall to the south-east, with shafted jambs to one window and pilaster buttresses; there is a round-headed window in the north wall also.

It seems probable that the 'little castle' of the five hides in the Ness of William fitz Osbern ('Domesday Book' I, 163a) was incomplete, since there is no mention of the castle in the campaign of 1088. The manor was granted to Robert fitz Harding about 1153–6, Henry II pledging himself to fortify a castle there to his requirements, according to documents exhibited at the castle (*Transactions of the Bristol and Gloucestershire*

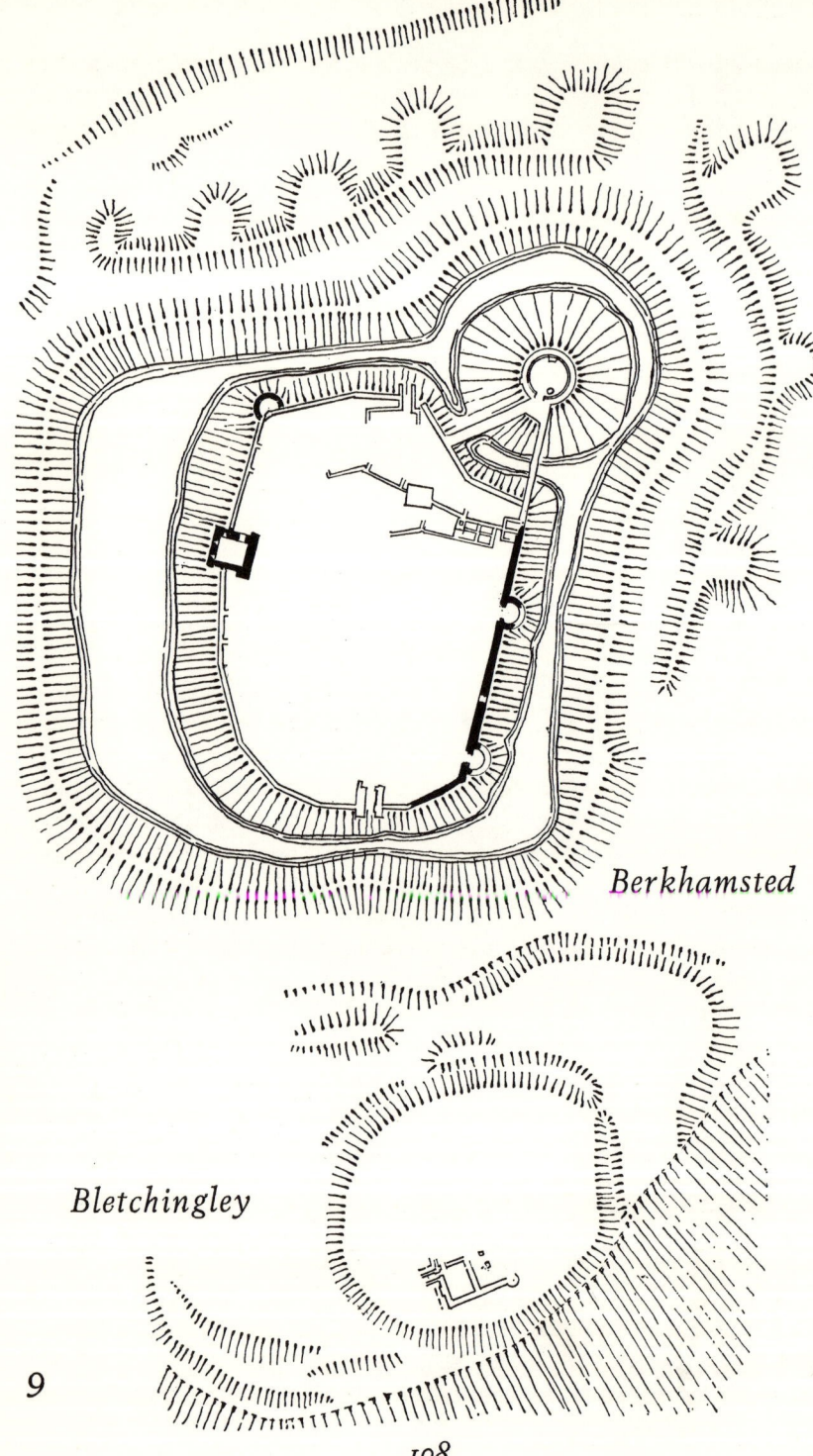
Berkhamsted

Bletchingley

108

Archaeological Society 48, pp. 133-79; 49, pp. 183-93. *Archaeological Journal* CXXII, pp. 197-200).* (Plate III; Fig. 8)

BERKHAMSTED   SP 995082   Hertfordshire

Motte and bailey (Ab3) with strong counterscarp to moat and outer bank with platforms attributed to the siege of 1216 (*Antiquaries' Journal* III, pp. 37-48) when the castle capitulated after a fortnight's bombardment by Louis of France.

The *fossarius* is mentioned in 'Domesday Book'. The castle was in the possession of Robert of Mortain in 1086 and the chapel of the castle is mentioned in a recapitulation of a charter of his son William (*Monasticon* VII, 1090) who was dispossessed for rebellion in 1104. Considerable expenditure on castle-works was incurred between 1155 and 1180 and again in 1200-1 and 1213-14 (*Pipe Rolls*). The identifiable works are (1157-60) King's houses on *motte* and chamber in bailey, and (1213-14) a tower.

The *motte*-top is surrounded by the lower courses of a circular flint rubble wall 8 ft thick with traces of a staircase and a stone-lined well. The entrance to the south-west had a forebuilding flanked by buttresses and a wing wall 12 ft thick running down the slope and carrying a stair. The bailey was surrounded by a flint rubble wall built in straight lengths and standing on a slight bank. The east wall had two hollow semicircular towers 30 ft across; (another tower at the north-west angle is not bonded into the curtain). The foundations of north and south gate-passages are simple in plan and may also be contemporary. A tower straddling the east curtain has corner buttresses (except to the east), and there were formerly traces of steps on the north side and in the south-west angle. Its date is uncertain; Richard of Cornwall built a three-storey tower in 1254 (*Annales Monastici* III, p. 191) and a great tower on the *motte* certainly existed (*Cal. Pat. Rolls* 1334-8, p. 366).

M.P.B.W. *Official Guide;* V.C.H. *Herts.* II, pp. 168 ff.* (Figs. 8, 9)

BERWICK   Northumberland

No traces survive of the castle handed over to Henry II in 1174 (*Foedera* I, p. 30; annotations in Cotton M.S. of Robert of Torigni; *Gesta Henrici Secundi* I, p. 96; *Newburgh* I, p. 98; *Torigny* IV, p. 267).

BICKLEIGH   SS 937068   Devon

Of the fortified house of twelfth century date (rebuilt in the fifteenth century) a chapel survives, opposite a gatehouse. (Norman bases to imposts) (W. G. Hoskins, *A New Survey of England: Devon*, p. 334).

BIGARZ   S 6698   Kildare

Low *motte* (B) on west bank of river Barrow opposite Ardree (q.v.) may be that of Robert de Bigarz mentioned in 1182 (Giraldus Cambrensis, *Opera* V, p. 356).

| BIGGLESWADE | TL 184445 | Bedfordshire |

Ring-work and bailey (Cb3) discovered by aerial photography (*Antiquity* XL, pp. 142–4). The ring of double ditches are regularly subdivided, and a trial trench produced early twelfth century pottery from the berm between the ditches (*Beds. Archaeological Journal* III, pp. 15–18).

| *BINBURY (THORNHAM)* | TQ 812602 | Kent |

Oval *motte* with faint traces of a small bailey (IBb4) adjoining Binbury Manor Farm. Some remains of a flint rubble curtain wall on the north side of the bailey with a projecting square tower (gatehouse?).

The castle has some resemblance to Godard's (1½ miles away, q.v.); a charter of 1215–19 mentions both places (but not this one as a castle).

BIRDSALL   see MOUNT FERRANT

BIRMINGHAM   see page 353

| BIRR | N 0504 | Offaly |

Motte (B) of castle erected in 1186, destroyed in 1207 and rebuilt in 1212 (*Irish Pipe Roll*).

| BISHOP'S CASTLE | SO 323891 | Shropshire |

Motte and bailey (Bb3) north of the Square. Fragments of a thin curtain wall have been uncovered at the junction with a ringwall on the *motte*, and a standing fragment nearby is battlemented. The blocked inturned bailey entrance exists behind a shop south of the hotel, while to the northeast is another fragment of rubble curtain. The castle is mentioned between 1150 and 1163 (Haughmond Cartulary, f. 136 (Morey and Brooke, *The Letters and Charters of Gilbert Foliot* (1966) p. 372) (*Transactions of the Shropshire Archaeological Society*, 49, pp. 245–9; 51, pp. 157–9).*

BISHOPS STORTFORD   see WAYTEMORE

| *BISHOPSTON* | SS 582900 | Glamorgan |

Oval ring-work on cliff above river with traces of bailey bank (ICc3). Excavation of the ringbank revealed several pointed stakes (the bark still adhering) 2½–4½ in. in diameter; the outer row were 9–12 in. apart, with a more irregular row 6 ft further in. The V-section ditch produced bones, leather and a bronze buckle, and the interior of the ring-work pottery, now in the Royal Institution of Swansea (*Archaeologia Cambrensis*, 5th series, 16, pp. 249–58).

GAZETTEER

BISHOPTON   NZ 368209   Durham

Motte and bailey (Ad1c3) possibly the house fortified in 1143 (*Symeon of Durham* I, p. 150) (*Victoria County History of Durham* I, pp. 353–4).*

(Fig. 6)

BISHOP'S WALTHAM   SU 552173   Hampshire

Three-storey square tower at south-west angle of moated site, of coursed rubble with ashlar quoins, chamfered-off angles. Most of the openings have been altered, but two have round heads which have lost their voussoirs. Chamfered offset externally at first floor level and an internal cross-wall. Beyond a narrow gallery to the north is the hall, with a wall-arcade at first floor level. Norman details also in the range running east from the angle tower. Excavations (*Medieval Archaeology* II, 194; V, 397; VI/VII. 319; VII, 248) within the enclosure have revealed a rectangular inner gatehouse with a late stair filled into the passage-way leading down to the crypt of an apsidal chapel with a central arcade. The first curtain stood within the present ranges.

The palace was begun about 1135–8 by Henry of Blois, Bishop of Winchester (*Anglia Sacra* I, 299; *Annales Monastici* II, 51) and perhaps demolished in 1155–6 (*Pipe Roll*) while the bishop was exiled. Royal councils were held here in 1182 and 1194. (*Hoveden* III, p. 250). (Plate II)

BLAEN LLYNFI   SO 145229   Brecknockshire

Rectangular moat with remains of curtain wall and overgrown foundations. Castle captured in 1215 (*Brut y Tywysogion*).

BLAENPORTH   SN 266489   Cardiganshire

Motte with long narrow bailey (IBb2) surrounded by streams. Norman castle captured in 1116 (*Brut y Tywysogion*).

BLATHACH   R 5858   Limerick

Site of castle built by 1210 (*Journal of the Royal Society of Antiquaries of Ireland* XXXIX, pp. 39–40).

BLETCHINGLEY   TQ 322506   Surrey

Ring-work on edge of greensand scarp with lobed bailey (Ce2). Parts of a rectangular building with walls 5 ft thick have been excavated (see V.C.H. *Surrey* IV, p. 255); it appears to have had some sort of forebuilding on the west side and to have been divided by a north-south cross-wall, the larger eastern part having an upper floor supported on masonry piers, with a spiral stair at the south-east angle. Gervase of Canterbury lists *Blechingele* in his *Mappa Mundi*, and *The History of Thomas Becket* (III, 131) records that it supplied men to prevent the escape of Becket in 1170. (Fig. 9)

| BLEDISLOE | SO 683082 | Gloucestershire |

Excavations in 1964 revealed that a low mound was thrown up over the post-holes of a dismantled timber building during the twelfth century (*Transactions of the Bristol and Gloucestershire Archaeological Society* LXXXV, pp. 57–69).

| BLEDDFA | SO 209682 | Radnorshire |

Altered *motte* and bailey (IBb4) south-east of church, with traces of masonry on the *motte*-top. A square tower with straight stair in the west wall was excavated in the mound immediately adjoining the church in 1962 (*Transactions of the Radnorshire Society* 32, pp. 1–17; 33, pp. 57–63). One of these was the castle of *Bledewach* repaired in 1195 (*Pipe Roll*).

BLYTH   see TICKHILL

BOLEBEC   see WHITCHURCH

| BOLINGBROKE | TF 348654 | Lincolnshire |

The old castlery is mentioned early in the reign of Henry III (*Lincolnshire Record Society* XVIII, p. 45), and may be the earthwork (IId) on Dewy Hill south of the church (*Medieval Archaeology* X, 152–8) which has produced eleventh–twelfth century pottery.

| BOLSOVER | SK 470707 | Derbyshire |

Site occupied by house of 1613–17 but certain traces of earlier work still visible. The Fountain garden wall is the refaced ovoid curtain (see *Journal of the Derbyshire Archaeological and Natural History Society* XXXVIII, plan opp. p. 5), and medieval foundations were found in the Little Castle forecourt in 1950.

Castle escheated to the Crown 1155. £116 spent in 1173–4 on Bolsover and the Peak and small repairs to tower etc. 1194–1216 (*Pipe Rolls*); £134 spent on Bolsover and Horston in 1208–9 (*Archaeological Journal* CXVIII, pp. 199–204).*

BON Y DOM   see CASTLE OF KING OLAF

BOROMHA   see KILLALOE

| BOUGHROOD | SO 132391 | Radnorshire |

Motte (B) beside farm is the site of the castle of 1205–6. (*Rot. Litt. Pat.* 56a).

| BOURN | TL 322562 | Cambridgeshire |

Ring-work and bailey (ICb3). Picot, the 'Domesday' sheriff of Cambridgeshire, gave 'the church of Brune and the chapel of the castle' to Cambridge (later Barnwell) priory (*Monasticon* VI, 86), and the identification seems more probable than Bourne, Lincs.

BOURNE   TF 095200   Lincolnshire

Motte (largely destroyed) with concentric baileys (Bd33) with an outer enclosure (for a village?) to the west.

The castle is mentioned in 1179–81 (*Pipe Rolls*). A keep with angle turrets is said to have stood on the mound, and the gatehouse had a round-headed opening between circular towers (Mackenzie, *Castles of England* I, pp. 428–9), but a trench through the site (*Lincolnshire History and Archaeology* I, p. 39) produced no pottery earlier than the mid-thirteenth century.

BOW AND ARROW   SY 697711   Dorset

The pentagonal tower overlooking Church Ope cove (Isle of Portland) has late medieval gunholes, but rests unconformably on an earlier foundation (to the north) and stepped plinth (to the west) which may have been a twelfth century keep.

Robert of Gloucester took *insulam Portland quam incastellauerant* in 1142. (William of Malmesbury, *Historia Novella*, p. 76) (*Proceedings of the Dorset Natural History and Archaeological Society* LXIX, pp. 65–7.)*

BOWES   NY 991135   Yorkshire

Keep in north-west angle of Roman fort, with ditch isolating it to south and west. On the north side there is a foundation on a slightly different alignment to the chamfered plinth of the keep. This foundation aligns with the lowest courses of a two-cell structure against the east wall of the keep, with differing chamfers, which are interpreted as the forebuilding. The keep is of sandstone rubble cased in ashlar, with clasping buttresses at the angles and a pilaster in the centre of each wall. The south-east angle contains a spiral stair serving all three floors and the south-west angle was a latrine block, the twin round-headed chutes being visible at the south end of the west wall, projecting beyond the line of the plinth. The north-south cross-wall was placed towards the west and the two parts of the basement were lit by three loops each: three in the south wall, two in the west and one in the north, each with stepped recesses. The first floor is marked externally by a string-course; internally the west room is carried on a set-back of the walls. The main entrance was in the east wall, a plain round-headed arch with a higher passage behind, with a side passage to a mural chamber. Another mural chamber in the north-east angle had a round-backed fireplace and a lobby. There are vaulted wall-passages, lit by square-headed loops, in the walls adjoining the south-west angle. The

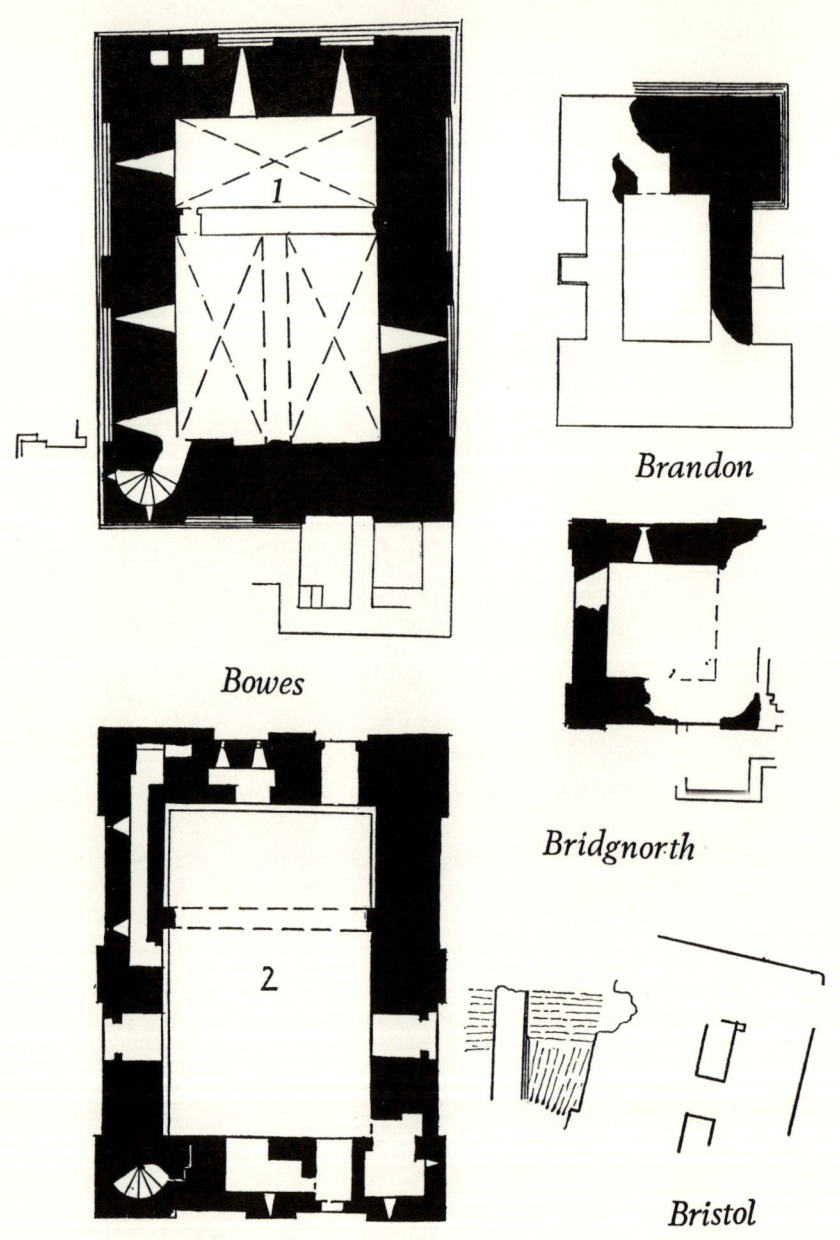

main windows (one each in the north, south and west walls) are in round-headed embrasures but the dressings have gone. The upper floor is fragmentary, but there are slight traces of an east-west roof of low pitch below.

Expenditure of £100 a year or more on the castle is recorded from 1171 (when it came into the hands of the Crown) to 1174, and again in 1179; the tower was mentioned in 1174, and was completed in 1187 (*Pipe Rolls*).

(Fig. 10)

BOYLE G 7903 Roscommon

Monastery fortified in 1202 (*Annals of Loch Cé*).

BRACKLEY SP 583367 Northamptonshire

Castle destroyed in 1173 (*Pipe Roll; Diceto* I, 404) the site being south-west of the town.

BRAMBER TQ 185107 Sussex

Motte in centre of pear-shaped bailey (Ab1) with strong western counter-scarp bank and small enclosure to south around eleventh century church; contemporary pottery was found during roadworks here (*Sussex Archaeological Collections* LXVIII, 241-4). The curtain wall of the bailey is of pebbles and flints with patches of herringbone-work and adjoining the present entrance is a square gate-tower with central internal pilasters. The west wall has a barrel-vaulted latrine passage and a round-headed window within a wide recess. There is a line of beam-holes above and below the window as well as for the gabled roof.

The castle is mentioned in 1073 (J. H. Round, *Calendar of Documents preserved in France* I, no. 1130, see also no. 1112) and extensive repairs were carried out while it was in the king's hands 1208–15 (*Pipe Rolls; Rot. Litt. Claus.* I, 142). (Fig. 6)

BRANCEPATH NZ 224378 Durham

Even before the rebuilding of 1796, the castle seems to have shown little trace of its early origin, although mentioned in 1216 (*Rot. de Oblatis et Finibus*, p. 572).

BRANDON SP 408759 Warwickshire

Rectangular moated site with concentric outer enclosure (except to the south) on north bank of River Avon between Wolston church and the railway station. Excavation of the eastern island produced a coin of Stephen, wavy-edged horseshoes and a prick-spur, doorhinge and knives and contemporary pottery, overlaid by builder's rubble, probably from the rectangular keep on an irregular mound attached to the other square 'island'.

The core of the keep walls was limestone rubble, cased in sandstone ashlar except the backs of the recesses in the north and south walls. The north-east corner of the keep was partly intact, and showed three chamfered courses of a plinth above a mortar 'concrete' base, the walls above sloping back to a roll-moulded string-course, above which the angles of the buttress were mitred off; the return into the northern recess is not sloped, but the top course is splayed back.

A platform opposite a gap in the wall in the centre of the recess, and a charred layer in front suggest that the entrance and its stairs lay here. The southern recess had a central pier and may have been arched over; finds here included a hoe, brooches, a seal and ivory draughtsman and short-cross pennies of *c.* 1196–1218.

The basement floor was of stone fragments in mortar, with a spiral stair in the south-west angle, and a charred east-west cross-beam was found on it, with traces of an upright post where the walls had been protected against the fire which ravaged the rest of the stonework. A vaulting-boss and string-course fragments showing roll-and-quirk mouldings were also found, with a series of arrow-heads (London Museum, *Medieval Catalogue*, types 7 and 13).

Excavation of the north side of the western enclosure produced sandstone blocks, lias 'slates' and green-glazed ridge-tiles with a hook on top with a counter of Edward I and short-cross penny of Henry III.

The castle appears to have been in existence by 1153 at the latest (Dugdale, *Warwickshire* p. 43; *The Ancestor* XI, p. 153) (*Transactions of the Birmingham Archaeological Society* LXXIII, pp. 63–83).* (Fig. 10)

BRECON   SO 043288   Brecknockshire

Motte and bailey (Bd3) with remains of polygonal tower on *motte* of uncertain date at junction of Honddu and Usk rivers. Mentioned in 1093 (*Florence of Worcester* II, p. 31).

BREDWARDINE   SO 335444   Herefordshire

Motte and bailey (IIBe3) beside river Wye south of church. Foundations of a keep 78 ft by 45 ft with a western projection on the mound overlooking a dammed stream. A square building on a mound is recorded at SO 336449 (*Transactions of the Woolhope Naturalists' Field Club* 35, p. 182). The castle is mentioned by 1189 (*B.M. Additional Charter* 20408) (R.C.H.M. *Herefordshire* I, pp. XXVI, 26).*

BRIDGEND   see NEWCASTLE (GLAMORGAN)

BRIDGNORTH   SO 717927   Shropshire

Castle on cliff beside River Severn. The curtain wall has gone, but an old drawing (reproduced in J. F. A. Mason, *The Borough of Bridgnorth*, p. 47) shows it of ashlar masonry, with a round-headed entrance arch of three orders, apparently billet mouldings between rolls. The square keep is of sandstone ashlar with pilaster buttresses at the end of each wall rising from a sloping plinth with two setsback carried right round the keep. The west face had a central pilaster, and was covered by a forebuilding to the entrance. A continuation south of the keep has a jamb backed by a portcullis groove. The first floor rested on an offset of the walling, the second floor on east-west joists and the top floor on north-south ones, with the weathering of a central gutter of the roof, below the wall-top. A fireplace jamb with abacus but no shaft remains in the south wall, and jambs of round-headed windows in the east and west walls (the latter double splayed, at second floor level).

The castle was surrendered to Henry I in 1102 (*Florence of Worcester*) and to Henry II in 1155 (*Gervase of Canterbury*, p. 162; *Chronicles of the reign of Henry II*, IV, p. 185). Over £300 was spent in 1166–74, particularly on the tower, and annual repairs to the castle thereafter (*Pipe Rolls*). A barbican (gatehouse?) and turning bridge were built in 1211–12 (*Pipe Roll; Rot. Litt. Claus.* I, p. 464; *Cal. Charter Rolls* I, p. 155). (Fig. 10)

BRIDGWATER   ST 305374   Somerset

Site of castle built under a licence granted to William Briwerre in 1200 (*Rot. Chartarum*, p. 70), apparently a square bank and ditch on the west bank of the River Parrett. (Site plan in *Somerset Record Society* XLVIII).

BRIDLINGTON   TA 176680   Yorkshire

William of Aumale expelled the canons from the priory church in 1143–4 (*Chronicles of the Reigns of Stephen* . . . I, pp. 46–8), presumably in order to fortify it, as his contemporaries had done at Coventry and Ramsey (q.v.). *Castleburun* occurs as a place name (Lancaster, *The Chartulary of Bridlington Priory*, pp. 18–20).

BRIDPORT see POWERSTOCK

BRIGHTWELL (SU 578908); *SOUTH MORETON* (SU 557880) Berkshire
One of these *mottes* beside their respective parish churches (Bd:Bd3) may be the castle built in 1145–6 within sight of Wallingford by the Earl of Chester (*Gesta Stephani*, p. 122). Brightwell is named in 1153 (*Chronicles of the Reigns of Stephen* . . . IV, 174).

BRINKLOW   SP 439797   Warwickshire

Motte and diamond-shaped bailey cut in two by inner bank and ditch (ACc3) south-east of church. In existence by 1130 (*Pipe Roll*). (Fig. 7)

BRISTOL   ST 594732   Gloucestershire

In excavations at the junction of Castle Green and Cock and Bottle Lane in 1948 a block of masonry some 40 ft square was discovered, of Pennant sandstone rubble with similar ashlar facing set in reddish sandy mortar, built across a shallow V-shaped rock-cut ditch 20 ft wide with a narrow flat bottom, running east-west. The outline of the masonry was irregular; the few remaining courses of the north side were trench built, the north-west angle having been destroyed about 1650. The south side appeared to be broken off, with a steyned well at the south-west angle producing thirteen century and later pottery. There were two rectangular shafts to the east of the central line of the block. To the west of the block the north slope of the ditch was faced with sandstone slabs butting against a wall of *petit appareil* (5 in. sandstone cubes in yellow sandy mortar) crossing the ditch on a slightly different alignment from that of the block, with two offsets on the east side.

The *castrum fortissimum* of Bristol is mentioned in 1088 (*Symeon of Durham* II, p. 215) and the keep is attributed to Robert, Earl of Gloucester (*Monasticon* II, p. 61; *Robert of Gloucester's Chronicle* II, p. 433) and the castle passed to Henry II in 1173-4; small sums were spent on its maintenance for the next half century (*Pipe Rolls*) — miners were working in the ditch in 1205-6 (*Transactions of the Bristol and Gloucestershire Archaeological Society* 70, pp. 13-21). See page 353.   (Fig. 10)

BROCARD'S and BROCKHURST   see CHURCH STRETTON

BROMWICH   see page 353

BRONLLYS   SO 149346   Brecknockshire

Motte and bailey (Be3) with round keep on *motte*; outer bailey rectangular. Some fragments of medieval building incorporated in stables. The fall of a stone from a tower (during a fire in 1175) is mentioned by Giraldus Cambrensis (*Opera* VI, p. 31) (*Archaeologia Cambrensis* 3rd series VIII, pp. 81-92).*   (Fig. 11)

BROUGH   NY 790140   Westmorland

Triangular enclosure made by cutting off part of rectangular Roman fort with a wide U-shaped ditch. The north curtain wall is of herringbone masonry (the central section has been rebuilt later) and has plain angles; that to the north-west beside the keep contains a straight stair. South-east of the keep the curtain is canted and the eastern half rebuilt, although the west side of the gatehouse passage and the springers of the three transverse ribs are probably eleventh or twelfth century in date, as may be the splayed window loop and plinth of the inner wall of a building running north along the east side of the enclosure.

Excavation of the keep showed a Roman foundation overlaid with a

Bronllys

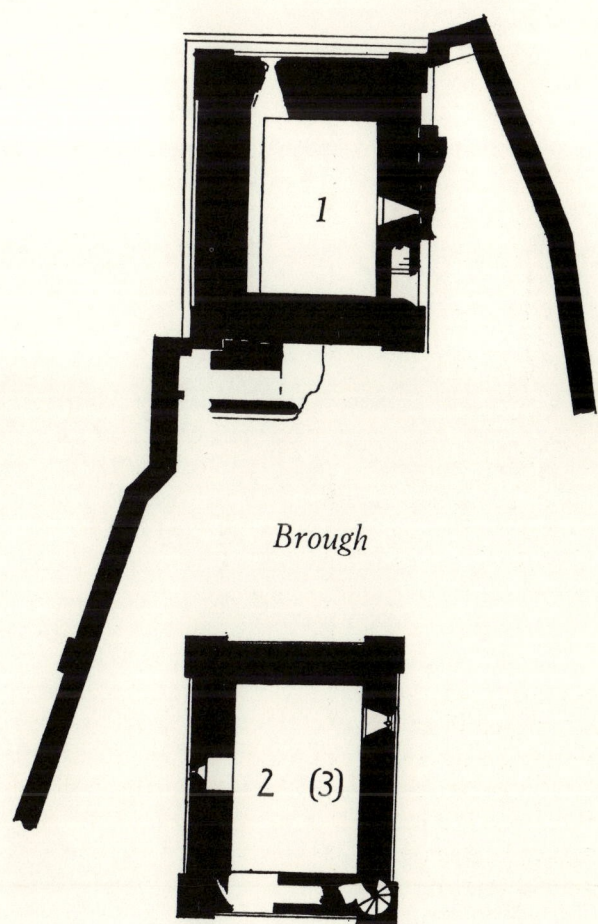

Brough

11

rectangular tower on which the present keep had been erected on a slightly different axis upon a raft of oak beams. The fragmentary foundation outside the north wall of the later keep contains herringbone work and may belong to its predecessor (*Transactions of the Cumberland and Westmorland Archaeological Society*, new series, XXVII, pp. 225-7).

The keep is of local rubble with sandstone dressings, having clasping pilaster buttessses at the angles and a central pilaster springing from the upper offset on the north and south walls, where the masonry is of slightly different finish (rather longer in the course). The basement is now entered by a round-headed doorway of uncertain date, breaking into a straight wall-stair from the floor above, which rises over a blocked loop. The eastern main entrance to the floor above has a similar stair. The first floor was lit by square-headed loops in the north and south walls, and that above by two-light windows — that in the north wall round-headed under a square outer arch, that to the south square-headed with a round-headed outer order resting on a central mullion with capital and side-shafts. The creasings of the gable can be traced in the east and west walls. The roof was later raised, and a spiral stair leads upwards in the north-west angle.

The castle is referred to in 1157 (see Appleby) and the tower was demolished in 1174 (*Chronicles of the reign of Henry II*, III, pp. 327-31) R.C.H.M. *Westmorland*, pp. 50-3.*   (Plate IV; Fig. 11)

BROUGHAM   NY 532290   Westmorland

Quadrilateral enclosure on south bank of River Eamont, with ditch round south half. The square keep is of sandstone rubble with ashlar dressings, with clasping buttresses at the angles except on the east wall, where a rectangular forebuilding projects from the south end. All floors are linked by a spiral stair in the north-east angle, with a latrine block in the north-west one. The basement had an inserted vault, and was lit by a loop in the north, south, and west walls, and entered through a doorway later extended through the outer wall of the forebuilding. One jamb of the original entrance survives above, with a jamb-shaft with moulded capital and base, and round-headed arch of two moulded orders. There are altered round-headed windows of two moulded orders with moulded splays in the north and west walls on both entrance and upper floors, and also square-headed loops in the south wall fragment of the forebuilding. The entrance floor has a square-headed loop beside the remains of a fireplace on the south wall, with an inserted wall arcade, and the north window has small cells entered from its jambs. The fireplace flue can be seen in the wall above, and the upper floor has a round-headed east window of two chamfered orders. (The top floor is an addition.)

Extending east from the forebuilding is a hall with clasping buttresses at the south-east angle and an east window jamb with dogtooth ornament,

GAZETTEER

also a loop in the west end of the north wall (R.C.H.M. *Westmorland*, pp. 57–60).* (Plate V; Fig. 12)

BRYN AMLWG   SO 167846   Shropshire

Ring-work (IC) with strong counterscarp bank; traces of walling on north and west slopes. Excavation revealed six structural phases from about the early twelfth century to the mid/late thirteenth century. Probably the 'Ruffin' of the 1160-4 *Pipe Rolls* (*Montgomeryshire Collections* 60, pp. 8–27).*

BUCKENHAM   Norfolk

The *castellum diruendum* of Buckenham was given to the Augustine Canons (B. M. *Harleian Charters* 83 Dg dated 1151–2 in *Facsimiles of Royal Charters* I, 27). This is usually taken to refer to Old Buckenham where there is a type IIbd2 site (TL 072927). At New Buckenham (TL 084904) there is a ring-work with bailey (Cb3) with a square village enclosure to the east. Heightening the ring-work has largely buried a gatehouse and round tower beside it. The tower is of flint rubble with freestone bonding courses; a string course has been torn out. The entrance has lost any details it may have had, and there is a slight internal offset. The cross-wall is bonded in with ashlar quoins having diagonal tooling, and is pierced by a round-headed doorway with similar quoins at the base. Three equidistant depressions may mark the position of the cross-beams for an upper floor, and the interior retains traces of plaster (*Norfolk Archaeology* XXXII, pp. 232–5).* (Fig. 18)

BUCKINGHAM   SP 695337   Buckinghamshire

Motte flattened to form churchyard; the foundations of a stone castle were found in digging in the slope of the *motte* (Camden (ed. Grose) *Britannia* I, p. 311).

The alleged prison of Hereward *c.* 1070 (Gaimar, *Chron.* 106 – *De Gestis Herewardi*). Mentioned in 1216 (*Histoire des ducs de Normandie*, p. 181).

BUDDUGRE   see TOMEN Y RHODWYDD

BUILTH   SO 044510   Brecknockshire

Motte (Ba/22) with narrow crescentic bailey (now cut in two segments); deep wide ditch with strong counterscarp bank encircling the whole site; buried masonry probably belongs to the Edwardian castle of 1277 – but the earthworks are mentioned as early as 1168 and frequently thereafter (*Brut y Tywysogion*) (G. T. Clark, *Medieval Military Architecture* I, pp. 304–8).*

BUNGAY	TM 336898	Suffolk

Motte and baileys (Bdd3), now largely built over, at waist of rectangular town enclosure in loop of River Waveney. The *motte*-top is now level with the inner bailey, and both have remains of flint rubble curtain walls entered by gate-houses flanked with half-round towers. The inner towers have open backs and ashlar plinths with a chamfered string-course, and there are traces of an angular tower projecting south from the inner curtain.

The rectangular keep on the *motte*-top was faced with sandstone rubble over a flint core, and had been buried in up to 12 ft of fine gravel (apart from the interior of the forebuilding). Parts of a sloping plinth were excavated, and also oolite quoins carrying a shaft, probably from the pilaster buttress at the end and middle of each wall. Two rounded masses outside the south half of the west wall have been interpreted as fallen walling, but their regular curvature invites comparison with the buttresses at Pevensey (q.v.). The basement and fore-building floors were of rammed lime, and fragments of columns with scalloped capitals and moulded bases probably came from an arcade above the north-south basement cross-wall. A vaulting fragment came from a multiple-bayed groined vault; all these ashlar dressings were in Caen stone. There was a spiral stair in the middle of the north wall, beside a latrine shaft, and two stepped loops survive in the east wall at entrance level. A rectangular forebuilding, projecting from the west end of the south wall had two rows of beam holes, a vaulted latrine at one angle (whose oak seat was found), and one end of a mine gallery under the south-west angle of the keep. A re-used string-course and shaft came from some earlier building; there is re-used ashlar in the inner curtain.

Hugh Bigod's castle was captured in 1140 (*Annales Monastici* II, 228) but he had regained it by 1166. Its destruction in 1174 is debatable (*Gesta Henrici Secundi*, pp. 48, 127; *Diceto* I, p. 404) as is the attribution of the curtain walls to the licence to crenellate of 1294 (*Proceedings of the Suffolk Institute of Archaeology* XXII, pp. 109-20; 201-23; 334-8).* (Fig. 12)

BURGH BY SANDS	NY 314592	Cumberland

When the thirteenth-century fortified manor-house was excavated in 1950, it was found to be built across the robbed Intermediate (Roman) wall and filled ditch; three ditch systems were found to precede the stone castle, the earliest not delimited, filled with clean boulder clay over sterile silt. Part of the north and western limbs of a later ditch 10-12 ft wide were traced, finally packed with cobbles for a foundation of a manor house Finally, a V-shaped ditch 16 ft across was traced, aligned with the foundations of a 7 ft 6 in. thick west curtain wall, on a different alignment from the earlier ditches and the later masonry. These three ditch systems (and the south-west curtain wall) are attributed to the twelfth century (*Trans-*

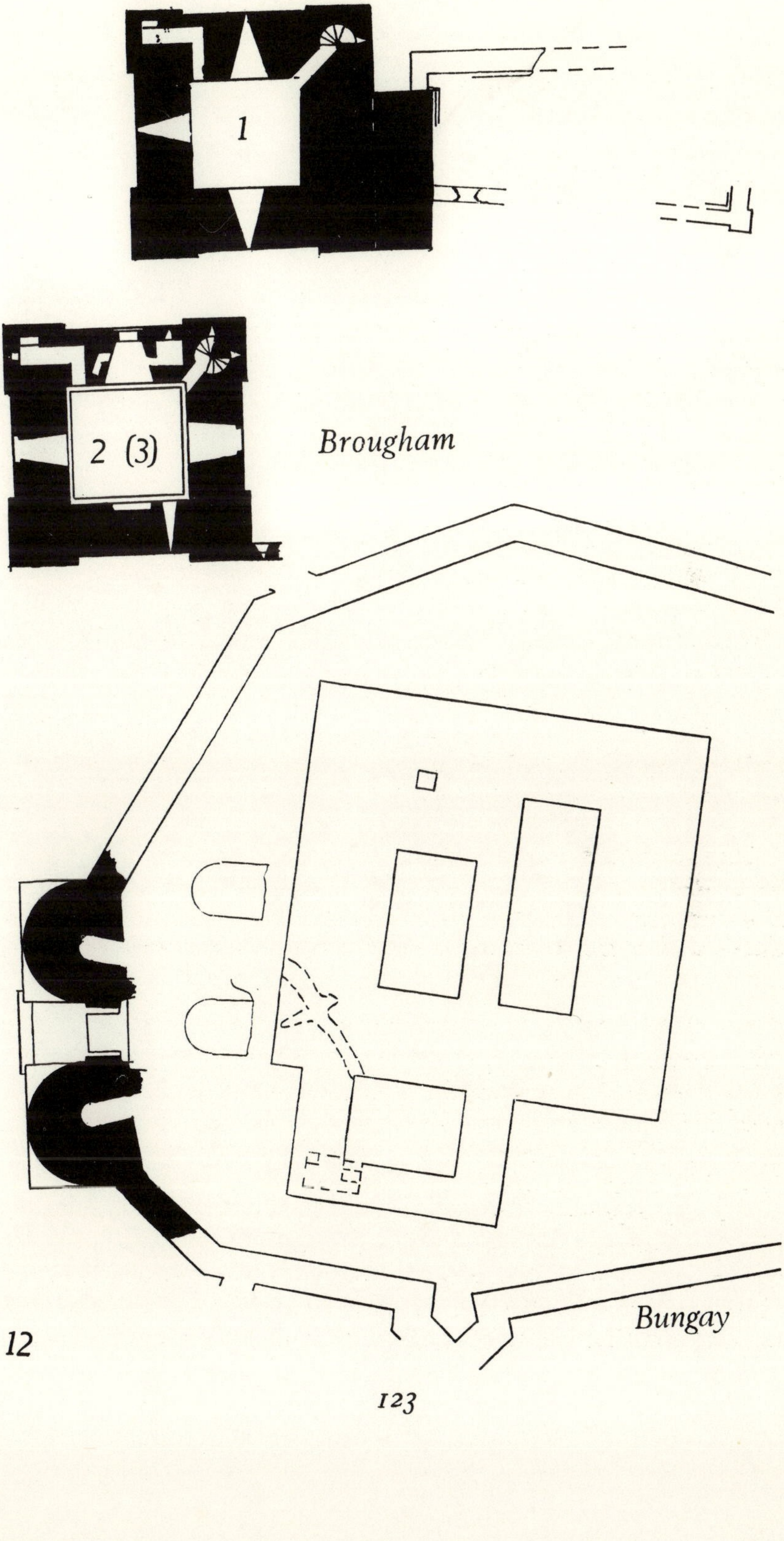

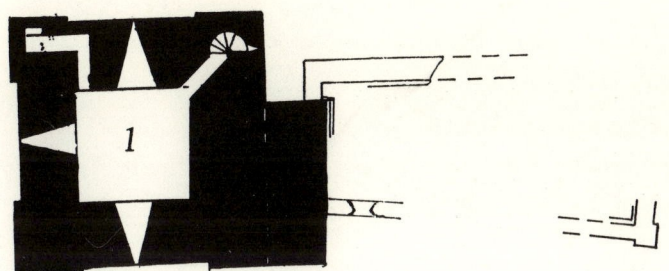

Brougham

Bungay

12

actions of the Cumberland and Westmorland Antiquarian and Archaeological Society, new series LIV, pp. 113–6).

BURGH CASTLE   TG 474044   Suffolk

Oval *motte* (IB) with V-shaped ditch built over south-west corner of Roman fort wall beside River Waveney. Excavations showed clay pads disturbing Saxon graves and slots in separate wall fragment, probably to support a timber tower (*Medieval Archaeology* V, p. 319).

BURLEY   SK 894119   Rutland

Excavation of this *motte* and bailey (Bf1) in 1935 produced much Saxo-Norman pottery, with axed oak logs from the flat-bottomed *motte* ditch cut in solid ironstone. The banks of the bailey and outer rectangular enclosures were low, and the bailey ditch extended only along the west and south sides (*Antiquaries' Journal* XVI, pp. 396–411).

BURROW see page 353

BURTON IN LONSDALE   SD 650722   Yorkshire

Motte and baileys (IBb3d2) with strong counterscarp bank in a gap of which a post and packing stone were found. Excavation of the *motte*-top revealed that the *motte* was of sand, thickly coated with clay and two superimposed pebble floors underlay a circular stone-built inner revetment, one splayed stone being probably the sill of a loop. An axe, key, quern, knives and arrow-heads were found, with two silver pence of the first issue of Henry II, although the pottery was dated to the thirteenth and fourteenth centuries (*Transactions of the Cumberland and Westmorland Archaeological Society* new series V, pp. 283–5, 309; *The Antiquary* XLI, pp. 411–17; *Yorkshire Archaeological Journal* 43, pp. 85–98).

The castle was in the hands of the Crown in 1129–30 (*Pipe Roll*).

'BURTUNA'

The castle was attacked by Henry of Anjou in 1147 (*Gesta Stephani*, p. 136) – the mound at SP 283029 is a possible identification near Black Bourton (Oxon.) but R. H. C. Davis (*English Historical Review* 77, p. 228) suggests Purton near Cricklade (Wilts.). See also STAFFORD.

BURWELL   TL 588661   Cambridgeshire

Rectangular mound surrounded by wide shallow ditch. On excavation the mound was found to be raised over a Romano-British building, and the ditch not to have been completed, with uncut terraces. A thick curtain wall of clunch faced with mortared flint nodules was traced on the south and east sides incorporating a square gate-tower with diagonally set buttresses,

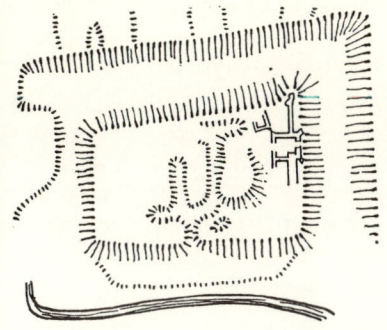
Burwell

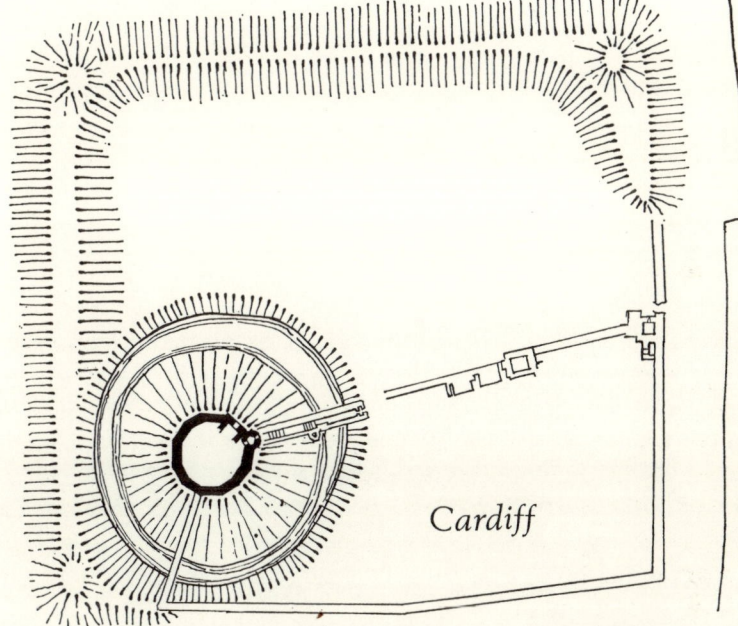
Cardiff

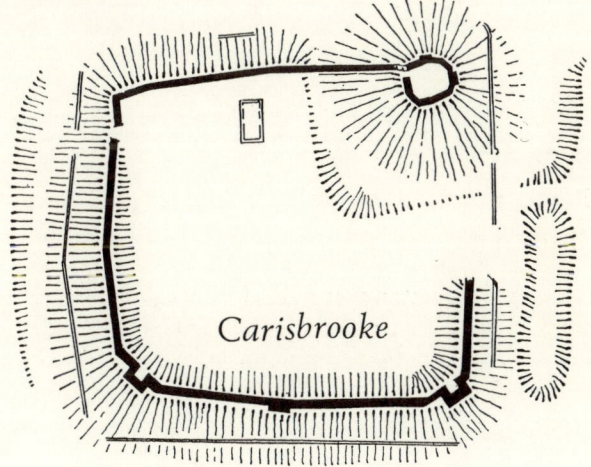
Carisbrooke

13

slightly projecting into the moat. The only detail surviving was a half column built into the north wall, and the bases of two latrine shoots in the curtain beside the gatehouse. Two post-holes midway across the moat probably supported a timber bridge. Both within and without the moat were dumps of builders' rubble (approached by ramps) with fragments of dressed clunch and flaked painted glass perhaps from a later chapel on the site (*Proceedings of the Cambridge Antiquarian Society* XXXVI, 121-33).

Stephen 'caused castles to be built in suitable places' to blockade Geoffrey de Mandeville, Earl of Essex, in 1143-4; (*Gesta Stephani*, p. 109). Geoffrey was mortally wounded during an assault on a royal castle in 1144 (*Chron. Ramsey*, 331; *Gervase*, 128 name it as Burwell). (Fig. 13)

BURY ST. EDMUNDS   see page 353

BUTTERCRAMBE   SE 733584   Yorkshire

Traces of mounds and a bank in Aldby Park may be the remains of the castle of William de Stuteville in 1200 (*Hoveden* IV, p. 17); the licence to fortify was granted in 1201 (*Rot. Chart.* p. 89).

BWLCH Y DDINAS   SO 179301   Brecknockshire

Hill-fort above the Rhiangoll Pass through the Black Mountains. A triangular inner enclosure is cut off by deep ditches and has the foundations of a drystone curtain wall, with square towers at the angles and middle of each side, two forming gatehouses. Foundations of a hall about 80 ft by 40 ft within a mantlet wall near the south-west angle. Possibly the 'Waynard's Castle' of 1143-55 (*Monasticon* III p. 265) (*Brycheiniog* X, pp. 15-27).*

BYTHAM   SK 990196   Lincolnshire

Angular mound above village (IIBd4). Foundations including a round-headed arch were excavated in the *motte* in 1870 (Wild, *History of Castle Bytham*). Stenton (*The First Century of English Feudalism*, p. 144, n. 4; 201, n. 3) suggests that 'Domesday Book' (I, 360b) indicates a castle at *West Bitham*, by analogy with Belvoir, and Wild (op. cit.) draws attention to the unusual mention of iron forges here. Castle here by 1141 (*Symeon of Durham* II, 307).

CABURN   TQ 444089   Sussex

Excavations in 1937-8 showed that the Early Iron Age ramparts had been heightened after the Roman period and again in the twelfth century with a row of large post-holes (up to 12 in. across) along the crest of the bank. (*Sussex Archaeological Collections* LXXX, pp. 203-10).

CADBURY

Money was paid towards the works of the castle in 1209 (*Rotuli de Liberate*,

p. 120) site uncertain (see Cary); perhaps the *burh* of South Cadbury (ST 6225) (*Antiquaries' Journal* XLVII, p. 75).

CADWALLON   ST 137969   Glamorgan

Motte (B) above village, in King's hands 1196–7 (*Pipe Roll*).

CAEREINION   SJ 163055   Montgomeryshire

Traces in churchyard of mound and bailey (Bd2) of the castle built in 1156 and burnt 1167 (*Brut y Tywysogion*) (*Montgomeryshire Coll.* XLIV, pp. 39–44).*

CAERLAVEROCK   NY 026656   Dumfriesshire

The 'Old Castle' forms a square enclosure within a wide moat and strong counterscarp bank. There are traces of a square tower set diagonally at the north angle of the enclosure, and excavation (reported by S. H. Cruden to the Scottish Summer School in Archaeology, 24 July 1954) revealed an ashlar plinth of three chamfered offsets, the middle one with diagonal tooling. (R.C.A.M. *Dumfriesshire*, pp. 10–11).*

CAERLEON   ST 342905   Monmouthshire

Motte with traces of bailey beside River Usk outside east wall of Roman legionary fortress (Ad3). Coxe (*A Tour of Monmouthshire*, p. 88) records the excavation of a foundation of mortared rubble 20 ft deep by 30 by 10 ft, with tiles and other building debris, perhaps of the gigantic tower mentioned by Giraldus Cambrensis (*Opera* VI, p. 55).

The *castellaria* is in 'Domesday' (I, 185b) and in 1158 and 1171–5 (*Brut y Tywysogion; Pipe Rolls*) (*The Monmouthshire Antiquary* I, pp. 70–1).*

CAERNARVON   SH 497627   Caernarvonshire

A *motte* in upper ward of later castle survived to about 1870 (photograph in *Antiquity* XXVI, plate IVb). Built by Hugh, Earl of Chester *c.* 1090–4 (*History of Gruffyd ap Cynan*, p. 132–3).

CAERWEDROS   SN 376557   Cardiganshire

Small *motte* (B) with very strong counterscarp bank, the site of a castle destroyed in 1136 (*Brut y Tywysogion*).

CAERWENT   ST 47093   Monmouthshire

Motte (B) overlying south-east angle of Roman fort; probably the *castell Gwent* of about 1150 (*Liber Landavensis*, p. 44).

CAESAR'S CAMP   see FOLKESTONE

CAHERCONLISH   R 6750   Limerick

Castle of Theobald fitz Walter (d. 1206), site uncertain (Armitage, *Early Norman Castles*, p. 333; Orpen, *English Historical Review* XXII, p. 452).

CAIRSTON   HY 263112   Orkney
Square curtain wall (now farmyard) with clay-set flagstones. There is a small square internal tower at north-west angle with wall-stair beside entrance gap. Possibly the castle attacked in 1152-4 (*Orkneyinga Saga*).

CAISLEN DOIRE PATRAIC   see DERRYPATRICK

CAISTOR   see page 353

CALDICOT   ST 487885   Monmouthshire
Motte and bailey (Bf3) beside stream. The round tower of gritstone ashlar on the *motte* has a chamfered string-course above a sloping plinth. The entrance arch is pointed, with a bar-hole; a wall-stair leads down to the basement and a spiral stair up to the first floor (on corbels; the upper floor has a set-back in the wall). There is a large hollow semicircular projection opposite the entrance. Each floor has four window-loops with side seats and a fireplace. A row of beam-holes for brattices remains below the tall narrow crenels of the parapet. Mentioned by 1197 (*Camden Miscellany* XXII, p. 67). (*Monmouthshire and Caerleon Antiquarian Association*, vol. 3).*   (Fig. 14)

CAMBRIDGE   TL 446582   Cambridgeshire
Altered *motte* (Ad3?) and bailey over Saxon graves (*Archaeologia* XVII, p. 228; *Archaeological News Letter* 7, pp. 222-6) inside Roman enclosure.

The castle of *Grontebrugae* was built by William I on his return from Yorkshire in 1068 (*Ordericus Vitalis* II, p. 185). Repairs were carried out in 1156-9, and work costing £31 in 1172-3 and £50 in 1190-1. Over £200 was spent on the hall and chamber in 1212-16 (*Rot. Litt. Claus.* II, p. 5) (V.C.H. *Cambridgeshire* III, pp. 116-17; R.C.H.M. *Cambridge* II, pp.304-6).*

CAMMEIS   SN 082401   Pembrokeshire
Motte and bailey beside gorge of River Gamman (Ac3); the bailey bank to the north has both an inner and outer bank in addition and the eastern angle is cut off by a rock-cut ditch with vertical sides 20 ft deep; the small triangular enclosure has thick walling of local shale, with traces of a square tower on the west side.

The castle is mentioned by Giraldus Cambrensis about 1190 (*Opera* VI, p. 111) and was to be rebuilt in 1197 (*Pipe Roll*) (*Archaeologia Cambrensis* CI, pp. 123-8).*

CANFIELD   TL 594179   Essex
Motte and bailey (Ae4) with triangular outer bailey, with a dam beside the River Roding to flood the ditches. Excavation on the axial line of the *motte* ditch revealed timber and pottery fragments. (*Transactions of the Essex Archaeological Society* 16, p. 138).

The castle is mentioned in 1214 (*Pipe Roll*) (R.C.H.M. *Essex* II, pp. 91-2).*

Caldicot

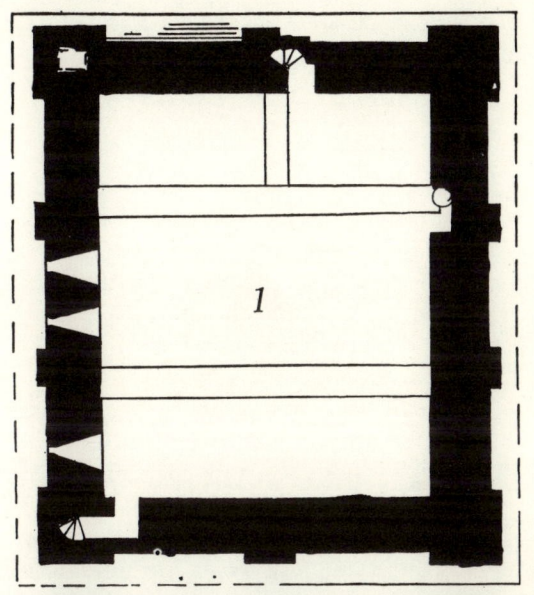

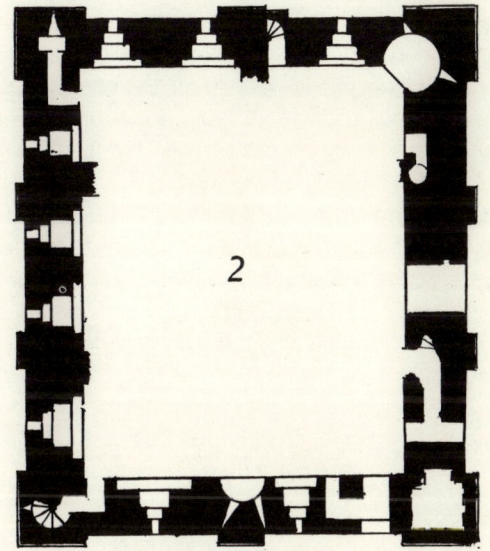

Canterbury

14

CANS   Shropshire (?)

Unidentified castle mentioned in 1134 (*Ordericus Vitalis, Historia Ecclesiastica* V, p. 43, cited by Eyton, *Antiquities of Shropshire*, V, 242). Ownership makes it unlikely to be Caus.

CANTERBOHHAN   see LLANDOVERY

CANTERBURY   TR 146575   Kent

Rectangular keep of flint rubble with Caen stone dressings (apart from some sandstone). Pilaster buttresses clasp each angle and there are two mid-wall buttresses on the south-eastern and north-western faces and one each to north and south, the last having a shallow extension covering one of the two spiral stairs (the other being in the eastern angle, vaulted in Roman brick). A fragment of plinth shows that it was chamfered with alternate courses of roll-and-fillet.

Internally the keep was sub-divided by two north-west/south-east walls, the outer compartments having further cross-walls. The more northerly cross-wall was built over a pit containing an early twelfth century cooking-pot rim (shown me by Professor S. S. Frere) and the southerly abutted against the well-pipe with drawing points on opposite sides on different levels. The ground floor was lit by three loops in the south-east wall. There was a wide entrance arch at the centre of the upper part of the north-west wall, of which a plain jamb and barhole remain, with traces of an adjoining wall-stair leading to the destroyed upper floor; a narrow blocked doorway (the original entrance?) lies at the north end of the north-east wall. There is no trace of a forebuilding. There were domed fireplaces in the western angle and centre of the north-east wall, with smoke-vents at the inner angles of the buttresses. There were 1, 2, 3, 4 windows in the north-west, north-east, south-west and south-east walls respectively, with wide stepped recesses turned in Roman brick and a latrine shaft in the southern angle One window voussoir has chevron ornament.

Houses 'in exchange of the castle' are mentioned in 'Domesday Book' (I, a2) and the Dane John has been suggested as a *motte*. Compensation for land taken for the castle was paid in 1169, and under £200 spent on the castle (chiefly the keep) in 1172–4 and again in 1190–3 and repairs thereafter (*Pipe Rolls*) (*Kentish Gazette and Canterbury Press*, reprint of lecture to Canterbury Archaeological Society by H. M. Enderby, 19 November 1932).*   (Fig. 14)

CANTREF BYCHAN   see LLANDOVERY

CAOLUISCE   see ASSAROE

CARDIFF   ST 180767   Glamorgan

Motte inside square bailey formed by walls of Roman fort (AdI); the north and east walls of the latter were ruined to the level of the Roman bank and then covered with a bank and ditch carrying a light wall. The south and west walls were rebuilt in stone nearly to the north-west and south-east angles — the alignment was altered to form an obtuse south-west angle just inside the Roman one. Foundations of other walls ran from the ends of these walls to the *motte* and up its slopes to a twelve sided shell-wall of rounded pebbles. All the work has been much altered; the shell has one side projecting slightly with return walls as if for a tower, and later buttresses, windows and turrets guarding the stair against the inner curtain wall up the motte. Built in 1081 (*Annales Monastici*, p. 4). The town had gates and a palisade by 1185 (*Annals of Margam* 17, *Pipe Roll*) (J. P. Grant, *Cardiff Castle*, Cardiff, 1923).* (Fig. 13)

| CARDIGAN | SN 164464 | Cardiganshire |

Rectangular area made by cutting off promontory with bank and ditch at Old Castle Farm. Built in 1093, captured and rebuilt frequently thereafter; rebuilt in stone by the Lord Rhys 1171 and sold to King John in 1199 (*Brut y Tywysogion*). It is not certain when the change to the present site in the town (Castle Green) took place.

| CAREW | SN 045037 | Pembrokeshire |

Immediately north of the present entrance to the inner courtyard is a rubble tower constructed from a rectangular gatehouse by blocking the ends of the passage and adding a latrine block to the south side. The floor above the barrel-vaulted passage has a round-headed doorway and loops (the external one much altered) with similar layout to the upper floor.

Traditionally built by Gerald of Windsor before 1116; seized by John in 1210 (*Rot. Litt. Pat. 92*) (*Archaeologia Cambrensis* CV, pp. 81–95; *Archaeological Journal* CXIX, pp. 270–307).*

| CARGILL | NO 157373 | Perthshire |

Motte (B) on south bank of River Tay. The castle is mentioned before 1199 in a document in the Dupplin Charter Chest (cited by G. W. S. Barrow in the *Bulletin of the Inst. of Hist. Res.* XXIX, p. 16, n. 1).

CARHAM see page 353

| CARISBROOKE | SZ 488878 | Isle of Wight |

High *motte* with two square baileys (Add3), the western one covering the walls of an earlier fortlet, the eastern one much altered. A sectional heading cut into the north-east slope of the *motte* in 1894 showed alternate horizontal layers of loose and rammed chalk above a layer of single stones — chiefly flint (*Proceedings of the Hampshire Field Club and Archaeological*

Society II, p. 258). The *motte*-top is surrounded by a squared rubble shell-wall of irregular polygonal plan; there is a wide buttress on the curved north side, and a round-headed latrine recess adjoining the later gatehouse. The multangular south side (with ashlar quoins) has traces of a plinth, and the whole surrounds a well 160 ft deep. The curtain wall of Binstead stone has bowed sides to north, west and south. The southern angles had projecting square towers and there may have been another at the north-west angle (now rebuilt); in the middle of the south side is a slightly projecting turret. The north curtain is now of varying thickness and ascends the *motte* as a flanker to the stairway.

The curtain wall turns inward on each side of the later gatehouse which is thus probably on the line of the original entrance. The southern part of the east curtain resembles that opposite, but there is a break in the alignment (with the foundations of a square tower) opposite the inturned entrance to the pre-Conquest fort wall, and further north the wall is thickened and rests on the fort wall.

Part of the basement of the great hall within the bailey is of twelfth century date. A Transitional capital of an engaged column with a beaded necking was found during restoration work and there is a two-light window with segmental heads under a circular opening; the mullion is columnar with a cushion base and quirked and moulded capital. There is a wide three-sided window seat below the Purbeck marble jambs.

Odo of Bayeux was arrested in the hall of Carisbrooke in 1082 (*Anglo-Saxon Chronicle*) and the castle is probably that mentioned under Alwinestone in 'Domesday Book' (I, 2a). The manor passed to Baldwin de Redvers in 1107 and he is described as having a castle ornately built of stone defended by a strong fortification when he was besieged here after his defeat at Exeter (1136). The castle surrendered when the water supply failed (*Gesta Stephani*, p. 29) (Stone, *Architectural Antiquities of the Isle of Wight* II, pp. 74–100).* (Fig. 13)

CARLINGFORD   J 1810   Louth

On rocky mound beside Carlingford Lough, A rectangular tower to the west has two loops in round-arched recesses in the north and west faces; the other walls, and a twin tower to the south have been destroyed. A straight curtain with two tiers of loops runs to a square tower with a splayed plinth whose external angles are chamfered off at first floor level (cf. Colton Tower at Dover). Beyond these towers the curtain curves round in short straight lengths, each length having one loop on each level.

Repairs to the castle are recorded in 1211–12 (*Irish Pipe Roll*) and in 1215 (*Rot. Litt. Pat.* 148). (Fig. 15)

CARLISLE   NY 396564   Cumberland

Triangular site north-west of city. Much of the lower part of the curtain

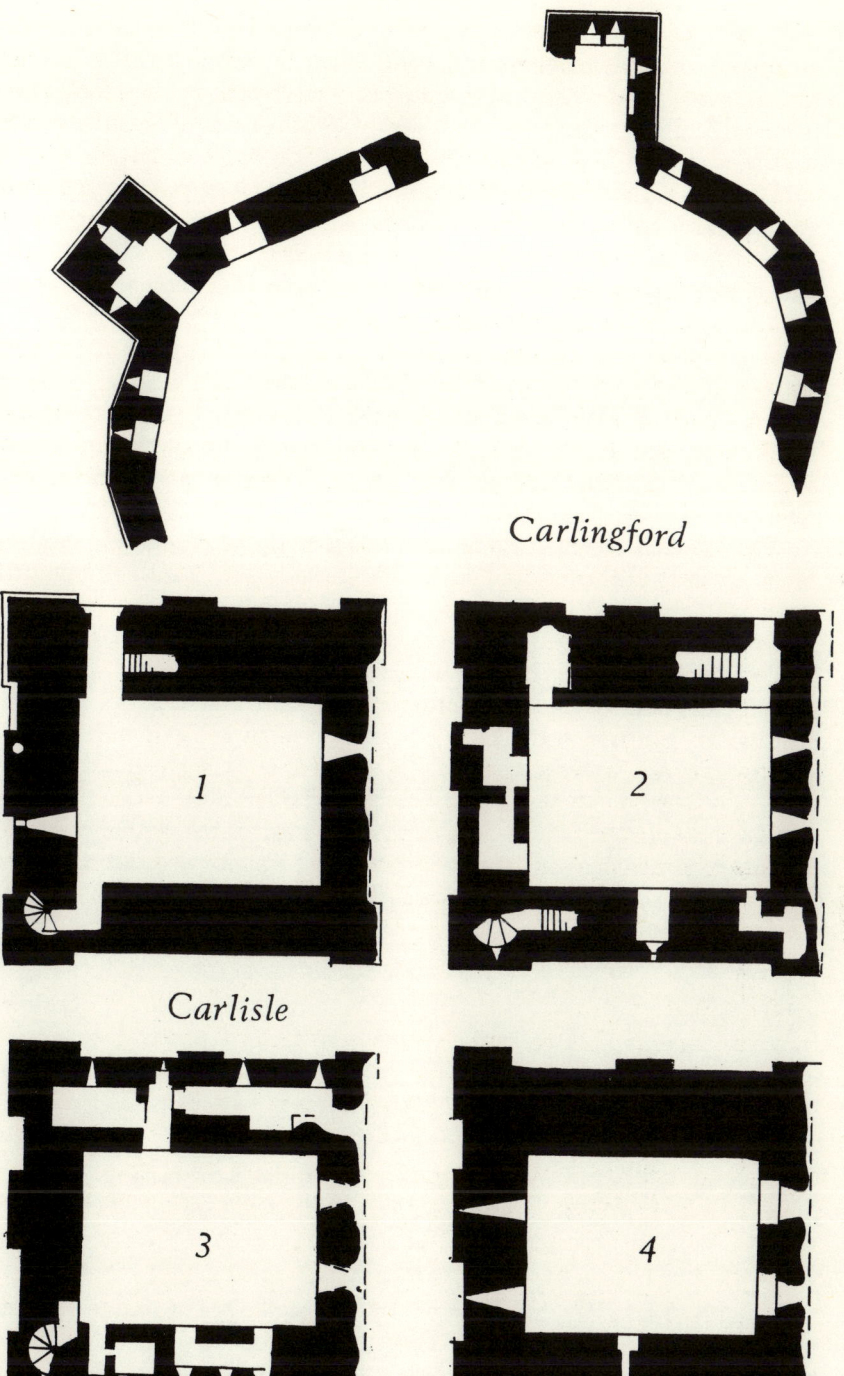

Carlingford

Carlisle

15

wall and rectangular turrets are built of small grey sandstone blocks. A gatehouse with round arches ornamented with chevrons formerly occupied the east angle, but probably went out of use when the inner (east) ward was separately walled, perhaps in 1167–8 (*Pipe Roll*). This and the other gates have been rebuilt.

The keep is almost a true cube, but has been much altered (particularly on the south and west sides). The original entrance (approached by a wooden stair on a stone base) was at the south end of the east wall, whence a straight wall-stair descended to the ground floor (the outer wall is now cut through for the present entrance); this was lit by loops, one in the north wall and two in each of the others. The entrance floor had a fireplace with shafts and nail-head decoration in the east wall, and a single window in the west wall with a wall-stair leading to the newel stair serving all floors in the north-west angle, and two windows in the other walls, one enlarged to form a drawing place for the well. Both entrance and second floors had a latrine in the south-west angle.

The second floor has two original windows in the south wall and several wall-chambers in the east and west walls (much altered), with a principal window in each. The top floor is lit similarly, with two loops in the north wall as well.

The castle was built by William II in 1092 (*Anglo-Saxon Chronicle*) and a 'castle and towers' were ordered by Henry I in 1122 (*Symeon of Durham* II, p. 267) but the keep is attributed to King David of Scotland (1136–57) (*Scotichronicon* V, p. 42). It was certainly the 'great old tower' of 1174 (*Chronicles of the Reigns of Henry II*, III, p. 256). The timbers of the keep were repaired in 1186–8 when a small tower and the king's chamber were being constructed; there was heavy expenditure early in John's reign too, and also on repairs after its capture by the Scots in 1216 (*Pipe Rolls* and *Rot. Litt. Claus.*) (*Transactions of the Cumberland and Westmorland Antiquarian Society* II, pp. 1–17).* (Fig. 15)

| CARLOW | S 7177 | Carlow |

Site of castle mentioned in charter of 1209 (quoted in the *Journal of the Kildare Archaeological Society* VI, p. 313).

| *CARLTON* | TF 395836 | Lincolnshire |

Overgrown site (Ba/23 ?) north-west of South Reston church.
The castle is mentioned in 1205 (*Rot. de Finibus*, 296).

| CARMARTHEN | SN 413420 | Carmarthenshire |

Motte and bailey (Be3) much altered by later walling. The traditional site of the Norman castle of 1094 at Rhyd y Gors (SN 408190) has no remains. Rebuilt in 1102, in 1145 (after its loss in 1137) and 1150. Considerably strengthened in 1181–3 (Pipe Rolls) it nevertheless fell to Llywelyn in 1215. (*Brut y Tywysogion*) (R.C.A.M. *Carmarthen*, pp. 249–51).*

CARREGHOFA   Montgomeryshire

A quadrilateral earthwork at SJ 255222 may be the castle built in 1101 (*Florence of Worcester* II, p. 50), although a large square room with plastered stone walls was found under Carreghova Hall in November 1871 (*Montgomeryshire Collections* VII, p. 386, quoting the *Oswestry Advertiser*). The castle was garrisoned and repaired in 1159–62, and a curtain wall was built in 1194–5 after its recovery from the Welsh. It was again fortified in 1212–13 (*Pipe Rolls*; *Rot. Litt. Pat.* p. 100).

CARRICK (AYR)   see page 354

CARRICK   T 0023   Wexford

Oval ring-work (IC) of 1169 (Giraldus Cambrensis, *Opera* V, 245), on opposite bank of River Slaney to the tower (Hore, *History of Wexford* V, pp. 22–34).

CARROCK   see page 354

CARRICKFERGUS   J 4287   Antrim

The castle occupies a rocky peninsular in Belfast Lough, with a curtain wall of basalt rubble. The round-arched entrance is flanked by round towers; the east one has an east window, externally splayed from triple shafts with voluted capitals supporting the round head (probably inserted). Excavations (reported in *The Times*, 1 August 1955) showed that there was an intermediate curtain wall with small square towers, one of which has triple arrowslits opening from single embrasures and single loops above on three sides. A loop was blocked when the outer curtain was added.

The inner bailey at the south tip of the peninsular is trapezoidal; the curtain wall has been much rebuilt with two round-headed windows and side seats and the square keep is built over the north angle. This latter has red sandstone dressings with yellow sandstone dressings higher up. A projection rises above the south angle as a turret projecting east, balanced by one at the west angle projecting west and south, containing spiral stairs, the former serving all floors and the latter the topmost and roof only, above a latrine block.

The keep was approached by a stair (now replaced) along the east side through a doorway (jamb survives) to a landing in front of the plain round-arched entrance with bar-holes. The basement has two groined-vaulted chambers with the well beside the cross-wall and a connecting doorway at the south end. The south wall has two loop-lit mural cells, one leading to a wall-stair rising to a double latrine beside a third, reached from the first floor, which retains a round-headed two-light window over the entrance, a narrow loop over the wall-staircase and a round-backed fireplace in the north-west wall. Another fireplace with a flat lintel remains on the upper floor, with pairs of windows in each wall. Those in the south-west wall, and the south one of the south-east wall are round-headed two-lights, set back in a round-headed external and internal embrasure. The roof above has been raised, but beam-holes remain in the north-west walls with rainwater gutters and a square loop at the west end of the south-west wall.

First mentioned in 1205 (*Calendar of Documents* I, 91, 104, 107.) Great tower mentioned 1212–12 (*Irish Pipe Roll*) (Ministry of Finance, *Official Guide*).* (Plate VI; Fig. 16, 26)

| CARRICKITTLE | R 2626 | Limerick |

Motte on natural rock, mentioned in 1199 (*Calendar of Documents* I, 14).

| CARRIGOGUNNEL | R 4655 | Limerick |

Natural rock *motte* of castle mentioned in 1210 (*Annals of Innisfallen*; *Annals of the Four Masters*) and restored to Richard de Burgh in 1215 (*Calendar of Documents* I, 91, identified in *English Historical Review* XXII, pp. 449–50) but see ESCLON.

| CARY | ST 641322 | Somerset |

Fragments of curving banks (Ca4 ?) to north and east of trapezoidal keep of local rubble with Doulting and Ham Hill ashlar face. Excavations showed that the keep was almost square, with a north–south cross-wall and projecting forebuilding to the north with a fragment of chamfered plinth surviving, and a pit below the entrance. The site was covered with a level layer of masonry chippings, with an occupation layer to the east between two concrete floors. Finds included a whetstone. (*Proceedings of the Somersetshire Archaeological Society* XXXVI, pp. 23–5, 168–74). The castle surrendered to Stephen for lack of food in 1138, and Robert of Gloucester levelled a siege-castle being built before it by Henry de Tracy in 1147 (*Gesta Stephani* pp. 44–6, 140). See CADBURY. (Fig. 16)

| CASTELL GWALTER | SN 622868 | Cardiganshire |

Small *motte* with rock-cut ditch on escarpment (Bd1) of a castle mentioned in 1114 (*R.R.A.N.* II, 1041) (*Archaeologia Cambrensis* (1946), pp. 156–7).

CASTELL TALIORUM see LLANHILLETH

CASTELL Y WAUN see CHIRK

CASTLE ... see under second name.

| CASTLECOMER | S 5273 | Kilkenny |

Altered *motte* (B) in garden east of village, burnt in 1200 (*Liber Primus Kilkenniensis*).

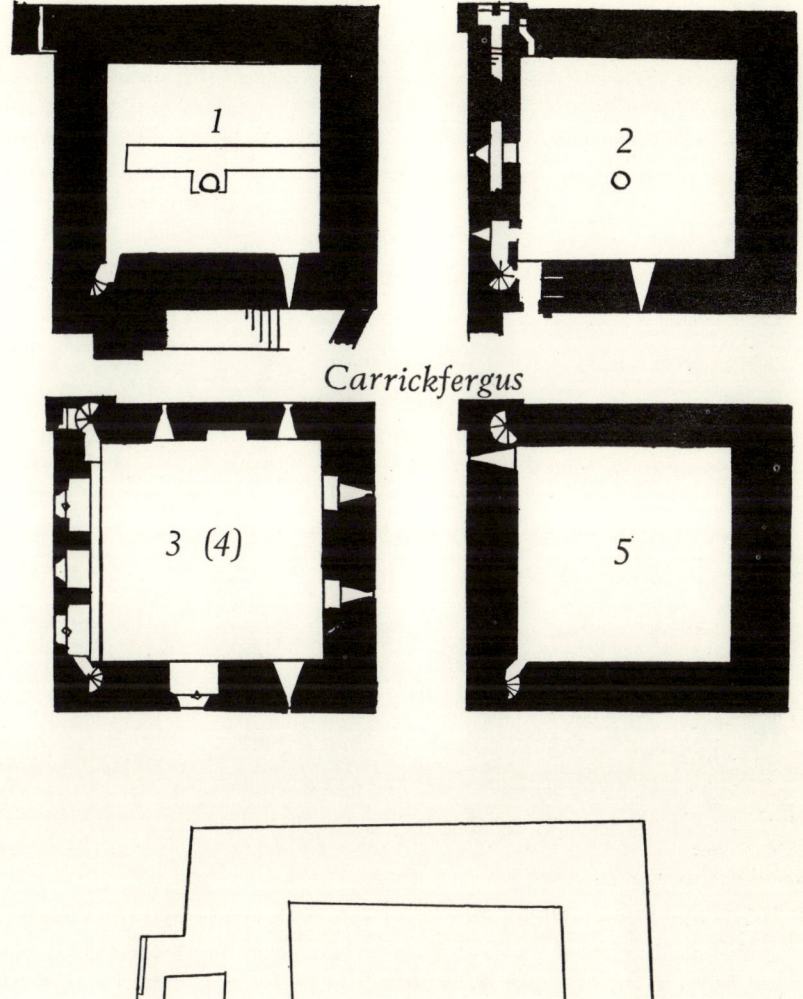

Carrickfergus

Cary

16

CASTLECONNELL   R 6563   Limerick
Motte south-west of village beside River Shannon, mentioned in 1200 (*Annals of the Four Masters*, 29) and 1211–12 (*Irish Pipe Roll*).

CASTLEDERMOT   see KILKEA

CASTLE HILL   see THETFORD

CASTLEKEVIN   T 1892   Dublin
Motte and bailey (IIBc2) possibly built by 1216 (*Memoranda Roll* of 1472, quoted in *Jl. of the Rl. Soc. of Antiquaries of Ireland* XXXVIII, pp. 17–27).

CASTLEKNOCK   O 0736   Dublin
Motte and bailey (Bb3) adjoining college, with strong double counterscarp banks. There are traces of polygonal keep casing the *motte* (see drawing of 1689, reproduced as plate VII (opposite p. 7) of the *Journal of the Royal Society of Antiquaries of Ireland* LXII). Castle of 1200, ordered to be destroyed in 1214 (as well as later) (*Calendar of Documents* I, 19, 81).

CASTLEMARTYR   see page 354

CASTLEMILK   NY 150775   Dumfriesshire
Rebuilt castle, site called *Casthelmilc* in 1174 (*Reg. Ep. Glaswegensis* I, p. 23). A drawing of 1547 (Hatfield House, Cecil Papers, Maps 2/27 reproduced in the *Transactions* of the Dumfries and Galloway Archaeological Society, XLIV) shows a cubical tower within a low wall with a square gateway on top of a *motte*. The tower had a gabled roof and was entered by a round-headed door reached by a ladder.

CASTLEMORE (TULLOW)   S 8574   Carlow
Motte and bailey (IBd4), Raymond le Gros's castle of 1181 (*Giraldus Cambrensis, Opera* V, 355); a mound producing hammer-dressed masonry 400 yards to the east may be contemporary (*Journal of the Royal Society of Antiquaries of Ireland* XXXVI, pp. 368–82). Radsillan and Tullow castles are mentioned separately in 1199 (*Reg. Abbey of St. Thomas, Dublin*, pp. 111, 113).

CASTLE OF KING OLAF (BON Y DOM)   Anglesey
The 'base of the tomen' visible in the twelfth century of the castle built by Olaf before 1012 (or 1034). (*History of Gruffyd ap Cynan*, p. 105). The name suggests a ring-work and a possible identification is Castell Bryn Gwyn (*Archaeologia Cambrensis* CXI, pp. 56–8) (SH 465670).

CASTELSKREEN   J 4740   Down
Oval *motte* on bank of circular ring-work (IAa3) of pre-Norman date.

Excavation showed that the bank surrounded a pond-like hollow, and had post-holes of a palisade. The entrance gap had stone gatepost sockets but was filled in and provided with a stone-built drain in the last phase. No discoveries were made on top of the *motte*, but an arrow-head, tanged knife and horseshoe nails were found under the toe of the *motte*; other knives, querns, spindle-whorls, twelfth-thirteenth century pottery and a cut halfpenny of 1205-18 were recovered from within the ring-work (*Ulster Journal of Archaeology* XXII, pp. 67-82).

CASTLETON   see DANBY

CASTLETOWN DELVIN   N 6062   Westmeath

Motte (B) in garden near later castle mentioned in 1182 (Giraldus Cambrensis, *Opera* V, 356).

CASTLETOWN   see DUNDALK

CATTHORPE   see page 354

CAUS   SJ 338079   Shropshire

Long oval ridge with embanked rim expanding into platform on east side, south-west of which is a *motte* and bailey (Ad3) with counterscarp bank on inside doubled back to form a third defensive line. There are some fragments of a shell-wall on the *motte* and of foundations of a curtain wall to the inner bailey. Castle named in 1198 (*Pipe Roll*).   (Fig. 19)

CAXTON   TL 294587   Cambridgeshire

Wide ditches surrounding square and rectangular islands (R.C.H.M., *West Cambridgeshire*, 40).*

CENARTH BYCHAN   see CILGERRAN

CENARTH FAWR   SN 269414   Carmarthenshire

Large mound (B) south-west of church, possibly the castle of Emlyn mentioned in 1184-9 and 1194-1204 (*Pipe Rolls*).

CENNANUS   see KELLS

CHALGRAVE   TL 009274   Bedfordshire

Low *motte* and bailey (ABd3) among other earthworks and strip-cultivation. The mound was found to be of clean clay-with-flints covered with a level 9 in. layer of gravelly earth containing twelfth century pottery. The bailey bank appeared to be stone-faced (*The Bedfordshire Archaeologist* 1, pp. 43-5). The *motte* was built over timber houses and abandoned by the early thirteenth century (*Archaeological Excavations*, 1970, p. 25).

CHARTLEY   SK 010825   Staffordshire

Motte and bailey (Bd4) with strong counterscarp bank and cross-ditch to make two baileys. Foundations of a round keep on the *motte* and of a curtain wall with half-round towers are generally attributed to *c.* 1220, although the castle was repaired in 1191–2 (*Pipe Roll*) (*Journal of the North Staffordshire Field Club* 39, pp. 143–9, revised from *Journal of the British Archaeological Association* new series II, pp. 53–9).*   (Fig. 20)

CHEPSTOW   ST 533941   Monmouthshire

Castle built on a natural leg-of-mutton shaped spur beside the River Wye. At the narrowest point is a long hall of sandstone blocks capped with lacing courses of tiles and then small coursed rubble with squared dressings. There are pilaster buttresses at the end of each wall and one in the centre of the eastern and western and four in the northern and southern walls, rising from a plinth. The north wall is considerably thinner than the others, and has a round-headed loop between each pilaster at ground level, with a string course. The first floor was supported on beams, and had a blind arcade of round-headed arches round the south and west walls; two original round-headed windows survive in the north wall. This level was approached by a rubble foundation on the east side in front of a square-headed door with a diapered tympanum and hood-mouldings; the inner arch (of two orders) has traces only of carving, and a straight wall-stair rises south from the passage to the angle and then spirals upwards. The upper part of the tower was reconstructed in the thirteenth century, but two circular splayed openings in the west wall remain.

The narrow space between the cliff and the north side of the tower is blocked by a narrow gallery, open to the sky. The east end has a pointed arch of two orders, the north wall has seven round-headed flat-sided embrasures and the wall-walk over was reached from an altered window at the west end of the tower's north wall.

The south curtain on either side of the tower has been rebuilt, but fragments remain of similar masonry to the tower, with a round-headed doorway just east of it. The rectangular tower at the south-west angle of the upper bailey has been altered internally, but retains two square-headed windows with a round roll-moulding to the head facing west, with window seats and a pointed rear arch; one of the pair facing south has a round head and rear arch. These light the main room above the basement. A row of beam-holes for brattices runs below the tall narrow crenels in the battlements, the southern merlons having arrowslits. There appears to be a re-used two-light window with moulded jambs in the inner wall of the upper gate.

The eastern curtain wall of the middle bailey is much altered but has two round towers with sloping plinths and plain arrowslits, one at the

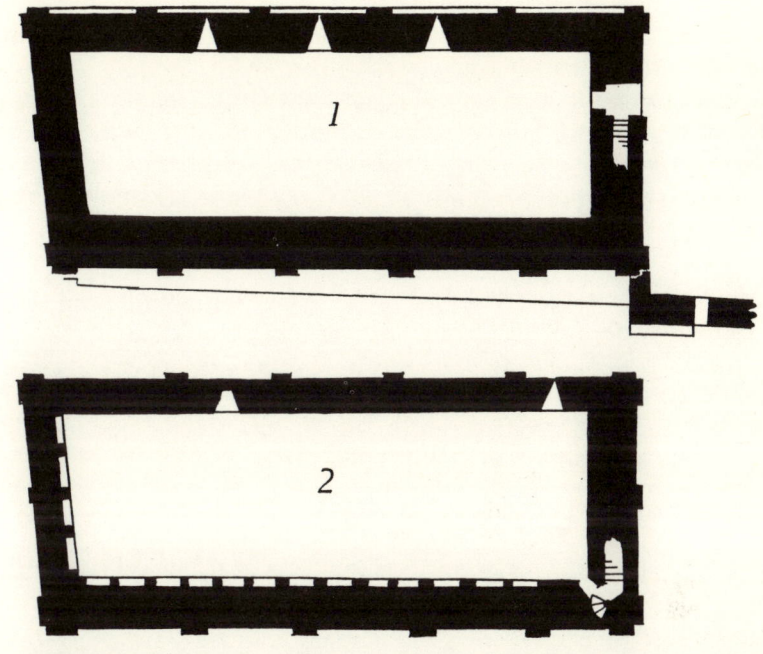

Chepstow

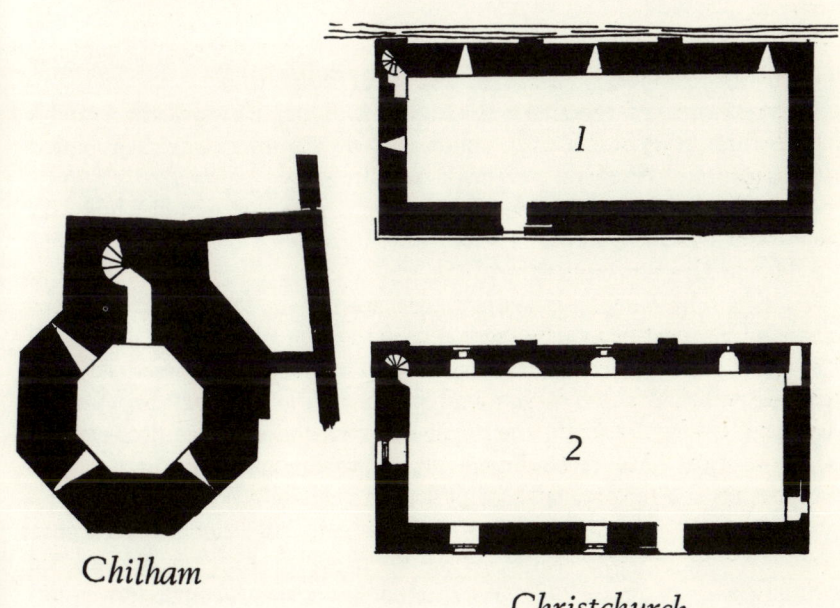

Chilham

Christchurch

17

southern end and the other (half-round) flanking a pointed arch of two orders with Romanesque moulded capitals.

The castle was begun by William fitz Osbern (1067–71: 'Domesday Book' I, 162a) and £10 was spent on repairs 1184–5 (*Pipe Roll*) (M.P.B.W. *Official Guide*: *Transactions of the Bristol and Gloucestershire Archaeological Society* LXVII, pp. 307–46).* (Plate VII; Fig. 17)

CHESTER   SJ 404657   Cheshire

Much altered *motte* and bailey (Bd4). The heavily-buttressed Agricola Tower may be of twelfth century date but old plans (*Journal of the Chester Archaeological Society* new series V, p. 244) show two other square towers on the curtain wall of the inner bailey which may be contemporary. Built by William I in 1070 (*Ordericus Vitalis* II, 181). Over £100 was spent on the castle in 1159–60 and £40 in 1182–3 (*Pipe Rolls*).

CHICHESTER   SU 862051   Sussex

Damaged *motte* in north-east corner of city wall, now Priory Park. A chapel in the castle is mentioned in 1142 (Liebermann, *Anglo-Normansiche geschichstsquellen*, p. 95 quoted in v.c.h. *Sussex* III, p. 79, n. 70). Small sums were spent on repairs from 1176, and the castle garrisoned in 1193–4 and a gaol built in 1198–9 (*Pipe Rolls*). Philip d'Aubigny was ordered to destroy the castle in 1217 (*Patent Roll* 1216–25, p. 57).

CHILHAM   TR 066535   Kent

Excavation in 1926 revealed a rectangular building of coursed flint rubble with a projecting stair turret, subdivided by a semicircular arch of thin pieces of red sandstone and ragstone alternately, supported on plain responds and by external pilaster buttresses. The southern bay had been demolished and the arch and a tall rebated entrance arch (with bar-hole) in the northern bay blocked, and a mound of earth piled against the north-west side. The remaining bay had been used as the foundation for a diamond-shaped annex to an octagonal keep to the west, one wall oversailing the early work on a timber bressumer. The keep, of coursed ragstone rubble, with ashlar quoins, had mid-wall buttresses (now cut back) with a rectangular stair-turret on the north-east side and a latrine projection to the south-east. The forebuilding wall above the arch was originally incorporated in a rectangular curtain (now much altered) with shallow projections at the angles. The basement was lit by three loops, and a shaft and respond remain on the upper floor, which has a round-headed window with two orders of roll-moulding and a string-course framing.

Over £400 was spent on the castle between 1171–4, and repairs in the 1190s (*Pipe Rolls*) (*Antiquaries' Journal* VIII, pp. 350–3).* (Fig. 17)

GAZETTEER

CHIRK (CASTELL Y WAUN)   SJ 291375   Denbighshire

Motte (A) above stream near church may be that mentioned in 1165 and 1212 (*Pipe Rolls*).

CHRISTCHURCH   SZ 160926   Hampshire

Motte and bailey (Bd3 ?) north of priory church. Rectangular keep of limestone and ironstone rubble, with splayed angles having ashlar quoins. The north and south walls are ruined to ground level; a door was found *below* the level of the *motte*-top in repair work (*Medieval Archaeology* IV, p. 88, n. 22). A Norman hall of about 1160 stands in the bailey. The thicker east wall was the curtain wall and has clasping angle buttresses and two mid-wall pilasters, with a spiral stair in the northern angle. The ground floor is lit by three loops in the east wall and one in the north, with entrances in each of the other walls. A timber staircase led up the side of the west wall to the main entrance; this floor is lit by five two-light windows with external chevron ornament to the round heads and internal jamb-shafts with sculptured capitals. The north window is further enriched with a patterned head and chevron ornament; the round south window is altered. Beam-holes for this floor and corbels for the roof are visible, and a fireplace with cylindrical chimney. The castle was captured by Walter de Pinkney in 1147–8 (*Gesta Stephani*, p. 140) (M.P.B.W. *Official Guide*).*

(Plate VIII; Fig. 17)

CHURCH STRETTON   SO 446925   Shropshire

Double enclosure made by ditching an egg-shaped area and subdividing with a cross-ditch, with a strong counterscarp bank provided by the natural spur of the site overlooking the Ludlow/Shrewsbury gap. Excavation in 1959 showed that the cross-ditch was V-shaped in section and a shale curtain wall had been built on the natural clay and partly buried in an earth bank, but later completely robbed.

Custody of the castle is mentioned in 1154–5 and repairs in 1194–5 (*Pipe Roll*) (*Transactions of the Shropshire Arch. Soc.* LVII, pp. 63–80).*

CHURCHOVER   see WAVREI

CILGERRAN   SN 195431   Pembrokeshire

On rocky promontory overlooking Teifi gorge with two successive rock-cut ditches isolating it to the south, forming a Type IIBc2 site. On the east side of the inner ward is a short length of clay-bedded stone walling; a similar piece is visible beside the later gatehouse at the south-west angle.

The short-lived castle of Cenarth Bychan (1108–9: *Brut y Tywysogion*) is a possible identification for Cilgerran, which is mentioned in 1165–6 and later; (*Brut y Tywysogion*) see CENARTH FAWR (M.P.B.W. *Official Guide*).*

CILLE FIACAL   see KILFEAKLE

CILLE SANTAIL   see MOUNT SANDEL

CIRENCESTER   Gloucestershire

The Empress built a castle 'next to the holy church of the religious' in the autumn of 1141, which was thereupon burnt and its earthworks levelled by Stephen (*Gesta Stephani*, 92). The abbey site was found in 1964 (*Antiquaries' Journal* XLV, p. 106), with a twelfth-century courtyard overlying the west end.

CLAHULL'S   see KILLESHIN

CLARE   TL 770452   Suffolk

Motte with two baileys (Aca/43), the railway station occupying the inner bailey. There is a curved fragment of a flint rubble shell-wall on the *motte* top (with later buttresses of pointed section) with its original wall-walk and three rows of putlog holes within, on clay-laid foundations. Some fragments of a curtain wall survive on the bailey bank and a gold cross, with pottery, tiles and glass were found here (*Archaeological Journal* VI, p. 190). Excavations in the outer bailey (*Proceedings of the Suffolk Institute of Archaeology* XXVIII, pp. 136–52) showed that the slight inturn in the bank was probably an original entrance.

The castle is mentioned in a confirmation of a grant of 1090 (*Monasticon* VI, pp. 1659–61; *B.M. Cott. M.S.* App. xxi f.63 v.) (*Proceedings of the Suffolk Institute of Archaeology* I, pp. 61–6).*   (Fig. 18)

CLAVERING   see page 354

CLEOBURY MORTIMER   SO 682760   Shropshire

The 'armchair' work on the hill-side above the river may be the castle destroyed in 1155 (*William of Newburgh* I, p. 105; *Torigny* pp. 184–5).

CLETWR   see HUMPHREY'S CASTLE

CLIFFORD   Herefordshire

A small *motte* and bailey at Old Castleton (SO 283457), cut across an oval hillock near the River Wye (Be4), may be the castle of William fitz Osbern (1067–71: 'Domesday Book' I, 183), rather than the complex site 1½ miles further west on the river cliff of the Wye (SO 243457) (Bf4) with its shell-wall on the *motte* studded with round towers. The foundations of a small rectangular keep are said to have been excavated in the centre of the mound (*Transactions of the Woolhope Field Club* (1956–8), p. 153).

CLIFTON UPON TEME   see HOM(M)E

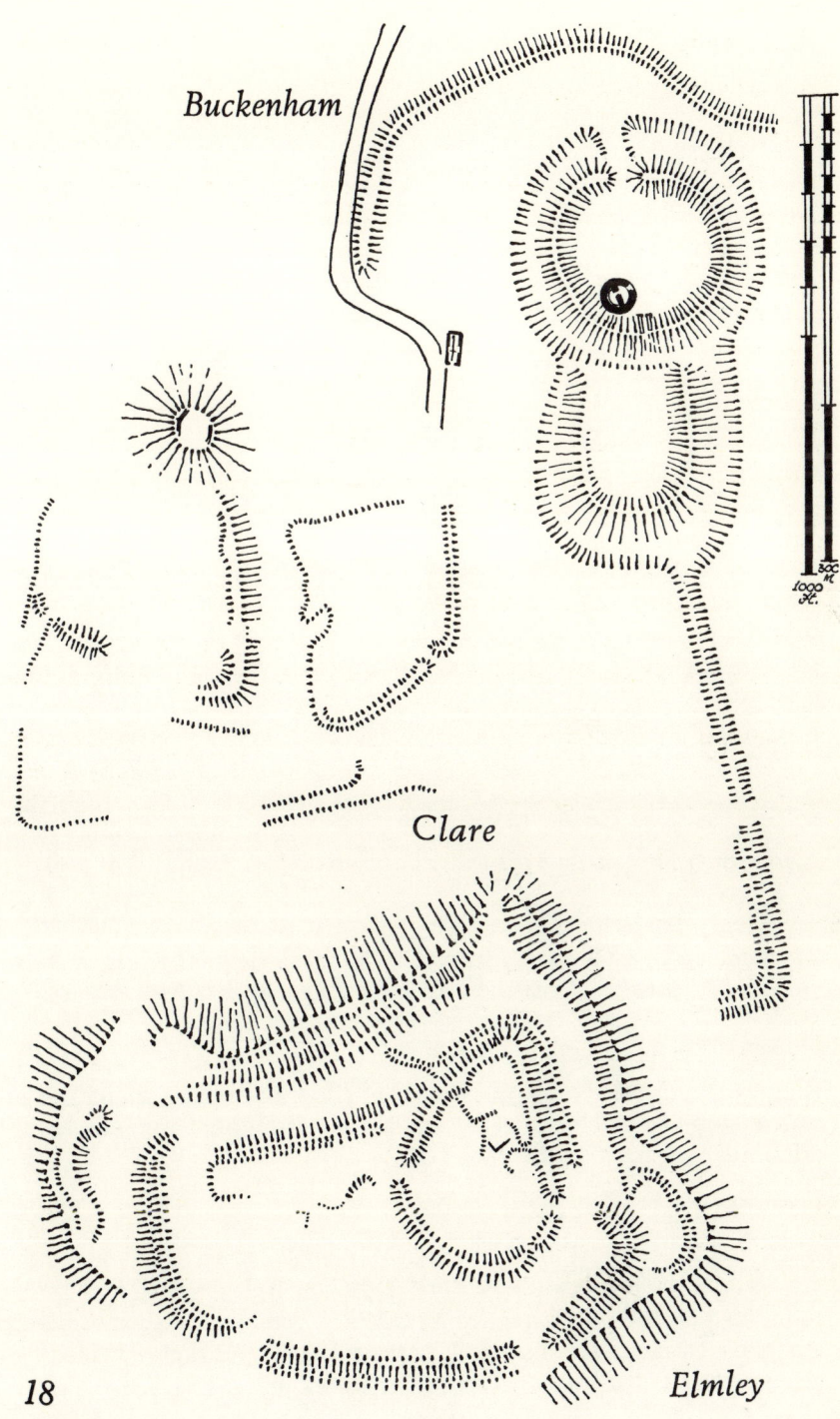

| CLITHEROE | SD 742417 | Lancashire |

A rock outcrop forms a natural *motte* with a triangular bailey to the south (Bc3). The keep is of limestone rubble with yellow ashlar dressings with wide pilaster buttresses enclosing the angles; later extensions have been made to those to east and south. The basement is lit by loops in round-headed recesses, one in each wall except the north-east which lay beneath the entrance stair. The entrance is a plain round-headed arch near the north end of the north-east wall; a smaller door opposite near the west end of the south-west wall gave access by a bridge to the rubble curtain wall, in plan like a sickle with its point near the west angle of the keep.

The first floor rested on an offset, with square-headed loops in round-headed recesses in the north-west and south-east walls. The former is flanked by a round-headed doorway leading to a barrel-vaulted mural chamber in the west angle and a square-headed doorway to the spiral staircase in the north angle which rises to the plain upper floor, again set back.

It has been argued that the *castellatu Rogerii pictaviensis* of 'Domesday' cannot be Clitheroe, which must have been built by Roger de Lacy (1177–94); (*Transactions of the Historical Society of Lancashire and Cheshire* 91, pp. 159–63; 93, pp. 45–53 quoting *Monasticon* V, p. 533), but the bailey is mentioned in 1102 (Farrer, *Lancashire Pipe Rolls*, p. 385) and the castle 1123–4 (Farrer, *Early Yorkshire Charters* III, 1486) (G. T. Clark, *Medieval Military Architecture* I, pp. 397–402).* (Fig. 21)

| CLONARD | N 6544 | Meath |

Motte (Bd3) built about 1182 (Giraldus Cambrensis, *Opera* V, p. 356).

| CLONES | H 4926 | Monaghan |

Motte and bailey built in 1211–12 and destroyed the following year (*Annals of Loch Cé*, *Annals of Ulster*; *Annals of the Four Masters*; *Irish Pipe Roll*).

| CLONMACNOISE | N 0130 | Offaly |

Ring-work and bailey (Cd2) beside River Shannon west of church, with square keep and gatehouse of uncertain date; castle built 1213 (*Calendar of Documents* I, 107; *Annals of Loch Cé*).

| CLOUGH | J 4140 | Down |

Motte and bailey (Ba3), the latter relatively small and ploughed out, with a V-shaped ditch to the *motte*. The *motte*-top had close-set post-holes round its perimeter with lines of replacement palisading here and there; a possible entrance was disturbed, but a posthole for a timber brace to a gatepost was found, and the palisading turned inward against the later

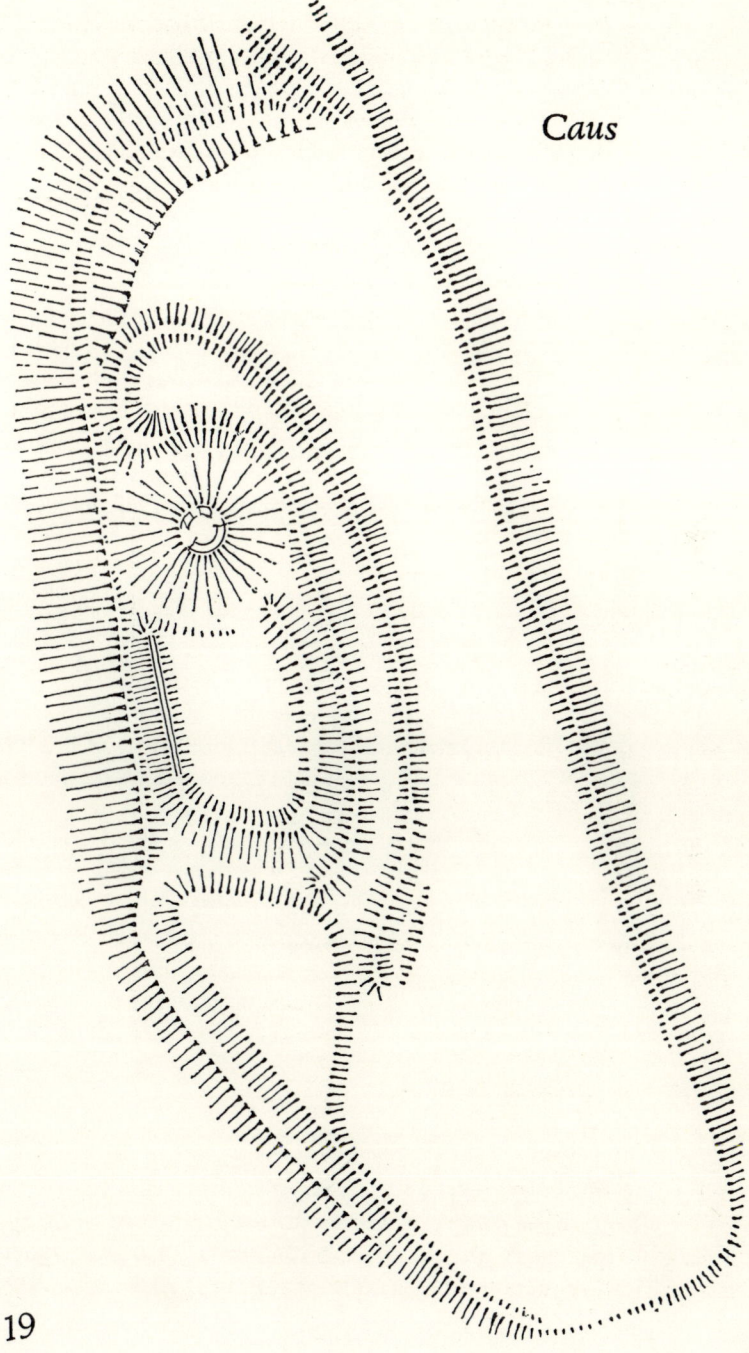

Caus

19

stone tower, perhaps indicating a timber predecessor. Just within the palisade were a series of pits, two of which had set-back postholes (and one rubble stone cheeks for an arrow-loop). The centre of the *motte*-top was depressed and the rubbish included a fragment of dressed sandstone, a quern-stone, wooden bowl, iron door pivot, gouge-bit, axe (?), socketed arrow-head and buckle, barrel padlock and a penny and halfpenny of 1199–1216, with ox-, pig-, sheep-, and fish-bones (*Ulster Journal of Archaeology* XVII, pp. 103–68).

CLOGHOUGHTER   H 3405   Cavan

Round keep of coursed rubble with trace of cross-wall on island in Lough Oughter. The south part is destroyed but the beam-holes of three floors remain, each lit by two loops in round-headed embrasures. The round-headed entrance was protected by a wooden brattice reached by a gap in the parapet between narrow crenels, and flanked by a round-backed fireplace with vent. (*Journal of the Royal Society of Antiquaries of Ireland* XXI, pp. 294–7; *Ulster Journal of Archaeology*, 3rd series x, pp. 83–6).*

CLUN   SO 298809   Shropshire

The two baileys are joined to the *motte* by narrow causeways (IIBb, d4), sited in the bend of the river, with a strong counterscarp bank cutting off the other two sides of a square enclosure. There are fragments of a curtain wall round the *motte*-top, with an entrance flanked by solid semicircular towers with sloping plinths. Projecting down the north slope of the *motte* is a rectangular keep of coursed slaty rubble with buttresses clasping the angles (the south wall has been destroyed), and rising from a sloping plinth on the north side, which has the remains of a window to each of three floors (the upper ones of two lights). The sub-basement has a loop in the east and west walls, the basement and *motte*-level floors two each, and the floor above two much wider embrasures in the east wall only.

Mentioned in the *Pipe Rolls* for 1160–4 and 1215, and in charters of 1140–50 and 1157 (Round, *Calendar of Documents preserved in France*... nos. 1127, 1145). (Figs. 20, 21)

CLUNARET   see CLONARD

CLUNGUNFORD   SO 396788   Shropshire

Mound (B) north-east of the church. Excavations revealed layers of wood ash and vivianite, with pottery (some pronounced Norman, with glaze) and fragments of a stone mortar (Hartshorne, *Salopia Antiqua*, pp. 102–6; *Archaeologia Cambrensis* 4th series V, p. 123; *J.B.A.A.* XIX, p. 317).*

CNUIC RAFFONN   see KNOCKGRAFFON

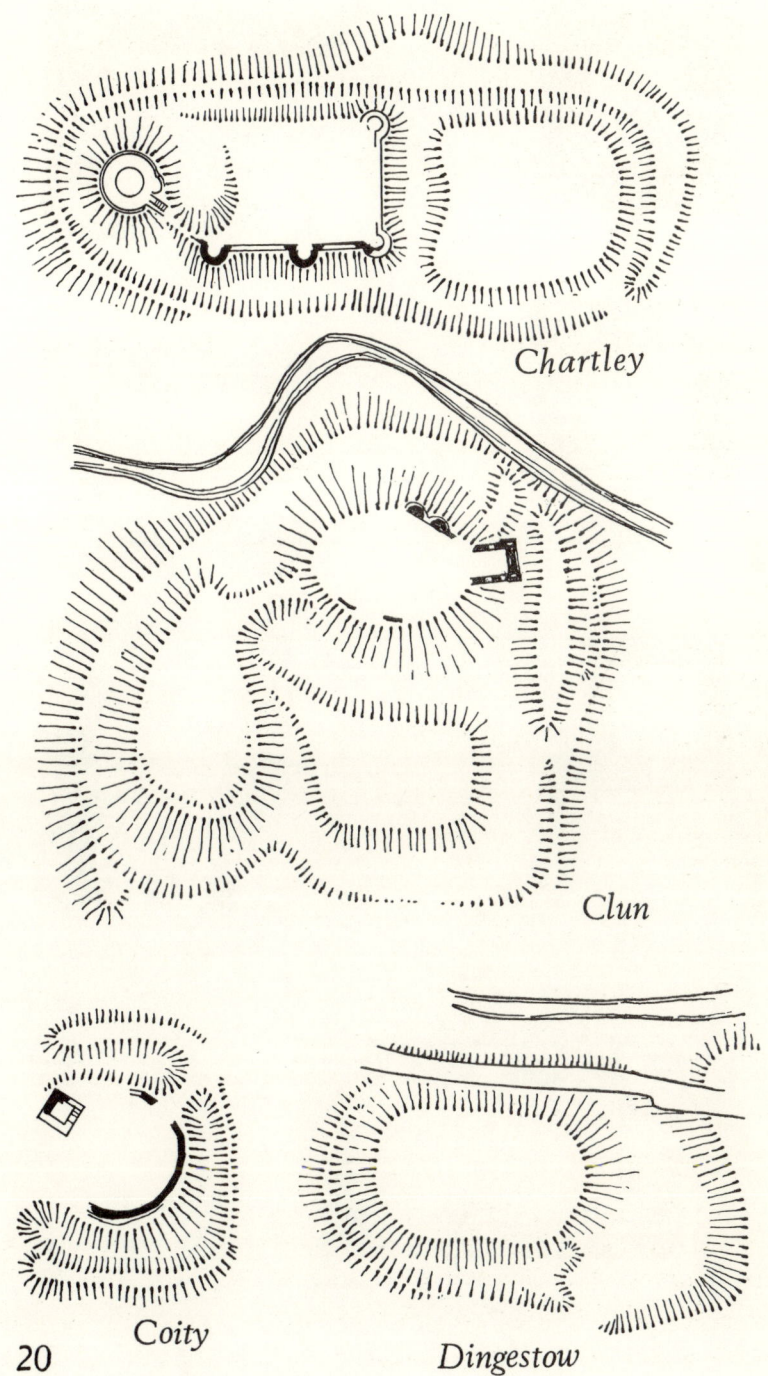

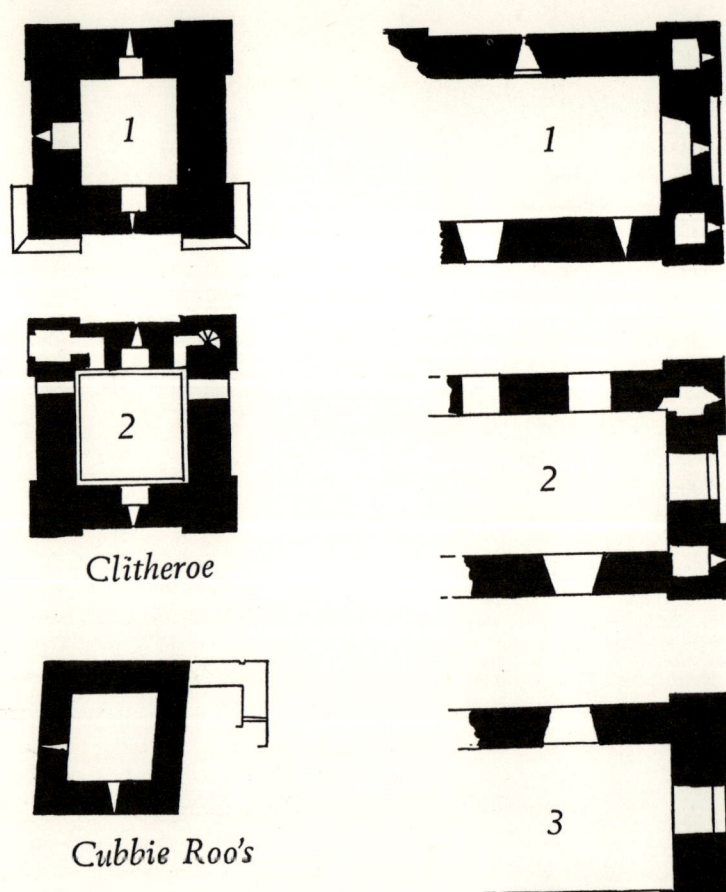

Clitheroe

Cubbie Roo's

Clun

Craigie

21

GAZETTEER

COED Y CWM (ST NICHOLAS) ST 083736   Glamorgan

Excavation of the entrance to this ring-work (C) produced pottery of the first half of the twelfth century sealed between two road surfaces (*Morgannwg* VIII, pp. 69–70; IX, p. 95).

COITY   SS 923816   Glamorgan

Ring-work (C) with strong counterscarp bank. The western outer enclosure is a late addition with slight ditches, and the original entrance was across the ditch from the east. The ring was surrounded by a curtain wall of coursed rubble in short straight lengths with alternating ashlar quoins; the north-western half of the circumference has been destroyed or altered, and the remainder raised (note narrow merlons embedded in the walling). The rectangular keep has been much altered.

The castle is mentioned in 1207. (G. T. Clark, *Cartae et alia munimenta quae ad dominium de Glamorgan pertinent* VI, 2306).

(Plate XII; Fig. 20)

COLCHESTER   TL 998252   Essex

Huge rectangular keep built around the vaulted base of a Roman temple, with a flat internal offset (wider to the south) overriding the robbed facing. The top course of the sloping plinth is of oolite with limestone above, then alternating courses of re-used septaria and tiles; Caen stone is used for the interior dressings. Besides intermediate pilasters, there are large clasping buttresses at the angles; those to the south are of different plan; that facing east is replaced by the apse of the chapel and that opposite, facing west, is thickened to balance the thrust and also take the spiral stair. (The turret over the stairs is eighteenth century.) The buttress at the west end of the south wall is only half the usual width above the plinth, to provide a landing for the staircase to the entrance door. There is the foundation of a simple rectangular forebuilding butted against the plinth; in turn surrounded with a loopholed mantlet wall entered between two solid D-shaped bastions, in which skeletons and medieval glass were found (*Antiquaries' Journal* XXX, p. 70). The south doorway appears to be an early insertion, of four round-headed orders (double billets outermost, rolls within) springing from chamfered imposts on four Corinthian capitals – the jambshafts are lost, one replaced by a stack of tiles. A small round-headed doorway remains in the east wall.

Built up narrow battlements can be traced in the walls, above which level stone quoins give way to tiles and the round heads of the loops are better finished. Each part of the interior of the keep is lit by loops with stone dressings, the rear arches being turned in tile. There are more loops at the upper level, with two round-headed and backed fireplaces with tile dressings, with short branching flues to the wall face.

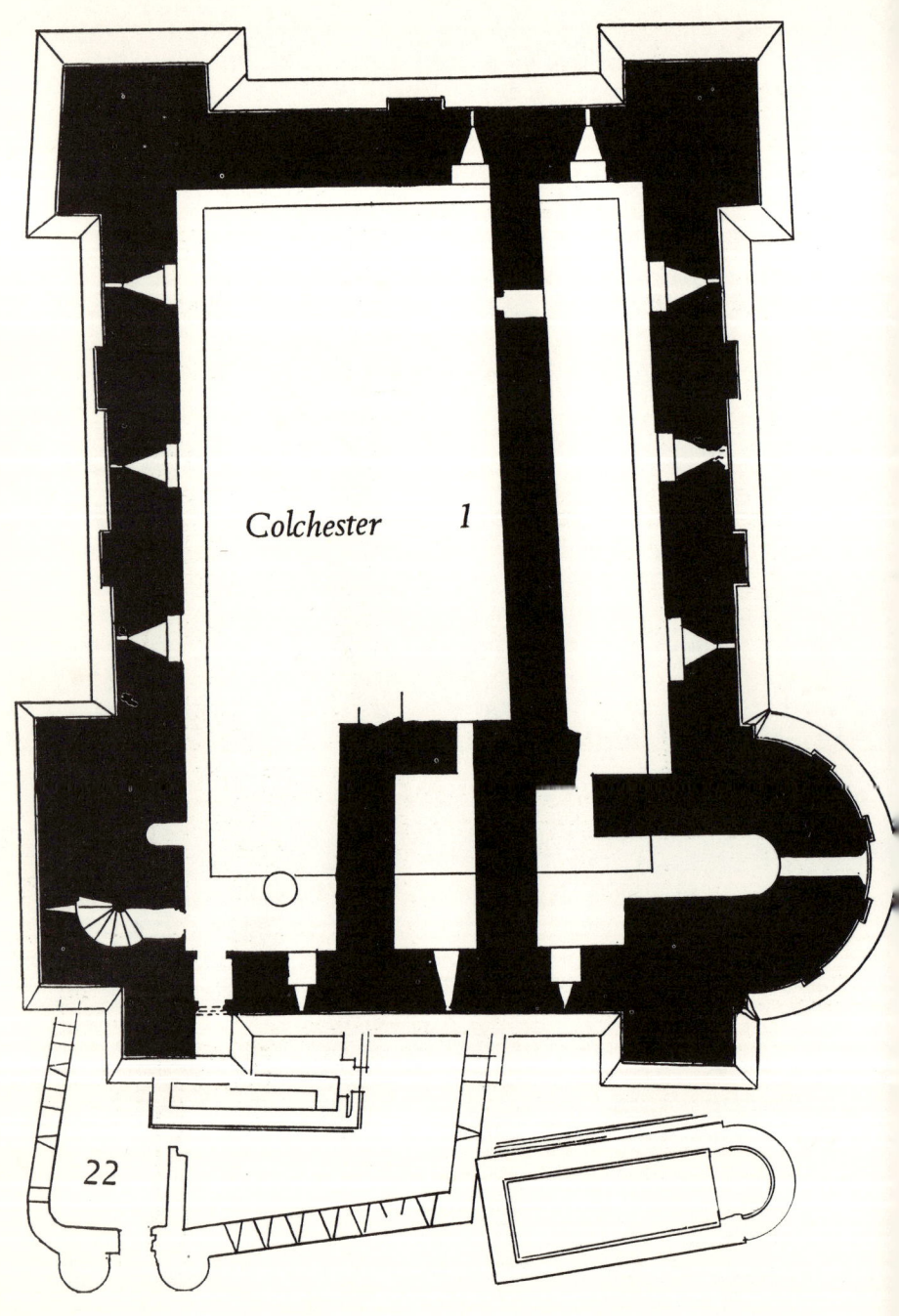

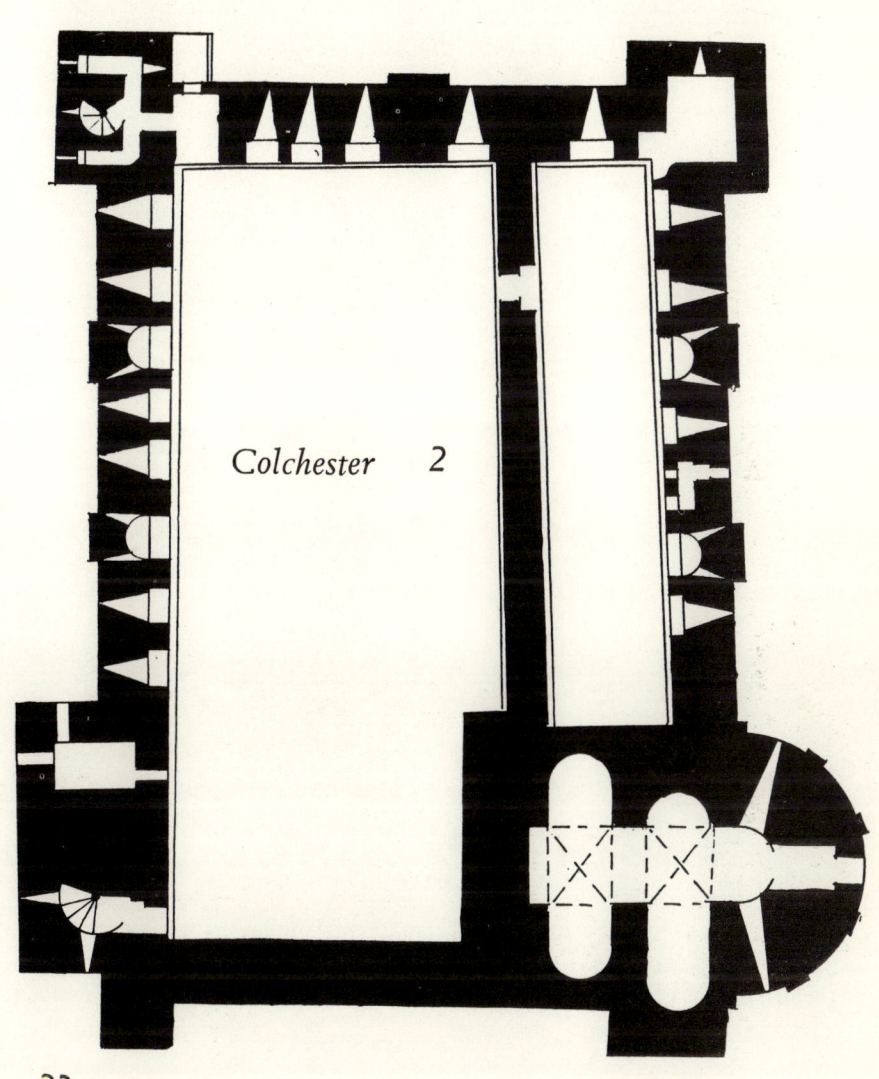
23

The interior of the keep is divided off into three southern compartments by thick walls to leave a square interior subdivided by a north–south cross-wall of coursed tiles and septaria as high as the first floor beam-holes, above which the wall is of herringbone-coursed tiles; there are faint traces of another division further west. The chapel basement has a barrel vault, the sub-chapel above has groined vaulting to double cross-apses and the chapel above had internal pilasters matching the external ones and an apsidal transept in the buttress. The corner turrets are hollowed out at first floor level, that to the north-west holding latrines and being cut back to provide a landing in front of a blocked round-headed entrance doorway. Before the partial demolition of 1683 the turrets rose above the main walls (*The History of the King's Works* II, p. 616, Fig. 51).

The temple precinct walls were robbed of their facing and buried in a bank based on a layer of level chalk over the Roman walling, the sand and gravel above being derived from the ditch. Under the turfline covering the bank was found a silver penny (Henry I, type X) (*Antiquaries' Journal* XLII, pp. 57–67). The foundations of an apsidal chapel have been excavated south of the keep chapel (on a different axis) and also part of a rectangular hall further south.

The burning of the town by the Danes in 1071 (*Oath Book* quoted by D. W. Clark, p. 12, see below) may have led to the building of the castle: certainly the charter of 1101 (*Cartularium Monasterii S. Johannis de Colecestria* I, 27; *B. M. Harleian M.S.* 312, f. 92) implies that it was built in the Conqueror's reign. A new bailey was made round the castle in 1173–4 and repairs to the walls made in 1182–3 and the castle strengthened in 1214–15 before its capture by the French (*Pipe Rolls: Rot. Litt. Claus.* I, 179 ff. (R.C.H.M. *Essex* III, pp. 50–4; D. W. Clark, *Colchester Castle* (1948); M. R. Hull, *Roman Colchester* (1958), pp. 160–91).*

(Plate IX; Figs. 22, 23)

COLERAINE   C 8532   Londonderry

A castle was built of stone from demolished buildings in 1213 and destroyed in 1221 (*Annals of Ulster, Annals of the Four Masters*). Geoffrey de Marisco was given twenty marks to fortify his house at *Katherain* in 1200 (*Rot. de Liberate*).

COLLACHT   see TULLOW

COLWYN   SO 108540   Radnorshire

Ring-work (now occupied by farm) with strong counterscarp bank within rectangular enclosure (Cd1). Mentioned in 1144, 1196 and 1215. (*Brut y Tywysogion*) (R.C.A.M. *Radnorshire*, pp. 108–9).*

GAZETTEER

COMBE   ST 837777   Wiltshire

Large pointed oval earthwork on ridge above By brook north of village, with counterscarp bank on east side and internal banks subdividing it into four successive enclosures, the southernmost being triangular with rounded corners. Scrope (*A History of Castle Combe*, pp. 6–10) states that traces of drystone walling were found during trenching of the bank, and that the keep had walls 10 ft thick, the lower storey of the two surviving measuring 16 ft by 10 ft. Carved stonework 'of a very rude style of Norman architecture' was found, with Saxon coins, arrow-heads, buckles and spurs. The engraving accompanying the description shows traces of a circular inner enclosure with the keep astride its south-east side.

CONISBROUGH   SK 517989   Yorkshire

Scarped natural hill north-east of church, with strong counterscarp banks except to west, where there is a small curved oblong bailey (IBd4). The hill has a curtain wall of coursed rubble built in straight lengths with ashlar quoins and a spreading plinth. The north side has a re-entrant to abut against the keep, with flanking latrines below stairs to the wall-walk. The other sides have solid semicircular towers carried above the parapet, with the foundations of a rectangular gatehouse projecting inward from the south side.

The cylindrical keep is of limestone ashlar, with a spreading plinth between chamfered string-courses carried round the six semi-hexagonal buttresses. The chamfer is repeated eight times as offsets on the buttresses. Internally the basement has a domed vault with a central hole above the well-shaft, which is ashlar-lined. The entrance above is square-headed, with a joggled lintel and segmental relieving arch, defended by bar-holes and traces of drawbridge pivots. The vaulted passage ends in a curve, unlike others which end tangentially to the curve of the interior; a curving stair rises in the thickness of the wall, with square ribs to the vault, lit by two loops between buttresses, to a lobby giving on to the second floor, supported on corbels and a setback of the wall face. A window of two square-headed lights under a joggled lintel with semicircular relieving arch has a horizontal bulge in the mullion for the shutter-bar, and the window-seats are reached by concentric segmental steps into the round-headed embrasure. The north-west buttress backs a fireplace with joggled lintel and sloping hood supported on triple columns with foliated capitals; the square chimney shaft rises vertically. A latrine passage is angled into the north-east buttress.

Both this floor and that above have small recessed sinks; the upper floor is reached by another curving wall-stair starting diametrically opposite that from the entrance level. The hood and lintel of the upper

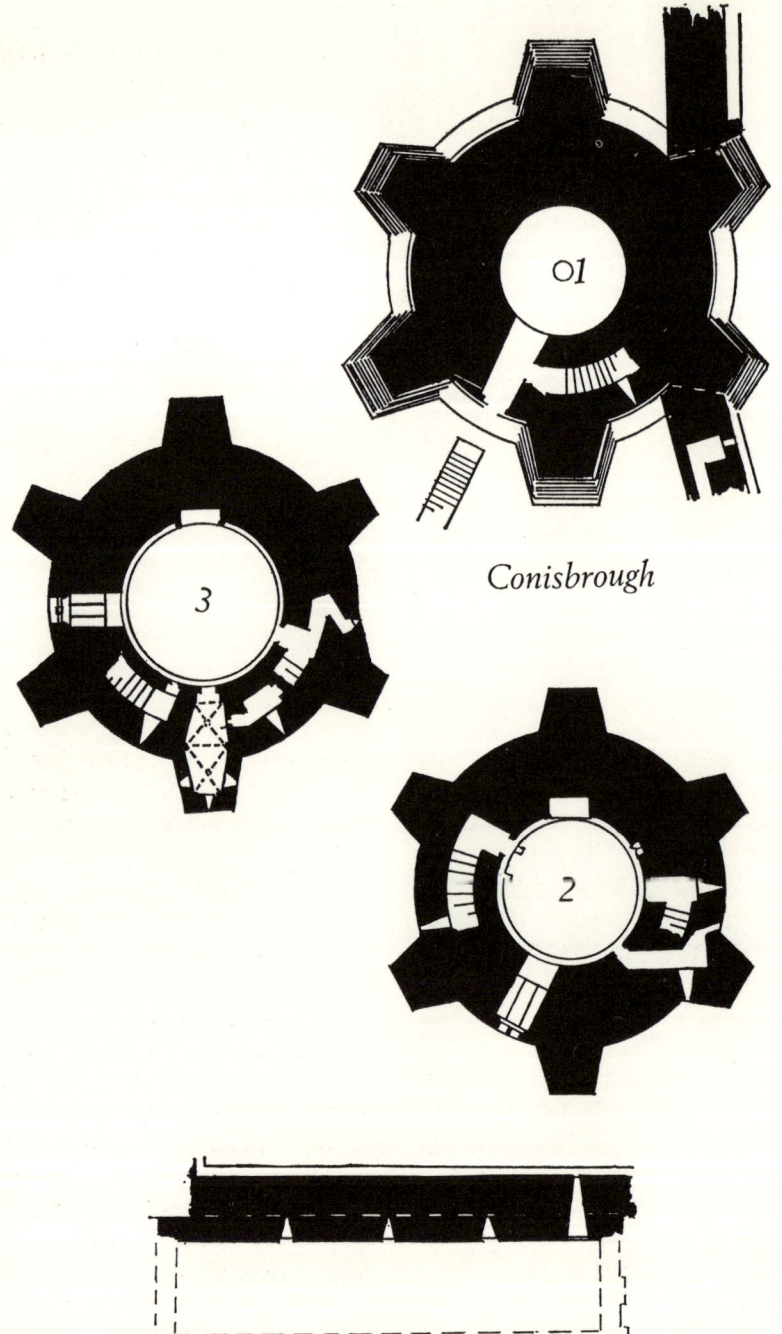

24   Conisbrough / Corfe

fireplace do not die back into the wall curve, and the shaft links with the lower one, but the other details are similar. There is another two-light window in the next clockwise bay between buttresses to that of the floor below. This floor is also supported on another wall offset. The south-east buttress is occupied by a long hexagonal chapel, entered through a square-headed doorway and vaulted in the bays. The cross-ribs rise from foliated capitals and nookshafts in the angles of the chapel, with bosses of a cross moline (west) and flowers (east), the transverse rib being decorated with chevrons and rising from triple moulded capitals with square abaci. The outer loop has a splayed recess with roll-moulded rear arch, within an arch with carved capitals and nookshafts under a chevron-decorated head. There are round quatrefoil windows with pellet-mouldings externally, a trefoil-headed sink under each; a small cell opens off the north side, beyond which the stair to the battlements rises with a latrine off its lobby, carried on an arch at the inner angle of the north buttress. The buttresses were carried above the main wall and hollowed out; the two to the west had curving stairs, that to the south an oven and its neighbour pierced with small holes, perhaps for pigeon roosts. The other two were lined as cisterns. The conical roof was carried on corbels, and the roof-space entered by a doorway in the parados wall.

The constable of the castle witnessed a document of 1174-8 (*Monasticon* III, p. 618) and the chapel is mentioned in 1180-9 (*Early Yorkshire Charters* VIII, p. 114-6); the castle is reasonably attributed to Hamelin Plantagenet, who held the castle from 1163-1202; a smaller version of the keep exists at Mortemer (Seine-Maritime) (*Yorkshire Archaeological Journal* 32, pp. 146-59) (*Yorkshire Archaeological Journal* 8, pp. 124-57, reprinted in G. T. Clark, *Medieval Military Architecture*, I pp. 431-53).*

(Plate X; Figs. 24, 27)

CORFE SY 958823 Dorset

Steep natural hill, the ear-shaped summit plateau surrounded with a plain curtain wall of coursed rubble. The lower slopes form a boomerang-shaped area, the central section of which was enclosed with a quadrilateral rubble wall and the western section with ashlar walling, including an octagonal tower at the apex and a semicircular tower on each flanking wall.

An early hall was examined in the western section in 1950-2; its south wall is of herringbone work with ashlar dressings, with three round-headed window embrasures; the slits themselves have square heads and are blocked by the later curtain built outside. The excavated west wall had three pilaster buttresses rising from a 10-in. offset at ground level. This overlies a retaining wall which may be associated with large post-holes further east and belong to an earlier timber building (*Medieval Archaeology* IV, pp. 29-55).

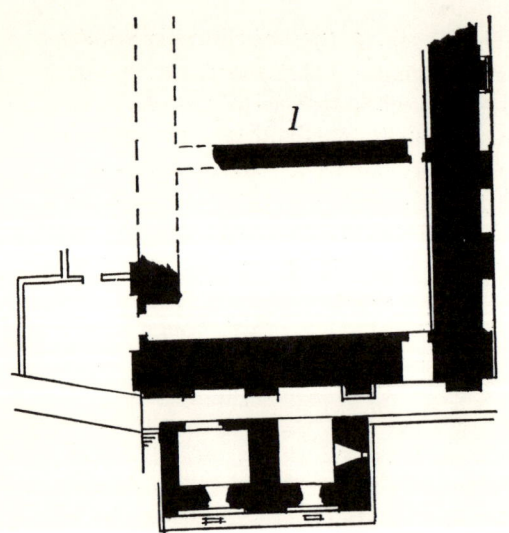
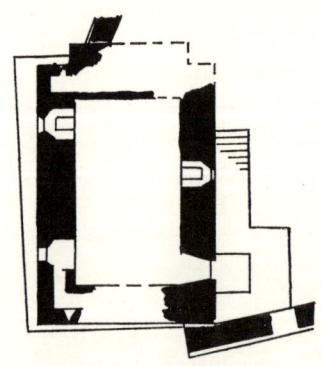
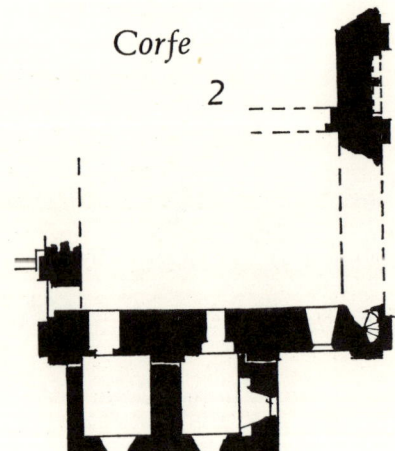
Corfe

Dolwyddelan

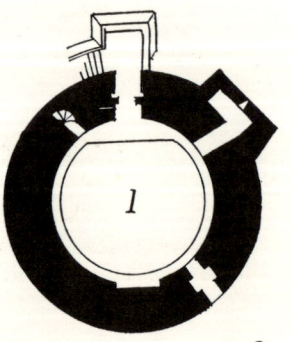
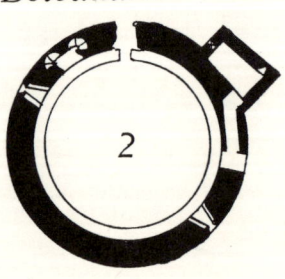
Dolbadarn

25

158

A rectangular keep was built in ashlar against the straight curtain of the plateau. The southern half remains standing above its foundations, indicating a building divided by four pilaster buttresses from east to west and at least five from north to south, with a blind arcade of round-headed arches between them below the parapet. Fragments of at least one east–west cross-wall remain, with one jamb of a round-headed arch of two orders, the higher with roll mouldings and an engaged shaft with volutes and diapered capital. The ground floor rested on beams above a basement, and the original entrance is uncertain; it may have been through the first floor round-headed archway (with a higher rear arch) at the west end of the south wall. When the latrine block was added, the adjoining window (engaged shafts with Corinthian capitals, billet and roll-moulding) was converted into a doorway to it, and a new entrance contrived by a staircase rising against the west wall to a pointed doorway offset under a semi-circular head. The keep was roofed in two north–south gables below the parapet, the hall having garrets over and the parapet being reached therefrom by a spiral stair in the south-east angle.

An exchange of land to build the castle at Wareham is mentioned in 'Domesday Book' (I f.78b); a later reference to the same exchange (*Testa de Nevill*, p. 164) replaces *Warham* by *de Corf*. The manor of Kingston included land near each of the two castles. The castle was garrisoned by Baldwin de Redvers in 1139 (*Gesta Stephani*, p. 56).

Little expenditure on Corfe is recorded in Henry II's reign, and less than £25 (on repairs) in Richard I's, but over £1,400 was spent in John's reign, particularly on digging the ditch separating the outer bailey from the rest of the castle and on the *domus regis* (*Pipe Rolls; Rot. Litt. Claus.* I).

This building was a hall, with a range of two-light windows in the north and south walls separated by pilaster buttresses, above a vaulted basement. There was a forebuilding on the south side leading to twin doorways into the hall and lower part of the western end; the upper part was reached by a wall-stair in the forebuilding. (R.C.H.M. *Dorset* II, pp. 57–78).*

(Plate XI; Figs. 24, 25, 27)

CORFE SIEGE-WORK   Dorset

Ring-work (Cb3) 400 yards south-west of the castle (SY 953820) may date from the siege of 1139 (*Gesta Stephani*, p. 56).

CORK

Work on the wall of Cork mentioned 1211–12 (*Irish Pipe Roll*).

CORNET   Guernsey

On the triangular rocky promontory on east side of island. Fragments of a rubble inner curtain wall with tapering buttresses remain near the north and south angles of the citadel and by the barracks beyond to the north-east. Both the first and last of these fragments include the lower parts of doorways. Before the explosion of 1672 there was a square tower at the south angle and a round keep in a ditch in the centre of the enclosure.

Brattices were shipped to Guernsey in 1206 (*Pipe Roll*) and may indicate the foundation date (B. H. St. J. O'Neil, *Official Guide; Quarterly Review of the Guernsey Society* V, 2; VI, 3).

CORNWALL   see page 354

| COTHERSTONE | NZ 015200 | Yorkshire |

Site of fitz Hervey's castle of 1200–1 (*Rot. Litt. Claus.* p. 89). V.C.H. *North Riding of Yorkshire* (I, p. 119) mentions a wall and re-used material in a nearby building, including a round-headed two-light window.

| COTTINGHAM | TA 040330 | Yorkshire |

Square mound. (IIB). William de Stuteville had licence to fortify his *domus de Totingeham* in 1201 (*Rot. Litt. Claus.* p. 89), but the castle is mentioned earlier (*Historians of the Church of York* I, 302).

| COVENTRY | | Warwickshire |

The priory was converted into a castle in 1143 with pits and trenches (*Annales Monastici* II, p. 230) by Robert Marmion, and the Earl of Chester had a castle here at the same time (*Coventry City Charters*, p. 7).

| *CRAIGIE* | NS 409318 | Ayrshire |

Overgrown foundations on mound, including ashlar hall with traces of a spiral stair in the south-east angle. There are three square-headed loops in the upper part of the north and south walls with stepped sills and round-headed rear arches having jamb shafts with moulded bases and caps, and round arched openings at the ground floor below. There are narrow crenels in the wall face (McGibbon and Ross, *The Castellated and Domestic Architecture of Scotland* III, pp. 296–301).*   (Fig. 21)

| CRAIL | NO 603074 | Fife |

Site beside Forth estuary. The castle chapel was granted by Malcolm IV (1153–65) (*Registrum Magni Regum Scotorum 1424–1513*, p. 136, cited by Barrow, *Regesta Regum Scottorum* I, p. 282).

| *CREWKERNE* | ST 421107 | Somerset |

The surface of Castle Hill has produced twelfth-century pottery now in the Taunton Museum; (*Proceedings of the Somerset Archaeological and Natural History Society* XCVIII, p. 9).

GAZETTEER

CRICKLADE   SU 098938   Wiltshire

The square town bank has been shown to have a stone revetment (*Wiltshire Archaeological Magazine* 55, p. 181; 56, p. 162; 58, p. 7).

The castle built in 1144 by William of Dover with water and marsh on every side (*Gesta Stephani*, p. 113) may have been at Castle Eaton, where there are some altered earthworks in Long Croft near Abingdon Court (SU 161965).

CROGEN   SJ 006370   Merioneth

Motte (B) behind the house on rock heightened in earth in loop of River Dee. Mentioned in 1202 (*Brut y Tywysogion*).

CROMETH

The castle of 1215 (*Rot. de Oblatis et Finibus*, p. 556; *Calendar of Documents* I, 91) may have been at Croom, Limerick (*English Historical Review* XXII, p. 458).

CRONDALL   see POWDERHAM

CRONK Y MUR   SC 204696   Isle of Man

Excavation in 1912 of a 30-ft high mound (partly natural) revealed a pit 18 ft by 10 ft revetted with upright stones, and drystone walling. One of the forts built by Magnus Barefoot after 1098? (p. 37) (*Proceedings of the Isle of Man Nat. Hist. and Archaeological Society* new series V, p. 398).

CRUG ERYR   SO 158593   Radnorshire

Small *motte* and bailey (Bb2) on mountainside with extensive view. The entrance causeway and *motte* ditch were excavated in 1936–7 (*Reports of the Congress of Archaeological Societies*). The castle was the *castrum Crukeri* of 1188 (Giraldus Cambrensis, *Opera* VI, p. 16).

CRUTA   see page 354

CUBBIE ROO'S, WYRE   HY 442264   Orkney

Basement of square tower within an oval ring-work with revetted banks and a medial ditch. The tower is not quite right-angled, with a narrow loop in the west and south walls and a water tank cut into the rock floor. A square annex was added at the north end of the east wall, with a latrine shoot from an upper floor (forebuilding ?). The masonry resembles that of the adjoining Romanesque two-celled chapel, and is considered to be the strong castle of Kolbein Hruga, mentioned in the Orkneyinga Saga 1153–8 (*Fl*: ii, 472) (R.C.A.M. *Orkney and Shetland* II, pp. 237–8).*   (Fig. 21)

CUCKNEY   SK 566713   Nottinghamshire

Motte west of mid to late twelfth century church. The north part of the church was built over mass burial trenches (*Transactions of the Thoroton Society* LV, pp. 26–9). The castle was built by Thomas of Cuckney during the 'old war' (1138–54 ?) (*Monasticon* VI, p. 873).

CUILE RATHAIN   see COLERAINE

'CULCHET'

A charter of about 1141 is dated *apud Novum Castellum de Culchet* (Lawrie, *Ancient Scottish Charters* CXXXIX). It might refer to Kelso (where Castle Hill is a place-name) or to Culgaith (Cumberland) or Culcheth (Lancashire).

CULGAITH   see CULCHET

CYMARON   SO 152703   Radnorshire

Oval *motte* with rectangular bailey at junction of streams (IAd4). Castle repaired in 1144 (*Brut y Tywysogion*), 1179, 1182, and 1195 (*Pipe Rolls*).

CYMMER   SH 732195   Merioneth

Motte (B) of the castle, built and destroyed in 1116 (*Brut y Tywysogion*).

CYNFAL   SH 615016   Merioneth

Steep sided low *motte* (B) with rock-cut ditch and rim-bank – small plateau may mark bailey. Castle built and destroyed in 1147 (*Brut y Tywysogion*).

DAMSAY   HY 390140   Orkney

Castle visited by Swein Asleifson in 1136 (*Orkneyinga Saga* ch. 70).

DANBY   NZ 691082   Yorkshire

Farm occupies site of castle exchanged by Adam de Bruce in the reign of Henry II (Bodleian MS. Laud Misc. 722 printed in *Thoresby Society Miscellanea* IV, p. 182). A Norman column is recorded from the site (Atkinson, *Cleveland Ancient and Modern* I, 263).

DANY   see KNOCKANY

DDU   see LLANDEILO-TALYBONT

DEDDINGTON   SP 472318   Oxfordshire

Rectangular ring-work with strong bailey enclosure (II Cd3). Excavation in 1947–8 revealed a polygonal inner curtain wall of ironstone rubble with early twelfth-century pottery in the foundation trench. A hall was built against the curtain *c.* 1160 of rubble with diagonally tooled oolite ashlar quoins overlying traces of a timber building; a solar was later added, and a series of stratified floors were found in the kitchen beside the gatehouse. A mound east of the bailey contained the sloping plinth of a rectangular tower of fine ashlar (*Oxoniensia* XI/XII, pp. 167–8).

The castle was in royal hands in 1204–5 (*Rot. Litt. Claus.* p. 7, *Rot. Litt. Pat* I p. 50). (H. M. Colvin, *A History of Deddington*, 12).*

| DEGANNWY | SH 781794 | Caernarvonshire |

Site consisting of two conical hills above River Conway, joined by banks and ditches to form a double *motte* and bailey (IIC/Ac3). Most of the remaining masonry is probably of 1245–54, but some fragments of walling south-east of the square quarry on the western hill (and a revetment against the north side of the hill) are on different alignments, and may be earlier. Excavations produced weathered arch-moulded stones and a carved crowned head, probably of pre-1216 date (*Archaeological Journal* CXXIV, 190–201).

Occupied since the ninth century, the fortification of the site was begun by Robert of Rhuddlan in 1088 (*Ordericus Vitalis* VIII, 3) and the castle rebuilt in 1210-2 (*Brut y Tywysogion*) (R.C.A.M. *Caernarvonshire* I, pp. 152–4).*

| DENBIGH | SJ 052660 | Denbighshire |

The site known as The Mount within the town (*Y Cymmrodor* XXXVI, p. 66) may be that mentioned in 1195–6 (*Pipe Roll*).

DENE see LITTLEDEAN

| DERVER (LOUGHAN) | N 6680 | Meath |

Motte (B) mentioned in 1215 (*Calendar of Documents* I, 95; *English Historical Review* XXII, p. 242).

| DERRYPATRICK | N 8272 | Meath |

Site of castle abandoned in 1176 (*English Historical Review* XXII, p. 234).

DESBOROUGH see *WYCOMBE*

| DEUDRAIT | SH 586371 | Merioneth |

Rocky site mentioned *c.* 1190 by Giraldus Cambrensis (*Opera* VI, p. 123).

| DEVIZES | SU 003613 | Wiltshire |

A later house occupies the site, west of the town. It appears to have been an oval mound on a promontory with concentric semicircular enclosures to the east forming the bailey and town enclosure (IBa/23). On the mound was a large hall with two arcades of round columns $3\frac{1}{2}$ ft across with responds, making six bays on each side. The service rooms formed a block at the west end, and there were porches at the east end of the north wall and the west end of the south. The east end of the south wall projected as a thick walled tower with loops protected by an outer apron wall (E. H. Stone, *Devizes Castle*, plate facing p. 114; confirmed by a sketch plan of 1858 in the Devizes Museum). The keep shown there is pure conjecture, based on Rochester, although the curtain wall with buttressed angles may be genuine. (See also *Wiltshire Archaeological Magazine* LI, pp. 496–9).

The keep was destroyed by fire in 1113 (*Annales Monastici* II, p. 44) but its wonderful architecture and strength were mentioned in its seizure from Roger of Salisbury in 1139 (*Gesta Stephani*, pp. 49, 52; William of Malmesbury, *Historia Novella*, pp. 24, 43–4). After Robert fitz Herbert's capture of the castle with leather scaling ladders in the following year, some of the defenders held out for a time in a very high tower (*Gesta Stephani*, pp. 69–70). The castle passed to the Crown in 1157 and £100 was spent in John's reign (*Pipe Rolls*). (Fig. 26)

DEVON

The licence of 1200 allowing William Briwerre to build castles at Bridgwater Ashley or Stockbridge (q.v.) added a third 'where he would in Devon' (*Rot. Litt. Claus.* p. 70). See *HARTLAND* (page 367).

DINAS EMRYS SH 606492 Caernarvonshire

Among the earthworks of this Romano-British and Dark Age fortress was found clay-laid rubble walling 3 ft 9 in. thick enclosing a space 32 ft by 23 ft full of charcoal, as if a timber superstructure had been burnt down. The most reasonable date seems to be the twelfth century (*Archaeologia Cambrensis* (1930), pp. 342–53; *Bulletin of the Board of Celtic Studies* 17, pp. 55–7).

DINAS POWIS Glamorgan

Excavation of the northern end of an oval hill-top (ST 148722) showed that it had been extensively occupied in the fifth and sixth centuries A.D. Later the area was fortified with a strong rubble bank with drystone revetments (producing fragments of a Norman cooking pot) with a rock-cut flat-bottomed ditch on the south side. The enclosure was approached by a winding path on to the steepest part of the hill, leading to a rock-cut passage defended by a gateway (sockets for posts found). The bank had a palisade on top, with traces of an inner row of posts in places.

Outside the ring-work to the south was a relatively slight crescentic bank, perhaps of earlier date, and then two further banks with revetments flanking a wide flat-bottomed medial ditch. At the east end of the outer bank were traces of an outer ditch, and a further bank and ditch at right angles along the edge of the slope as if to delimit a bailey.

The lower (south) end of the hilltop was cut off by a right-angled bank

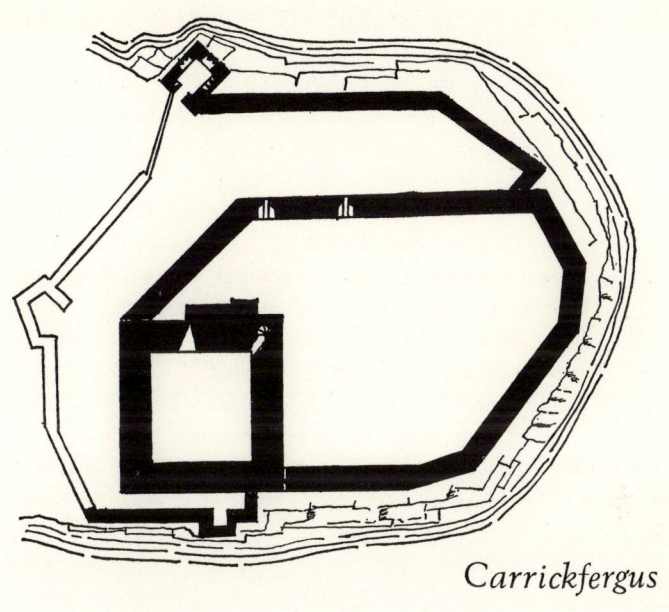

Carrickfergus

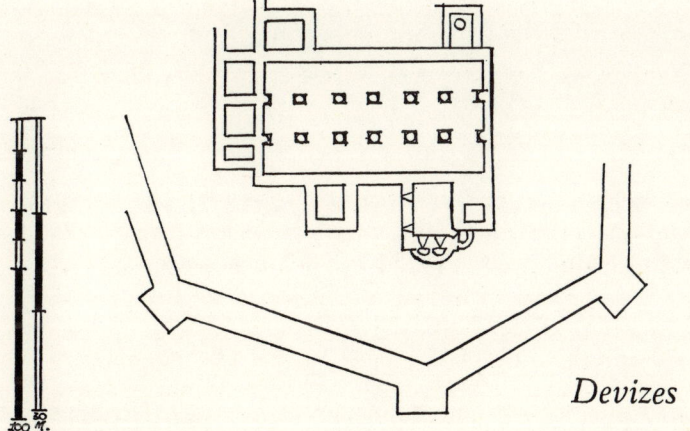

Devizes

26

and ditch with an earlier bank and ditch beyond it, perhaps a siege-work of the masonry castle further south-east (ST 152716). The rubble stump of a square tower inside the enclosure appears to be the earliest part of this, mentioned in a document of 1193–1218 quoted in *Transactions of the Cardiff Naturalists' Society* 42, p. 71; G. T. Clark *Cartae et alia munimenta quae ad Glamorganici pertinent* I, 224 (L. Alcock, *Dinas Powys*, Cardiff 1964).*

DINEFWR   SN 611217   Carmarthenshire

Pentagonal enclosure on protruding bluff in Dynevor Park, with rock-cut ditch to north, where the hall block and curtain were rebuilt in the fifteenth century. The earlier curtain has a plain round tower at the north-west angle, a rectangular latrine turret and angle tower to the south-west. Foundations of an oblique entrance passage to an archway in the south-east curtain survive, with a round keep inside the east curtain. This has a half-round string course above a battered base, through which an entrance has been cut. The window loops have wide pointed embrasures, and the first floor is carried on a setback of the wall. There is a relatively modern 'folly' on top.

The castle is mentioned in 1163–1213 (*Brut y Tywysogion*), but was dismantled in 1220 (*Letters of Henry III*, I, 176) (R.C.A.M. *Carmarthen*, 107–8).*   (Fig. 32)

DINGESTOW   SO 455104   Monmouthshire

Motte and bailey (IIBb2) west of church beside River Trothy, being constructed in 1182 (Giraldus Cambrensis, *Opera* VI, pp. 51–3; *Gesta Henrici Secundi* I, p. 288).   (Fig. 20)

DINIERTH   SN 495624   Cardiganshire

Motte and bailey (IBb) at confluence of two rivers. The *motte*-top has traces of masonry. Destroyed in 1136, the castle was rebuilt in 1158 and 1203, and finally destroyed in 1208 (*Brut y Tywysogion*).

DINWEILER   see PENCADER

'DINYETHA'

Unidentified site, perhaps in Radnorshire, mentioned in about 1100 (*Monasticon* VI, p. 349).

DIXTON   SO 520135   Monmouthshire

Mound north-east of church; excavation produced metalwork (including a knife) and bone comb of eleventh/twelfth century date (*Bulletin of the Board of Celtic Studies* 13, pp. 251–2).

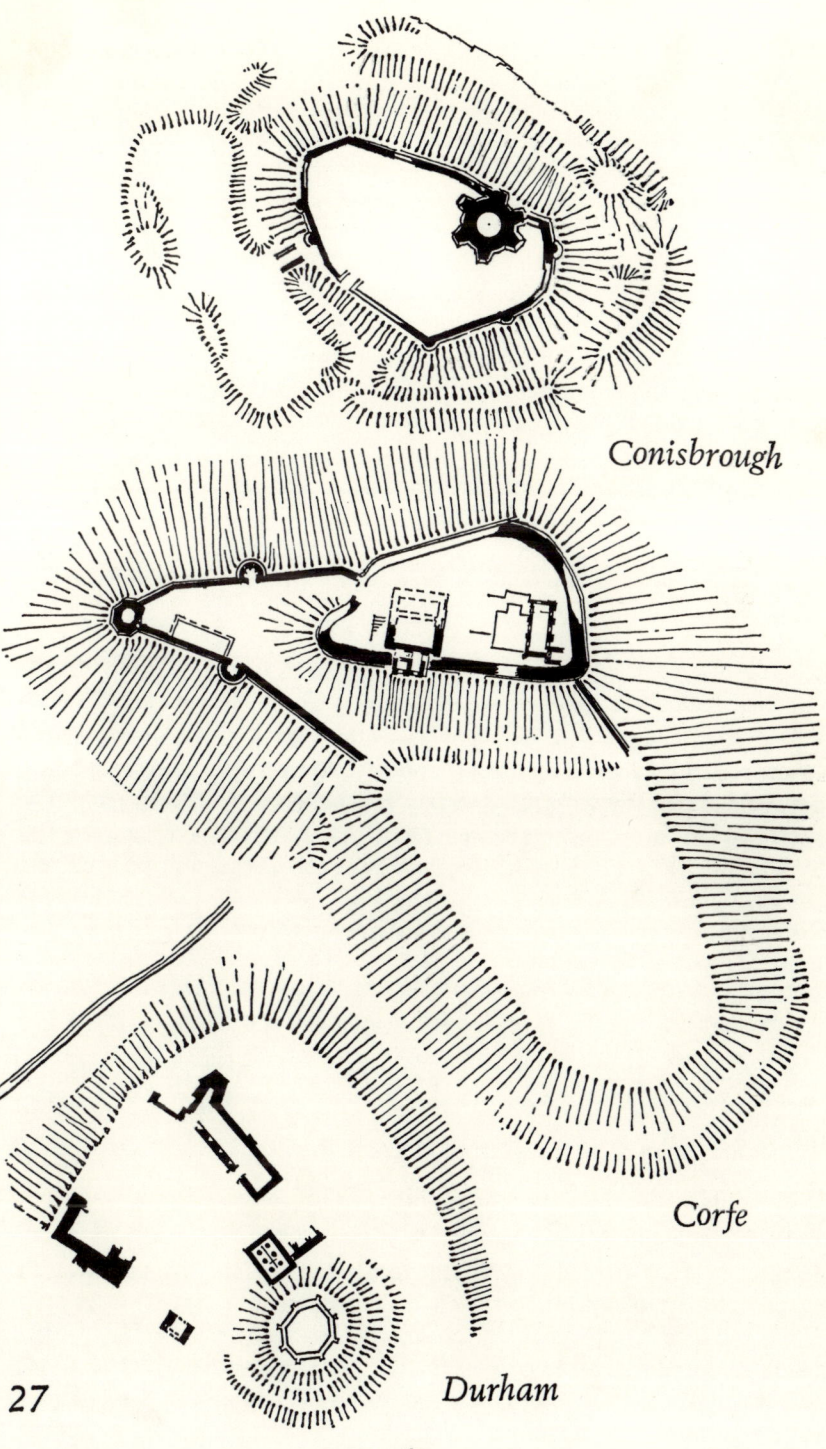
27   Conisbrough / Corfe / Durham

DOLBADARN   SH 586598   Caernarvonshire

Triangular platform overlooking Llyn Padarn/Peris isthmus. The round keep of local slate and grit rubble, has a sloping base. The basement had a small square tunnel for light and air, and no stair. A modern staircase curves round to a platform in front of the restored two-centred door-arch, defended by a portcullis and an inner door (drawbar slot). The floor was supported on a wall offset and parallel beams; the chimney of the damaged fireplace opposite the entrance leads to the outside high in the wall; a tall window-opening has recessed seats on either side. The upper floor (reached by a spiral stair which continues — across a small lobby — to the battlements) is similarly supported and has four window-openings with flanking seats and another damaged fireplace with vertical chimney. The roof appears to have been based on two parallel roof trusses and four pairs of corbels, with a string course and roof gutter. The upper floors each had access to a projecting rectangular latrine block.

Dismantled in 1284 (*P.R.O. Exch.* A/C 351/9); the reign of Llywelyn Fawr (1200–40) is the most likely time for its erection (R.C.A.M. *Caernarvonshire* II, pp. 165–8).*   (Fig. 25)

DOLWYDDELAN   SH 722523   Caernarvonshire

Rectangular keep (altered and partly rebuilt) with plain polygonal curtain wall of slightly later date. A slight projection beside the ruined entrance covers a latrine block. The keep is approached by a stair interrupted by a drawbridge pit; the entrance doorway has a simple chamfered arch. The basement has three rectangular loops for light, and must have been reached by a ladder. The windows of the main floor have seats and pointed rear arches, and the crease for a steep roof gable can be traced on the inside of the south-west wall; below this a wall passage leads to a latrine. The upper floor is an insertion.

Traditionally the birthplace of Llywelyn Fawr, 1173.

A mound nearby (SH 725522) has traces of a 25 ft square tower (R.C.A.M. *Caernarvonshire* I, pp. 81–3).*   (Plate XII; Fig. 25)

DONAGHMOYNE   H 8506   Monaghan

Motte and bailey (Bd4) built in 1193 (*Annals of Loch Cé*) (*Journal of the Royal Society of Antiquaries of Ireland* XXXVIII, pp. 263–5).*

DONNINGTON   SK 448276   Leicestershire

Ring-work (C) with strong counterscarp bank. The manor of Castle Donnington is mentioned as such in a document of 1102 (or 1155?): B.M. *Harl. M.S.* 568 cited by Nichols, *History of Leicester* III, p. 770. Nichols reproduces an engraving (plate CVIII opposite p. 781) of a long hall with pilaster buttresses and a round-headed opening in the end wall.

The castle was in royal hands in 1214, and was destroyed in 1215 (*Wendover* II, 165; Matthew Paris, *Hist. Ang.* II, 171; *Hist. Maj.* II, 639).

DOONMORE   D 1842   Antrim

Traces of timber revetments and the postholes of a 12 ft square tower were excavated on a rocky outcrop, with a twelfth/thirteenth century cooking-pot (*Ulster Journal of Archaeology* third series, I, pp. 122–35).

DORCHESTER   SY 690908   Dorset

Former *motte* and bailey (Bb3 ?) containing a hall with two rows of columns on Portisham stone bases with Norman arches destroyed in 1794 (*Proceedings of the Dorset Natural History and Archaeological Society* LXVI, p. 67). A castle may be implied by the reference to destroyed houses in 'Domesday Book': one certainly existed by 1175 (*Pipe Roll*).

DORLES   see THURLES

DOUNE OF INVERNOCHTY   see INVERNOCHTY

DOVENBY HALL   NY 096334   Cumberland

Norman window in vaulted tower within house (Pevsner, *Buildings of England* 33, p. 78).

DOVER   TR 326417   Kent

The main earthworks probably date from the Early Iron Age (*Antiquity* XXXIII, pp. 125–7) in which a Roman *pharos* and Saxon church were built before the Conquest. A bank and ditch excavated just south of the church (*Medieval Archaeology* VIII, p. 254) may have been part of the *castrum* that Harold promised to build 1064–6 or the additions ordered by William in 1066 (*William of Poitiers*, pp. 104, 212). Between 1166 and 1180 over £750 was spent on the castle, the £260 of the last year at least being on the curtain wall alone (*Pipe Rolls*). This might be the Avranches tower (semi-octagonal with a vaulted fighting gallery) with flanking walls with a sloping plinth and open-backed rectangular towers along and across the ditches of the E.I.A. entrance, of ragstone rubble with Caen ashlar. Three arrowslits of each tower open from a single embrasure. The ditch south of the church was filled in and a second bank built across it and subsequently cut into for the foundation of a stone wall (destroyed) and largely rebuilt in the thirteenth century.

The next phase of building was the rectangular keep within a pear-shaped inner curtain (of similar stone to the earlier phase) and ditch. The curtain has 14 projecting square open-backed towers; two to the northeast and south are placed close together to form gatehouses, the former having a triangular barbican enclosure (with a *turning* bridge-pit) at the

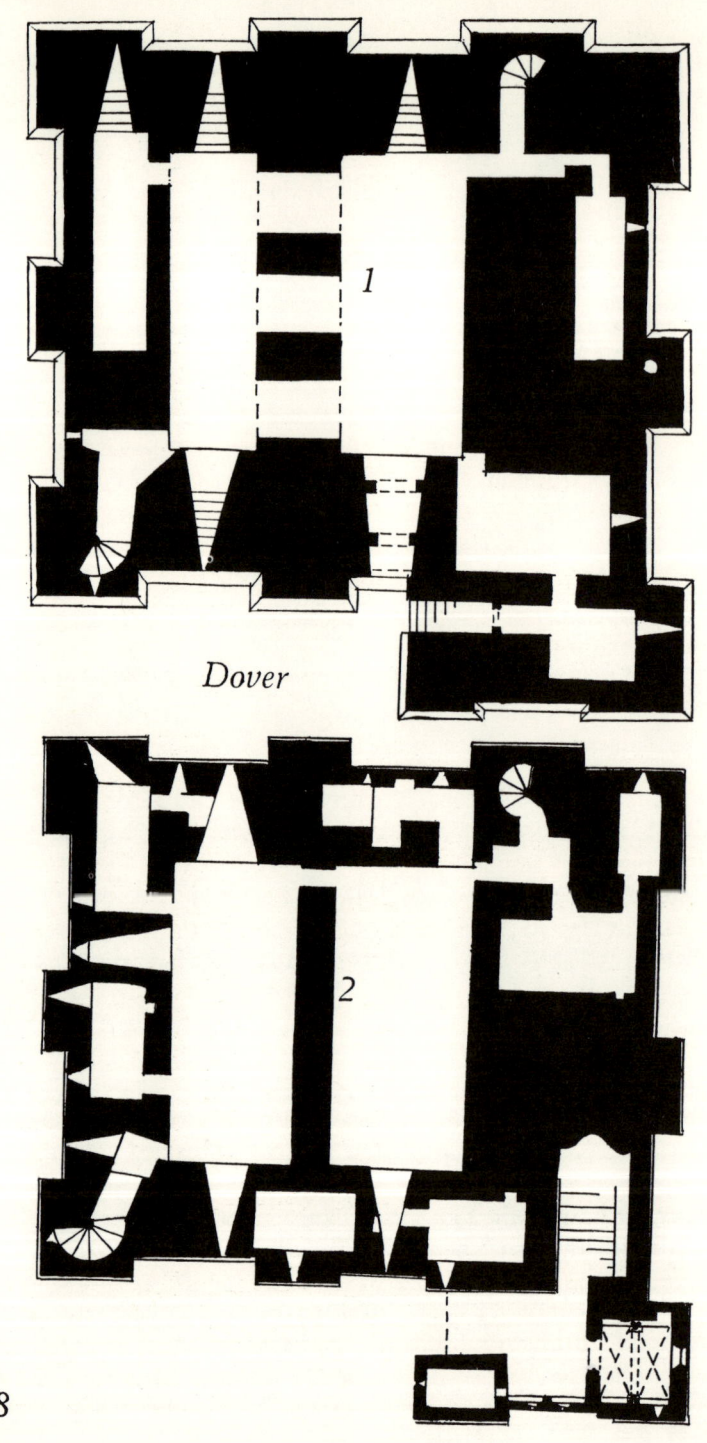

Dover

28

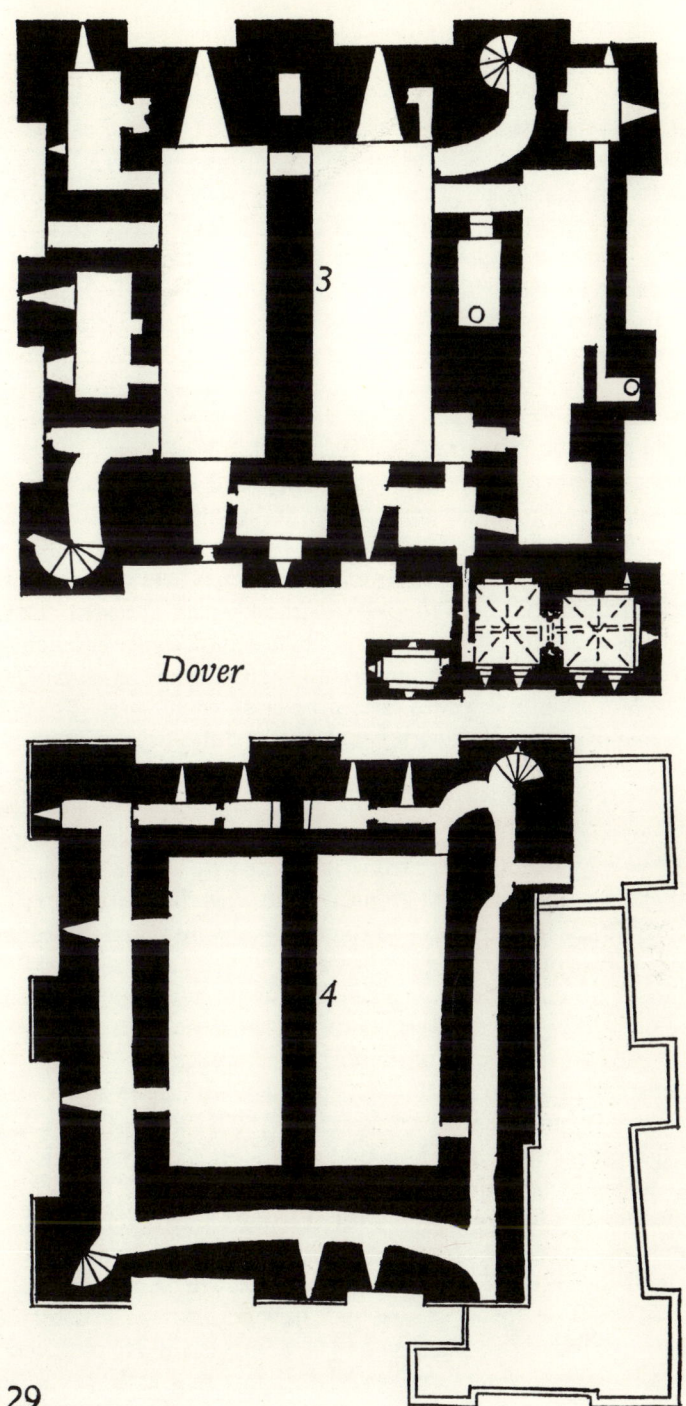

Dover

29

'stalk' of the pear. This work, costing nearly £6,300, was carried out between 1180–90 (*Pipe Rolls; Hoveden* II, p. 5). A rectangular tower was demolished when the curtain was completed (*Journal of the British Archaeological Association,* third series, XXX, pp. 87–121; XXXII, 54–104).

The rectangular keep is almost cubical (95 ft (including 12 ft turrets) × 98 ft × 96 ft) excluding the forebuilding. There are broad and deep buttresses clasping the angles and in the centre of each disengaged face, the sloping plinth capped with a roll-moulding and sets-off above, the moulding on the buttresses alone. The forebuilding covers the north-eastern side and turns along the eastern angle; the steps lead to a modern entrance to the basement and through a segmental arch, then up to the lower chapel, with a doorway of two orders, chevrons between roll-mouldings with engaged shafts with floriated capitals. The same scheme is found inside with a two-bay arcade separated by a further shaft and an east window with a chevron and roll-moulded arch. A loop and cupboard occupy the adjoining bays. The landing in front of the lower chapel has a two-bay arcade with loops, and a flat timber ceiling like that of the chapel. A barrel-vaulted chamber stands to the west of the chapel. The stair then turns north-westward through a much-altered door and passage (carried up as a turret) past a passage ending in a round shaft (for raising stores?) to end in a loop-lit vaulted room, also carried up as an open turret. The entrance door, a round-headed arch with jamb-shafts (stiffleaf capitals) gives on to the main floor of the keep, with a room at the eastern angle giving access to the chapel and a further chamber with roll-moulded groined vaulting rising from angle shafts and lit by loops. The chapel and ante-chapel also have a two-bay arcade. The chapel is entered by a taller version of the arch of the lower chapel, the groined vault (dogtooth between rolls with a flowered boss) is supported on corbels adjoining and reflecting the floriated capitals of the arcade jamb-shafts.

All floors are connected by spiral stairs at the north and south angles, and are divided by a north-west/south-east cross-wall, the basement level being pierced with three plain round-headed arches.

The basement is entered through a passage with three doors, and is lit by two loops in stepped recesses in each of the north-west and south-east walls; the other walls, the forebuilding and the eastern angle contain vaulted rooms lit by loops. The first floor has a series of wall-chambers, each opening off a window recess with a separate loop of its own, and there is a similar layout in the plan of the entrance floor above. A vaulted room opening off the entrance passage contains a well, lined with Caen stone to a depth of 172 ft and going at least 70 ft further down in the natural chalk. Beside it were found two lead pipes $3\frac{1}{2}$ in. across leading to rough conduits in the walls. (*Archaeologia Cantiana* XLIII, p. 167). A gallery runs through the thickness of the walls, with a break in the middle of the north-west wall where it forms two ranges of latrines with external loops. Side doors give access to the turrets over the forebuilding, and two loops in each of the southern walls have internal embrasures lighting the interior of the keep. The floors have been altered and the roof vaulted for cannon, but the angle turrets may be original.

Between 1190–1207, small sums were spent on repairs, but over £1,000 was spent in 1207–14, much of it on completing the outer curtain, defended by D-shaped towers; two close together at the north angle formed a gatehouse, blocked and altered after the siege of 1216–17. One wall-tower (Godsfoe's) and a gatehouse (Colton's) on the return wall to the internal earthwork round the church were rectangular (M.P.B.W. *Official Guide*).*

(Plates XIII, XIV, XV; Figs. 28, 29)

DOWNEND   see PURITON

DOWNPATRICK   J 4944   Down

Unfinished *motte* with ovoid bailey with strong counterscarp bank (Bb1 ?). The sites of John de Courcy's castles of 1176–7 (Giraldus Cambrensis, *Opera* V, 343; *Annals of Ulster*) are debatable (*Ulster Journal of Archaeology*, 3rd series I, pp. 198–200; III, pp. 56–63) (*Archaeological Survey of County Down*, pp. 202–3).*

DOWNTON   SU 181214   Wiltshire

Ring-work and baileys (Ca/2a/23) beside River Avon, now largely altered by landscape gardening. Foundations and Saxon axes have been found nearby, and a gravel-pit to the south contained Saxon pottery. (*Wiltshire Archaeological Magazine* 29, p. 103; 88, pp. 118–55).

The castle was built by Henry of Blois in 1137 (*Annales Monastici* II, p. 51) and recovered by him in 1148 after another castle had been built nearby (possibly Godshill near Fordingbridge a type ICd4 site (SU 166162).

DRAX   SE 676260   Yorkshire

Castle captured by Stephen in 1154 (*Hoveden* I, p. 213; *Chronicles of the reign of Stephen* I, 32).

DRIFFIELD   TA 035585   Yorkshire

Motte and bailey (Bd3). The foss of the bailey against the Nafferton Road is mentioned in a fine of John's reign (*Surtees Society* 94, no. 120).

DROGHEDA   O 0976   Louth

Motte and bailey (Aa4) in existence by 1192 (*Calendar of Documents* I, 93, 145) (*Journal of the Royal Society of Antiquaries of Ireland* XXXVIII, pp. 246–50).*

| DROMORE | J 2153 | Down |

Motte and bailey (Ad3) in loop of River Bann with outer bank and ditch further north and east. Excavation of the *motte*-top showed two lines of palisading, the post-holes underlying burnt planking and a stone kerb (of a perimeter track?) over which a rimbank had been thrown up, surrounding a central hollow. The *Irish Pipe Roll* of 1211–2 mentions new buildings at Dromore (*Ulster Journal of Archaeology* 4, 57, 61; XVII, pp. 164–8. *Archaeological Survey of County Down* pp. 203–4; Plate 40).*

| DRUMCULLEN | N 0007 | Offaly |

Castle mentioned 1211–2. (*Irish Pipe Roll*).

| DUBLIN | O 1734 | Dublin |

Castle sited near the confluence of the rivers Liffey and Poddle. The plan (Phillips, *Report on Fortifications of Ireland*; see *Journal of the Royal Society of Antiquaries of Ireland* LVIII, p. 46) was quasi-rectangular with round towers at the angles and half-round towers flanking the entrance and in the centre of the south curtain opposite. The surviving fragment of the south-west curtain is canted, and the south-west round tower (of limestone rubble with a sloping plinth) had a small rectangular tower to the west; these may derive from a previous fortification. There was some sort of fortification here in 1172 (*Song of Dermot; Reg. St. Thomas, Dublin* 369) and a strong tower was ordered in 1204 (*Close Roll; Calendar of Documents* I, 80; *English Historical Review* XXII, pp. 460–4).

| DUDLEY | SO 947908 | Worcestershire |

Flattened *motte* and oval bailey (Bb3) with counterscarp bank except to south, also scarpings of natural hill on which the castle stands. The inner part of the gate passage is barrel-vaulted, with diagonally tooled quoins at three angles and some remains of round-headed arches at front and rear. There is also a blocked round-headed arch springing from plain jambs in the later service block north of the hall.

William fitz Ansculf's castle is mentioned in 'Domesday' (I, 177) and it was attacked in 1138 and demolished in 1173 (*Chronicles of John of Worcester*, p. 50; *Diceto* I, p. 404) (*Archaeological Journal* LXXI, pp. 1–24).*

| DUFFIELD | SK 343441 | Derbyshire |

Remains of *motte* and bailey (IBd2). Excavations in 1957 showed that the ditch south of the *motte* had been recut as a wide flat-bottomed moat. The natural rock had been levelled and scarped to form the *motte*; several post-holes were sealed by the large almost square keep erected upon it, excavated in 1886. Little more than the foundations survive; the west wall facing was built on rock, but the south wall was trench-built with an inter-

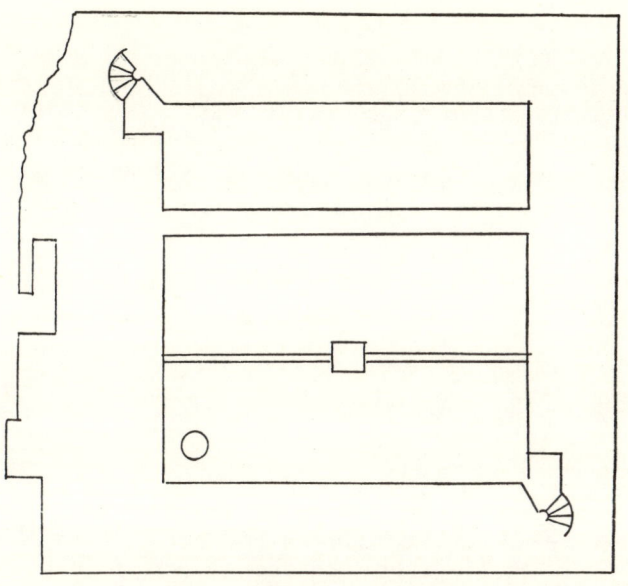

Duffield

Dundrum

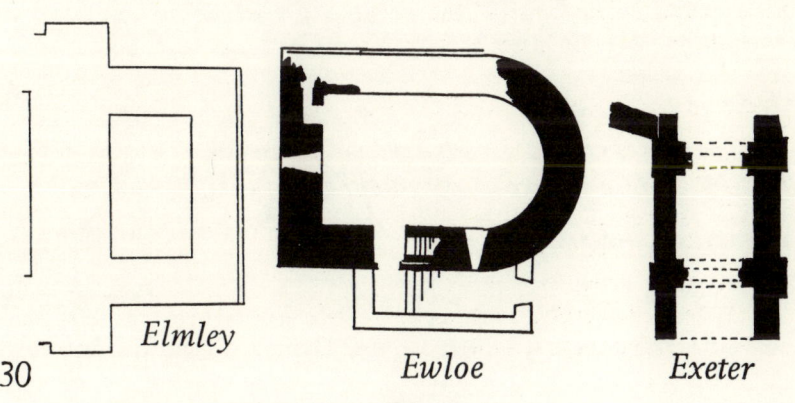

Elmley *Ewloe* *Exeter*

30

nal offset. Five courses of 7-in. high sandstone ashlar were recorded at one place on the inner face. There was an external buttress at the south end of the extremely thick west wall, outside which was a thin layer of concrete. The site was covered with charcoal, and the rubble showed signs of intense heat.

The interior was divided from north to south into three compartments by a wall (with traces of a doorway), and a channel running under a central square pier, with upper angles were chamfered to take a round column. Spiral stairs open off the east and west walls at the south and north ends respectively. The well in the south-west corner is square for the first ten feet and circular below, cut through the shale at the side of the rock outcrop. A wooden spade, bucket (with iron handle) and pottery were recovered from the well together with moulded capitals of engaged columns.

Henry de Ferrers (d. 1089) is said to have built a castle here (*Derbyshire Archaeological Journal* IX, 120, quoting an unspecified MS. in the Duchy of Lancaster office). The castle was surrendered to Henry II in 1173 (*Gesta Henrici Secundi* I, p. 48). Ralph Diceto (p. 588, n. 20) states that it was then demolished, but its mention in a deed of Robert de Ferrers (1245-78) (*Great Cowcher* of the Duchy of Lancaster II, f. 98, n. 41) and the thirteenth century pottery from the site suggests that occupation continued until perhaps Ferrers' attainder in 1266. However the finds from the keep area (a prick spur and bridle bit, knives and Stamford ware (Saxo-Norman) pottery) need not be later than 1173, and the suggestion that William de Ferrers built the keep between 1177-90 must be treated with reserve (*Journal of the Derbyshire Archaeological and Natural History Society* IX, pp. 118-78; LXXIX, pp. 1-21). (Fig. 30)

| DUFFUS | NJ 189673 | Morayshire |

Ovoid ditch enclosing *motte* and bailey (Bd3) said to have been that erected by Freskin the Fleming in 1151 (Giovanni Ferrerio, *History of Kinloss Abbey*, quoted in the *Official Guide* (M.P.B.W.); certainly the lands were in his hands by 1153; Scottish Record Office, *Cartae variae*, f. 299).

| DULEEK | O 0468 | Meath |

Site of castle restored in 1174 (Giraldus Cambrensis, *Opera* V, 313) at confluence of streams (*English Historical Review* XXII, p. 234).

DUMATH see DUNAMASE

| DUMFRIES | NX 970764 | Dumfriesshire |

Two *motte* castle sites, much altered (Castle Dykes and Dumfries Academy) beside the River Nith. One may be the *vetus castellarium* of a charter of 1179–85 (*Regesta Regum Scottorum* II, p. 265).

DUNAMASE   S 5797   Laoighis (Leix)

Ring-work and bailey, the former of rounded triangular shape, with a small forework completing an oval trace (ICb2?). Site on rocky plateau with precipitous slopes to north and west. The rectangular keep is of squared rubble with two round-headed windows at ground level and a projecting forebuilding to the west. Mentioned in 1215 (*Calendar of Documents* I, p. 106; *Histoire Guillaume le Marchal; Patent Roll*). This may be the castle of *Dunmalc* of 1211–12 (*Irish Pipe Roll*), unless this was Dunboyke, Wicklow.

DUNBAR   NT 678792   East Lothian

Late medieval masonry on site of castle mentioned in 1216 (*Histoire des Ducs de Normandie*, p. 163).

DUNDALK   J 0507   Louth

(?) Ring-work and bailey (Cd4) mentioned in a document of 1205–10 (*Reg. St. Thomas' Abbey, Dublin*, p. 9, quoted in the *Journal of the Royal Society of Antiquaries of Ireland* XXXVIII, pp. 256–61).

DUNDEE see INVERGOWRIE

DUNDONALD   J 4274   Down

Motte (IB) west of church, taken in 1210 and repaired in 1211–12. (*Irish Pipe Roll*).

DUNDRUM   J 4037   Down

Large mound with rock-cut ditch and outer enclosure to south-east. The oval mound top is surrounded by a curtain wall of split-stone rubble, built in straight lengths with an internal offset. Excavation showed that there were traces of an earlier earthwork bank, and that the curtain had been built in a foundation trench on a double flagstone course with a simple entrance and bridge pit to the east, and with the remains of an angular and a semi-circular dry-stone revetment within the enclosure to the north-west. Soon afterward the circular keep had been built, its footings packed into a foundation trench.

The round keep has a splayed plinth and has a spiral stair in the north-east part of the wall linking all floors. The first floor is entered by a segmental-headed passage from the east, with a doorway nearly opposite to a bridge leading to the parapet of the curtain, with a square-headed loop with window-seats and a segmental rear-arch on either hand, and a fireplace with square flue to the north. This floor is supported on a setback of the wall — the rebuilt upper floor has a row of beam-holes. The basement was lit by a stepped loop below each of those of the entrance floor, the floor space being excavated to form a square rock-cut cistern.

Castle besieged in 1205 by John de Courcy (*Chronicle of Man* I, pp. 80–82; *Calendar of Documents* I, 95) (*Ulster Journal of Archaeology* XIV, pp. 15–29; XXI, pp. 63–6; XXVII, pp. 136–9; *Archaeological Survey of County Down*, pp. 207–11).* (Fig. 30)

DUNDUNNOLF   see BAGINBUN

DUNGARVAN   X 2593   Waterford

Castle west of town, mentioned in 1215 (*Calendar of Documents* I, 89, 91, 94; *Rot. de Oblatis et Finibus*, p. 556). (*Ulster Journal of Archaeology* n.s. 33, p. 66).

DUNHAM MASSEY   SJ 734874   Cheshire

Flattened mound beside Dunham Massey Hall, ditch flooded as an ornamental lake; the Hall probably occupies the bailey.

In 1173 Hamo de Masci held the *castellum de Duneham* against Henry II (*Gesta Henrici Secundi* I, p. 48) (*Transactions of the Lancashire and Cheshire Antiquarian Society* XLII, pp. 53–60).

DUNHEVED   see LAUNCESTON

DUN LAGAIDH   see page 354

DUNMALC   see DUNAMASE

DUNNOTTAR   NO 882839   Kincardineshire

Oval *motte* (IB) at neck of peninsular, mentioned *c*. 1209 in the *Roman von Guillaume le Clerc* (see SOMERLED'S).

DUNSCATH   NH 820694   Ross and Cromarty

Motte (B) built by William the Lion in 1179 (*Chronicle of Melrose*, p. 88; *Reg. Dunfermline*, p. 32); it is not clear whether another two castles were built in Ross in 1211 (*Scotichronicon*, VIII, c. lxxvi).

DUNSTER   SS 992433   Somerset

No early masonry appears to survive on this scarped natural hill, held by William de Mohun against Henry de Tracy in 1139, nor any trace of the siege-work built by Stephen to help de Tracy (*Henry of Huntingdon*, p. 261; *Gesta Stephani*, p. 54). Mentioned in 'Domesday Book' (I, 95) as the castle of Torre.

XVII *above* The wall of the first hall at FRAMLINGHAM, its ashlar chimneys with smoke vents fossilized in the later curtain wall.
right The keep at GOODRICH, its upper doorway converted into a window. A carved string-course runs below the top floor Norman window.

XVIII GUILDFORD keep is built against the side of the *motte*, with ashlar buttresses and ornamental rubble coursing including herringbone work.

XIX At HEDINGHAM the entrance doorway (*left*) has scalloped capitals and chevrons on the arch. The windows become more elaborate as the keep rises (*right*) and the stair-turret rises highest of all. The creasing of the forebuilding roof can be seen, and also the regular pattern of small putlog holes in the ashlar.

xx The keep at KENILWORTH has large angle-turrets. That nearest the camera conceals the entrance doorway, later elaborated with a forebuilding.

XXI Lunn's Tower of the curtain wall at KENILWORTH is almost circular, with pilaster buttresses dying into the sloping plinth.

XXII The squat round keep at LONGTOWN had three rounded buttresses. Note the corbelled-out latrine in the centre.

XXIII At LUDLOW the great gatehouse had its entrance blocked (note the irregular masonry in the centre) converting it into a keep.

XXIV *above* Part of the blind wall-arcade of the entrance passage survives inside the keep at LUDLOW.
below The round nave of the Norman chapel at LUDLOW, with its ornamental west door and window above.

xxv *left* A close-up of the west doorway of the chapel at LUDLOW—billet-moulding surrounding chevrons on the arch, diapering on the abaci and scalloped capitals. *right* The diapered soffit of the chancel arch.

XXVI Six capitals from the blind arcade within the nave of LUDLOW castle chapel.

XXVII *above* The late keep at LYDFORD, with double-splayed windows to the lower floor above the *motte*-top.
below The rectangular keep at MIDDLEHAM with its lancet windows out of reach of stone robbers, who have removed the lower ashlar facing.

XXVIII *above* The narrow loops of the basement contrasting with the late medieval windows above on the inner wall of the hall at MONMOUTH.
below The gatehouse at NEWARK, with billet-moulded arch and string-course. Blocked Norman windows can be traced beside the later two-light openings.

XXIX The top storey of the round keep at NENAGH is modern. The small doorway halfway up led out on to the wall-walk of the curtain wall, the toothings of which can be seen.

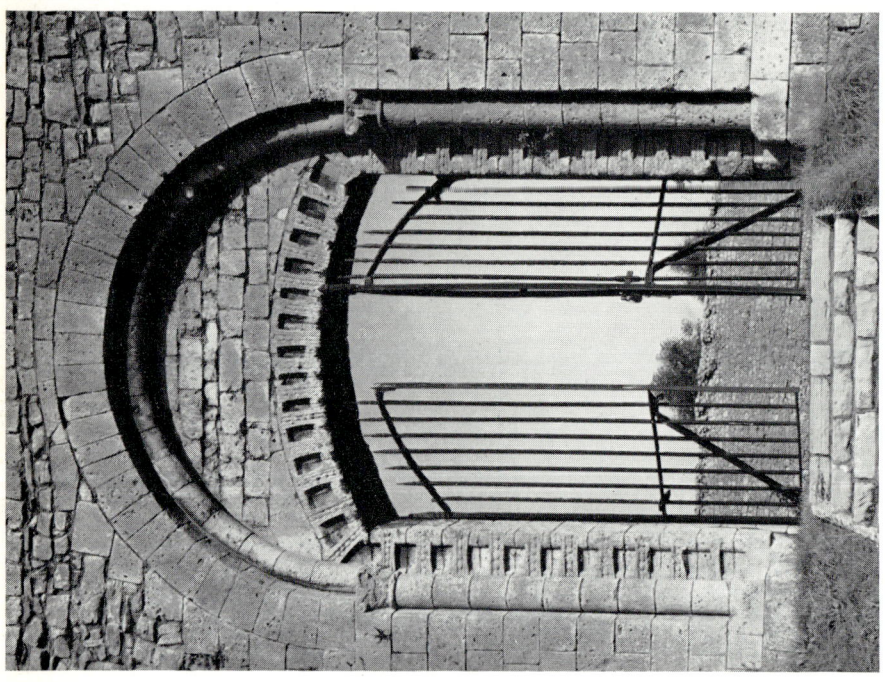

xxx *left* The remarkable gateway at NEWCASTLE BRIDGEND; *right* The ornamental arches of the chapel in the keep at NEWCASTLE UPON TYNE (compare plate XV, right) with water-leaf capitals on the right.

XXXI The entrance and postern doorways to the keep at NEWCASTLE UPON TYNE can be seen above and beyond the front turret of the forebuilding.

XXXII   Although harshly restored, the ornamental details of the keep at NORWICH are accurate copies of the originals.

DURHAM NZ 274423 Durham

Motte and bailey (Ac3) backed against cliff at neck of loop of River Wear. The sandstone keep on the *motte* is an irregular octagon with angle pilasters, largely rebuilt in 1840. The account of Laurence of Durham (1144–9) (I, 367–78), *Surtees Society* 70) suggests a timber tower on four posts within the shell-wall. Excavation of the *motte* in 1951 showed tipped layers of sand and earth, with two turflines above an occupation layer (*Antiquaries' Journal* XXXIII, p. 56). The basement of the chapel has six pillars of veined local stone, with square responds north-south and semicircular east-west, with grotesquely carved capitals supporting slightly stilted semicircular arches. Formerly approached by a spiral stair, the basement is lit by plain loops in the north and east walls. The floor is of rhomboidal slabs apart from a central line of square flags.

The north range is masked by a sixteenth century gallery. Originally the range had square basement piers with plain abaci, but their failure led to the filling of the basement and the revetting of the slope with clay-set rubble on stepped foundations, using cubical ashlar with wide joints. The Lower Hall above has an elaborate doorway of three shafted orders, having elaborately scalloped capitals with moulded abaci, and squared bases to the chamfered plinth (the innermost order triple-shafted). The innermost arch has rectangular sunk panels beaded diagonally, the middle double billets and the outer octagonal sunk panels. Between the first two orders is a string of repeated roses flanked by pellets, between the next a lattice overlying pellets, and outside all a pelleted lattice. The rest of this hall is much altered, but a spiral stair leads to the Upper (or Constable's) Hall. The south wall of this hall is constructed as a continuous arcade with windows in alternate bays, the chevron-ornamented arches each standing on a scalloped capital supported on two plain columns with moulded bases raised to form seats between the windows. A later staircase has preserved the two-light windows under semicircular heads.

The great hall (west range) is largely rebuilt, but the north-west angle and the north end of the undercroft are probably original work, and a Norman window has been found in the kitchen at the south end of the range. That the square southern gatehouse was Norman is clear from a picture of *c.* 1790 (reproduced in V.C.H. *Durham* III, opposite p. 84) where the arch is of four orders, with cable mouldings; a sunk star string course remains on the west side.

The castle was built by William I on his return from Scotland in 1072 (*Symeon of Durham* II, p. 199) as a fortress for the bishop. Symeon attributes the keep and north range to Bishop Flambard (1099–1128), and the west hall and rebuilding of the north range to Bishop Pudsey (1153–95) (*op. cit.* I, 140; II, 260). The castle was in the king's hands in 1211–12 when a portcullis and watch-tower were built, possibly at the north-west angle of the castle (*Pipe Roll*) (V.C.H. *Durham* III, pp. 64–94).*

(Plate XVI; Fig. 27)

DURROW   N 3131   Offaly

Motte and bailey south of abbey (Bc2). Hugh de Lacy's murder took place during its erection in 1186 (Giraldus Cambrensis, *Opera* V, 387; *Annals of Clonmacnoise, Annals of Ulster; Annals of the Four Masters*) (*Journal of the Royal Society of Antiquaries of Ireland* XXIX, pp. 227–32).*

DURSLEY   Gloucestershire

Said to have been built by Roger de Berkeley after his loss of Berkeley (1153), but Henry, Duke of Anjou spent a night at the castle of *Durslea* in 1149 (*Gesta Stephani*, pp. 143–4). Possibly the Drakestone earthwork (ST 737980).

DUVELESCENSE   see DULEEK

DYMOCK   SO 713294   Gloucestershire

Motte (B) south-east of village, granted temporarily to William de Braose by Roger, Earl of Hereford (between 1148 and 1154). (*Cambridge Historical Journal* VIII, p. 185).

DYNEVOR   see DINEFWR

EASTON   TL 608254   Essex

Motte with traces of rectangular bailey, partly altered into moated site (Ad2?). Excavations in 1964 (*Transactions of the Essex Archaeological Society*, third series, I, p. 265) produced eleventh/twelfth-century pottery from the bailey. See also *Medieval Archaeology* X, p. 190.

EARDISLEY   SO 311491   Herefordshire

Motte inside rectangular moat (Bd2?); there is now no trace of a motte-ditch or bailey bank, but there is a strong counterscarp bank on the south side intersecting a western counterscarp prolonged to the south and wider but lower at the northern end. Further west a curving bank and ditch makes a segmental outer enclosure.

A *domus defensabilis* is mentioned in 'Domesday Book' (184b, 2), and the castle is named in 1182–5 (*Pipe Rolls*) and 1209 (*Rot. Litt. Pat.* 91a) R.C.H.M. *Herefordshire* III, pp. xxix, 52–3.   (Fig. 31)

EARLS BARTON   SP 852637   Northamptonshire

The Saxon tower of the church stands within the line of the outer lip of

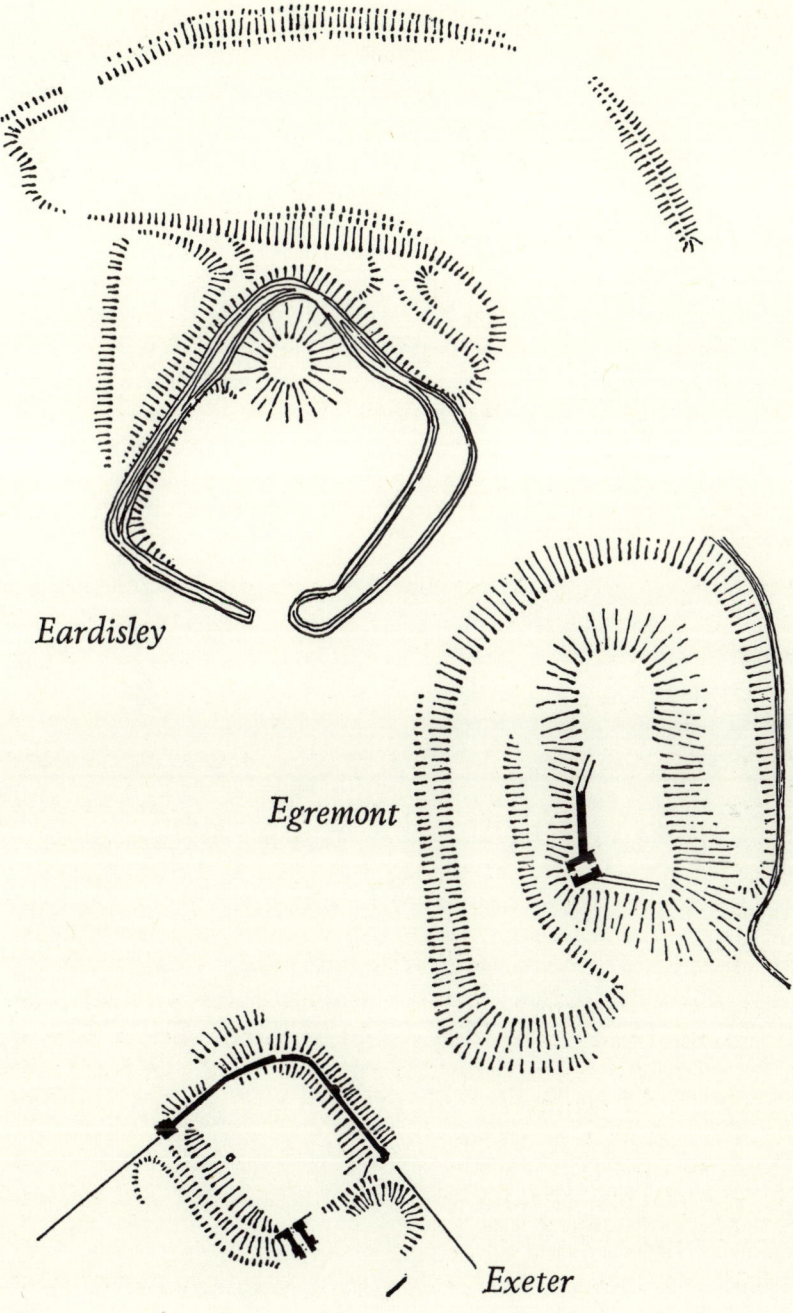

31

the *motte* ditch, and it has been argued that the *motte* must have been built before the church tower (see p. 31).

EATON SOCON   TL 173588   Bedfordshire

Earthworks (IICe2) on Ouse river terrace. A section through the east side of the main southern enclosure showed a collapsed clay gravel wall sealing St Neots' pottery and a clay floor revetted on the river side. On the other side of the wall rose a small mound containing coloured window glass and pottery of Saxon to late medieval date, based on a layer of mortar and plaster. A trench across the northern enclosure revealed disturbed burials below a layer of large stones, including a pilaster strip, with St Neots and Thetford pottery. A rectangular building existed at the south-east angle. A Saxo-Norman house has been excavated subsequently further west, beyond the castle moat which was revetted with beech planking and an alder dowel, with post-holes on top of the bank overlying another house.

The remodelling of the house as a castle may have taken place between about 1120 and 1156, when the manorial history is obscure. (*Bedfordshire Historical Record Society* II, pp. 61–72) (*Proceedings of Cambridge Antiquarian Society* XLV, pp. 48–60; LVIII, pp. 38–73).*

ECCLESHALL   SJ 828296   Staffordshire

Altered site (apparently originally a semicircular enclosure) beside stream, of the manor house which John licensed Bishop Muschamp to fortify in 1200 (*Rot. Chart.* I, p. 60).

EDEN see page 354

EDERDOVER   NH 584495   Ross and Cromarty

Castle on south shore of Black Isle, built by William the Lion in 1179 (*Chronicle of Melrose*, p. 88; *Reg. Dunfermline*, p. 32).

EDERNION see RUG

EDINBURGH   NT 251735   Midlothian

The only early survival is the lower part of St Margaret's chapel, of coursed ashlar with a restored doorway at the west end of the north wall, with scalloped capitals and shafts supporting a round head carved with chevrons inside a pellet-moulding. The chancel arch is of two similar orders but with nail-head moulding; the chancel is apsidal internally, with a small round-headed east window and three similar ones in the south wall of the nave.

The *Castro Puellarum* of 1093 (R.C.A.M. *City of Edinburgh*, p. xxxv) and the chapel is mentioned about 1130 (Lawrie, *Early Scottish Charters*, LXXII, XCII). The castle was surrendered to the English Crown in 1174 and fortified in the following year (*Foedera* I, p. 30; *Pipe Roll*) (R.C.A.M. *City of Edinburgh*, pp. 1–25).*

GAZETTEER

EGREMONT   NY 010105   Cumberland

Scarped hillock, rectangular gate-tower in fine ashlar bonded into curtain wall of slabs laid in herringbone coursing. The round-headed entrance arch with roll-moulding springs from plain imposts; the inner arch is segmental. The Bucks' engraving shows a keep on the north side of the site. Castle mentioned in 1203 (*Curia Regis Rolls* II, 274).   (Fig. 31)

ELDBOTLE   see page 354

ELGIN   NJ 212629   Morayshire

Rectangular tower of uncertain date on *motte* (IB) at west end of burgh. Knight service at the castle was required for a grant of land in 1160 (Sixteenth century transumpt cited by Barrow, *Regesta Regum Scottorum* I, p. 220).

ELLESMERE   SJ 403346   Shropshire

Motte and bailey (IBc3), mentioned in 1138 (*Ordericus Vitalis* XIII, cap. 37). £4 spent on it in 1171–2 and frequent references in 1203–8 (*Pipe Rolls; Rot. Litt. Pat.* I, pp. 51, 88).

ELMLEY   SO 980403   Worcestershire

Complex earthworks on the slope of Bredon Hill in the park of Elmley Castle. A triangular promontory from the slope has a double bank and ditch to the north and a scarp to the east; a re-entrant to the south-east has been strengthened with an inner ditch. The widest part of the promontory has an oval ring-work with a counterscarp round its pointed end and a long pentagonal bailey to the south with counterscarp (except to the north where the double bank runs fairly close) — say a I/II Cf3 site. Near the centre of the ring are the rubble remains of an oblong building with a plinth on one side; the other extends beyond the return walls, with irregular outer ends to the outer face, as if return walls running south have been destroyed, so that the structure may have been a rectangular keep of which only the basement of the forebuilding survives. The keep and curtain wall were excavated (*Reports of the Congress of Archaeological Societies* for 1932–3) but no report seems to have been published, although there is a plan of the keep in the Sands Collection of the Society of Antiquaries in London.

    Mentioned in 1216 (*Rot. Litt. Pat.* I, 192).   (Figs. 18, 30)

ELY   TL 540800   Cambridgeshire

Motte and bailey (Be3), possibly the *praesidio* of 1070–1 (*Liber Eliensis*, p. 194) but the *castle* mentioned is Alrehede. A castle was however fortified by Nigel, bishop of Ely in 1138–9 as well as a strong-fort by the river (*Ibid.*, pp. 314, 328).

EMLYN see CENARTH FAWR

ENGLISH BICKNOR   SO 581157   Gloucestershire

Motte and bailey (Bd2) with outer enclosure surrounding church, mentioned in 1217 (*Patent Roll* 127) (*Transactions of the Bristol and Gloucestershire Archaeological Society* IV, p. 301).*

ERDIGG see WREXHAM

ESCLON

Castle mentioned in 1212 is not Carrigogunnel (*Ulster Journal of Archeology*, third series IV, p. 71 and note 263).

ESTRAHANENT see ANNAN

ESSLEFORD see SLEAFORD

ETHERDOUR see EDERDOVER

EWLOE   SJ 290673   Flintshire

Masonry castle on small ear-shaped tongue of land at junction of two stream-valleys cut off by a wide ditch on the south with extra counterscarp. Most of the masonry dates from soon after 1256 (P.R.O. *Plea Rolls Chester*, 29/23, n. 48) but bridge abutments at the south-east angle of the enclosure indicate an earlier castle of which the Welsh Tower may be part. This roughly coursed rubble tower is rectangular with an apsidal east end and a sloping plinth on the north side. There was a forebuilding on the south side with a lower doorway leading up to the segmental arch of the entrance. A wall stair opening off this rises to the wall top, where traces of the west gable and gutter may be seen, the walls being carried up higher to screen it; there are holes for a wooden gallery at the top of the south wall. The basement has now no openings, and the entrance floor, supported on beams, is lit by a square-headed window in the south wall (pointed internal arch), with traces of a similar window in the west wall. Beside the latter is the chamfered jamb of an entrance to a wall-passage, perhaps to the latrine shaft in the north wall.

The references to *Eggelawe* in 1212–13 (*Pipe Roll*) are associated with castles further south and may refer to Kinnerley (q.v.) (*Y Cymmrodor* XXXIX, pp. 1–19).*   (Fig. 30)

EWYAS HAROLD   SO 384287   Herefordshire

Motte and bailey (IAa3) west of church, the *motte* being at the base of the spur, with no visible sign of a ditch on the bailey side. G. T. Clark records robber trenches on the *motte* as of a shell-wall with twin-towered gatehouse to the west (*Archaeologia Cambrensis* fourth series VIII, pp. 116–24).

The castle was *refortified* by William fitz Osbern (i.e. between the end of 1066 and his death in February 1071) ('Domesday Book' I, 185–6) R.C.H.M. *Herefordshire* I, pp. 63–4.*

EWYAS LACY   see LONGTOWN

EXETER   SX 921929   Devon

Almost square earthwork in north angle of Roman town wall; traces of a bailey have been found (IICd2) (*Proc. Devon Archaeological Exploration Committee* II, pp. 181–2). The earthwork carries a curtain wall (much rebuilt but with herringbone work inside the north wall), with a gatehouse projecting at the south end of the south-east side. The flanking walls of the gatehouse are spanned by three semicircular arches of two square orders: the outer at a high level, lighting a pair of triangular-headed windows (with cushion capitals) above the middle arch (now blocked), braced with pilaster buttresses outside, as is the inner arch which has simple chamfered capitals and piers. Towers with pilaster buttresses on each face cover the junction of castle and town walls. That to the west is square, with triangular-headed lights to the stair-turret; that to the east is polygonal, with a half round tower further north.

The castle site was chosen by William I after the surrender of Exeter in 1068 (Ordericus Vitalis, *Historia Ecclesiastica* II, p. 181) and a stone curtain wall existed at the time of Stephen's siege in 1138 (*Gesta Stephani*, pp. 22–3). Over £200 was spent on the castle in 1169–77, nearly £50 on the king's chamber there in 1180–1 and more than £50 in 1207–8 on ditchworks and transport of stone and lime (*Pipe Rolls*), possibly for an outer (southern) bailey wall, of which a fragment survives (*Transactions of the Devon Association* 27, pp. 137–42; 98, pp. 327–48).* (Figs. 30, 31)

EYE   TM 147738   Suffolk

Motte and bailey (Ab3) west of church, with former traces of flint rubble curtain walls, one running up the *motte* with a round projection (*Proceedings of the Suffolk Institute of Archaeology* II, pp. 119–20). The castle was built by William Malet before 1086 ('Domesday Book' II, p. 379) and was in the hands of the Crown from 1157–98, and small amounts were spent on brattices and heightening the walls as well as repairs (*Torigny*, p. 192; *Pipe Rolls*).

EYNSFORD   TQ 541658   Kent

Low mound with bailey on terrace beside River Darent. Excavations have shown that the mound carried a timber tower about 35 ft square covering a well. Later the mound was surrounded by an oval shell-wall of coursed

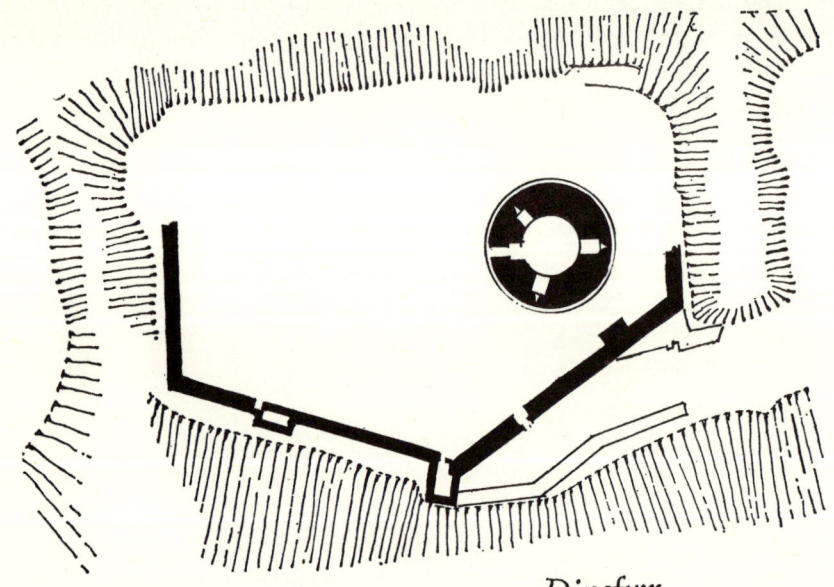

Dinefwr

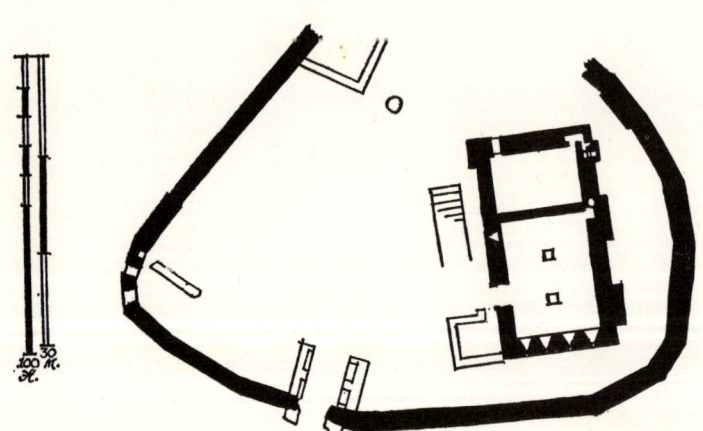

Eynsford

32

flint rubble with a sloping plinth, with an entrance between slight buttresses and latrines in the salient south-west angle, with tufa dressings. When a hall was built across the site of the tower, the levelled platform was raised, as was the curtain to which a shallow turret was added to the north-east, and also beam-holes for a timber boarding flanking the salient. The gate was extended with two internal bays and a kitchen contrived in the east angle. The hall was of flint with greensand and tile dressings, and built in the first half of the twelfth century. Its basement was divided by a narrow cross-wall, with steeply sloping loops in the southern walls and an upper floor supported on an arcade of three round arches. The smaller part of the basement was fitted up as a self-contained room with the old well, a fireplace and wall-stair to a buttress-latrine. Later the hall was approached by a stair on a stone base leading over an enclosed pit to a square forebuilding. (*Archeologia Cantiana* LXXXVI, 109–171). (Fig. 32)

| FAIRSEAT | TQ 628614 | Kent |

Excavation in 1964–5 of a mound at the angle of a square enclosure, with an oval one to the west, produced mid-twelfth century pottery and evidence of a timber tower burnt down in the mid-thirteenth century. (Kent Archaeological Research Group's Council *Newsletter* May 1966).

| FARNHAM | SU 837473 | Surrey |

Motte and bailey (Bc3) within D-shaped enclosure of ditch and bank. The outer enclosure wall is of chalk blocks, with projecting rectangular towers, several of which have been destroyed (see the Bucks' view of 1737). Excavations in 1958–9 showed that a circular well-shaft was extended upward from the original ground level in mortared chalk rubble as a square interior (with ashlar quoins) to a tower 37 ft square externally, around which a flange of chalk rubble blocks was first freebuilt and then the upper part of the flange integrated to form a base for a tower 51 ft square. A mound of natural marl was packed hard up to the flange and covered with loose rubble, and the mound completed in marl with a hard top layer level with the top of the flange; above this layer the tower has been removed. The *motte* is surrounded with an almost circular shell-wall of chalk (repaired in sandstone) with a wide shallow gatehouse entered through a roll-moulded segmental arch, with a bar-hole and portcullis; the room over the passage is lit by two loops. Four rectangular turrets survive on the shell-wall, formerly with round-headed windows lighting the rooms level with the *motte*-top. With the gatehouse and other junction of the bailey curtain, they divide the perimeter into six segments, each with two pilaster buttresses rising from the sloping plinth.

The bailey buildings have been much altered, but the double-splayed loops and angle buttess to the south-west appear to be of twelfth century

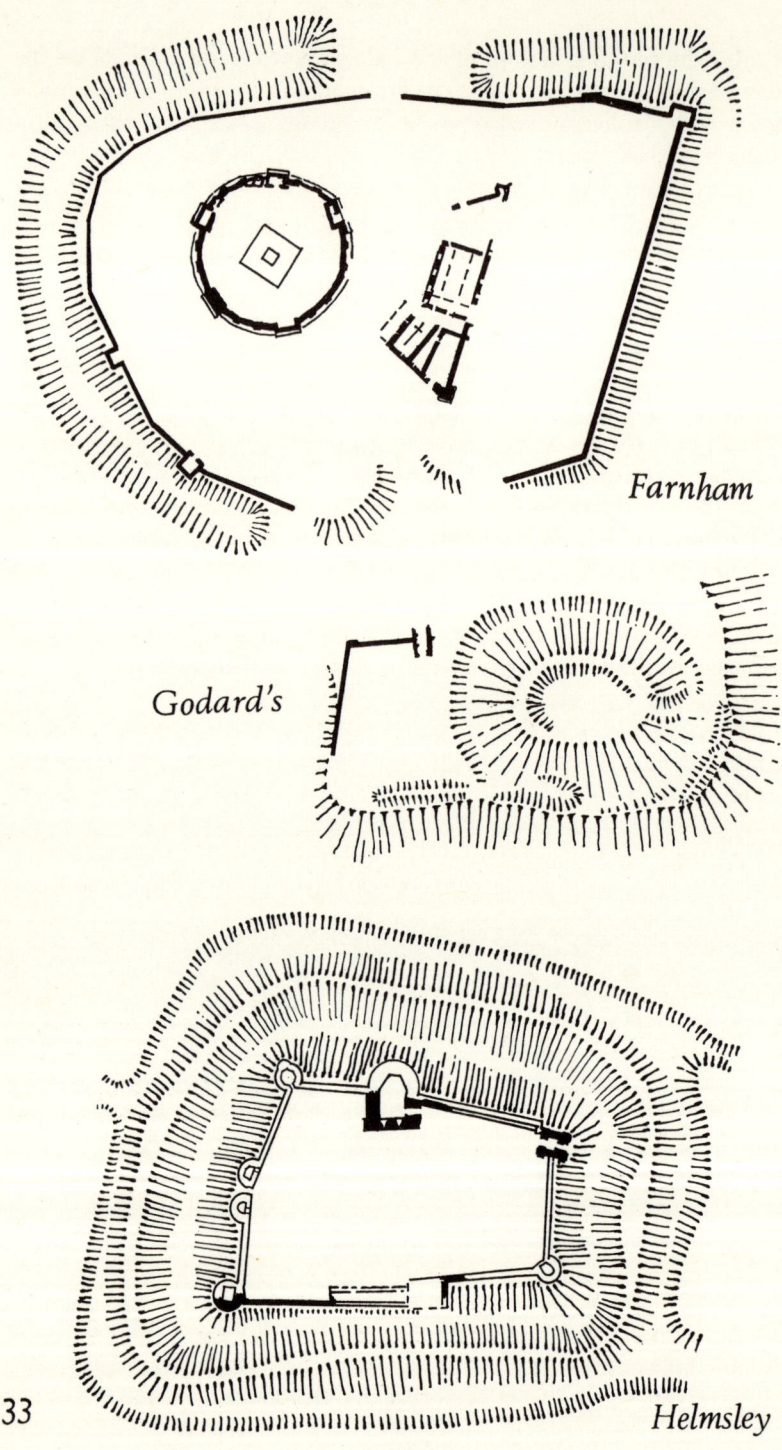

33

date, also the round windows of the hall basement (the hall had timber aisles of which two square scalloped capitals survive), and the screens doorway with a roll-moulded segmental head and palmette capitals to the Purbeck marble shafts.

The castle was built in 1138 (*Annales Monastici* II, 51) and seized by Henry II in 1155 and the tower may then have been destroyed (if it ever was completed) (Matthew Paris, *Chronica Majora* II, 210; *Torigny*, 186; *Diceto* I, p. 301) (M.P.B.W. *Official Guide; Medieval Archaeology* IV, pp. 81–94).* (Plate XVI; Figs. 1, 33)

| FARINGDON | SU 297957 | Berkshire |

During the erection of a tower at Faringdon Clump in 1935, an oval clay platform (30 ft by 40 ft) with laid stones at two points was found, with two concentric clay bands and an outer ditch. The entrance was marked by a gap in the bands, with a stone spread over the gravel. A crescentic crop mark (*Oxoniensia* XIX, pl. VIIb) in the field near the allotments has not yet been investigated.

This has been equated with the castle built by Robert of Gloucester in 1144 and destroyed by Stephen in 1145 (Matthew Paris, *Hist. Ang.* I, 275; *Annales Monastici* II, pp. 230–1; *Chronicles of the reigns of Stephen . . .* III, 115–16) but nearly all the pottery from the site is of thirteenth century type (*Oxoniensia* IV, p. 140; *Berks Arch. J.* 50, p. 70). The *Gesta Stephani* (pp. 120–1) states that the castle and Stephen's camp were defended by bank and ditch. (*Antiquaries' Journal* 16, pp. 165–78; 17, pp. 294–8).*

FAVORIE see FORE

FERNS   Wexford

Castle built near here in 1186 (Giraldus Cambrensis, *Opera* V, 326).

FLANDRENSIS see ARDREE

| *FLEET* | TF 385232 | Lincolnshire |

A mound excavated in 1913 produced Saxo-Norman pottery (*Reports and papers of the Lincolnshire Architectural and Archaeological Society* VI, pp. 11–12).

FLEMISH see LLANIO

| FOLKESTONE | TR 214379 | Kent |

Ring-work and bailey (ICc2) on spur of North Downs. Both ring and bailey have strong counterscarp banks, and the bailey bank is cut across at one point by a further bank and ditch almost to the ring-work counterscarp. Excavation in 1878 showed that the ditches were V-shaped, cut in solid chalk to an angle of 45° without revetment. A well within the ring-work had footholds on opposite sides spiralling downward (one containing an iron piton) to a depth of 84 ft at least; a similar pit nearby was 16 ft deep, and contained an almost complete cooking-pot 'with the entire bones of a fowl', and an iron arrow-head (London Museum Type 1). Other excavations within the ring-work produced a penny of Stephen. Chalk fragments including a carved man's head, a font (?) with Romanesque arcading and a pinnacle with an upper quernstone and a tubular padlock were found in the occupation level at the back of the ring-bank. Wheel-made pottery (chiefly hard red sandy coarse ware with large grains) was found in most of the trenches excavated, some having a green glaze. Metal finds included knives, lozenge-shaped bolt-heads, 'fiddlekey' nails and sinuous-edged horseshoes, with ornamental bronze strip. A rubble wall was found in 1949 on the south side of the eastern causeway across the ring-work ditch.

The removal of the priory church from the *castello de Folkestan* to a new site *extra castellum* is mentioned in 1137 (*Monasticon* IV, 673). This may refer to the built-up Bayle site immediately east of the parish church (TR 230359) on a sharp headland overlooking the harbour. (*Archaeologia* 47, pp. 429–65; also notes in Folkestone Public Library).*

FONMON   ST 048682   Glamorgan

A rectangular building 45 ft long and high by 25 ft wide externally with 5 ft thick walls is plastered over and encased in later work. Even if Norman it may have been a hall rather than a castle (*Country Life*, 18 March 1949, pp. 606–9).*

FORDHAM   Cambridgeshire

Fortified during the rebellion of the Earl of Essex 1143–4 (*Liber Eliensis*, p. 328). For the castles built by Stephen in opposition, see Burwell.

FORE   N 5270   Westmeath

Motte and bailey (IBb2) garrisoned in 1211–12 (*Irish Pipe Roll*).

FORFAR   Angus

The *vetus castellum* is mentioned before 1200 (*Liber Cartarum Prioratus Sancti Andree in Scotia*, p. 354, cited by Barrow; *Regesta Regum Scottorum* I, p. 48, n. 4).

FORRES   NJ 034587   Morayshire

Motte (B) south-west of church. A plan of 1798 (reproduced in Mackenzie *The Medieval Castle in Scotland*, plate III) shows a seven-sided shell-wall round the summit, with angle pilaster buttresses.

GAZETTEER

FOTHERET ONOLAN   see CASTLEMORE, TULLOW

FOTHERINGAY   TL 062930   Northamptonshire

Motte and bailey on north bank of River Nene (IBd2) with traces of a concentric enclosure (except to the south). First mentioned in 1212 when Earl David was ordered to surrender it to the king; it was finally given up in 1215 (*Patent Roll*; *Close Rolls*).

FRAMLINGHAM   TM 286637   Suffolk

Motte and bailey (IBc3) on south bank of River Ore, in east angle of town ditch. The earthworks are extensive ditches, apart from the banks of the Lower Court, and the stream was dammed to provide water defences to the west. Excavations have shown that a castle was thrown up over a Saxon burial ground and there may have been a Saxon fortress here, as tradition asserts (*Proceedings of the Suffolk Institute of Archaeology* XXVII, pp. 65–88).

The east wall of the original hall survives, built into the later curtain. It had two floors, the upper resting on beams, each having a fireplace and chimney-stack, one of which retains its smoke vents. The upper floor had two round-headed windows with moulded rear arches, extended through the later curtain, which overlapped the first roof. To the south, the impression of the east wall of a chapel remains, with central and flanking pilaster buttresses. The round-headed east window has flanking recesses and the rebuilt gable is high-pitched and the wall above ornamented with an arcade of round-headed arches of two sizes. The curtain runs south to a hollow angle tower, its projecting angle cut off with a solid rectangular tower to either side. Beyond this second one is a hollow tower and then the rectangular gatehouse astride the curtain; this has two inner triangular arches with joggled lintels, enclosing the portcullis slot. The upper floor (of timber) was reached by an external stair and had a latrine passage. The three lengths of walling between the gatehouse and angle tower have embrasures with twin arrow-loops – the first three with round rear arches, the other two pairs with timber lintels. The rest of the circuit between the gatehouse and north end of the first hall has seven hollow rectangular towers; that immediately next to the gatehouse is a latrine block (also in the curtain beyond) and between the next two towers are two walls roughly bonded into the curtain and linking it to a square tower on the bank of the Lower Court. This tower has only a loop at ground level, but the floors above are linked by a spiral stair, and a door with bar-hole leads to the wall-walk of the northern spur wall, with a similar ground-floor door in the southern wall, overlooked by two arrowslits in the north wall, from which a timber stair rose to another similar door in the inner curtain wall. There is a shallow tower with a spiral stair blocking the other junction of Lower Court bank and curtain.

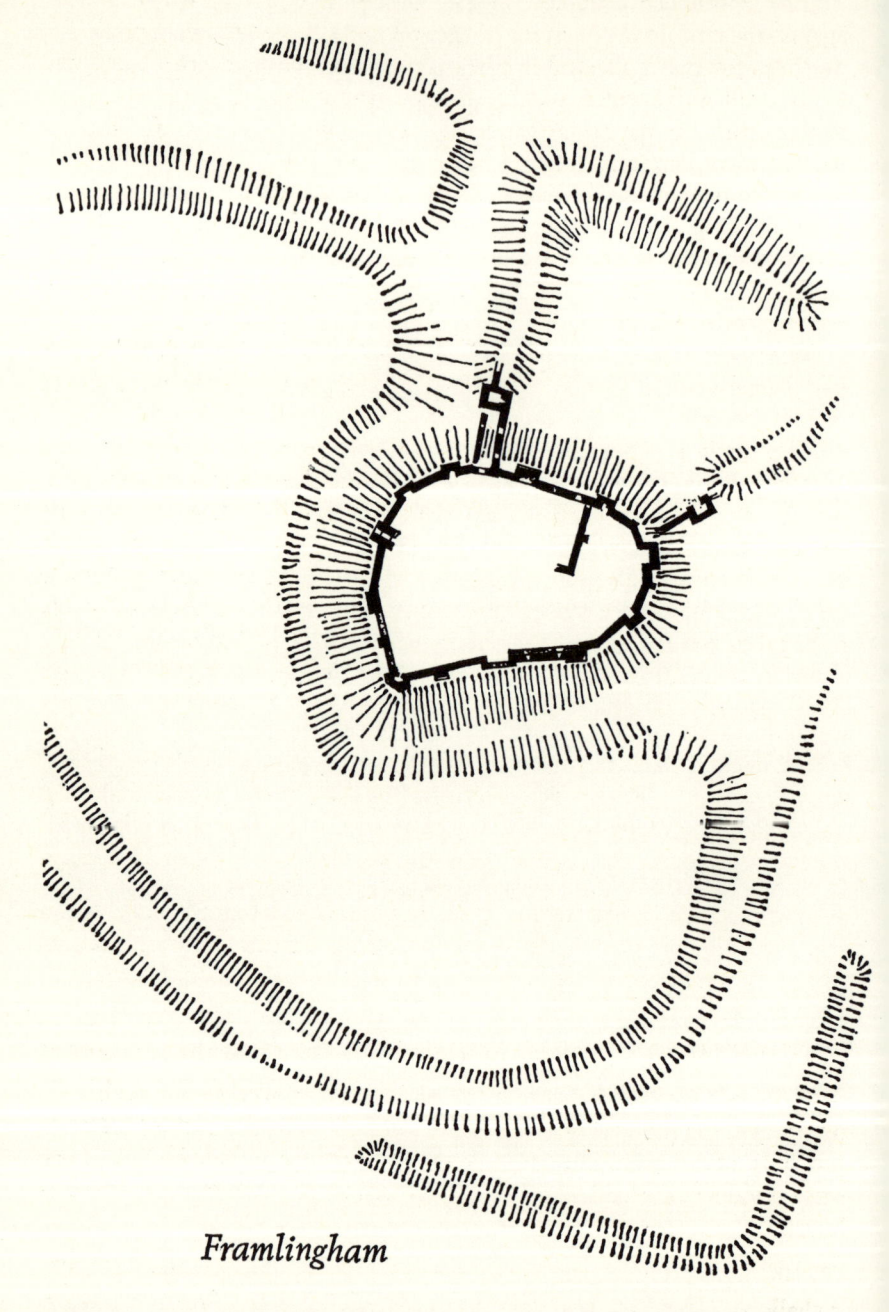

Framlingham

The Poorhouse occupies the site of the second hall which abutted against the curtain to the north of the spurwork, between two towers. The northern tower has a round-headed window and the southern a spiral stair to the wall-walk, which passed through round-headed doorways in the towers, with timber bridges over the hollow backs. The merlons of the parapet have long arrowslits. The second hall has a row of four round-headed embrasures in the curtain, three being windows and the southernmost opening on to a wall-stair leading to the spiral stair already mentioned. Part of the north wall of the solar block survives, with the jambs of a doorway and a loop in the wall below — the east wall is reduced to foundations.

The tower immediately north of the first hall is skewed to avoid it, with two barrel-vaulted floors. The flints and septaria rubble walling had clunch dressings.

The castle was surrendered to the Crown in 1157 (*Torigny*, p. 193; Matthew Paris, *Chronica Majora* II, p. 214) and again in 1173 (*Diceto* I, pp. 377–85; *Hoveden* II, p. 54) and demolished (*Gesta Henrici Secundi* I pp. 48, 127; the *Pipe Roll* accounts for 1173–6 make reference to the *prosternendum* and also *ad perequandum fossatum eiusdem castelli*) but the castle was bought back by Bigod in 1189 (*Foedera* I, p. 49; *Pipe Roll*) only to be taken and garrisoned by John in 1216 (*Rot. Litt. Claus.* I, pp. 254–; *Rot. Litt. Pat.* I, p. 169) (*Proceedings of the Suffolk Institute of Archaeology* XXV, pp. 127–48; M.P.B.W. *Official Guide*).*   (Plate XVII; Fig. 34)

FRAMPTON　　　　　　TA 327391　　　　　　Lincolnshire

Square moat south of village, perhaps the site of the castle mentioned in 1216 (*Rot. Lit. Pat.* 167).

FRAOCH EILEAN　　　　NN 108252　　　　　　Argyll

A long rectangular hall in this castle has a very thick north wall, with a straight wall-stair in its thickness and pilaster buttresses rising from its plinth. (*Transactions of the Glasgow Archaeological Society* new series, XV, pp. 111–28.)

FRODSHAM　　　　　　SJ 518776　　　　　　Cheshire

The Bucks's engraving (reproduced in Ormerod's *History of Cheshire* II, opposite p. 52) shows a long narrow hall with semicircular headed windows probably of Norman date, like that at Halton (q.v.). Foundations of the early buildings are said to survive in the cellars of the eighteenth-century house.

FROME　　　　　　　SO 670458　　　　　　Herefordshire

Motte with traces of bailey (Bd3?) in existence soon after 1162 (*Herefordshire Domesday* (Balliol MS. 350), p. 44).

FUTEPOI   see SKREEN

GAINS   see ASHLEY

GAINSBOROUGH   Lincolnshire

Castle confirmed to the Earl of Lincoln in 1146 (*Regesta Regum Anglo-Normannorum* III, 494).

Moor (*History of Gainsburgh*, p. 61–2) recites this charter and cites Caskgate Street and the Castlestede of an *inquisito post mortem* of 1327. The *motte* and bailey at Thonock (*Archaeological News Letter* I, 8, p. 15) is a possible site (SK 818917) (Ca2).

GAITTECASTELLUM   see page 354

GALCLINT   see RUSHTON

GALTRIM   N 7949   Meath

Motte and bailey (IIBf3) in grounds of Galtrim House, abandoned in 1176 (*English Historical Review* XXII, pp. 233–4); but garrisoned in 1211–12 (*Irish Pipe Roll*).

GANNOCK   see DEGANWY

GARN FADRUN   SH 278352   Caernarvonshire

Stone walling enclosing an irregular wedge on the summit of the hill-fort is very regular in plan, and probably represents the castle, mentioned as new in 1188 by Giraldus Cambrensis (*Opera* VI, 123 (R.C.A.M. *Caernarvonshire* III, p. 69–71).*

GAUSA   see GOXHILL

GEASHILL   N 4322   Offaly

An earthwork enclosure south of the village may be the castle mentioned in 1201 (*Calendar of Documents* I, p. 30).

GEISIL   see GEASHILL

GELLIGAER   see CADWALLON

GLASBURY   see page 354

GLASTONBURY   see page 355

GLOUCESTER   SO 828185   Gloucestershire

Site of castle beside River Severn south-east of cathedral, destroyed in

1791. It is mentioned in 'Domesday Book' (I, 162) and the king's tower was in existence by 1105 (*Regesta Regum Anglo-Normannorum* II, 706).

From accounts in the Pipe Rolls £7 was spent on 'the works of the tower of Gloucester' in 1129–30 and £20 in 1158–9 *in operatione frame turris de Gloucestria*. £98 was spent on the castle in 1172–4 and extensive repairs to walls in 1180–90 (including a tower over the gateway and the bridge, 1184–5). The keep was derelict after the siege of 1263 for over a century, but a fourteenth century sketch (B.M. *MS. Royal* 13A iii f. 82, reproduced in *The History of the King's Works* II, p. 655) shows a crenellated three-storey tower (probably square) with angle turrets rising above the main walls.

GODARD'S (THORNHAM) TQ 808582   Kent

Oval ring-work with small square bailey to the west (ICd4) occupying spur of North Downs north-east of church. Remains of flint rubble curtain wall to north and west sides of bailey, the angle being marked by a wide clasping buttress. In the north wall are the remains of a rectangular gatehouse with traces of three bays of vaulting.

A Cumbwell Priory charter of *c*. 1215–19 (quoted in *Archaeologia Cantiana* V, p. 215) mentions land *inter muros castri de Thorneham et Beyngbi*. (Fig. 33)

GODSHILL   see DOWNTON   Hampshire

GOODRICH   SO 577200   Herefordshire

The fine Edwardian castle above the River Wye encloses a square keep in sandstone ashlar, with slight mid-wall and clasping pilaster buttresses rising from a sloping plinth. A doorway (now converted into a window) at first-floor level has a round head of two square orders, the outer with jamb-shafts with scalloped capitals and moulded bases. The upper floor is marked externally by a chevron-ornamented string-course, at which level the mid-wall buttresses stop. The floor was reached by a spiral stair in the north-west angle, being lit by windows in the north and west walls resembling externally the doorway below, but having an inner order with chevron-ornamented jambs and a shafted mullion separating the two lights. Some traces survive of a curtain wall predating the mainbuilding (see foundations within the south-west tower, and details of the east curtain).

Godric's castle is mentioned *temp*. William I (?), in 1101–2 and 1146 (Round, *Calendar of Documents preserved in France*, I, nos. 1133, 1136 and 1126) and may take its name from Godric Mappestone, the 'Domesday' tenant of *Hulle* near by. It also occurs in the Pipe Roll for 1178 (M.P.B.W. *Official Guide*).* (Plate XVII; Fig. 35)

GOREY see MONT ORGUEIL

GOXHILL   Lincolnshire

A charter of William, Earl of Lincoln (before 1148) mentions the gift of the *capitalis curia* where Peter of Goxhill's castle was. (*Facsimiles of royal charters in the British Museum* 24). Possibly the *motte* and bailey (Bc3) at Barrow End (TA 065225) which is mentioned later in the twelfth century as is a castle at Barton (*Monasticon* I, p. 631; VI, p. 327) or on the site of Newhouse Abbey (TA 128132).

GRANARD   N 3382   Longford

Motte and bailey (Ac3), built in 1199 (*Annals of Innisfallen; Annals of the Four Masters; Song of Dermot; Calendar of Documents* I, 95). Vaulted rooms of square mortared masonry are said to have been found within the *motte* (O'Donovan's edition of *Annals of the Four Masters* p. 1262, n.o.) and there are traces of a round keep and curtain wall on the *motte*-top.

GREAT . . . see under second name

GREENAN see page 355

GRIFFINI see KNOCKTOPHER

GRIMSBY   Lincolnshire

Most of the £80 allocated to build a castle here in 1200 was not spent, and in 1214 the stone and lime stocks were sold off (*Pipe Rolls; Rot. de Oblatis et Finibus*, p. 107).

GROBY   SK 524076   Leicestershire

Excavation of the quarried mound in 1962 showed that it was thrown up over a rubble-walled building (the walls butted together) with stairs leading up to an entrance doorway. There was a 50-ft wide ditch round the *motte* (*Medieval Archaeology* VIII, p. 255). The castle was destroyed in 1176 (*Diceto* I, 404; *Gesta Henrici Secundi* I, 126).

GROSMONT   SO 405244   Monmouthshire

D-shaped mound (II B) with traces of outwork protecting entrance bridge to south. Long hall on west side, of coursed sandstone rubble with a sloping plinth and pilaster buttresses clasping the eastern angles and in the centre of the north and south walls, with another near the south end of the eastern wall supporting a fireplace internally. The western angles have ashlar quoins, vertically tooled, and loose early thirteenth-century mouldings were found within. The hall is entered by a pair of doorways in the centre of the west wall, with a fireplace in the south wall, rising as a straight chimney. The hall is lit by long thin loops (one in the north wall, two in the south walls and four to east and west); the upper floor has a similar layout of lancet windows with segmental-headed embrasures, being reached by an outside stair against the west wall; the floors are linked by a spiral stair in the south-east corner.

The castle was in existence by 1154 (*Regesta Regum Anglo-Normanorum* III, 314). (M.P.B.W. *Official Guide*).* (Fig. 35)

GUIDDGRUG   see MOLD

GROTON   see LELESHAY

GUILDFORD   SU 997494   Surrey

Motte with traces of bailey (Bc2 ?) south of ditch with thick clunch wall found 30 yds south of the High Street. The *motte*-top carries part of polygonal shell-wall in clunch and a square keep, built down the eastern slope, with the springing of the entrance beside the latter.

The keep is of Bargate rubble slabs with scappled flints and chalk forming a sequence of courses (*Surrey Archaeological Collections* LV, p. 4). There are pilaster buttresses in the centre and end of each wall, the angle buttresses being carried above the wall-head, particularly above the spiral stair at the north-west angle. The ashlar plinth is modern. The basement has a steeply sloping round-headed loop in the north and south walls, and the modern stair is on a rubble base including a re-used Norman capital. Excavations revealed an internal offset 18–24 in. wide except to the east where the shell wall foundation was used (*Surrey Archaeological Collections* XVI, pp. 32–3). The entrance is by a pointed arch of two orders in the centre of the west wall, the outer order carrying a buttress on corbels. The rubble barrel-vaulted passage has ashlar sides with a bar-hole. Beam-holes remain for a landing outside, the threshold being the cut-off buttress. The south-west angle contains an L-shaped chamber with a barrel-vault, with an arcade on the outer sides of round-headed arches with carved scalloped and palmette capitals and shafts, lit by loops and entered by a doorway (formerly round-headed). There are other mural chambers in the north part of the west wall and the east part of the north wall, the latter altered for the insertion of a round-backed fireplace venting at the pilaster angles. There are two-light windows (with round heads with a solid tympanum under a round-headed arch and a stepped embrasure) in the centre of the east wall pilaster and the north and south walls. The floor above rested on an internal offset and is lit by a (restored) two-light window in the centre pilaster of each wall (apart from that to the north,

Goodrich

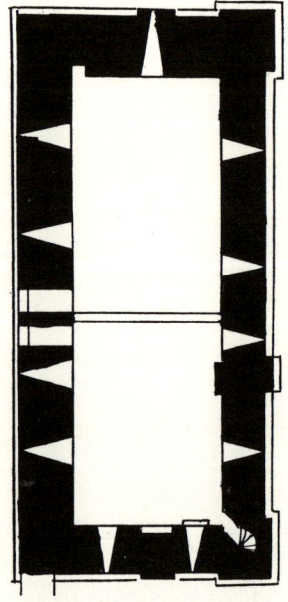
Grosmont

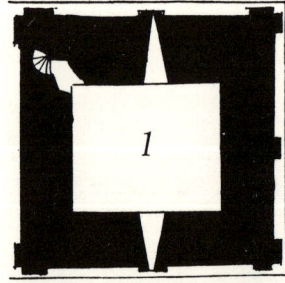

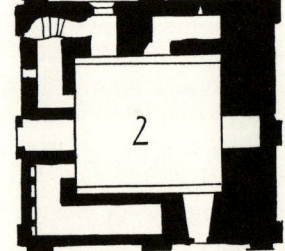

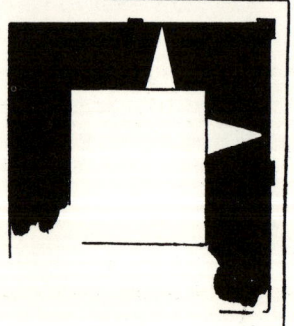
Kenfig

Guildford

35

offset for another central fireplace). Mural passages lead to the spiral stair and a corbelled-out latrine shaft in the east end of the south wall.

Among the walls south-west of the *motte* is one with a round-headed loop in a wide embrasure. The castle was put in a state of defence in 1173–4 and repaired in 1181–2 and later (*Pipe Rolls*) (V.C.H. *Surrey* III, pp. 554–60).* (Plate XVIII; Fig. 35)

HADDON   SK 235664   Derbyshire

In 1195 Richard Vernon obtained a licence to surround his house with a wall 12 ft high. (Historical Manuscripts Commission, *MSS. of the Duke of Rutland* IV, p. 24).

HAGANET   see HAUGHLEY

HAILES   Gloucestershire

Ralph of Gloucester fortified a castle and built a church here 'when war was violently raging' (i.e. 1139–48) (*Lanaboc . . . de Winchelcumba* I, 65). There is a square moat south of Hailes Green Farm (SO 048299), but the site was probably close to the existing twelfth century church (SO 050301) and destroyed when the abbey was founded in 1246.

HALSTEADS (WHARTON)   SD 516726   Lancashire

Much altered *motte* and bailey (Bc2 ?) with retaining walls, perhaps the castle of *Morhull* surrendered in 1216 (*Proceedings of the Society of Antiquaries of London*, Second series XXI, pp. 413–9; Farrer, *Lancs. Pipe Rolls and Early Charters*, p. 258, n. 1; *Calendar of Charter Rolls*, p. 221).

HALTON   SJ 539821   Cheshire

The Bucks' engraving shows a long narrow hall with semicircular headed windows which supports Ormerod's dating the foundation of the castle to the reign of Henry II (*History of Cheshire* I, p. 111; plate opposite p. 688); the capital from the site with a necking row of upright leaves (*Transactions of the Chester Archaeological Society* Vol. II, frontispiece) looks Romanesque. Perhaps the *Haiton* of 1151–7 (Round, *Calendar of Documents preserved in France*, 412).

HAM   see HOM(M)E

HAMPSTEAD MARSHALL   Berkshire

Motte and bailey (Ae2) with another mound (B) nearby (SO 421669) and a third (ring-bank enclosing what appears to be an unfinished *motte*) half a mile away (SO 430666). These are documentary references of 1227–34 (*Close Rolls*), but pottery (*Berkshire Archaeological Journal* 44, pp. 72–5) suggest that occupation may have commenced in the twelfth century. (*Transactions of the Newbury District Field Club* VI, pp. 114–26).

HANLEY   SO 838414   Worcestershire

Oblong moated site (probably altered) built in 1207–12 at a cost of nearly £750 (*Pipe Rolls*; *Rot. Misae*; *Rot. Litt. Claus.* I, 211b; *Rot. Litt. Pat.* 162).

HANSLOPE   SP 798446   Buckinghamshire

Ring-work partly scarped into a *motte* adjoining church (C or Ba2 ?); the earthworks further south and west are probably remodelling after the 1292 licence to crenellate. The castle was captured in 1215 (Matthew Paris, *Chronica Majora* II, 638). (Fig. 37)

HARBOTTLE   NT 933048   Northumberland

Motte and bailey (Bb3) on bank of River Coquet. The western half of the bailey was walled, and a square gatehouse and tower at the north angle can be traced. Some of the foundations on the *motte*-top, (overlaid by later walling) may belong to a rectangular keep, and a fallen mass of masonry in the ditch has a chamfered plinth about 8 ft high.

The castle was built about 1157 on the orders of Henry II (*Letters of Henry III*, 1, p. 141) and mentioned in 1174 (*Gesta Henrici Secundi*, p. 64) (*History of the Berwickshire Naturalists' Club* XXVIII, pp. 215–31).*

HARPTREE   ST 562556   Somerset

Fragments of a masonry wall in a wood south-west of East Harptree Church. The castle was captured in 1138 by a feint attack elsewhere, after a siege-castle was to have been built in front of it (*Gesta Stephani*, pp. 43–6), but retaken in 1140 (William of Malmesbury, *Historia Novella*, p. 42).

HARTLAND   see page 355

HARTSHILL   SP 324944   Warwickshire

Irregular pentagonal curtain wall of granite with sandstone quoins south of *motte* (Bf3?). The splayed plinth of the chapel has a roll-moulding at the top. Perhaps in existence by 1148–53 when Hartshill was one of the boundaries of the 'demilitarised zone' (see p. 52). (*Transactions Birmingham Archaeological Society* 53, pp. 206–10).

HASTINGS   TQ 820095   Sussex

The earthworks of this site, largely destroyed by the sea, are complex. The surviving inner enclosure is triangular, with a steep fall to the north-west and a broad ditch separating it from a square outer enclosure to the north-east, which has a bank cutting off an inner triangular area. At the junction of these is an oval mound occupying the north angle of the inner enclosure without a separate ditch (IAc2).

The rubble curtain wall appears to be partly of early date, since the northern of the two western towers of the Norman church blocks a loophole through it, and there is herringbone coursing nearby.

The thick wall crossing the *motte*-top is based on a foundation of slabs following the contour of the surface, and an inner *motte* of sand containing an early Norman potsherd was revealed in 1968; a mortar layer found near the south-east angle may have been the site of the keep (Dawson, *History of Hastings Castle*, pp. 523-5.)

Several writers state that William built a castle at Hastings before the battle of 1066 (*Anglo-Saxon Chronicle*; *Henry of Huntingdon*, p. 200; the *Chronicon Monasterii de Bello* (p. 3) specifically refers to it as *ligneum* and the Bayeux Tapestry shows men digging and shovelling earth on to a mound through which a palisade protrudes). There are however some grounds for thinking that the first castle may have been sited elsewhere, either further east (around TQ 829098) or beyond the Priory Valley (around TQ 815095) the better to protect the ships. (*English Historical Review* LXXI, pp. 61-9; *Sussex Archaeological Collections* LVII, pp. 119-35). The present castle was often in the hands of the Crown, after being held by Robert, count of Eu between 1069 and 1088. Small sums were spent in 1160-1 and 1170-4 (less than £100, so that the stone keep mentioned could hardly have been begun then) and a further £100 in 1181-3. John had the castle demolished in 1216 (*Annales Monastici* III, p. 46) V.C.H. *Sussex* IX, pp. 14-19.*

| HAUGHLEY | TM 024626 | Suffolk |

Motte and bailey (Ad3) with traces of outer enclosure. The castle was seized by the Crown in 1163 and destroyed in 1173 (*Pipe Rolls*; *Gesta Henrici Secundi* I, p. 60; *Diceto* I, p. 377).

| HAVERFORDWEST | SM 953157 | Pembrokeshire |

Nothing appears to survive of the castle mentioned by Giraldus Cambrensis (*Opera* V, p. 288) in 1172. (See also *Rot. de Oblatis et Finibus*, pp. 499, 522).

| HAWARDEN | SJ 319653 | Flintshire |

Motte and bailey (Bb1) with round keep, hall and elaborate barbican of thirteenth or fourteenth century date, later than the attack of 1205 (*Pipe Roll*).

| HAWICK | NT 499140 | Roxburghshire |

Motte (B) on spur between Rivers Teviot and Slitrig. Excavations revealed a small flat-bottomed ditch, on the bottom of which was found a short-cross penny of the first issue of Henry II (*Proceedings of the Society of Antiquaries of Scotland* XLVIII, pp. 18-24).

HAY   Brecknockshire

The castle of 1121 (Pipe Roll Soc. *Ancient Charters*, p. 8) destroyed in 1216 (*Brut y Tywysogion*) might be the type B *motte* near the church (SO 226422) or the type C ring-work underlying the masonry at SO 229423. A square tower of coursed rubble beside the entrance has been much altered, but the inner face has a round-headed window (of two lights with a solid tympanum; the mullion has gone) at first floor level.

HEDINGHAM   TL 787359   Essex

Large ring-work (with 'wishbone' counterscarp banks) and bailey (ICf4). Rectangular keep in the middle of area, of oolite ashlar with a splayed plinth chamfered at the top. The shallow central wall pilasters die into the plinth, but those at the angles have a recessed angle and are broader, splaying out in a separate plane from the main walls. A straight stair along the west wall gives access to the forebuilding; of this the flint rubble base remains with traces of a gate at the foot of the stairway and of roofs of various dates in creasings in the keep wall. The round-headed entrance is of two orders: the internal one plain, the outer with a double chevron head and scalloped capitals and beaded abaci to the jamb shafts. There are slots for a portcullis and drawbar, and internal angle-shafts. An adjoining spiral stair in the angle leads down to the basement, lit by two loops in each wall, with round-headed rear arches. This plan is repeated in the upper floors, but the embrasures are square in plan, with roll-moulded heads and cushion capitals to the shafted jambs. Side chambers lead from them and the window openings are more ornamental and open from the angle turrets as well. On the entrance floor they have roll-moulded heads and chamfered capitals to the half column supports. The gallery windows are of two lights with roll-mouldings, scalloped capitals and beaded bases to the half-columns and those in the garret below the present roof have chevron and roll ornament. There are round-headed fireplaces in the east wall on each floor above the basement with short flues to the wall face. The top one has a square back and is plain, but the round-backed ones below have chevron decoration round the head, supported on engaged columns with billet (entrance floor) or scalloped (above) ornament to the capitals. The entrance floor is spanned by a plain arch to carry the next floor which has two levels, being spanned by a roll-moulded arch supported by scalloped capitals on multiple half-columns. There are angle-shafts to support the wall-plates of an earlier ceiling. The upper level has a continuous barrel-vaulted gallery in the wall, with a spiral bead moulding on the engaged shafts of the doorway. A chamfered roof corbel suggests that the garret above (rubble-faced, unlike the rest of the keep) may be an alteration, although the stair rises through it to a corner turret with another at the opposite corner.

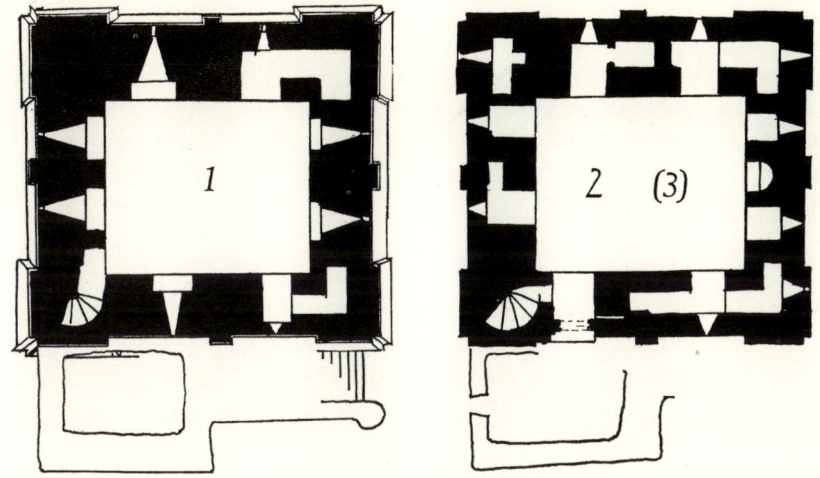

Hedingham

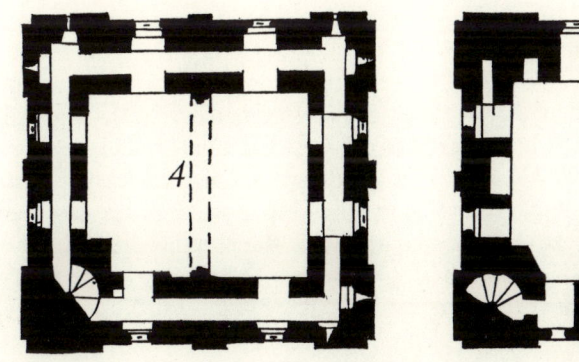

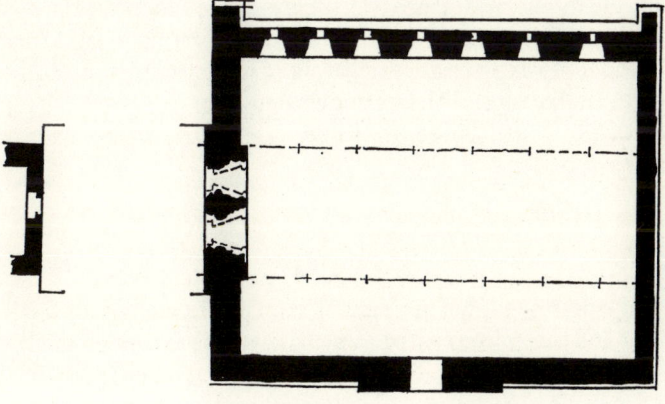

Leicester

36

The great hall stood south-west of the keep on a vaulted basement; traces of a chapel immediately south of the keep have been excavated, but all is now covered over again. Stephen's queen died in the castle in 1151 (Matthew Paris, *Chronica Majora* II, 188). (R.C.H.M. *Essex* I, pp. 51–7).*

(Plate XIX, Fig. 36)

HELGOT see STANTON

HELMSLEY   SE 611837   Yorkshire

Quadrilateral enclosure with double ditch, tapering toward the south-east where the outer ditch branched around a rectangular bailey (IICd4); a branch running north may have enclosed another. The enclosure has a curtain wall of coursed rubble, with round towers at the angles, except that at the east where there is a square gatehouse with portcullis-slot and chamfered jambs in the outer arch (see Newark). The west curtain runs north-west from the outer, and south-east from the inner wall of a square tower largely rebuilt, but with a ribbed barrel-vault and lancet over the north-east doorway. The north-west angle tower has a square interior and a sloping plinth continuing south-east; the north-east angle tower is seven-sided within, and has an external bulge with a loop. The curtain between these towers has a doorway with portcullis-slot flanked by half-round towers entered from the bailey; that to the west has a half-round interior, but the other is semi-hexagonal. In the north part of the north-east curtain are three narrow loops, beyond which is the keep, apsidal to the east but rectangular to the west, later raised to twice the original height. The original work is greyish-white limestone rubble with galleting of the joints and yellow ashlar quoins; the irregular lay-out suggests that the apse may be a modification of the original plan. A spiral stair in the west angle links all floors, and there are round-headed doorways into the basement from the north berm and the bailey. Originally the basement had a vault from a central pillar, and was lit by two square-headed loops in the south-west wall: above them are three lancet windows at first floor level (reached by round-headed doors from the wall-walk of the curtain) and another lancet above in the gable roof, with interior corbels.

The castle is attributed to Robert de Roos (1186–1227: *Rievaulx Chartulary*, p. 360).   Fig. 33

HELY see HYMEL

HEREFORD   SO 512396   Herefordshire

Motte (now destroyed, but see plan of 1677 in *Transactions of the Woolhope Field Club* 1883–5, p. 162) with strong bailey bank except on the River Wye side.

This may be the *aene castel* in Herefordshire in 1051 (*Anglo-Saxon*

Chronicle). Repairs to the houses *in mota* were paid for in 1165 and 1169, and the walls partly rebuilt in 1181–2. Brattices were erected in 1173–4 and a small tower built in 1202–3 (*Pipe Rolls*). The town was walled in 1189 (*Report of the Historical Monuments Commission* 13 App., part 4, p. 204).

HEREFORD SIEGE-WORK   SO 508398   Herefordshire

In the siege of 1140, an earthwork was built in the cemetery and catapults and arrows were shot from the cathedral tower (*Gesta Stephani*, pp. 72–3). The wall and ditch containing Saxo-Norman pottery found west of the cathedral might be associated with this (*Transactions of the Woolhope Field Club* XXXVI, pp. 117–25).

HEREFORDSHIRE BEACON   SO 760400   Herefordshire

On top of one of the Malvern Hills, the main plateau has a surrounding bank and ditch with counterscarp; an inner bank and ditch cuts off the slopes of the highest part of the hill-top, on which the oval ring-work stands, with traces of an outer bank and ditch in front of the south entrance. Excavated in 1897; the pottery from the bank (in the Hereford Museum; see R.C.H.M. *Herefordshire* III, pp. xlvii–xlviii) is now regarded as twelfth century (*Antiquaries' Journal* XXXIX, p. 241, n. 1), as is the ring-work (*Archaeological Journal* CIX, pp. 146–8) (*Journal of the Royal Anthropological Institute* X, pp. 319–31; *Antiquity* XXXIX, pl. XLI).*

HERTFORD   TL 325125   Hertfordshire

Motte and bailey (Af3) beside river. A few boulders *may* mark the foundations of a round tower about 30 ft across crowning the small *motte*. The ditches have been largely filled in, but the eastern limits of the bailey are marked by three lengths of flint rubble walling 7 ft thick, patched with bricks and worked stone; the first length runs eastward down the slope of the *motte* and is broken through for the entrance path on the site of an original entrance, then turns south-eastward to an angle bastion (destroyed) where the wall turns through 90° as far as a late medieval octagonal turret. The western curtain has gone, but a mass of flint rubble forming part of the foundation of the gatehouse (of 1463–5) may be part of it.

Peter of Valognes was appointed constable of the castle by William I and the post became almost hereditary – his son Roger was confirmed in the appointment in 1141 (*Cartae Antiquae*, p. 144). £191 was spent on the castle works in 1171–4 and the castle was garrisoned in 1173–4. Repairs were carried out in 1183–4, 1194–6, and 1198–9, and work costing £36:10s. was done in 1190–1. In 1236–7 the 'tower that is covered in lead' was unroofed and the lead and timber stored (*Pipe Rolls*); it is not clear where this tower stood, nor whether the whole tower or merely the roof timbers were taken down, but the context suggests an old work (H. C. Andrews, *The Chronicles of Hertford Castle*, Hertford, 1947).*

HINCHLEDER   see INCHELFYRE

HINCKLEY   SP 428935   Leicestershire

Ring-work (IIC) in garden east of church, perhaps in existence by 1148–53 as Hinckley was one of the points limiting the 'demilitarised zone' (see p. 52).

HINNEKESTI   see ASKEATON

HINTON WALDRIST   SU 376991   Berkshire

Conical *motte* outside banked enclosure (Ae4) produced eleventh century pottery on excavation. The *motte* of sandy clay had been built over a channel and pit cut in the original ground surface (*Berkshire Archaeological Journal* 44, pp. 49–60).

HOLGATE   see STANTON

HOLYWELL   SJ 186762   Flintshire

Small *motte* above church with ditch cutting off spur as bailey (Ac2). Built in 1210 (*Brut y Tywysogion; Pipe Roll*).

HOM(M)E   SO 713618   Worcestershire

Motte and bailey (IBd3) beside stream, mentioned in 1207 (*Rot. Litt. Pat.* 73b).

HOOD see page 355

HORNBY   SD 583698   Lancashire

Motte and bailey (Ab3) overlooking bridge across River Lune. This (rather than the later castle) is probably that seized from Roger de Montbegon III by John in 1205 but returned three months later (*Close Rolls* I, 16, 22; *Patent Rolls* I, 486); probably also the *Orneby* of 1200 (*Rot. de Oblatis et Finibus*, p. 275).

HORNCASTLE   TF 260696   Lincolnshire

The castle was said to have been demolished in a charter of 1146 (Dugdale, *Baronage* I, 39; *Registrum Antiquissimum of Lincoln* I, p. 287.) This may be an error for Thorngate (in the same hands), but considerable remains of the Roman wall still survive there. (*Arch. Jl.* CXII, pp. 38–9).

HORSELEAP   see ARDNURCHER

HORSTON   SK 373432   Derbyshire

Site on rocky spur, cut off to north and east by ditch. The ashlar north wall of the keep survives, with a fragment of the west wall, showing a sloping plinth and corner towers, together with a square mural chamber. Excavation in 1852 and later produced fragments of beams, a small bell, a boar's tusk and a pair of antlers. The outer face of the keep had been partly covered with loose stones grouted with mortar. Many moulded ashlars were built into the old park wall, and a capital in the form of a wolf's head swallowing the column is recorded (*Journal of the Derbyshire Archaeological and Natural History Society* X, pp. 16–27).

Hugh de Buron (d. 1155–6) was described as 'sometime lord of the castle of Horeston' (*Letters Patent*, 20 March 1337, quoted in *Ibid.*, LIX, p. 5). In 1198 the castle passed to King John in exchange for lands elsewhere, and £700 was spent on it in 1200–3 (*Pipe Rolls*); there is a mention of crenellating the tower in 1205 (*Rot. Litt. Claus.* I, 53).

HOSELEY   see ROFFT

HUGH'S   see LLANDEILO-TALYBONT

HUMPHREY'S   SN 440476   Cardiganshire

Motte (IA) made by ditching off the point of a natural spur. Destroyed in the Welsh rising of 1136, it was rebuilt in 1153 (*Brut y Tywysogion*).

HUNSINGORE   SE 428532   Yorkshire

Square mound (IIB) mentioned *about* 1190 (*Yorkshire Archaeological Journal* 8, p. 298).

HUNTINGDON   TL 241715   Huntingdonshire

Damaged *motte* and bailey on north bank of River Ouse (IBd2) with strong bailey bank at east corner. Scarp marks another rectangular bailey on west side of *motte*. About 400 yds away to the west is a large mound 10 ft high beside the Mill stream, with scarps of an angular enclosure which may link with a bank and ditch beyond the railway.

The castle was built in 1068 (*Ordericus Vitalis* II, 185) and destroyed in 1174 (*Diceto* I, 404). But the *Pipe Roll* also records *in operatione novi castelli de Hunted*, so that the second mound might be a siege-work (R.C.H.M. *Huntingdonshire*, pp. 149–51; 157; 162).*

HURSLEY   see MERDON

HUTTONS AMBO   SE 763674   Yorkshire

Triangular enclosure on spur above River Derwent, enclosing a timber hall with opposed entrances in the short sides. Later the hall was rebuilt in sandstone rubble and extended, with a line of posts to support the roof-ridge. The earthworks were remodelled as a squarish ring-bank with a revetted entrance passage with gateposts, and a causeway across the steep-sided flat-bottomed ditch. A deep cylindrical pit was found at the south angle of the earthwork. The pottery found indicated occupation from 1150 to 1300: metal finds included a bronze pin, an iron knife, horseshoe and arrow-heads (*Archaeological Journal* CXIV, pp. 69–91).

HUTTON CONYERS — Yorkshire

Earthworks on Hutton Moor or north of village (SE 325735), may be the castle of Earl Alan built in 1140 (*Symeon of Durham* II, p. 306) (see also Walbran, *Memorials of Fountains* I, p. 79n.).

HYMEL — SP 973976 — Northamptonshire

Traces of earthworks surrounding site of Fineshade Abbey may be remains of castle demolished at the start of John's reign (*Monasticon* VI, p. 450).

HYWEL see HUMPHREY'S

IAL see TOMEN Y FAERDE

ILBERT'S see PONTEFRACT

INCHCONNELL — NM 976119 — Argyll

Remains of early walling with pilaster buttresses like those at Sween have been found in the later castle (*Discovery and Excavation in Scotland* 1965, p. 7).

'INCHELEFYRE'

Castle of Walter de Lacy in 1215, perhaps at Inchleffer, Meath (*Calendar of Documents* I, 95; 1211–12 *Irish Pipe Roll*) or possibly Cloughouter (q.v.).

INCHIQUIN — X 0176 — Cork

Round keep of limestone rubble with sloping plinth beside River Womanagah. Basement lit by three loops in round-headed embrasures, with a wider splayed arch of entrance to south. A wall stair opens off one jamb and rises to the first floor, which has three (four ?) round-headed windows with side seats and a latrine passage with plank-centred vaulting. The second floor (reached by a spiral stair continuing the wall stair) had a main beam supporting nine cross-beams; little remains except traces of a window and a long low corbelled-out hood (*Journal of the Cork Historical and Archaeological Society* 50, pp. 42–5).* (Fig. 42)

INKBERROW — SP 017573 — Worcestershire

Wood for repairs of the castle was ordered in 1216 (*Rot. Litt. Claus.* I, 280b).

INSULA see OWSTON FERRY

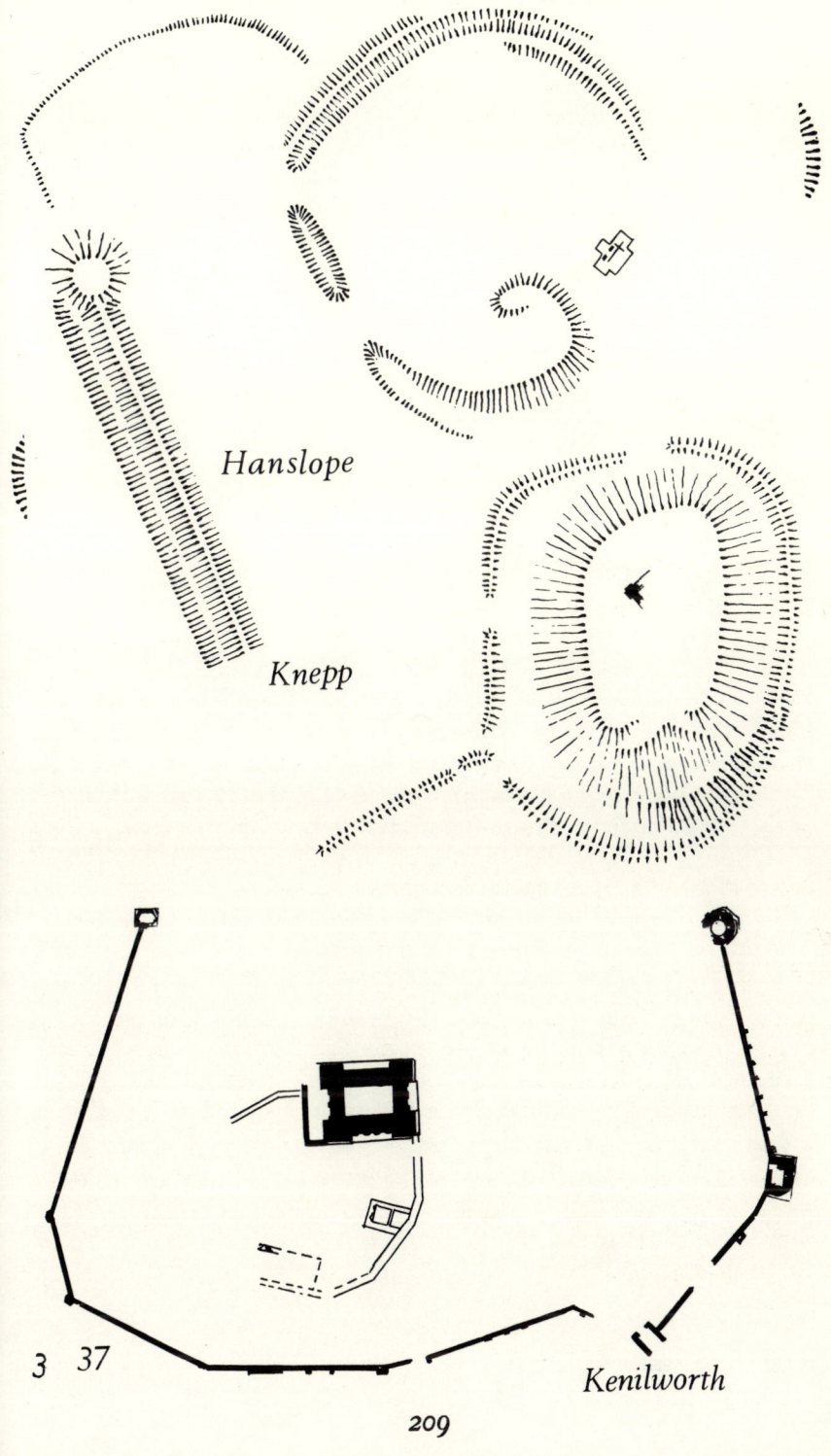

INVERGOWRIE	NO 395307	Angus

Stone castle of King Edgar (d. 1107) (Boece, *Scotorum Historiae Prima Gentis Origine* XII, p. 262), now vanished.

INVERKELLOR see LUNAN BAY

INVERNESS		Inverness-shire

Castle mentioned in 1187 (*Gesta Henrici Secundi* II, pp. 7–9; Fordun, *Gesta Annalia* XVI (1, p. 268).

INVERNOCHTY	NJ 351129	Aberdeenshire

Oval mound with strong counterscarp continuing north as dam at junction of River Don and waters of Bardoch and Nochty. A mortared stone wall 6 ft thick ran round the top of the mound on an irregular foundation, with a short straight south face flanking the entrance gap, with a plinth and an internal square tower. Some remains of a rectangular chapel were found across the north part of the mound with a reused scalloped capital (*Proceedings of the Society of Antiquaries of Scotland* LXX, pp. 170–81).

INVERURIE	NJ 782206	Aberdeenshire

Recut *motte* and traces of bailey (Ab3?) in churchyard, beside River Urie. Remains of an oak gangway or bridge were found on the south side of the *motte* (Davidson, *Bass of Inverurie*, p. 15, quoted by W. M. Mackenzie, *The medieval Castle in Scotland*); a mask-like pottery spout from the castle is recorded in the *Proceedings of the Society of Antiquaries in Scotland* LIII, pp. 46–50. Davidson (*Inverurie*, p. 2) states that the castle was built before 1176 but does not quote his source.

IPSWICH		Suffolk

The site of the castle besieged by Stephen in 1153 (*William of Newburgh*, p. 189) is uncertain: earthworks in the Arboretum grounds or the Mount near St Stephen's church have been suggested. Excavations in Shire Hall yard revealed an eleventh-century boundary ditch about 20 ft wide and 5 ft deep with squared central slot, covered by an 8 ft bank and ditch 20 ft wide and 10 ft deep, constructed in 1204 (*Ipswich Borough Records: Little Domesday*). Further north at Cox Lane a broad U-shaped ditch contained caltrops, mortared stone blocks and Saxo-Norman pottery, apparently defending a single property (*Proceedings of the Suffolk Institute of Archaeology* XXIX, p. 233–303).

IRVINE see page 355

ISABEL see SHRAWARDINE

GAZETTEER

| JEDBURGH | NT 647202 | Roxburghshire |

Motte of castle mentioned in two charters of 1147–52 (Lawrie, *Ancient Scottish Charters*, CLXXXIX, CXC).

JEDWORD   see JEDBURGH

KARAKITEL   see CARRICKLITTLE

KARKAULIS   see CAHERCONLISH

KARKINLIS   see CAHERCONLISH

KARRECH   see CARRICK

KATHERAIN   see COLERAINE

KELBERY   see KILBIXIE

| KELLS | S 4643 | Kilkenny |

A *motte* with a walled bailey (Ab2) remains near the King's river, and is mentioned in a charter of *c.* 1210–20 (quoted in the *Journal of the Royal Society of Antiquaries of Ireland* XXXIX, pp. 327–8; and the *Irish Pipe Roll* of 1211–12).

| KELLS | N 7476 | Meath |

The round and square bell towers of about 1161 (*Monasticon* VI, p. 1141) predate the castle begun and abandoned in 1176 (*Annals of Ulster*; Giraldus Cambrensis, *Opera* V, p. 337).

KELSO   see CULCHET

| KENDAL | SD 523924 | Westmorland |

Ring work with strong counterscarp bank and small outwork on ridge east of town (Cd4). The fragments of curtain wall and towers are of uncertain date, but the Bucks' view (reproduced in the *Transactions of the Cumberland and Westmorland Archaeological Society*, new series VIII, pp. 84–94) suggests that the projecting square tower to the north-east may be Norman, with its several offsets and round-headed windows.

| KENFIG | SS 801827 | Glamorgan |

Motte with large bailey (Bd2) — perhaps a village enclosure — on low-lying ground beside river. An originally free-standing square keep of local Pennant rubble with Sutton ashlar quoins was excavated in 1927; this had small clasping and mid-wall pilaster buttresses with chamfered bases above a sloping plinth. The first floor was supported on an offset and beam-sockets; traces of stucco remained on the inside walls. Later the south wall had been rebuilt only half as thick as before, with a re-entrant angle, loopholes and an entrance cut in the other walls, and a rectangular latrine turret added to the north-west corner. The basement was vaulted and the mound thrown up to cover it, with a revetment wall.

The town was mentioned in 1157, but the earliest reference to the castle is the carriage of wood thence in 1185–6 (*Pipe Roll*) (*Archaeologia Cambrensis*, seventh series, VII, pp. 161–82).* (Fig. 35)

KENILWORTH SP 279723 Warwickshire

The inner enclosure is surrounded by a curtain wall running from the north-west and south-east corners of the keep to enclose a circular area in straight lengths; the setback jamb (with portcullis groove) and springer of an entrance arch remain on the south side of the south-east corner turret of the keep. The keep is of sandstone ashlar, with a vertical-sided base below a chamfered plinth of fourteen offsets, which is returned along the outer faces of the angle turrets at ground level. There are pilaster buttresses at the inner angles of the turrets, and two more on the south side and one central one to the east and west; the north wall has been destroyed. The western pilasters do not rise the full height of the wall, and there is an offset round the others and the turrets. The basement is vaulted but now filled with earth; the north-east turret carries a spiral stair lit by loops in the east angle pilaster; the north-west tower was a latrine block. The south-west tower has two vaulted cells, one above the other, and the well-shaft was at the south end of the east wall; it was reached through a doorway with a tympanum, and at first floor level through the jamb of an altered window. The east wall has a double-splayed loop with round heads in and out; there were probably three in the south wall, now cut back into tall parallel-sided openings. There is a round-headed doorway in the west wall.

The keep was entered at a higher level through a narrow segmental-arched doorway at the south end of the west wall, with a vaulted passage off which a door opens into the south-west turret, with a simple round-headed window in the west wall. The floor was carried on an offset; the rear arches of the windows (round-headed the pairs to east and west; segmental to the south) are original, as may be the two square orders outside the west windows. The low-pitched creasing of the roof can be seen in the east and west walls (joists to south), with a fighting gallery above with steeply sloping square-headed loops above each window and around the south-west turret (two on the outer faces, one on the returns). These loops now have a cross-slit and 'fishtail' bases.

The forebuilding on the west side of the tower is rather awkwardly fitted against it, carrying on part of the plinth. Above the round-headed doorway in the south wall is a square string-course and the jamb of an

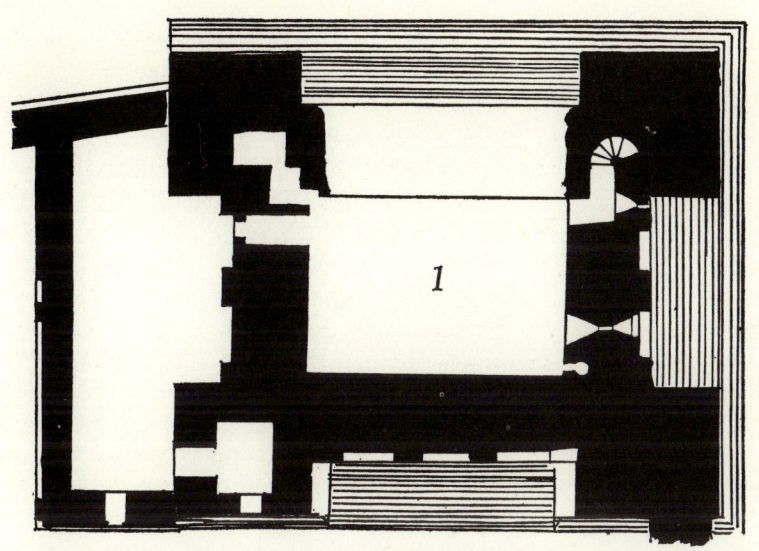

Kenilworth

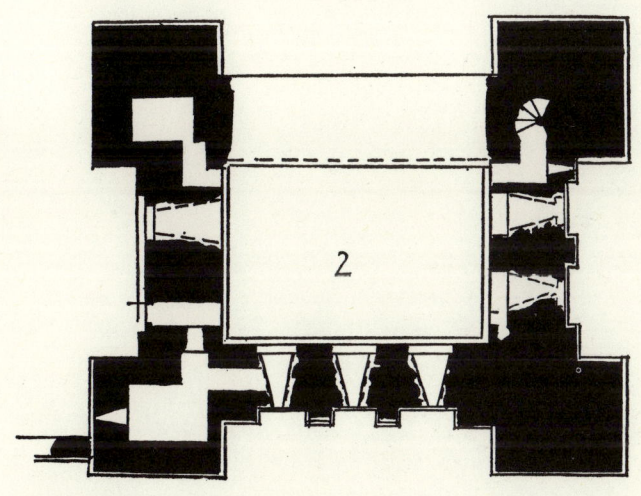

Kirkwall

upper window, with flat beam-holes for a floor and square ones at a higher level for the roof over the entrance stair.

A blocked window in the north angle of the later Great Chamber may date from about 1200, as may the foundation of a two-celled building abutting against the line of the inner curtain south of the entrance. A small Norman font was found in the enclosure (*Archaeological Journal* XI, p. 297), and the Norman capital found in the later chapel in the outer enclosure (Clark, *Medieval Military Architecture* II, p. 141) may have come from here. Excavation to the south of the inner enclosure showed a U-shaped ditch of the twelfth century replaced by a V-shaped one in the early thirteenth; the curtain wall foundation trench produced mid-thirteenth century pottery, and that to the north had a chamfered inner plinth with four offsets (*Transactions of the Birmingham Archaeological Society* 81, pp. 55–73). This outer curtain is much rebuilt, but the section with three round-headed loops and a return wall to the south of the keep looks early, as does the inner part of Mortimer's Tower to the south-east, two parallel walls across the curtain wall with a portcullis slot. The northern towers have early features too: the Swan Tower has a solid square base and octagonal upper floor, and Lunn's Tower has four pilasters rising from a circular sloping plinth, with fantail arrowslits above.

About 1122, Geoffrey de Clinton retained land from a grant to make his castle and park (*Monasticon*, VI, pp. 220–1; *Cal. Charter Rolls* III, p. 275). The castle passed into the hands of the Crown in 1173 (*Archaeological Journal* CX, pp. 120–4) and the keep and other buildings repaired in 1184 and 1190–3; over £1,000 was spent during John's reign, mainly 1210–15 (*Pipe Rolls*). (Plates XX, XXI; Figs. 37, 38)

KIDWELLY SN 409070 Carmarthenshire

Semi-circular ring-work within triangular *burgus* beside river; the hillock in front of the main gatehouse may be the remains of a *motte*. The site may therefore be either (C/2) or (Ba/24?). Excavation showed that the outer curtain wall of the castle stood on an earlier shale bank which faded out on the line of the gate-passage, and was overlaid by a midden containing twelfth century pottery. The (recut) ditch had a sharp V-shaped profile, although the bottom was flat for a width of 5 ft or so. The only masonry earlier than about 1275 was a small Norman capital built into the later hall.

A charter of about 1114 was signed *in domo castelli de Caduelli* (*Monasticon* IV, 65) and the (re-?) building of 1190 by the Lord Rhys was followed by its recovery by the Normans and burning by the Welsh in 1215 (*Brut y Tywysogion*) (*Archaeologia* 83, pp. 93–138).* (Fig. 39)

KILBIXIE N 3162 Westmeath

Motte (B) with traces of shell-wall surrounding a square foundation. Built in 1192 (*Song of Dermot*; *Annals of Loch Cé*).

GAZETTEER

KILBRIDE see page 355

KILDREENAN   O 2525   Dublin

Site of castle beside stream south-west of Killiney church, in existence by 1200 (*Journal of the Royal Society of Antiquaries of Ireland* LXVI, pp. 172-4).

KILFEAKLE   R 9938   Tipperary

Motte and bailey (Ad4) beside church with traces of wall running down *motte* to a small tower in ditch. Built in 1192, destroyed in 1196 but restored in 1203 (*Annals of the Four Masters, Annals of Innisfallen; Rot. de Liberate*) (*Journal of the Royal Society of Antiquaries of Ireland* XXXIX, pp. 275-6; LXXX, pp. 263-8).*

KILKEA   S 7497   Kildare

Motte (B) near later Kilkea Castle may be that of 1181 (Giraldus Cambrensis, *Opera* V, 355; *English Historical Review* XXII, p. 248).

KILKENNY   S 5056   Kilkenny

Castle destroyed in 1173 but mentioned again in 1192 (*Annals of Tigernach, Annals of Innisfallen*).

KILLALLON   N 6468   Meath

Motte (B) near later Kilkea Castle may be that of 1181 (Giraldus Cambrensis, *Opera* V, 355; *English Historical Review* XXII, p. 248).

KILLALOE   R 7074   Clare

Unfinished *motte* of 1207, built over the ringwork of Beal Boru destroyed in 1116 (*Annals of Clonmacnoise, Annals of the Four Masters*). Identification supported by excavation (*Jl. of the Cork Hist. and Arch. Soc.* 67, pp. 1-27).

KILLAMLUN see KILLALLON

KILLANY see ARDEE

KILLARE   N 2748   Westmeath

Motte (B) built in 1182, burnt in 1187 (Giraldus Cambrensis, *Opera* V, p. 356; *Annals of Ulster, Annals of the Four Masters*).

KILLEANNAN see ETHERDOUR

KILLESHIN   S 6777   Laoighis (Leix)

John de Clahull's castle of 1181 (*Song of Dermot; Giraldus Cambrensis, Opera* V, p. 355) site identified by Orpen (*English Historical Review* XXII, p. 248) as between Leighlin and Ardree.

KILMEHAL (Ireland)

Unidentified castle of 1206 (*Calendar of Documents* I, 44).

KILMESSAN   N 8755   Meath

Motte (B) perhaps that of 1215 (*Calendar of Documents* I, 110; *English Historical Review* XXII, p. 243).

KILMORE   H 3804   Cavan

Motte (Bb3) in existence by 1212 (*Irish Pipe Roll*) and mentioned in association with Cloughoughter in 1224 (*Ulster Journal of Archaeology* third series x, pp. 78–81).

KILPECK   SO 444305   Herefordshire

Motte and bailey (Be2) with strong counterscarp banks above combe to south, and flanking baileys to north-west and south-east and rectangular village enclosure (around the Romanesque church to the east) of bank and ditch. Parts of a polygonal rubble shell-wall remain on the *motte*, with a round-headed fireplace and circular flue to the north, two drains to the east and an interior cross-wall. The shell may have been circular internally; it has a sloping external plinth.

The chapel within the castle was given to Gloucester Abbey in 1134 (*Chron. St. Petri Glouces.* I, p. 16); the castle is mentioned in 1189 (*Pipe Roll*) (R.C.H.M. *Herefordshire* I, pp. 158–9).*   (Fig. 39)

KILSANTAN   see MOUNT SANDEL

KILTINAN   S 3728   Tipperary

Rebuilt castle on cliff beside River Glashauney mentioned in 1215 (*Patent Roll; Calendar of Documents* I, 95; *Rot. de Oblatis et Finibus*, p. 557).

KILTON   NZ 702177   Yorkshire

Natural promontory cut off by a ditch; the description of Kilton castle in the *Yorkshire Archaeological Journal* XXII, pp. 55–125, gives no sources for the dates there quoted, but a round-backed fireplace with roll-moulded imposts may be of the twelfth century.

KINCARDINE   NO 671751   Kincardineshire

Rectangular curtain wall with sloping plinth and remains of interior buildings on three sides and rectangular gate-towers in the fourth, on island in marsh. Castle and manor referred to in 1212 (Fordun, *Gesta Annalia* I, 278) (Macgibbon and Ross, *The Castellated and Domestic Architecture of Scotland* III, pp. 111–2).*

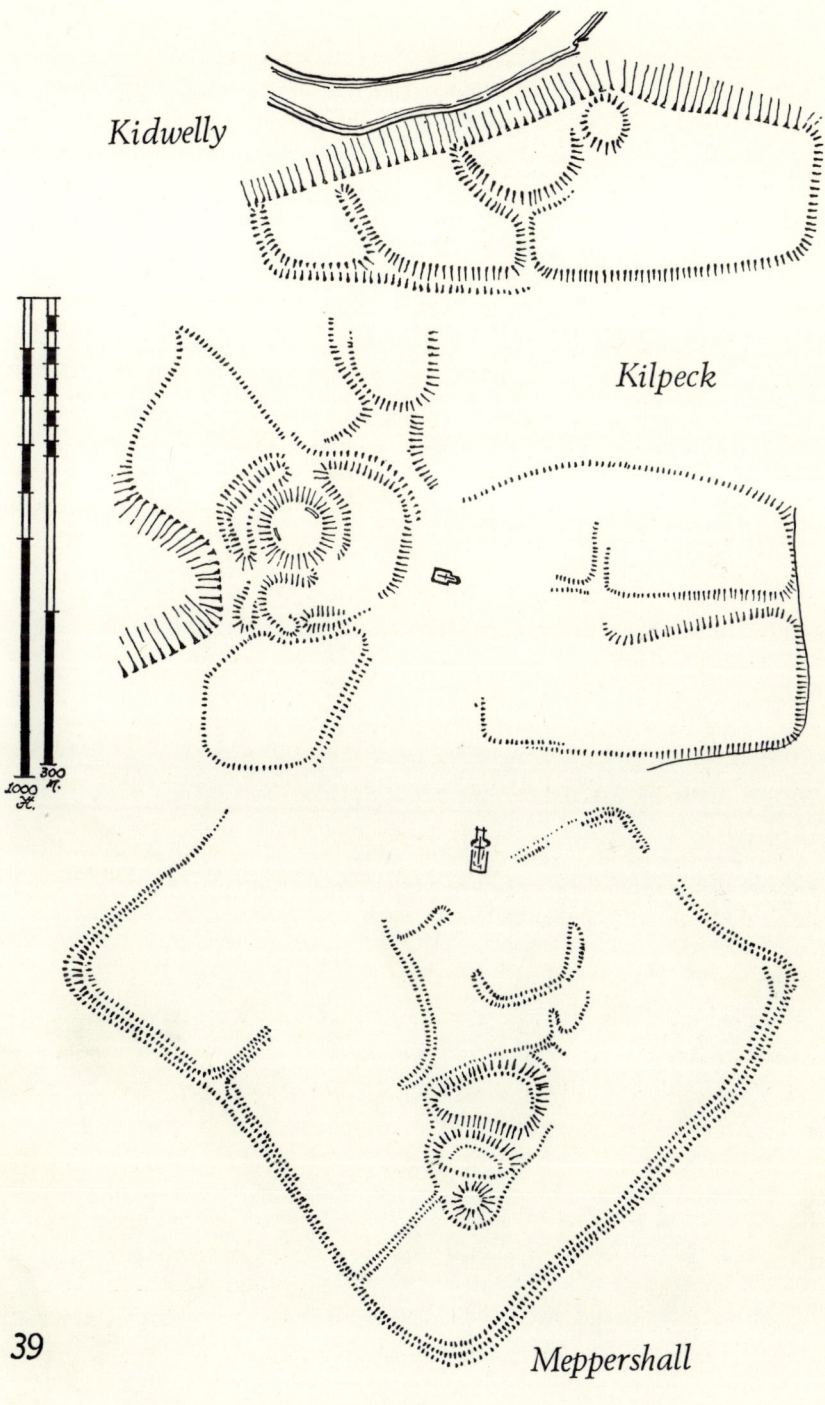

KINCLAVEN   NO 158376   Perth

Square walled enclosure with traces of entrance near one angle and a dog-legged passage through the adjoining wall. Compare Kincardine, also in Strath More (Macgibbon and Ross, *The Castellated and Domestic Architecture of Scotland*, I, pp. 67–70).

KINGERBY   TF 056928   Lincolnshire

Motte inside square moat before rebuilding of house, possibly of the castle burnt in John's reign (*Patent Rolls* I, 182) and rebuilt in 1216 (*Rot. de Oblatis et Finibus*, pp. 595–6).

KINGSHAUGH   SK 765735   Nottinghamshire

Fragmentary remains of a rectangular earthwork with outer enclosure (IICd?) (see V.C.H. *Nottinghamshire* I, p. 301) at Darlton used as a castle in 1193–4 (*Rot. Curiae Regis* I, p. 47; *Pipe Roll Society* XIV, p. 23). A new house was built on the site in 1210–11 at a cost of nearly £600 (*Pipe Rolls*).

KINGTON   SO 291569   Herefordshire

Damaged site north of the church on cliff above Back Brook. Mentioned in 1187 (*Pipe Roll*).

KINNARD FERRY   see OWSTON FERRY

KINNCLARE   Offaly

Site of castle (near Clara?) built in 1213 (*Annals of Clonmacnoise*).

KINNITTY   N 1508   Offaly

Site of castle built in 1213 (*Annals of Clonmacnoise*).

KIRKBY MALZEARD   SE 236745   Yorkshire

Site of castle mentioned in 1130, destroyed in 1174 (*Pipe Rolls*; Bodleian Library, *Dodsworth M.S.* VIII ff., 51d, 83d; *Gesta Henrici Secundi* I, p. 48).

KIRKOSWALD   NY 560410   Cumberland

Rectangular moat round late medieval castle with square projection to the north-west which may indicate the outline of a former *motte*-and-bailey layout (II Bd4)

A licence to fortify the site was granted in 1201 to Hugh de Morville (*Rot. Chart.* 89).

KIRKWALL   HY 448110   Orkney

The west range of the Bishop's Palace incorporates the lower part of a long narrow hall of coursed flagstone, with eight loops in the west wall and three in the south part of the east wall (the north part has been altered). These loops have polychrome dressings internally, like three square recesses in the south wall, resembling the early masonry of the cathedral, begun in 1137 (M.P.B.W. *Official Guide*).* (Fig. 38)

KNAPWELL   see page 355

KNARESBOROUGH   SE 349569   Yorkshire

Triangular site with rounded angles on promontory with rock-cut ditch. Traces of a north-south cross-wall of coursed rubble which have been excavated suggest an inner enclosure at the west end, later covered with a layer of rammed marl. At the south end the finds included a bone comb and pins, with wavy-edged horseshoes. A basement floor in the later keep is composed of fragments of a twelfth century pillar (*Yorkshire Archaeological Journal* XXX, pp. 200-24; XXXI, pp. 114-31), and early thirteenth century pottery was recovered from the primary silt of the ditch (*Antiquaries' Journal* XXXIII, p. 211).

Royal work here was paid for in 1129-30 and over £1,300 spent in 1203-12, much of it on ditching (*Pipe Rolls*).

KNEPP   TQ 163209   Sussex

Large *motte* (IIB) with counterscarp bank forming a wider ditch to the west with a bank beyond in marshy land. The fragment of a rectangular keep on the mound is of sandstone ashlar, with traces of two round-headed doorways (one above the other). The angle is covered by pilaster buttresses extending beyond the sloping plinth, with an angle-nook of only half their depth.

The castle was repaired in 1209 (*Pipe Roll*) and its destruction was ordered in 1215 and again in 1216 (*Rot. Litt. Pat.*, pp. 137, 187). Its (wooden?) towers were to be taken to Dover (*Rot. Litt. Claus.* p. 142).

(Fig. 37)

KNIGHTON   Radnorshire

The castle mentioned in 1182 and 1191-3 (*Pipe Rolls*) may be the *motte* (B) in the town (SO 284722) or the *motte* and bailey (Bd2?) 500 yds away beside the river (SO 290722).

KNOCK   see CASTLEKNOCK

KNOCKAINY   R 6738   Limerick

Castle D'Any was included in the Carricklittle grant of 1199 (q.v.).

KNOCKGRAFFON   S 0241   Tipperary

Motte and bailey (IIAe1) with foundations on *motte*-top of square building; other foundations in bailey. Built in 1192 (*Annals of the Four Masters*; also *Patent Roll* 1202). See Kilfeakle for references.

| KNOCKIN | SJ 334223 | Shropshire |

Motte and bailey (IIBd2) east of church, with fragments of rubble walling on south side of bailey. Mentioned in 1165, 1196–7 (*Pipe Rolls*).

| KNOCKTOPHER | S 5337 | Kilkenny |

Motte (A), perhaps that of 1181 (Giraldus Cambrensis, *Opera* V, p. 255; *English Historical Review* XXII, 247–8).

KNOWTH   see page 355

LACFORD   see SLEAFORD

LAGELACHON   see DERVER (LOUGHAN)

LAMPETER   see STEPHEN'S CASTLE

| LANCASTER | SD 473619 | Lancashire |

The square keep is of short square ashlars with open joints, with pilaster buttresses in the centre and end of each wall and an east-west cross-wall. Little detail survives, but there is a spiral stair in the south-west angle and the round-vaulted embrasures of two loops at two levels of the eastern wall with nook-shafts. Part of a curtain wall survives built into the later buildings, with a round tower of ashlar at the south-west angle abutting on a rectangular hall (cf. Pembridge). The tower is approached from the hall basement by a pointed arch with moulded capitals and shafts, with two flanking spiral stairs and loops on the ground floor. The circular moat is largely filled in.

The keep is traditionally attributed to Roger of Poitou (before 1102) and it may be the *castellatu Rogerii pictaviensis* of 'Domesday Book', although Dugdale (*Baronage* I, p. 99) attributes it to Roger de Lacy II (see Clitheroe). Over £600 was spent in the reign of John, including ditch-work and perhaps the curtain wall and towers (*Pipe Rolls*) (*Transactions of the Historic Society of Lancashire and Cheshire* XLVIII, pp. 95–122).*

(Fig. 40)

| LAUDER | | Berwickshire |

There seem to be four possible sites for the castle mentioned in 1173–4 (*Gesta Henrici Secundi* I, pp. 48–9): the forts at NT 526468 and 570484; or the later stone castles at NT 534479 and 564474.

| LAUGHARNE | SN 302107 | Carmarthenshire |

Late thirteenth-century castle, on site of one mentioned in 1189 and 1215 (*Brut y Tywysogion*).

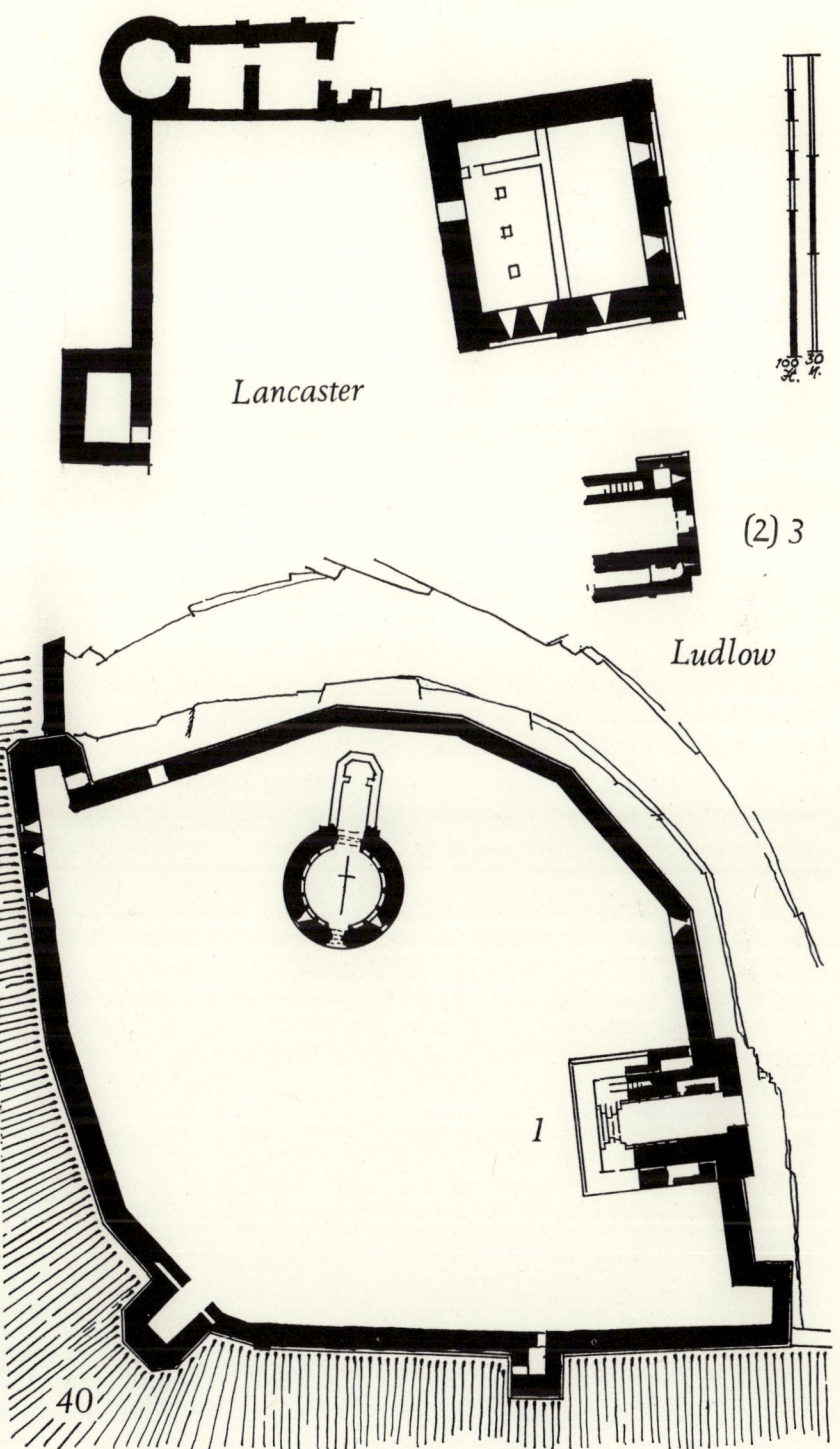

Lancaster

(2) 3

Ludlow

40

221

LAUNCESTON	SX 331847	Cornwall

Motte and bailey (Ad3) with traces of pearshaped *burgus* to north and east. It is very difficult to date the masonry (in local slate and Polyphant stone) in the absence of details. The fragments of curtain wall may be of the twelfth century, as may the solid drum towers of the south gate, which have sloping plinths below a round string-course. The *motte*-top was surrounded by a mantlet wall just outside the existing shell; its foundations were found recently and it is shown on Norden's drawing (*B.M. Harl. M.S.* 6252, f. 70). The shell is slightly oval and of irregular thickness, rising from a sloping plinth capped with a round string-course. The entrance has been altered and lowered; a plain chamfered impost marks the original gate. There are two opposing wall-stairs (one entered from the side of the gate-passage) and a small cell with air vent also in the thickness of the wall.

Excavation (*Cornish Archaeology* 3, pp. 63-9) has shown that the central round tower is later than the shell, and its attribution to Richard, Earl of Cornwall (1227-72) may be accepted. Certainly the Pipe Roll expenditure from 1175 refers only to repairs of the King's Chamber and other houses. The 'castle of Cornwall' is mentioned in 'Domesday Book' (I, 101b, 2; 121b) (*Archaeologia* 83, pp. 207-17).* Launceston castle is mentioned in 1122 (*Regesta Regum Anglo-Normanorum* II, 1363).

LAVAGH	S 3283	Laoighis (Laix)

Motte and bailey (Ba/23) cut off from ridge with triple bank and ditch. In existence by 1207 (*Annals of Clonmacnoise*).

LAVENDON	SP 917543	Buckinghamshire

Motte with three rectangular baileys (Bd4); much twelfth century pottery was found when the *motte* was destroyed in 1944 (*Antiquaries' Journal* XXXIX, p. 239, n. 1).

Henry of Clinton received twenty loads of wheat in 1192-3 *ad muniendum castellum de Lavendon* (*Pipe Roll*).

LEA	N 5312	Laoighis (Leix)

Oval mound covered in masonry debris south of River Barrow, the site of castle mentioned in 1201 (*Calendar of Documents* I, p. 30).

LECHLIN see LEIGHLIN

LEEDS	TQ 836533	Kent

Of the castle of *Slede* taken in 1139 (*Henry of Huntingdon*, p. 265) the only possible traces are two round-headed arches of Caen ashlar in a cellar, and perhaps the inner curtain wall with two square towers near the north end. C. W. Martin (*A History of Leeds Castle, p.* 94) records a traditional date of before 1119.

LEGA   see LEA

LEICESTER   SK 583041   Leicestershire

Motte and bailey (Bb3) beside River Soar. A small piece of rubble masonry near the *motte*-top may be original. The bailey is largely built over, but its outline is preserved in the parish boundary, and excavations in 1939 (*Transactions of the Leicestershire Archaeological Society* XXVIII, pp. 22–9) revealed a V-shaped ditch 40 ft wide containing eleventh/twelfth century pottery, with remains of a collapsed curtain wall. A plain sandstone hall on the river front has two tall chevron-ornamented windows with scalloped capitals to the nook-shafts in the south wall, and a reset arch in the west wall. The chamfered tie-beams support struts to the principal rafters; one scalloped capital from the six-bay timber arcade is preserved in the hall, with the end of the square pier below and roll-and-fillet carving of the arch above.

The castle was damaged in the 1101 rebellion (*Monasticon* VI, 466; see J. H. Round, *Feudal England*, pp. 347–8) and was captured by the king in 1173–4 and then demolished (*Gesta Henrici Secundi* I, 61; *Diceto* I, 404; *Hoveden* II, p. 101; *Pipe Rolls*) (*Transactions of the Leicestershire Archaeological Society* XXII, pp. 125–70).*   (Figs. 1, 36)

LEIGHLIN   S 6465   Carlow

Motte (B) built in 1181 (Giraldus Cambrensis, *Opera* V, p. 355, identified in *English Historical Review* XXII, p. 245).

LELESHAY   Suffolk

The castles of Lelesey, W. of Milden and W. of Ambli were near the manors of Groton and Semer in the time of King Stephen (*B.M. Harl. M.S.* 1005, f. 163) and Thomas de Burgh had licence to fortify his house at Leleshay in 1204 (*Liberate Roll; Fine Roll* 3 Henry III). There are earthwork castles at Lindsey (TL 980441: Bd2) and Milden (TL 950461: Bc2). W. of Ambli's castle might have been Pytches Mount in Groton Park (TL 965425: B) or the moated site at Offton (TM 064492: IIBd2).

LEWAN   see NEWCASTLE LYONS

LEWES   TQ 415101   Sussex

Ovoid bailey with *motte* at each end (ABb3) of roughly squared chalk blocks. There is a fragment of a shell-wall of flint rubble on the north-east

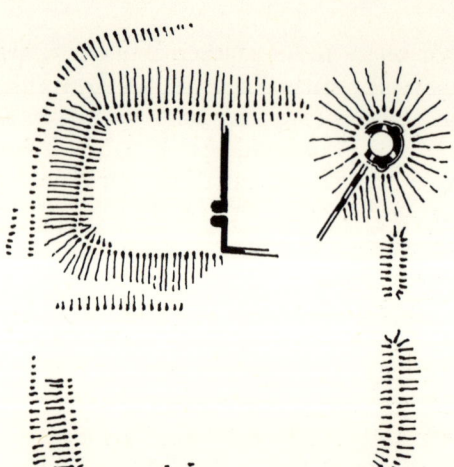

Longtown

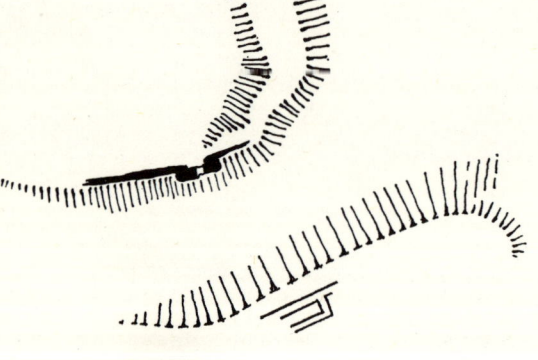

Launceston

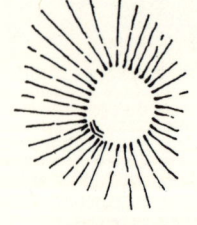

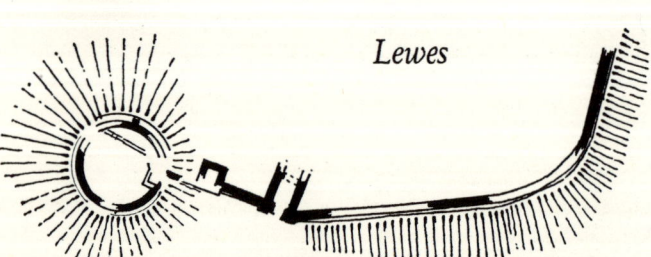

Lewes

41

motte-top, with the southern half of another shell-wall on the other *motte*. This is elliptical in plan, built of flints with a knapped facing laid in herringbone courses (the semi-octagonal towers are later), with corbels for the roofs of interior buildings. A timber tie-beam hole is visible in a modern recess to the south-east. The foundations of a rectangular building were excavated in 1884 on the north side, and appear to pre-date the shell and connect with a square tower whose foundations survive at the top of the modern steps.

The eastern curtain partly revets the bailey bank, and is of flint rubble with a square internal tower in the *motte*-ditch and a two-bay rectangular gatehouse also projecting inwards, behind the later barbican. The round arch has Caen stone dressings, with a later segmental inner arch. The northern part of the entrance has been destroyed, but there are remains of an upper storey. A fragment of the western curtain has been built into a house and there is said to be a plain barrel-vault in the basement.

Mentioned indirectly as the *castellum Delaquis* in 1086 ('Domesday Book' II, 157, 163, 172) (*Sussex Archaeological Collections* XXXIV, pp. 57–70).* (Fig. 41)

'LEYLAND' see page 355

| LICHFIELD | SK 118096 | Staffordshire |

The castle of between 1129–48 (B.M. *Cott. MS. Cleopatra* D, ix; *Anglia Sacra* I, i, 434) probably stood in the Ware/Frog Street area. (*Proceedings of the North Staffordshire Field Club* XLVIII, pp. 123–8).

| LIDDELL | NY 402742 | Cumberland |

Motte and bailey (Bd3) beside Liddel Water on Scots border. Held by Ranulf de Soulis in 1174 (*Gesta Henrici Secundi* I, 65) (*Transactions of the Cumberland and Westmorland Antiquarian and Archaeological Society* X, pp. 91–101).*

'LIDELEA' Hampshire (?)

This castle of the bishop of Winchester was captured by a trick, and finally surrendered to Stephen in 1147 after the bishop had built two castles in front of it (*Gesta Stephani*, pp. 138–9). The castle has been identified with BARLEY POUND (p. 100), the siegeworks being at POWDERHAM (p. 285) and a ploughed-out *motte* near Bentley (SU 794463) (*Antiquaries Journal* LI, p. 301).

| *LIDGATE* | TL 722582 | Suffolk |

Rectangular mound and bailey (IIBd3) surrounding the church, with outer enclosures beyond to north and east. Rubble walls of uncertain date in bailey. (See p. 50)

NORMAN CASTLES IN BRITAIN

LIMERICK   R 5758   Limerick

The quadrilateral enclosure on the east bank of the River Shannon has round towers at the angles and flanking the gate-passage. A former square tower on the river front and the short lengths of a curtain at an angle to the principal 'run' may be evidence of the castle of 1202 (*Archaeological Journal* XCIII, pp. 178–80). Over £700 was spent in 1211–12 (*Irish Pipe Roll*). The castle was built in 1177 (Giraldus Cambrensis, *Opera* V, p. 349).

LINCOLN   SK 975718   Lincolnshire

Two *mottes* on the south side of a rhomboidal enclosure (ABd3); ditch only to south. The larger mound carried a polygonal shell of oval plan. There are fifteen external faces, each capped with a pilaster buttress with a roll-moulding as well as the offset which runs round the shell, which has a sloping plinth. The round-headed entrance arch is set in a projecting north-east buttress with a restored hood-mould and bar-hole. A doorway on the opposite side of the shell has a segmental head, although the Bucks' sketches show it as round-headed. The sketches also show four bands of stone revetting the *motte*. The curtain wall running down opposite sides of the *motte* has mural chambers at its junction with the keep, and is of herringbone coursed rubble founded on timber frames. It runs as an arc to the lesser *motte*, which carries an ashlar rectangular tower of two storeys linked by a wall-stair and thence to the east gate, which projects slightly forward with a round-headed arch. An underground passage runs west from a spiral stair descending into the lesser *motte*. The north and west curtain walls are straight, except that the north west angle is slanted back to avoid the Roman west gate. The medieval west gate was a rectangular tower astride the curtain, with a round-headed arch and portcullis groove with two small round-headed windows over.

The Bucks' sketches show round Norman arches to the city gates called Little Bargate and Clasketgate.

One hundred and sixty-six houses were destroyed to make room for the castle built in 1068 ('Domesday Book' I, 336b; *Ordericus Vitalis* II, p. 185; *Anglo-Saxon Chronicle* p. 202; *Florence of Worcester* II, p. 2). A stone curtain is indicated by the term *murus* used in 1115 (*Registrum Antiquissimum of Lincoln* I, p. 267), and the shell-keep known as the Lucy Tower after the countess of Chester, who died about 1136; in an agreement of 1149 with Stephen, Ranulf, her son, was to fortify one of his towers in the castle and to hold until given possession of Tickhill, when he was to retain only the tower that his mother had fortified (*Registrum Antiquissimum of Lincoln* I, pp. 287–8). He had seized the castle by a trick in 1140, and was forced to surrender it in 1146. Repairs were paid for in 1190–1 and 1199–

1200; over £80 was spent strengthening the bailey in 1193-4 (*Pipe Rolls*) J. W. F. Hill, *Medieval Lincoln*, Cambridge, 1948.* (Fig. 43)

LINCOLN SIEGE-WORKS

Stephen turned St Mary's church into a siege-castle in 1140-1 (William of Malmesbury, *Historia Novella*, p. 48); this may have been either the cathedral, St Mary Crackpole or St Mary le Wigford. The *munitio* of his siege of 1144 (*Henry of Huntingdon*, p. 277) is said to have been the square earthwork outside the westgate of the castle (J. W. F. Hill, *Medieval Lincoln*, pp. 177-80).

LINDSEY see LELESHAY

LINLITHGOW   NT 002773   East Lothian

Romanesque capital in the Palace from the castle possibly mentioned in 1147-50 (*de castello et de Linclito*; Lawrie, *Ancient Scottish Charters* CLIII).

LISMAHON   J 4339   Down

Oval mound (IB) of pre-Norman date, raised further with piled boulder clay. A regular light palisade was found on the north-west side of the *motte*-top, with an iron-smelting workshop within. The north-east part contained the sleeper walls of a square house with rounded corners (later extended west) with a central post and hearth. At the north-east angle four large post-holes enclosed a 6-ft square, perhaps the base of a turret. A large figure-of-eight pit north of the house had vertical walls, and an outer-splayed slot had been cut through the peripheral bank; a burnt deposit contained a silver halfpenny of 1185-99 (*Medieval Archaeology* III, pp. 139-76).

LISMORE   X 0498   Waterford

Motte and bailey (Bd2?) beside ford of River Blackwater, built in 1185 although Henry II had intended to build one previously (*Annals of Loch Cé*; *Song of Dermot*; Giraldus Cambrensis, *Opera* V, 386).

LITTLEDEAN   SO 677135   Gloucestershire

Small ring-work (C) with strong bank; part of bank isolated to form a guardpoint mound. Excavation revealed a key and pottery like that from Lydney Castle (q.v.) with a bone knife-handle in and below a rough floor of sandstone pitching covering the interior.

This may be the 'old castle of Dene' mentioned in a charter of 1153-4 (*Cartae Antiquae Rolls* 11-20, p. 133) (*Transactions of the Bristol and Gloucestershire Archaeological Society* 77, pp. 48-60).*

LIVERPOOL   see WEST DERBY

LLANDOG   see LLYCHEWIN

LLANDEILO-TALYBONT   SN 587027   Glamorgan

Small *motte* with traces of tiny bailey (Ba2?) south of loop of Loughor River, belonging to a castle destroyed in 1215 (*Brut y Tywysogion*).

LLANDINAM   SO 046905   Montgomeryshire

Motte with two U-shaped baileys in echelon (Be3), perhaps built in 1162 (*Brut y Tywysogion*).

LLANDOVERY   SN 767342   Carmarthenshire

Motte and bailey (Be3) beside river. D-shaped tower with fragments of twin-towered gatehouse and curtain on *motte*. Part of the curtain rests unconformably on a stepped foundation near the north angle, perhaps of twelfth century date.

First mentioned in 1116, when the Welsh took the *rac-castell* but failed to capture the *twr*. Its destruction in 1158 (*Brut y Tywysogion*) was followed by strengthening and garrisoning at royal expense in 1160-2 (*Pipe Rolls*) R.C.A.M. *Carmarthenshire*, pp. 94-5.*

LLANEGWAD   Carmarthenshire

Motte and bailey near ford (SN 516214) (Bc2) with traces of masonry on the *motte*-slope, is perhaps the castle of 1203 (*Brut y Tywysogion*), but the fine site of Allt y Ferin (SN 522233), on a promontory (Ac3) must be considered as an alternative (R.C.A.M. *Carmarthen*, p. 116-17).*

LLANELLY   SN 501004   Carmarthenshire

Mound in Old Castle works reservoir — traces of bailey. Probably the castle of Carnwillion, mentioned in 1190-1215 (*Brut y Tywysogion*).

LLANFAIR RHYD CASTELL   Denbighshire

The castle given to the monks of Aberconway by Llewelyn ap Iorwerth in 1198 (see *Archaeologia Cambrensis* XCIV, p. 144) is probably Voelas (SH 870522).

LLANGADOG   SN 709276   Carmarthenshire

Motte and bailey (Ab3) beside ford. Iron key said to have been found on mound. Destroyed in 1209 (*Brut y Tywysogion*).

LLANGENYDD   see page 355

LLANHILLETH   SO 219020   Monmouthshire

Foundations excavated east of St Illtyd's church included part of a large round tower with central pillar, and a square tower with recessed corners, the re-entrant angles having oblique buttresses. The cruciform interior had canted angles and each turret had two steeply shelving loops opening off a single embrasure; round-headed windows reconstructed from the fallen debris had moulded heads externally and chamfered inner arches (*Archaeologia Cambrensis* 79, pp. 385-7; 80, pp. 372-80).

LLANIO   SN 661579   Cardiganshire

Small *motte* (B), probably the castle of Richard de la Mare destroyed in 1136 (*Brut y Tywysogion*). For the tentative identification with *Castello i Flemis* of 1184 (*Monasticon* V, p. 632) see *Proceedings of the British Academy* XLII, p. 167, n. 2.

LLANRHYSTYD   SN 552696   Cardiganshire

Ring-work projecting from large crescentic enclosure. (ICb/23). Built in 1148 by Cadwalwdr ap Gruffyd (*Brut y Tywysogion*).

LLANSTEPHAN   SN 351101   Carmarthenshire

Ridge at confluence of Twyi and Tav rivers, cut off by double ditch with bank between. The oval inner ring-work (ICd2) is largely levelled; the bank was revetted with a polygonal curtain wall with rounded angles of roughly coursed mortared rubble, of which the western part remains; a square gatehouse tower was inserted in the mid-thirteenth century, but a barhole in the original curtain fragment suggests it replaced an earlier gate on the same site. The whole curtain was later raised in height. The entrance passage had doors and an outer portcullis. The first floor is reached from the curtain wall-walk, and a straight wall-stair leads to the upper floor; both have rectangular loops.

First mentioned in 1136 on its capture by the Welsh (*Brut y Tywysogion*); William de Camville borrowed money to fortify the castle in 1192 (*Pipe Roll*) (M.P.B.W. *Official Guide*).*

LLANTILO   see WHITE

LLANTRITHYD   ST 045727   Glamorgan

4 × 5 rows of post-holes, partly recut for drystone hall with rounded corners inside a timber-revetted bank, and rock-cut ditch. Excavation produced seven Henry I pennies (type XI, *c.* 1125-8) and a cut halfpenny of 1110-13. (*Morgannwg* VI, pp. 98-100; VII, pp. 126-7; VIII, pp. 70-1).

LLANWADEIN   see LLAWHADEN

LLAWHADEN   SN 073174   Pembrokeshire

Oval ring-work (IC). On the west side are the foundations of two round towers and traces of a curtain wall underlying the fourteenth-century work on the line of the bank. The site is mentioned about 1175 (Giraldus Cambrensis *Opera* I, p. 26) and more explicitly in 1190 (*Pipe Roll*) and its capture and destruction are recorded in 1192–3 (*Brut y Tywysogion*) M.P.B.W. *Official Guide.**

LLYS EDWIN　　　　　　SJ 235697　　　　　　　　Flintshire

Moated site at Celyn Farm excavated in 1931. The counterscarp bank had been palisaded with oak logs 7 to 9 in. in diameter, and an outer bank and ditch had a strong gate and bridge through the double bank to the north-east.

The rectangular northern quarter of the 'island' was cut off by a curtain wall with square towers to the north, east and west. That to the west protruded to protect the entrance abutment and cobbled passage with a portcullis slot, and contained pottery and roofing fragments: three impacted javelin-heads were found outside, also an iron plate and rivetted bronze bowl (cf. Clough). The other angle towers enclosed the angle of the curtain. A timber hall (later rebuilt in stone) crossed the enclosure at an angle, and a substantial timber kitchen building stood against the outside of the south-east wall. Bones, a chopping-block, several knives, and a whetstone were found here together with the well.

There was a burnt-out detached tower at the west angle of the 'island'; post-holes at the south and east angles may have been timber towers – or a palisade only.

The suggested identification is with Eadwine who lost *Castretone* 1070–1 but whose son regained possession. Some of the details of the rebuilt hall suggest an early thirteenth-century date for the last phase. (T. A. Glenn, *The family of Gryffith of Garn*, pp. 44–63; summary in *Bulletin of the Board of Celtic Studies* VI, pp. 96–7).

LOCHMABEN　　　　　　NY 089812　　　　　　　Dumfriesshire

Earthworks underlying masonry of uncertain date (IICd4?) on a promontory into the loch may be the castle mentioned in 1173 (*Gesta Henrici Secundi* I, pp. 47–9) or the *motte* at NY 083823 (MacGibbon and Ross, *The Castellated and Domestic Architecture of Scotland* I, pp. 78–80).*

LOCKING　　　　　　ST 364609　　　　　　　　Somerset

Excavation of a mound with a rectangular enclosure (Bd2?) at Lockinghead Farm revealed a 9-ft square cellar of oolite laid as drystone walling, containing a sword, oxbone and pottery fragment (*Proceedings of the Somersetshire Archaeological Society* XLIX, p. 186).

LOGSEVETHY　see LOXHUNDY

LONDON　see BAYNARD'S: MONTFICHET: RAVENGER'S: TOWER

The Jews' houses were used to repair the city wall in 1216 (*Coggeshall*, p.

171; *Walter of Coventry* II, p. 222). Stow (*Survey of London*, ed. Kingsford, I, p. 38) mentions Hebrew inscriptions found in rebuilding Ludgate.

LONG BUCKBY   SP 625677   Northamptonshire

Oval ring-work within triangular bailey (ICc1), excavated in 1955 to show that it partly overlay an earlier enclosure, with a curtain wall of limestone rubble added later but before a stone-revetted bank and V-shaped ditch were cut. Much Saxo-Norman pottery was found, with schist hones, a prickspur and gilt bronze strip (*Journal of the Northamptonshire Natural History Society and Field Club* XXXIII, pp. 55–66).

LONGTOWN   SO 321292   Herefordshire

Motte and bailey (Ad3) occupying the western half of a square enclosure of bank (no ditch). Round keep (on *motte*) of shaly sandstone rubble with two string-courses around sloping plinth, and another at the level of the second floor. Three symmetrical hemicylindrical buttresses — one beside the (destroyed) entrance contains the spiral stair to the upper floor (supported on an offset with corbelled-out struts to the main beam) which is lit by rectangular loops (with beam-holes for an external timber gallery), and has a corbelled-out latrine beside another buttress. The third buttress backs a fireplace recess. The ground floor windows, one beside each buttress, have side seats and square heads; the semi-circular arch over one window has beaded rosettes on soffit and outer face. The plinth has been damaged, possibly to tooth-in the rubble curtain descending the *motte* and flanking the eastern side of the bailey, with a cross-wall with rounded ends to the gate-passage walls.

The mention of Newcastle and Ewyas Lacy in 1187 (*Pipe Roll*) may refer to Longtown and Ponthendre (Ac3, at SO 326281) in turn (R.C.H.M. *Herefordshire* I, 181–4).*   (Plate XXII; Figs. 41, 42)

LORRHA see page 355

'LOSKE'   (Ireland)

Unidentified castle of Theobald Walter (d. 1206) (*Cal. of Documents* I, 81).

(LOTHIAN)

Robert fitz Godwin was attacked while building a castle in Lothian between 1099 and 1103 (Fordun, *Chronica Gentis Scotorum* I, p. 225).

LOTHRA see LAVAGH

LOUGHOR   SS 564980   Glamorgan

Mound with traces of bailey surrounding church to west (Bd3?). There are the remains of a square tower (with the stub of a curtain wall attached) in coursed slate slabs on the mound, but the pointed arch to the inside doorway and embrasures to the loop on each external face look rather later than the castle destroyed in 1151 and again in 1215 (*Brut y Tywysogion*). The ringwork was filled in late in the twelfth century to provide a rebuilding platform.

LOUGHSENDY (or LOUGHSEWDY)   see LOXHUNDY

| LOUTH | N 9800 | Louth |

Motte (Fairy Mount) with strong counterscarp bank (A) probably the castle burnt in 1196 but reoccupied by 1204 (*Annals of Innisfallen; Calendar of Documents* I, 30). See MOUNT ASH.

| LOXHUNDY | N 1853 | Westmeath |

Motte (B) mentioned in 1212 (*Irish Pipe Roll*).

| LUDGERSHALL | SU 265513 | Wiltshire |

Ring-work (Cc3) with double ditch enclosing the south face (with return walling) of a small rectangular tower of flint rubble. Large holes mark the site of timber tie-beams in the walls. The quoins have been robbed, but there are traces of round-headed windows in the south and east walls, and a chimney-shaft in the south-west angle. Extensive foundations have been excavated to the south-east of the tower. (*Medieval Archaeology* IX, p. 192). Early twelfth century pottery and a cut halfpenny of the first issue of Stephen were found in a rectangular pit in the southern 'bailey' with timber structures, some underlying the drystone-revetted bank. Tripod pitchers were found in the rapid silt of the ditch, and the lid of a bone casket, with ornamental strips and iron fittings was also found. (*Medieval Archaeology* X, p. 192 and pl. XV; *W.A.M.* 61, pp. 104–5).

| LUDLOW | SO 508746 | Shropshire |

The inner enclosure of this castle is formed by a rock-cut ditch isolating the north-west corner of the hill, defended by coursed rubble curtain walls with a sloping plinth built in straight lengths to enclose a pointed oval enclosure. Four square wall-towers project from the north-west wall, the two northerly ones having the angles mitred off. The small tower on the west side has two round-headed doorways in the north and east walls at ground level; the others have open backs, and wall passages at first floor level (there are wall passages at ground level in the curtain flanking the north-west tower as well). The enclosure was originally entered through a T-shaped gatehouse projecting only slightly beyond the south curtain, with an outer arch of two square orders and an inner door of one order (with a narrow side passage to avoid it) and a flanking blind arcade of round-headed arches on crude capitals and shafts. The floor over the barrel-vaulted passage was reached by a straight wall-stair, being lit by two windows (one head survives) and two loops (one with an outer arched head supported on shafts) in the south wall. The top floor branches of the T contain a spiral stair and small room, each lit by loops. An annex was soon added to the north-west to make the tower almost square, and the archway was blocked and another entrance cut through the adjoining curtain wall beside another annex to the north-east.

The gatehouse is ashlar faced; the north part was later demolished and rebuilt further south to make a smaller tower.

The chancel of the chapel within the enclosure has been destroyed, but the battlemented circular nave of coursed rubble still stands. The lower part of the exterior is plastered as high as a double billet-moulded stringcourse, above which are round-headed windows with jamb-shafts facing north, south and west. The west doorway has a plain inner order, the outer ones having jamb shafts with cushion capitals and diapered imposts. Reading outward, the mouldings are roll, chevron and billet. There is an internal blind arcade of round-headed arches (alternatively chevron and wavemoulding) on shafts. The eastern arch is somewhat similar to the western, except that the innermost order has double shafts under cushion capitals (wave-moulded to the north and diapered to the south) with cabled necking. The soffits of the outer orders are also diapered.

The curtain wall of the square outer enclosure has an open-backed square tower on the east side.

The castle is mentioned in 1139 (*Chron. Normann.* p. 977) and frequently in the *Pipe Rolls* of 1177–93. The keep was traditionally the prison of 1148–54 (Eyton, *Antiquities of Shropshire* V, p. 247) so that the gatehouse may have been converted by then, after the 'war' of 1143–8 (Wightman, *The Lacy Family*, p. 205) (*Archaeologia* LXI, pp. 257–328).*

(Plates XXIII, XXIV, XXV, XXVI; Fig 40)

LUDLOW SIEGE-WORKS   Shropshire

Two siege-castles of 1138–9 (*Chron. Normann.* p. 977; *Florence of Worcester* II, p. 110); one may have been the mound removed to extend the parish church.

LULWORTH   SY 855821   Dorset

The foundations excavated west of East Lulworth church (Hutchins, *History of Dorset* I, p. 371) may be the castle of *Lulleworda* captured by Robert, Earl of Gloucester in 1142 (William of Malmesbury, *Historia Novella*, p. 76).

LUNAN BAY   Angus

Two sites – a *motte* (B) to the west (NO 689510) and a promontory to the

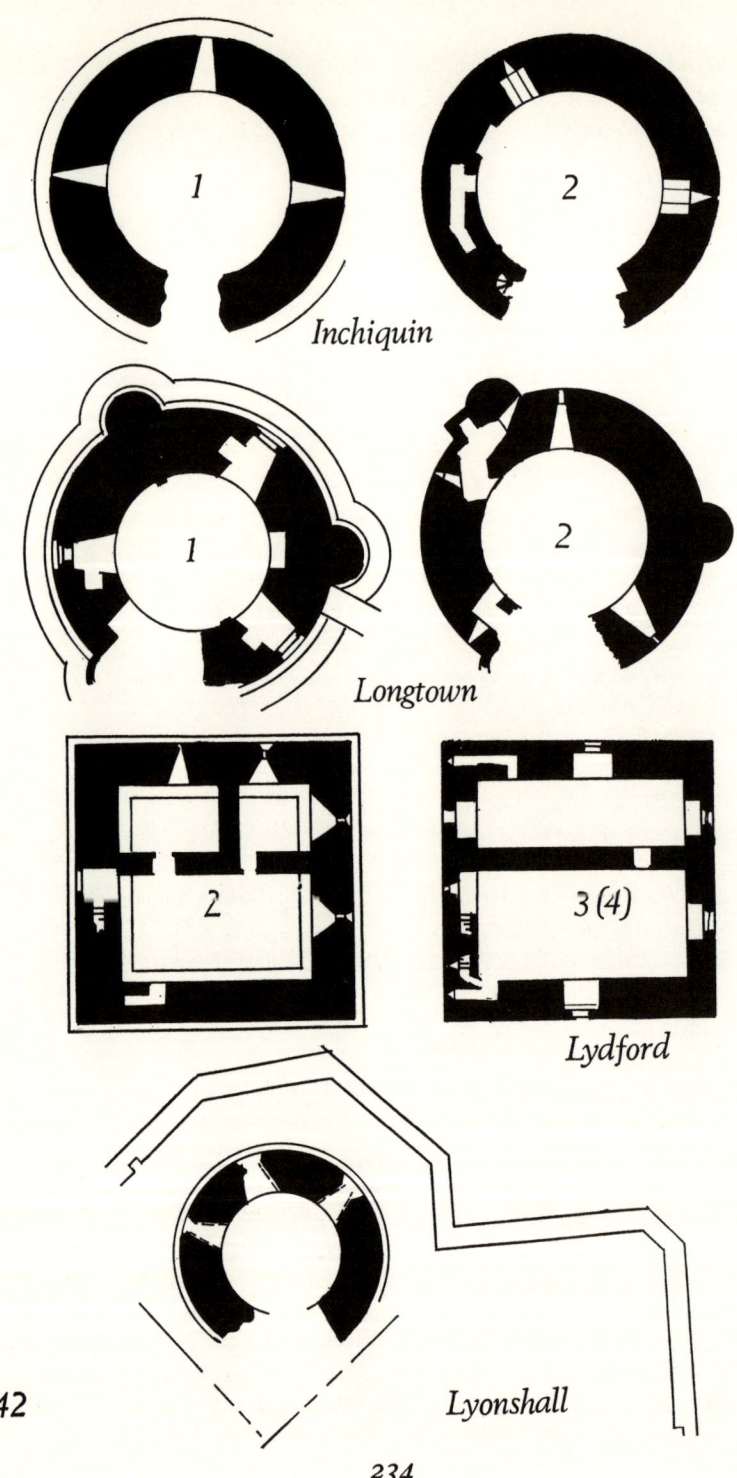

42

north (NO 700512) with straight curtain wall — one of which may be the castle of William de Berkeley after 1165 (*Proceedings of the Society of Antiquaries of Scotland* LXXV, pp. 115–22).

| LUNDY | SS 137442 | Devon |

A wall 7 ft thick with a blocked alcove was excavated in 1964 in a ditched mound at Bulls Paradise, overlying an occupation layer and covered in turn by a cobble spread containing late twelfth-early thirteenth-century pottery (*Medieval Archaeology* IX, p. 216; *Lundy Field Society Report*, forthcoming).

LUURE see OSWESTRY

LUVETH see LOUTH

LYDBURY NORTH see BISHOPS CASTLE

| LYDFORD | SX 510848 | Devon |

The promontory site of the town was defended in Saxon times by a steep stone-faced bank to the north-east continued round the natural gorge and valley on the other sides. There are two earthworks north-east and south-west of the church. The former (Bc3) has a bailey made by two straight banks (one overlying a ditch) and the gorge. An almost square keep was built, the basement (lit by three loops) being buried in the *motte*. The pointed entrance arch leads to a wall-stair. The eastern walls each have two double-splayed windows and there are latrines in the western angle on three levels. A rectangular well-sinking (with a later circular shaft beside it) has been excavated, together with a pickaxe and spade iron. (*Trans. Devon Association* 91, pp. 176–7; *Medieval Archaeology* II, p. 195; III, p. 307; VIII, p. 252; IX, p. 188). The cross-wall seems to be an insertion, and it is difficult to distinguish how much of the work above the ground is original. A wall-stair from an embrasure leads up to the parapet, the roof being carried on corbels.

Excavation of the quadrant earthwork cutting off the angle of the gorge south-west of the church showed that the revetted bank had been thrown up over early twelfth century pottery, the loose shale being derived from a U-shaped ditch. Four contiguous rectangular huts of squared timber and wickerwork occupied the east half of the enclosure with a loose stone paving front. The site had been burnt and the top of the bank sliced off later. Finds included a quantity of grain and a penny of Stephen's first issue (1135/42) in a late deposit of pottery.

Forty houses were laid waste in the town between 1066–86 ('Domesday Book'), which may indicate castle building; a strong building for prisoners was built in the town (for £74) in 1194–5 and the castle garrisoned in

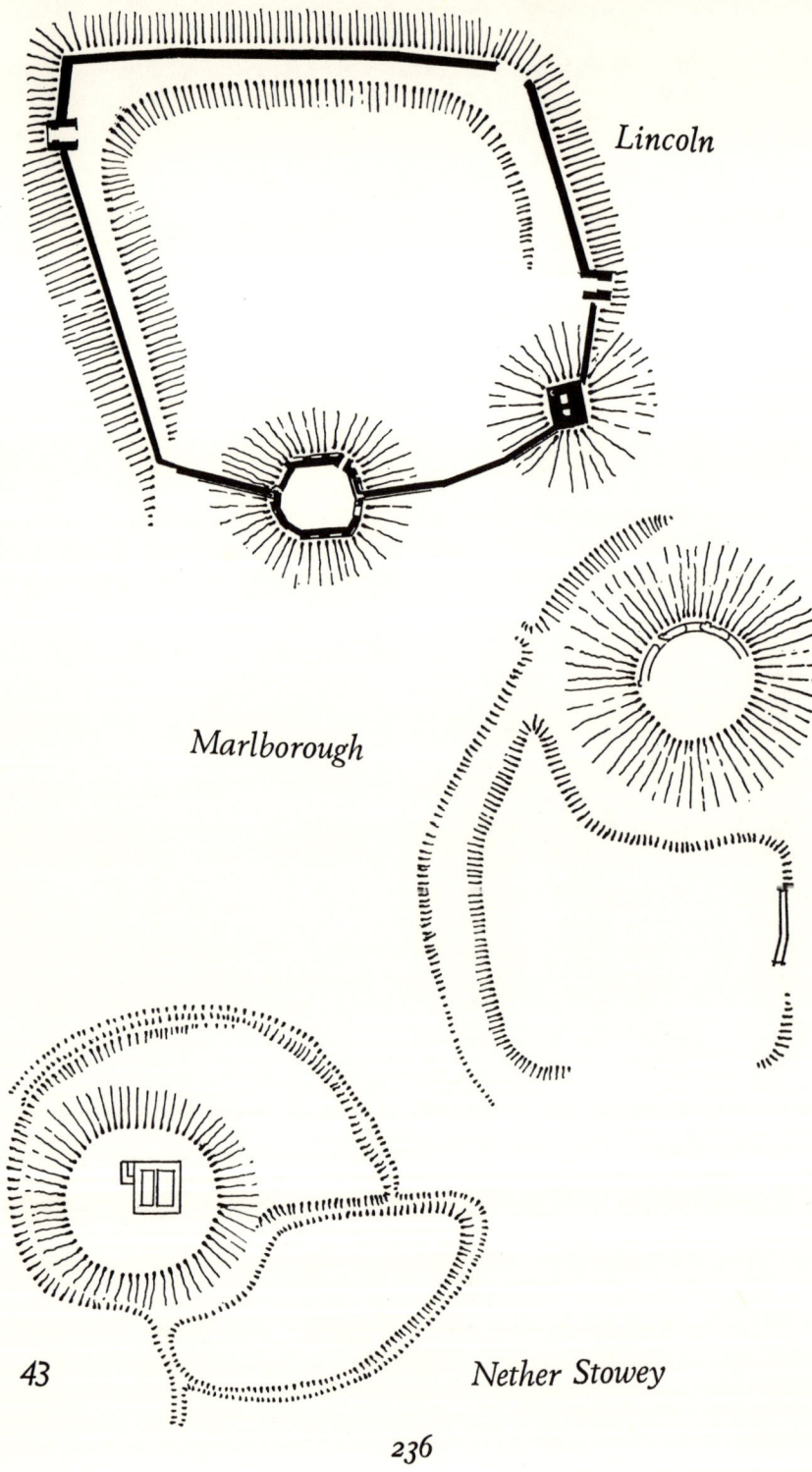

43 Lincoln / Marlborough / Nether Stowey

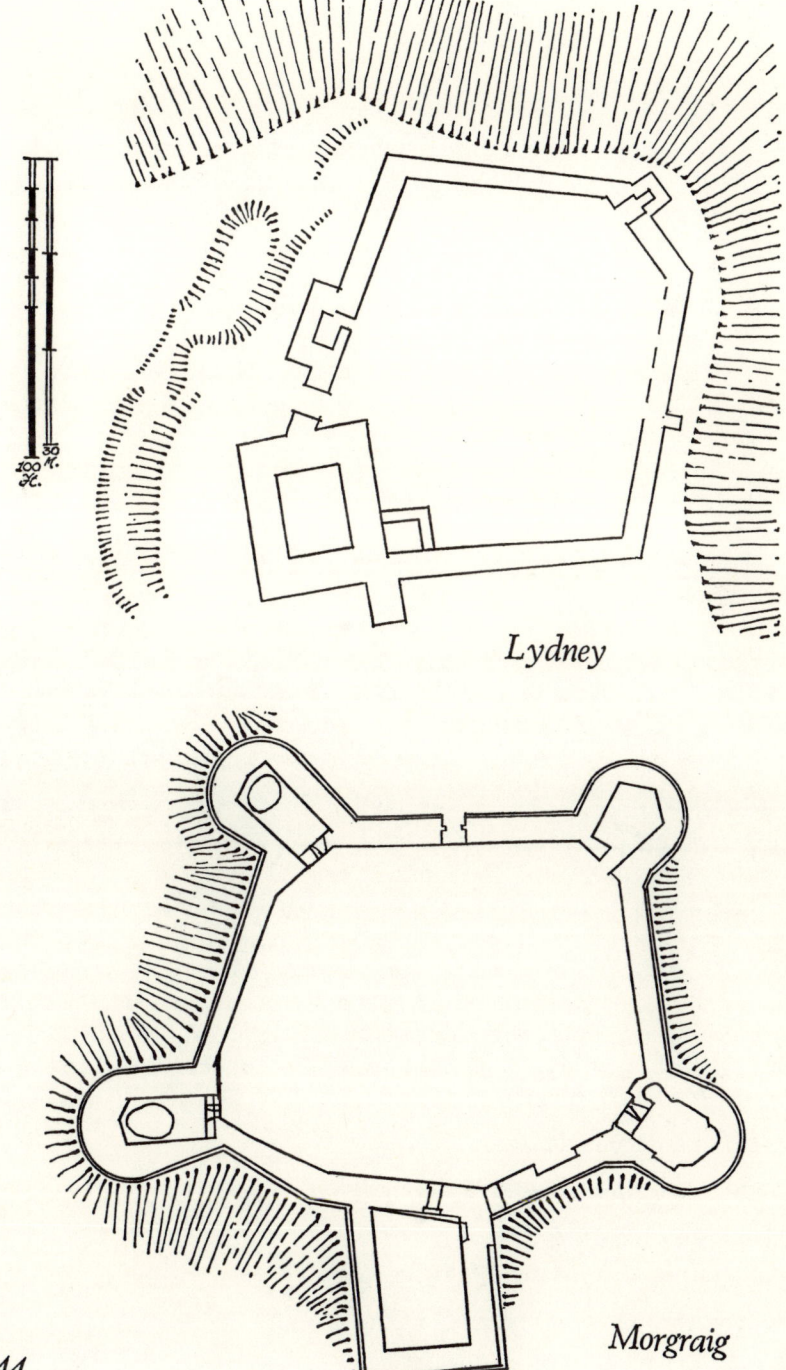

Lydney

Morgraig

1198–9 and repaired in 1208–9 (*Pipe Rolls*) (*Archaeological Journal*, forthcoming).* (Plate XXVII; Fig. 42)

LYDNEY SO 617025 Gloucestershire

On Little Camp Hill, immediately south-west of Lydney Park. A kite-shaped area of the hill-top is cut off by a bank and flat-bottomed rock-cut ditch using the natural steep slope to the south, with a similar internal ditch enclosing the stone castle (excavated in 1930) of local limestone rubble with roughly squared sandstone facing. The rectangular keep has a sloping plinth, and a large solid projection from the north-west angle. Two occupation levels were distinguished, and a 1-ft square post-hole of the earlier period found near the centre of the east wall, which had been rebuilt on a series of off-sets which overlapped the original masonry with a straight joint. A curtain wall runs in a diamond-shaped trace from the centre of the south side of the keep at an angle, with an entrance gap guarded by a shallow rectangular tower to an angle; the next is cut off with a short length of wall containing a small square turret. At a later date an angle of the keep and gate-tower was filled with a small annexe. A stone with a double roll-moulding was found in the entrance, coping stones and voussoirs near the curtain wall and a small capital and fragment of chevron moulding elsewhere. The pottery found included a glazed jug. Iron buckles, keys and nails were found, together with strapwork from a wooden door, shears, a padlock bolt, boathook, single-ended pick, lead plumb-bob and bone flute (*Antiquaries' Journal* XI, 240–61). (Fig. 44)

LYONSHALL SO 331563 Herefordshire

Ring-work and bailey (Cd2) beside churchyard, with further square bailey beyond to the north-east. The stump of a round keep, with roll-moulding above a sloping plinth, stands on a slight mound on the north side of the ring-work, with traces of a retaining wall to the south; the jambs of three loops survive. Parts of a curtain wall surround the ring, being inturned toward the keep and then carried round it as a mantlet in a semi-octagon.

Probably one of the two castles of John of Evreux mentioned in the *Pipe Roll* for 1188; named as *Lenhaul* in 1209 (*Rot. Litt. Pat.* p. 91) (R.C.H.M. *Herefordshire* III, p. 142–3).* (Fig. 42)

MABUDRUD see PENCADER

MABWYNION see STEPHEN'S CASTLE

MADOC see page 356

MAENCLOCHOG SN 083272 Pembrokeshire

No traces of the castle destroyed in 1215 (*Brut y Tywysogion*).

MAGH COBHA see BALLYRONEY

GAZETTEER

MAIDEN'S   see EDINBURGH

MAINCORE   see page 356

MALMESBURY   ST 933873   Wiltshire

A castle was built in the churchyard by Roger of Salisbury in 1118, not a stone's throw from the abbey. The site is probably that now occupied by Castle House which contains medieval walling of uncertain date. The castle was recaptured in 1139, when it was to be destroyed (William of Malmesbury, *Gesta Regum* II, pp. 547–57; *Historia Novella*, p. 24). An agreement between Henry of Anjou and Stephen to destroy it in 1153 was broken by a traitor selling it to Henry (*Gesta Stephani*, p. 154). £20 was spent on the walls in 1173–4 (*Pipe Roll*) but the monks were allowed to demolish it in 1216 (*Rot. Chart.* p. 222). The ringwork at Cams Hill (ST 941858) probably dates from the siege of 1144 (*Gesta Stephani*, p. 113).

MALTON   SE 792717   Yorkshire

Castle on site of Roman fort (see *Antiquity* II, p. 70) in existence by 1138 (Henry of Huntingdon, 261) and destroyed in 1214 (*Pipe Roll*).

MANCHESTER   Lancashire

Mentioned in 1184–7 and 1215–16 (*Pipe Rolls*; *Rot. Litt. Pat.* I, p. 165).

MANORBIER   SS 064978   Pembrokeshire

Immediately north of the present entrance to the castle courtyard is a square tower of three storeys, with a round-headed doorway at first-floor level on the west side. A hall and solar block was built opposite this across the point of the promontory with round-headed doorways reached by an external stair; a similar doorway gave access to the ground floor storage. The solar has a round-headed window beside a fireplace with a sloping head on corbels below a round chimney-stack. A twelfth-century bone draughtsman was found in the hall (*Archaeologia Cambrensis* fourth series XI, p. 288). Giraldus Cambrensis was born in the castle about 1146 (*Opera* I, p. 21).

MARLBOROUGH   SU 184686   Wiltshire

Motte and bailey (Ac2) in grounds of Marlborough College. Rubble footings have been found of a fragment of a shell-keep on the *motte* (curved, with pilaster buttresses), and of parts of the curtain wall (with an oak peg) (*Wiltshire Archaeological Magazine* 47, p. 543; 48, pp. 133–43). The *motte* produced Norman pottery (*Reports of the Marlborough College Nat. Hist. Society* LXXXII, pp. 66–104; LXXXV, pp. 42–7; XCVII, pp. 13–20)

The castle is first mentioned in 1138 (*Annales Monastici* II, p. 51; *Gesta Stephani*, pp. 70, 111) and the building work was carried out in 1175–9, and repairs from 1194 onwards including a *cingulum* round the *motte* in 1209–11 (*Pipe Rolls*). Tower mentioned in 1215 (*Histoire des ducs de Normandie*, p. 150). (Fig. 43)

MARSHWOOD SY 404977 Dorset

Low *motte* in moated enclosure (Bd2) with a concentric outer enclosure to the south-west. The *motte* carries the stump of a rectangular keep of coursed rubble; the external facing has gone, but internal ashlar quoins survive, with traces of an opening in the north wall.

Earliest mention of site 1215 (*Proceedings of the Dorset Natural History and Archaeological Society* LXVI, p. 70) (R.C.H.M. *Dorset* I, p. 157).*

MARTON see MORE

MATEFELUN Shropshire (?)

William de Boterells was given 10 marks to fortify his *domus de Matefelun* in 1195 (*Pipe Roll*). Possibly the *Moretoin* of 1215; see MORE.

MATHRAFAL SJ 131107 Montgomeryshire

Oval *motte* within square earthwork beside River Banwy (IBd2) built and destroyed in 1212 (*Pipe Roll; Brut y Rywysogion*). (*Montgomeryshire Collections* XLIV, p. 150).

MATILDA'S see PAINSCASTLE

MAUD'S see PAINSCASTLE

MAYNOOTH N 9338 Kildare

The castle occupied a square enclosure on the south side of a loop of the River Lyreen. The east front has a square solid tower with narrow entrance passage at the north end and a projecting square tower at the south-east (cf Trim). The main gatehouse to the south has a round-arched entrance of one plain order.

The keep on the west side has a chamfered plinth of six offsets, with wide buttresses in the centre of each wall rising to the first floor, except to the west, where the entrance stair rose to the forebuilding. The basement is lit by pairs of square loops in each wall except the north, and the first floor has round-headed windows flanking mural chambers in the buttresses to west and south. The north wall has a door to the wall-walk of the curtain beside the buttress chamber, and a higher doorway leads to a wall stair giving on to a mural passage round the other sides of the keep, with beamholes for an external wooden gallery. Below this are the beam-holes and rainwater gutters of an early roof. The east wall has a round-headed window south of two doorways, the one being the entrance and the other giving on to the upper part of the forebuilding. Changes in the masonry suggest three phases of building (*Journal of the Royal Society of Antiquaries of Ireland* XLIV, pp. 281–94).* (Fig. 45)

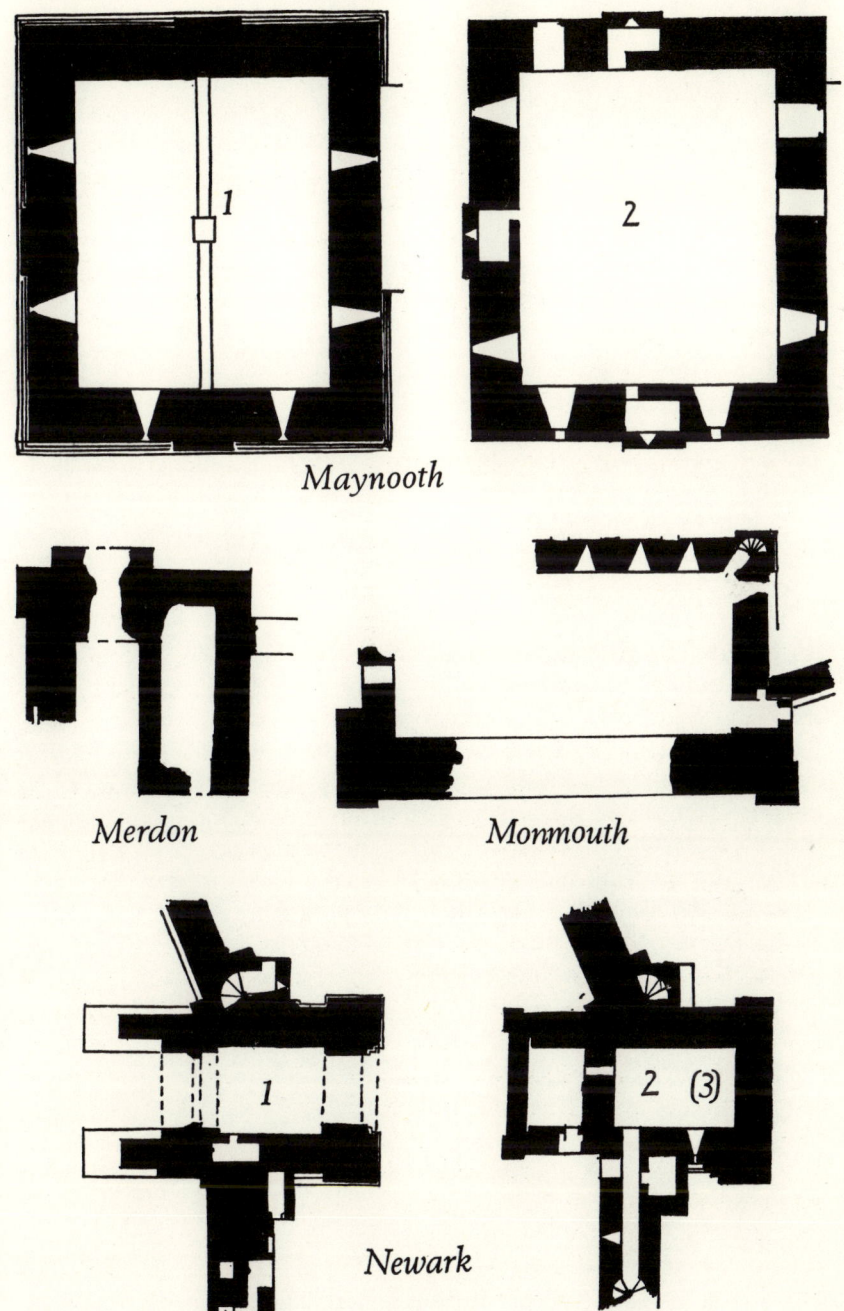

Maynooth

Merdon   Monmouth

Newark

45

| MEELICK | M 9314 | Galway |

The church was filled up to the gables and a *motte* built around it in 1203 (*Annals of the Four Masters; Annals of Loch Cé; Song of Dermot*).

| MEMBURY | SU 305745 | Wiltshire |

Excavation of a rectangular earthwork revealed what appeared to be a square twelfth-century keep underlying a manor-house, the latter defended by a round tower at one angle of the defences (*Antiquaries Journal* XXVIII, p. 33 for preliminary note; full report forthcoming in Professor W. F. Grimes' *Excavations upon defence sites 1939–45, III: Medieval*).

| MEPPERSHALL | TL 132358 | Bedfordshire |

Motte and baileys (Bcc2) with further ditches west of remarkable twelfth-century church, all within large square village enclosure, two sides of which form the parish boundary. The only evidence of date is an *inspeximus* of a charter of Stephen dated *apud Mapertes Halam in obsidione* (*Proceedings of the Cambridge Antiquarian Society* XLV, plate 1). (Fig. 39)

| MERDON | SU 421265 | Hampshire |

Ring-work (IIc) with partial subdivision to provide a bailey in the south part; the whole earthwork cuts across another ear-shaped enclosure (Iron Age?) of lower profile. The northern part of the western bank has an inner revetment of a flint wall at least 3 ft thick which ends in a small internal chamber (repaired in brick) and probably connects to the rectangular gatehouse on the north side. This is of flint rubble with clunch quoins and has a chamber in the eastern half, the passage occupying the other half. Buttresses flank the entrance, and traces remain of an upper level floored in timber, with a loop and latrine passage from the chamber. An oak mazer was found in the well south of the gatehouse (*Archaeological Journal* III, p. 361) which has a clunch ashlar lining.

The castle was built by Henry de Blois in 1138 (*Annales Monastici* II, p. 51) and was probably destroyed in 1155 (*Pipe Roll*) since we hear no more of it. (Fig. 45)

| MERRINGTON | NZ 263315 | Durham |

William Cumin built a *vallum* round the church in 1144 (*Symeon of Durham* II, p. 316).

| MEURIG | | Cardiganshire |

Site of keep marked by trench 60 ft square and fallen masonry, overlooking ditch cutting off promontory (SN 702675). There is a *motte* (Ib) a mile further east (SN 717677). One site is mentioned in 1116, and destroyed in 1137; the rebuilding in 1151 and destruction of 1208 (*Brut y Tywysogion*) may relate to the other.

MIDDLEHAM   SE 128877   Yorkshire

Large rectangular keep within concentric ditch; a *motte* and bailey 500 yds south-west may be of earlier date. The keep is faced in limestone ashlar, with a chamfered plinth and clasping buttresses, except on the east side where there is a stone base the whole length carrying the entrance stair to a plain round-headed door beside the south-east angle, where there is a spiral stair with round-headed doorways to all floors. Square latrine turrets project from the middle of the south and west walls. There is a north–south cross-wall with five round-headed openings at basement level and two above. The eastern part had a groined barrel-vault supported on a central row of five cylindrical columns, and is lit by two stepped square-headed loops in the end walls, with three recesses in the outer wall. The western basement had a pointed groined vault of six bays with a single loop at each end and seven in the west wall.

The entrance floor has deep round-headed windows – four in the longer (east–west) walls, and one to the north and two to the south on either side of the cross-wall, the south pairs each flanking a drain shaft. Round-headed doorways lead into mural chambers at the angles (except to the south-east); that to the north-east had a groined vault springing from semi-octagonal capitals, with twin loops in the north wall; a single loop in the east wall is flanked by an oblique passage to a door over the entrance stair. The billet-moulded corbels and beam-holes suggest a double-gabled roof on the cross-wall, later raised when an upper west floor was added.

The castle was built by the grandson of the 'Domesday' tenant (*Monasticon* VI, p. 920) probably in the late twelfth century; it was occupied for the king in 1216 (*Rot. Litt. Claus.* I, p. 248).   (Plate XXVII; Fig. 46)

MIDDLETON STONEY   SP 531233   Oxfordshire

Motte and bailey (IBd1) east of church. Twelfth-century pottery was found here in 1948 (*Oxoniensia* XIII, pp. 69–70). The castle is mentioned in 1215–16 (*Rot. Litt. Pat.* p. 127; *Rot. Litt. Claus.* I, p. 273) – the latter being an order for its destruction.

MIDHURST (ST ANN'S HILL)   SU 889215   Sussex

Triangular mound east of church beside River Rother, with inner ditch cutting off oval area and leaving narrow bailey to north-west (ICc2). Excavations in 1913 showed that the inner area was enclosed with a 5 ft thick coursed rubble wall, slightly inturned for the entrance, beside which was an inner wall with three pilaster buttresses cutting off a shield-shaped

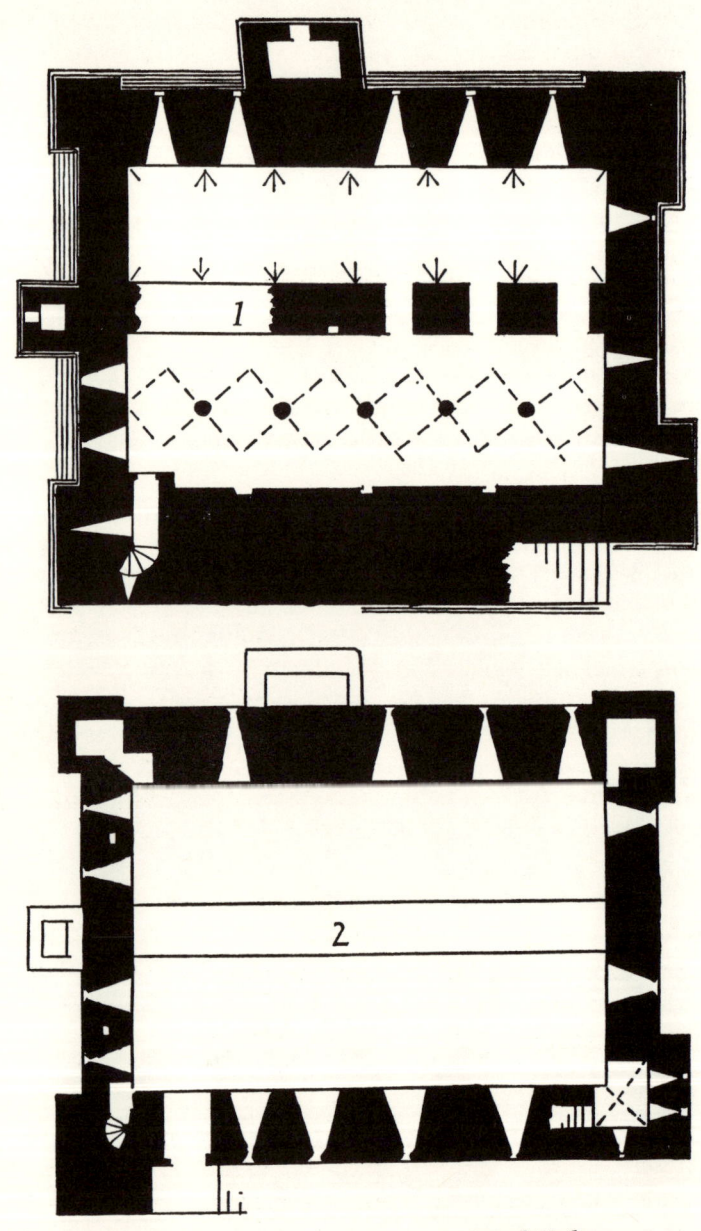

Middleham

area. There were two deeper buttresses on the outer wall. The east curtain wall had a hall butting against it, and was interrupted by a square-naved chapel (with a narrower square chancel) just north of the shell-keep. Fragments of moulded stonework suggested a mid-twelfth century date (W. H. St. J. Hope, *Cowdray and Easebourne Priory*, pp. 3–4). (Fig. 47)

MILDEN   see LELESHAY

MILDENHALL   see page 356

MILEHAM   TF 917194   Norfolk

Mound with two baileys, the inner perhaps a recutting of the original (Ba3 → Bb2 + a/23). The lower part of a square keep of flint rubble projects from top of mound, the interior being dug out but overgrown (see the engraving in the *Gentleman's Magazine* for June 1819, p. 513). There are traces of a plinth on the west side, and a buttress at the east end of the south side. Mentioned 1153 (Madox, *Formulae Anglicanum*, 154). (Fig. 47)

MINSTER COURT   TR 312643   Kent

The site of a monastic grange after 1030. The apsidal church has a strong west tower with a spiral stair in the surviving north-east angle, lit by a loop in a round-headed recess with cushion capitals to the shafts and a roll-moulded head like a window in the east gable of the north range. This latter was a hall of four bays, the pilaster buttresses cut back and a floor inserted internally. The west range, linking hall and church, looks earlier, being of flint rubble with some herringbone coursing, whereas the hall is of diagonally-tooled ashlar. A passage between the tower and the range has a groined vault, being entered by a round-headed doorway with a plain tympanum (*Archaeological Journal* 86, pp. 213–23).

MIRFIELD   see page 356

MISERDEN   SO 944093   Gloucestershire

Motte and bailey (Bd2), beside stream in Miserden Park, the castle of Robert Musard which he surrendered in fear of his life in 1146 (*Gesta Stephani*, p. 123). The interior of a shell-keep 60 ft across was partly excavated about 1907 by D. Montgomerie (letter in Sands collection).

MITFORD   NZ 170855   Northumberland

Pointed oval enclosure with strong counterscarp bank and outworks on south bank of Wansbeck, with a similar shaped *motte* on one side (IBb3). The *motte*-top is surrounded by a high D-shaped shell-wall of roughly coursed squared rubble, with a sloping plinth. There is a round-headed doorway of two square orders rising from imposts on the west side and a

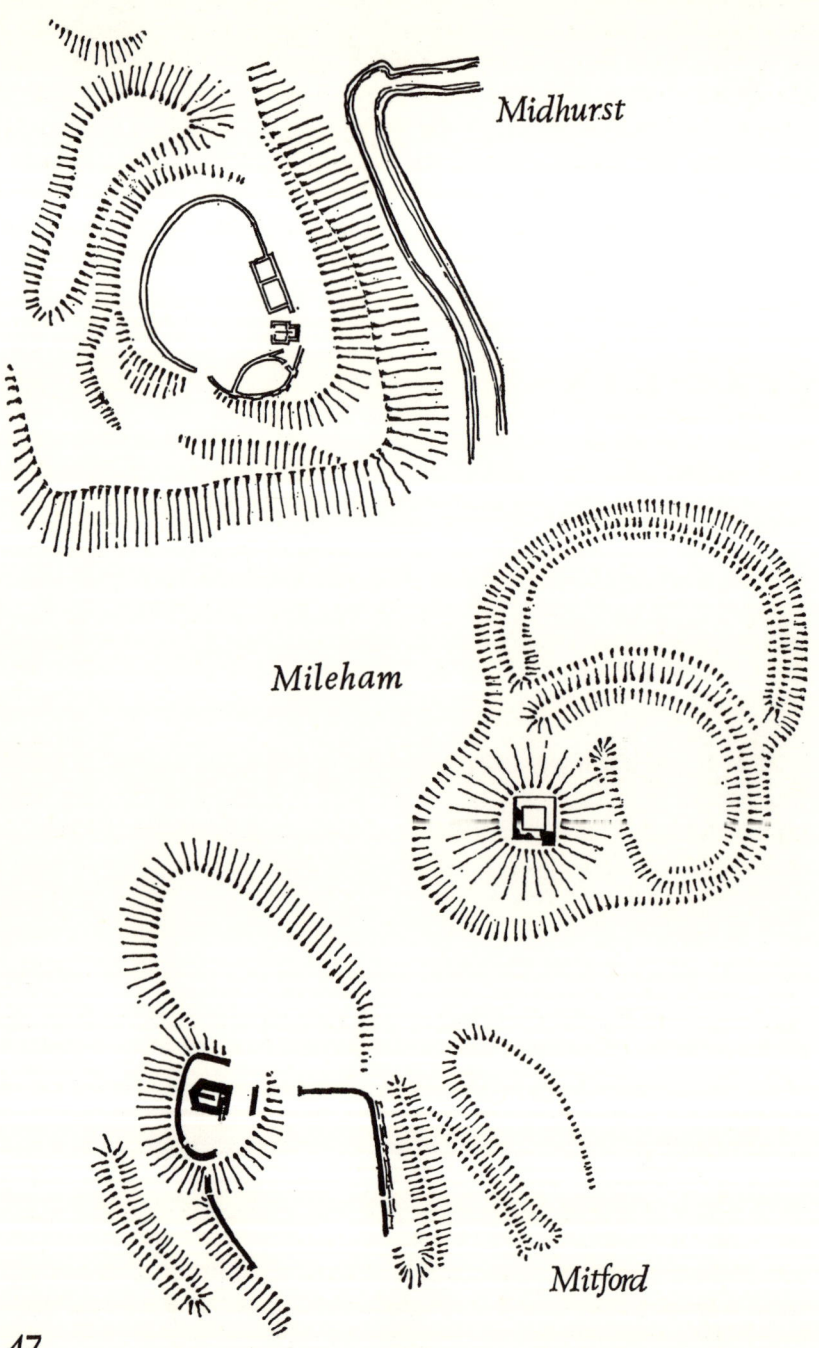

47

similar (but rebuilt) one in the opposite side. Within is a pentagonal keep, rectangular but with a salient angle, the surviving basement being divided by a cross-wall into two barrel-vaulted rooms lined with ashlar with chamfered plinths and imposts, lit by high-set loops and entered through a segmental-headed doorway from a straight wall stair in the wall opposite the salient. The southern half of the bailey was walled; part to the southeast is built of straight lengths of ashlar walling incorporating a round-headed doorway opening on to a rock-cut ditch. Excavations inside the bailey in 1938 revealed a chapel with mid-twelfth century mouldings covering an earlier burial ground.

William Bertram's *oppidum* at Mitford is mentioned in 1138 (*Chronicles of the reign of Stephen* III, p. 158) and was confiscated in 1215 by John (*Cal. Patent Rolls* 1216-25, p. 122; *Close Rolls* I, 246) (*Archaeologia Aeliana* fourth series XIV, pp. 74-94; XXXIII, pp. 27-34).* (Fig. 47)

| MIXBURY | SP 610341 | Oxfordshire |

Square banked enclosure with bailey (IICd3); the evidence of date is circumstantial; the Norman French name *Beaumont*, the finding of fragments of Norman masonry (Blomfield, *The History of the Deanery of Bicester: Mixbury*, p. 4) and the granting of the manor to Oseney Abbey in 1213 (*Cartulary of Oseney Abbey* V, pp. 387-400).

MOIRA   see DUNDRUM

| MOLD | SJ 235644 | Flintshire |

Motte and bailey, the latter altered (Ad2 ?). Two walls 30 ft apart were excavated south-west of the mound in 1872 (R.C.A.M. *Flintshire*, p. 63).

The capture of Guiddgrug in 1147 (*Brut y Tywysogion*; *Annales Cambriae*) may refer to this site. Mold is mentioned in 1167 and thereafter (*Pipe Rolls*).

| MONMOUTH | SO 507129 | Monmouthshire |

Oval ring-work at root of peninsula at junction of rivers Wye and Monnow (IC) scarped from low cliff, adjoining a square enclosure (with bowed sides) enclosing town to east. A large round tower stood on a slight mound on the north side of the ring-work until 1647 (Speed, *Theatre of Britain*). The rectangular keep on the west side is of coursed sandstone rubble with diagonally tooled ashlar dressings of the same material. The west wall is thicker than the others, but the main part has collapsed, as has the northeast angle. Pilaster buttresses clasp the angles, rising from a sloping plinth, but the buttresses in the east wall have been cut back. The basement and spiral stair in the south-east angle are lit by narrow loops, and there is a larger segmental headed window with a stepped embrasure in the south wall above a simple string-course. The original entrance was through a thickened buttress at the west end of the south wall; part of a contemporary curtain wall runs south.

The castle was built 'in the time of Count William' (*Liber Landavensis*, pp. 277–8), supported by a document of the reign of William I, (Round, *Catalogue of Documents preserved in France* No. 1133; and 'Domesday Book' I, 180b) (M.P.B.W. *Official Guide*).* (Plate XXVIII; Fig. 45)

MONT ORGUEIL   Jersey
On rocky promontory at eastern end of island. The square gatehouse of rubble masonry protecting the outer bailey has pointed arches, the outer being recessed with a round-headed arch over, springing from imposts. The inner curtain wall has an inward projecting gatehouse (much altered) with barhole and portcullis. Within the inner bailey is a rebuilt crypt with a groined vault springing from a central row of four round pillars and two corbels with plain square abaci and bases. It is entered through a round-headed doorway with double row of voussoirs. Two granite altar slabs were found near by; the floor above the vaulting was of red clay. Another crypt further north-east has a rubble vault springing from four round piers, three of rubble but the fourth a granite column; a small lancet survives on the upper floor. This may be the castle of Jersey mentioned in 1212 (*Patent Roll; Rot. Litt. Claus.* p. 126) (E. T. Nicolle, *Mont Orgueil Castle*).*

MONTACUTE   ST 494170   Somerset
St Michael's Hill forms an egg-shaped bailey, with combes running inward toward the oval *motte* which has a counterscarp bank to the west (1Be1). In 1069, those occupying the hill were attacked by the Saxons (*Ordericus Vitalis* II, p. 193), and Robert of Mortain's castle is mentioned in 'Domesday Book' I, 93a, but was given to the priory founded near by between 1091 and 1104 (*Somerset Record Society*, VIII).

MONTFICHET   TQ 318811   London
Probably the tower which stood between Baynard's castle and Ludgate (*Calendar of Charter Rolls* II, 180), and existed by 1137, being strengthened 1173–4 (*Chronicles of the reign of Henry II*, III, p. 338). See references under Baynard's (London).

MONTGOMERY   SO 214980   Montgomeryshire
Motte with strong counterscarp bank to bailey (Ab2). Excavations in 1960–7 revealed traces of five successive bridges between *motte* and bailey, the ditch having been recut. The bailey was palisaded and a large timber-revetted pit was excavated, with an apsidal timber building. Mentioned in 'Domesday Book' I, 253b, 254a.
Med. Arch. V, p. 322; VI/VII, pp. 326–8; VIII, p. 262; IX, p. 193.

GAZETTEER

MONTROSE   see page 356

MORE   SO 339914   Shropshire

Motte with two square baileys in echelon (Bdd4) beside marsh. The *motte* overlay a post-Conquest ring-work (*Antiquity* XXXIV, p. 229).

Possibly the *Moretoin* of 1215 (*Rot. Litt. Claus.* I, pp. 199a); the site (Ad2) at Marton (SJ 291026) is less likely. The *castelli Moretoin* of 1025–6 (*Cartulaire des Iles-Normandes*, p. 7) was in France.

MORETON   see MATEFULUN and MORE

MORETON CORBET   SJ 561231   Shropshire

One wall and fragments of two others of a rectangular keep of squared sandstone rubble. The angles have clasping pilaster buttresses, the angle being mitred off below the parapet. Mentioned in 1215 (*Rot. Litt. Claus.* I, p. 199) and 1216 (*Rot. Litt. Pat.* p. 166). Fireplace hood with stiffleaf capitals to polygonal columns.

MORGRAIG   ST 160843   Glamorgan

Pentagonal curtain wall with oval angle towers with polygonal interiors, apart from rectangular keep-like tower at angle opposite entrance gap. Square-headed windows, formerly with iron grilles and wooden shutters and pointed arches within. Built of local conglomerate, sandstone and limestone rubble, with dressings of the latter and also Sutton stone. Excavation in 1903–4 produced a few iron fragments, cooking pots and a whetstone, and the castle was attributed to the early thirteenth century, a date supported by the broad leafmoulded stopchamfer of one doorjamb (*Trans. of the Cardiff Naturalists' Soc.* XXXVIII, pp. 20–58).*   (Fig. 44)

MORHULL   see HALSTEADS

MORPETH   NZ 198857   Northumberland

Triangular hill (Ha' Hill) between River Wansbeck and the spur bearing the later castle which may have formed its bailey (Ab4). Excavation in 1830 revealed scalloped capitals and billet mouldings on the hill (Hodgson, *History of Northumberland* II, ii, p. 381).

The castle was taken by William II in 1095 (Gaimar, *Lestorie des Engles* 6151–4) and is also referred to in 1138 (*Symeon of Durham* II, 299).

MOTE OF URR   see URR

MOULTON   TF 314214   Lincolnshire

Oval *motte* (IB) in Kings Hall park, perhaps the castle of Thomas de Moulton of 1216–7 (*Rot. Litt. Pat.* p. 164; *Rot. Litt. Claus.* I, p. 313b).

| MOUNT ASH | H 9514 | Louth |

Motte (Ad2) with traces of hexagonal tower on top; excavation produced pottery and a Norman gilt-bronze prick-spur (*Journal of the Royal Society of Antiquaries of Ireland* XIII, pp. 322–6; XXXVIII, pp. 252–6; XL, pp. 203–8). See LOUTH.

| MOUNT FERRANT | SE 795639 | Yorkshire |

Narrow ridge cut off by cross-ditches (Cb4), site of the castle razed about 1155 by William of Aumale, the timber being given to Meaux Abbey (*Early Yorkshire Charters* IX).

| MOUNT SANDEL | C 8530 | Londonderry |

Large *motte* (B) beside River Bann, built by John de Courcy in 1197 (*Annals of Ulster, Annals of the Four Masters, Annals of Loch Cé*). The correct site may be the *motte* and bailey (Ad2) three miles upriver at Mill Loughan.

| MOUNTSORREL | SK 581149 | Leicestershire |

Oval hillock on ridge cut off by bank and ditch, with scarps to end of ridge, south of village. The castle and village were given to the Earl of Leicester by the Earl of Chester about 1148 (*Lansdowne MS.* 415, f. 41, quoted by Stenton, *The First Century of English Feudalism*, appendix 47) who also quotes (p. 250–6) *Cott. MS. Nero* C. III, f. 178 of 1148–53) and was confiscated in 1173–4 (*Hoveden* II, 65, 101) and the tower over the well and other buildings repaired in the 1190s and in John's reign (*Pipe Rolls; Rot. Litt. Claus.* I, pp. 16, 23, 35).

MOYCOVE   see BALLYRONEY

| MULGRAVE | NZ 839117 | Yorkshire |

Polygonal enclosure on ridge, isolated by ditches. The curtain wall acts as a revetment, and two lengths making a slight angle on the south-west side have a chamfered plinth, which together with the lower parts of the north and south walls of the altered keep within may be contemporary with the erection of the castle in 1214 (*Chron. de Melsa* I, p. 106) (V.C.H. *North Riding of Yorkshire* II, pp. 390–3).* The *castrum de Mulgreit* of 1133 (*Monasticon* I, 410) may be the *motte* at NZ 832117.

| NAAS | N 8919 | Kildare |

Much altered *motte* (B ?) with modern house on top. Mentioned by Giraldus Cambrensis, about 1180 (*Opera* V, p. 100).

GAZETTEER

NAIRN NH 885566

William the Lion (1165–1214) exchanged land in order to fortify a castle and burgh (*Registrum Episcopatus Moraviensis*, No. 25).

NARBERTH Pembrokeshire

The castle destroyed in 1116 (Brut y Tywysogion) is probably the type A *motte* known as Sentence Castle (SN 110116) rather than the later site (SN 109144).

NARRAGHMORE N 7402 Kildare

Site of castle of Robert fitz Richard, mentioned in 1182 (Giraldus Cambrensis, *Opera* V, p. 356).

NEATH SS 753977 Glamorgan

A castle west of the river existed in 1129 (G. T. Clark, *Cartae et alia munimenta quae ad Glamorgancia pertinent* (2 ed.) I, 75), and Neath is mentioned 1182–5 and later (*Annales Monastici* I, 18; *Pipe Rolls*) but the surviving masonry appears to be later than 1216.

NEILSTON see page 356

NENAGH R 8679 Tipperary

Large round keep originally at north apex of an irregular pentagonal curtain wall with smaller round towers at the angles. The southern pair formed the front gatehouse; practically all of the east one has gone, together with the walls and tower between it and the keep. The base of the west one survives with two narrow loops and the jamb of the gate-passage with a portcullis slot. The inner part of the gatehouse is rectangular, of two storeys with segmental rear-arches to the windows in the east part of the inner wall, with the hood-mould of an upper doorway and a central gap marking the line of the entrance. A fragment of the west tower of the curtain remains with the jamb of a doorway adjoining.

The round keep is of coursed limestone rubble with ashlar dressings and a high sloping plinth; a forebuilding was contrived between the west curtain (with latrine shaft) and a radial south wall, leading to a (destroyed) door at first floor level. A spiral stair, reached from the entrance passage, links the upper floors which were supported on wall offsets. A main north–south beam strengthened the first and second floors, which are lit by narrow loops plunging below first floor level. The two loops on the first floor have round rear arches, as have those to south and west on the floor above; the south one has chevron ornament, and a dog-legged passage from the west embrasure leads to a round-arched doorway giving on to the west curtain, of which only the ragged toothing remains. The other two embrasures are pointed, with window seats to the east one. The original top floor has four pointed windows with segmental embrasures, that to the south having jamb shafts with moulded capitals and bases, and that to the west with a latrine passage opening off the jamb. Adjoining the west window of the upper storeys are hooded fireplaces with separate shafts, the upper having a hood supported on columns with moulded capitals and bases.

Coins of Henry II and John are said to have been found under the foundations during the demolitions of 1790; the castle is usually attributed to Theobald Walter (d. 1206) (*Journal of the Royal Society of Antiquaries of Ireland* LXVI, pp. 247–69).*   (Plate XXIX; Fig. 48)

NEROCHE   ST 271158   Somerset

Excavations have shown that the spur of the Blackdown Hills was first cut off by a bank and ditch to form a rectangular enclosure with rounded ends. In the late eleventh century an inner square enclosure was made, and finally in the early twelfth a *motte* was built on the bank of the latter, an outer bank and ditch added (Ad3). The pottery included local imitations of Normandy types and diamond rouletted pieces, with gilt-bronze strip and D-shaped buckles (*Proceedings of the Somersetshire Archaeological Society* XLIX, pp. 23–54; *Medieval Archaeology* VIII, pp. 258–9).

NETHER STOWEY   ST 187396   Somerset

Motte and baileys, (Ba/22, a/24) with foundations of a rectangular tower about 60 ft by 50 ft, with north–south cross-wall and subdivisions, also trace of forebuilding at south end of east wall (*Proceedings of the Somersetshire Archaeological Society* XLIII, pp. 29–34). Possibly the castle of William fitz Odo, captured by Henry de Tracy in 1139 by throwing torches through the tower loopholes (*Gesta Stephani*, p. 55), although Torrington (Devon: ss 499189) (Bd3) has also been suggested. (*English Historical Review* 77, p. 228). Mentioned in charter forged before 1154 (*Regesta Regum Anglo-Normannorum* III, 373)   (Fig. 32)

NEVERN   see CAMMEIS

NEWARK   SK 796541   Nottinghamshire

Trapezoidal enclosure of bank and ditch with early masonry on the west side, beside River Trent. An excavation on the east side (*Transactions of the Thoroton Society* LX, pp. 20–33) showed that the bank had been thrown up over a Saxo-Norman occupation layer. A rectangular tower of slight projection remains at the south-west angle with a later plinth. There is an altered loop in each wall at each of the floors above the basement (which has a long narrow loop in the outer walls only). Each floor was entered from a wall passage in the south curtain. A little further north is a patch of walling with an internal round-headed arch, originally giving on to another wall passage rising to the upper floor of the tower. The crypt of the hall near the north-west angle has a central arcade of four round-headed arches, with a groined vault rising by chamfered ribs from imposts.

The north gatehouse is at a re-entrant angle of the curtain wall, with projecting flanking buttresses which have been recased. The front and rear round-headed arches are of two square orders springing from imposts on pilaster buttresses. There are clasping buttresses of ashlar on the inside of the gatehouse, and turrets at the angle with the curtain carry a spiral stair and a remodelled guardroom, with a latrine block and spiral stair in the curtain further west, where there are round-headed windows at two levels. The upper part of the outer part of the gatehouse has been remodelled, although Norman window mouldings can be traced in the blocked-up masonry. Internally there was a round window in a round-headed embrasure; the side windows have square heads under a round arch, and the stepped embrasures have nook-shafts with scalloped capitals and roll-moulded heads with an outer roll-moulding and pellet hood now spring from rubble corbels (the dressings and quoins are ashlar, in contrast to the coursed rubble slabs used elsewhere).

The Bishop of Lincoln was allowed to make a ditch and *calceta* (rampart ?) here in 1133, and one-third of the Lincoln knights were released for castleguard at Newark by 1135 (*Regesta Regum Anglo-Normannorum*, No. 1770; *Registrum Antiquissimum of Lincoln*, I, 23, 33-5, 38, 191) and it was called a magnificent castle of very ornate construction in 1139 (*Henry of Huntingdon*, p. 266) (*Transactions of the Thoroton Society* XXXIX, pp. 53-91). * (Plate XXVIII; Fig. 45)

NEWBURY   SU 472672   Berkshire

The site of Newbury Castle has been identified as The Wharf, east of the town centre. Its one appearance in history is the siege of 1152 (*Henry of Huntingdon* 284,; B. M. *Cott. M.S. Claud.* A VIII f. 110, quoted by Money, *The History of Newbury*, pp. 79-99).

NEWCASTLE   see KILDREENAN

NEWCASTLE (BRIDGEND)   SS 902801   Glamorgan

The coursed rubble curtain wall and the two square towers within have sloping plinths. The long straight east curtain stands against a steep slope, and the south wall turns at a right angle as far as the first tower, which is set obliquely on the axis of the first of seven shorter lengths of wall (with alternating quoins) which link the south and east walls in a roughly semi-circular trace. The second tower, half way round the trace is generally similar to the first, with ground-floor splays to a loop like that on the upper floor of the first tower, which also has traces of fireplaces. The entrance doorway, in a patch of ashlar walling just east of the first tower, has an inner order with a segmental head and roll-moulded jambs crossed by beaded billet ornament, and an outer order with a roll-moulded round arch supported on shafts with Corinthian capitals and moulded bases.

Apart from the *novo castello* of 1106 (see OGMORE), the first references are those of 1183–5 (*Pipe Roll*; G. T. Clark, *Cartae et alia munimenta quae ad Glamorgancia pertinent* I, pp. 21, 39; J. H. Round, *Calendar of Documents preserved in France*, No. 1129) (M.P.B.W. *Official Guide*).*

(Plate XXX; Fig. 54)

| NEWCASTLE LYONS | O 0234 | Dublin |

Placename mentioned 1211–2 (*Irish Pipe Roll*).

| NEWCASTLE MACKYNEGAN | O 2903 | Wicklow |

Ring-work (C) at end of natural ridge. Placename mentioned 1211–2 (*Irish Pipe Roll: Reg. St. Thomas Dublin*, pp. 166, 293) (*Journal of the Royal Society of Antiquaries of Ireland* XXXVIII, pp. 126–40).*

| NEWCASTLE UNDER LYME | SJ 844460 | Staffordshire |

Mound near the junction of Silverdale and John of Gaunt's Road, originally in extensive lake made by damming Lyme brook. Foundations of a long narrow building were excavated south-west of the mound, with ashlar dressings to pilaster buttresses and the jamb of an entrance. North of the mound a long wall with chamfered plinth and buttress with offset was found, with morticed timbers of a bridge (*Journal of the North Staffordshire Field Club* LXVIII, p. 170; LXIX, pp. 65–70; LXX, pp. 71–6).

The new castle of Staffordshire was restored to the Earl of Chester in 1146 (*Regesta Regum Anglo–Normannorum* III, 178) and the bridge and palisade were repaired in 1168–9 and 1189–90. The tower and other buildings were repaired, and others built in 1190–3 and over £200 spent by John during his reign (*Pipe Rolls*). The tower is probably that described in the seventeenth century as 20 paces square and 70 ft. high (Pape, *Medieval Newcastle*, pp. 124–5). See also TRENTHAM.

| NEWCASTLE UPON TYNE | NZ 253639 | Northumberland |

Triangular enclosure made by cutting off a headland at the confluence of the Lort Burn and River Tyne with a bank and ditch, the former *motte* had a polygonal shell-wall with buttresses (*Proceedings of the Society of Antiquaries of Newcastle-upon-Tyne*, fourth series, X, p. 297). Excavation of the south curtain wall (*Archaeologia Aeliana*, fourth series, XLIV pp. 79–145) showed it was ashlar-faced with stepped plinths and a wall-stair.

A barrel-vaulted passage through the wall is entered from one round-headed recess. Fragments of the curtain wall (with chamfered plinth) exist at the rear of the Black Gate and outside the great hall found in 1906. The hall was of four bays with aisles and arcades having roll-moulded bases to the circular columns; the north wall had a blind arcade of seven pointed arches, the three central ones having doorways.

A drawing of the great gate to the west of the keep before its demolition showed a round-headed arch of two orders sprung from chamfered imposts continued as a string-course, with a cross-wall running south of the keep. The keep is of irregularly coursed sandstone slabs (squarer within). It is nearly square in plan, with broad buttresses clasping the angles and in the centre of the east and west walls with narrower and shorter pilasters in the north and south walls rising from a chamfered plinth with a roll-moulding at the top. The north-west angle is not square but semi-dodecagonal in plan, and the forebuilding on the east side has two intermediate pilasters, but otherwise continues the design of the other sides of the keep. The chapel is in the basement of the forebuilding, approached by a square-headed door with round relieving arch and bar-hole to an L-shaped barrel-vaulted lobby vaulted in three bays, the outer ones with ball flower ornament between rolls on the ribs and the central bay with chevron ornament springing from corbels. The wall arcades have chevron decoration, supported on voluted capitals (one scalloped) with shafts and moulded bases; the chancel arch has two rolls with chevron between and externally, with square jambs and a quirked hollow impost.

All floors are linked by a spiral stair in the south-east angle, the latrines being grouped in the west wall. The basement has a central column with scalloped capital supporting an eight-ribbed vault springing from chamfered corbels and lit by two shelving loops; three wall chambers remain, one having a loop converted into a door 12 ft above the ground. The floor above is lit by a loop in the west wall and a two-light window to the south, the lights having roll-moulded heads within a double roll-moulded head supported on volute capitals with a continuous abacus and moulded bases. A chamber in the north wall has a round-headed fireplace with a chamfered cornice, repeated in the flanking window embrasures. There is a similar chamber in the south wall of the floor above but the fireplace has billet and roll-mouldings to the segmental head, with a short flue to the outer face of the wall. This floor is entered from the main stair, first through a segmental arch with an outer roll-moulded order supported on shafts with cushion capitals and moulded bases to a lobby with chevron-decorated wall arcades with volute capitals, and a fireplace, and a main door of two (restored) orders, the inner of chevrons continued as jamb panels, and the outer of chevrons divided by a roll-moulded impost on moulded shafts. There are four two-light windows, the two to the south

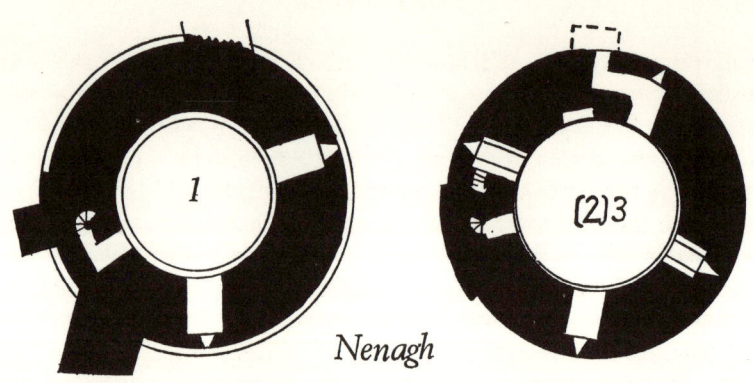

Nenagh

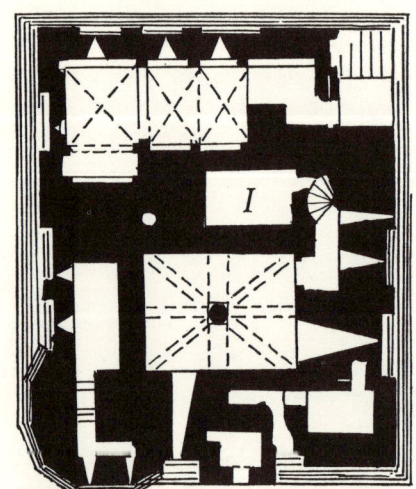

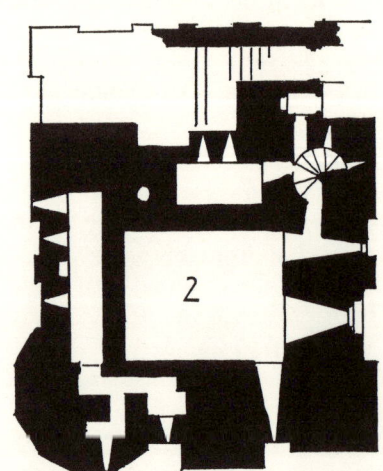

Newcastle upon Tyne

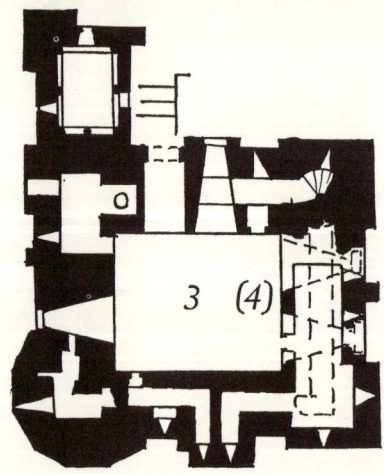

48

256

being placed over the wall-chamber and linking with a wall passage from the spiral stair, which was abandoned as a consequence of a change in design (*Archaeologia Aeliana*, new series, XXV, p. 96). A wall chamber in the north-west angle has an external bar-hole to the door, and the chamber in the north-east angle gives access to the ashlar lined well, 100 ft deep to the timber base-frame covered in lead (*Archaeologia Aeliana*, third series, IX, p. 263). Another wall-stair runs north from the spiral stair above the entrance to another spiral stair at the north-east angle, whence a gallery runs right round the upper part of the tower below the roof (runnels in east and west walls), lit by square-headed loops. There were internal doors, two in the east and west walls and one in the others, the beam-holes for an internal gallery.

The castle was founded in 1080 (*Symeon of Durham* II, p. 211) but the expenditure of over £1,100 in 1168–78 dates the existing masonry; there was a pause in 1173–4 during the Scots invasion, and over £100 was spent in 1211–12 (*Pipe Rolls*) (*Archaeologia Aeliana*, fourth series, II, pp. 1–51).*

(Plates XXX, XXXI; Fig. 48)

| NEWPORT | ST 312884 | Monmouthshire |

No remains survive of the castle mentioned in 1172 (*Brut y Tywysogion*) and 1185 and later (*Pipe Rolls*).

| NEWPORT | SN 057389 | Pembrokeshire |

Ring-work (C) underlying later stonework may be of the castle captured in 1215 (*Brut y Tywysogion*).

| *NEWTON LONGVILLE* | SP 842306 | Buckinghamshire |

Twelfth century pottery found in the *motte* ditch. (Report forthcoming in the *Newsletter* of the Wolverton and District Archaeological Society).

| NOBBER | N 8286 | Meath |

Motte and bailey (Bb3) in existence by 1186 (*Calendar of Documents* I, p. 110).

| NORHAM | NT 906474 | Northumberland |

Beside Tweed ford, with square ring-work and quadrant bailey (IICa/42). The west gate of both enclosures are barrel-vaulted with internal pilasters. The south gate has a round arch flanked by semicircular buttresses, and part of the curtain wall (particularly that to the east) may be of similar date; the south curtain was built on foundation piers penetrating the bailey bank (now gone). The eastern curtain is bonded into a pilaster buttress of the rectangular keep, which had clasping angle buttresses and intermediate pilasters, three to north and south and one to east and west.

The west wall and the whole upper part have been rebuilt, but the north wall retains a hollow moulding at its base and traces of a straight stair in its thickness. There is the start of a jamb to a ground floor entrance. The east–west cross-wall to the basement has a barrel-vault to the south and a four-bay vault to the north with ribs springing from pilasters, a narrow loop in each bay, with another in the south wall of the keep opposite the entrance and one in each half of the east wall. The floors were also linked by a spiral stair in the north-west angle; the upper floor has a round-headed fireplace in the south wall and recess in the east, and the twin-gabled roof can be traced above.

The castle was built by Ranulf Flambard in 1121, but it was ordered to be destroyed in 1138 (*Symeon of Durham* II, pp. 260, 291) and was rebuilt after 1157 (*Surtees Society* IX, p. 12). Over £700 was spent on Norham and Tweedmouth in 1208–12 (*Pipe Rolls*) (M.P.B.W. *Official Guide*).*

(Fig. 49)

NORRACH   see NARRAGH

NORTHALLERTON   SE 364941   Yorkshire

Motte and bailey (Bd4) with counterscarp bank and traces of ring-work beyond Willow Beck to north-west. One may be that mentioned in 1068 (*Symeon of Durham* I, p. 100) and the other that built by Bishop Pudsey in 1174 and destroyed in 1176 (*Hoveden* II, pp. 57, 65, 101).

The excavations mentioned in the 1938 Report of the Congress of Archaeological Societies have not been published.

NORTHAMPTON   SP 750604   Northamptonshire

Excavations in 1863–79 and 1961–3 have shown that the castle (now largely built over by the railway) was thrown up over late Saxon houses, many pits containing Saxo-Norman pottery, bone chessmen and draughtsmen, bells, arrow-heads and horseshoes being recovered (*Reports and Papers of the Associated Architectural Societies* XV, pp. 198ff; XVI, pp. 243ff; *Medieval Archaeology* VI/VII, p. 322; VIII, pp. 257–8; IX, p. 191). The earliest *motte* (IB) was buried in the huge bailey bank of the second phase (*c.* 1100), together with traces of timber buildings. Re-used ashlar blocks were incorporated in the undercrofts of buildings set within the north-east angle of the second phase (Bd2 ?). Moulded arches and carved corbels were found.

The castle was built before 1111 (*Lives of Anglo-Saxons and Others* ed. Giles, p. 54; V.C.H. *Northamptonshire* III, p. 3, n. 57) and compensation for land taken for the castle was paid in 1130; repairs to the keep were paid for in 1173–4, 1181–3 and 1192–3, and considerable sums were spent on it after the sieges of 1215 (*Pipe Rolls*).

XXXIII The elaborately sculptured arcades of the hall at OAKHAM.

XXXIV At ORFORD the polygonal keep has three large turrets (*left*) and twin window openings (*right*); the shutters are modern, but may represent the original method of closing.

XXXV A contrast in keeps: *left*, the plain stepped tower at OXFORD. *right*, the domed round tower at PEMBROKE, with its two-light window over the door.

XXXVI The additional upper storeys to the keep at PORTCHESTER can be detected by the changed shape of the windows and the pattern of putlog holes for the scaffolding, and also by the finishing-off of the pilaster buttresses.

XXXVII The original gateway at RICHMOND (background, left) was converted into a tower with a separate upper entrance.

XXXVIII RICHMOND castle from the south, showing the early hall (right) with the holes for a timber gallery below the windows of the lower storey, and the curtain wall on a low cliff above the river scarp.

XXXIX   *above* At CASTLE RISING the forebuilding (right) is highly decorated externally; *left* The entrance stairs and middle doorway, with simple cubical capitals.

XL *above* The keep at ROCHESTER with its forebuilding (left) and the ranges of hall and gallery windows.
below The arcaded crosswall with one of the doorways to the well-pipe (right).

XLI *above* The surviving half of the keep at SCARBOROUGH and its early curtain walls on a promontory above the North Sea.
below The gatehouse at SHERBORNE.

XLII The timber gallery at STOKESAY is Jacobean, but may well replace an earlier one contemporary with the Norman tower below.

XLIII CASTLE SWEEN, near the isthmus of the loch (left) with its central round-headed entrance.

XLIV Two original windows survive in the WHITE TOWER OF LONDON—top storey, extreme left. The parallel lines in the foreground indicate the line of the Roman city wall, one of whose turrets is incorporated in the Norman tower (under the first tree).

XLV   TRIM from the air. The square keep with mid-wall turrets stands on a slight mound. Beyond the River Boyne is a hummocky area, perhaps the quarry for the stonework of the castle.

XLVI *above* The thirteenth-century round tower at TRETOWER stands in the middle of the angular Norman residential block.
below The keep at USK, with its twin splayed windows (centre).

XLVII St Leonard's Tower, WEST MALLING, with blind arcading halfway up and simple windows at the top.

XLVIII Although modernized and re-windowed, the lower part of the Round Tower at WINDSOR preserves the plan of the Norman original.

containing a late twelfth/early — thirteenth-century masonry hall (*Medieval Archaeology* VI/VII, p. 326).

PENCADER   SN 444362   Carmarthenshire

Motte and bailey (Be2) at confluence of streams. Perhaps the castle of Mabudrud and Dinweilir built in 1145 (*Archaeologia Cambrensis* 1963, pp. 123–4).

PENCELLI   SO 095248   Brecknockshire

Triangular enclosure, made by cutting off a natural promontory with a bank and ditch. The point is covered with debris from an irregular building some 50 ft square with walls nearly 10 ft thick. The castle was captured in 1215 (*Brut y Tywysogion*).

PENDRAGON   NY 782026   Westmorland

Keep in circular enclosure (C ?) beside River Eden at Mallerstang. The tower is of rubble with very slight clasping buttresses at the angles and a turret projecting diagonally from the south-west angle. On the ground floor are round-headed loops in the south and west walls, and small barrel-vaulted cells at the south end of the west wall and the east end of the north one. There are wall passages extending from each angle of the first floor, that to the south-west extending into the turret and having a moulded arch to the doorway. Remains of two-light windows with an outer arch of two orders (moulding and chamfer) exist at two places in the east wall and one to the west. (R.C.H.M. *Westmorland*, pp. 163–4).* (Fig. 55)

PENEVERDANT   see PENWORTHAM

PENKRIDGE   see RODBASTON

PENLLYN   SS 979761   Glamorgan

The stable block contains herringbone laid walling a few feet high, perhaps the base of an early hall or tower.

PENMAEN   SS 534880   Glamorgan

Promontory cut off by curving bank and ditch to form oval ring-work (Ic). Excavations showed a rectangular timber gatehouse which had been burnt down and the entrance passage revetted in drystone masonry. A small timber hall was replaced by a larger one further south on drystone footings (*Antiquaries' Journal* XLVI, 178–210).

PENRICE   SS 492879   Glamorgan

Ring-work (IC) west of village, built by Henry de Beaumont in 1099 (Aberpergwm *Brut* cited in *Archaeologia Cambrenis* XC, p. 71) Wooden stakes were found in (or under) the bank about 1927 (*Antiquaries Journal* XLVI, p. 207).

PENWORTHAM   SD 525290   Lancashire

Motte and bailey (Bd4) north of church beside River Ribble. Excavation of the mound in 1856 produced evidence of a circular wooden structure round a central oak post, with a cobbled floor. The mound was raised 5 ft with layers of sand and clay and another floor laid and then the mound raised a further 7 ft. Among the finds was a Norman prick-spur; it is not certain which level it came from (Hardwick, *History of Preston*, pp. 103–11). The castle of *Peneverdant* is mentioned in 'Domesday' (I, 270).

PERTH   Perthshire

The castle chapel is mentioned in a grant of 1157–60 (National Library of Scotland *Advocates*' M.S. 34.1.3 (A) f.x. cited by Barrow, *Regesta Regum Scottorum* I, p. 209).

PETERBOROUGH   TL 194987   Northamptonshire

Mound (IIB) north of cathedral, named Mount Thorold after the Norman abbot (1069–98) who built it, according to a fourteenth-century interpolation in *The Chronicle of Hugh Candidus* (ed. W. T. Mellows) pp. 84–5, 173.

PEVENSEY   TQ 644048   Sussex

The Normans narrowed the west gate of the oval Roman fort with a wall in front of the guard-chambers, and cut away a curving ditch in front which produced early cooking pots on excavation (*Sussex Archaeological Collections* XCI, p. 64). The arch of the east gate was also repaired and fighting platforms added to the top of the two bastions further north. A long collapsed section of the Roman wall to the south-east was closed partly by a rubble wall and partly by an earth bank.

    A pit containing a wooden ladder, cask, bowls, and spades with four eleventh-century jugs from Normandy has been excavated in the outer bailey (*Antiquaries' Journal* XXXVIII, pp. 205–17).

    A square inner bailey was made cutting off the eastern angle of the Roman fort with a bank and ditch. The line of the bank can be traced in the rough foundations of the early thirteenth century gatehouse, and the ditch was narrower than the present moat (see plan in *Sussex Archaeological Collections* LXXIV, p. 7). A rectangular keep is based on the Roman wall, using one of the earlier bastions and adding two more round-fronted bastions facing east, one north (containing a square well-shaft), and two west. The drain chamber beside the Roman bastion has produced a bascinet visor, and a twelfth-century spoon was found under the stair foundation on the west side (*Antiquaries' Journal* XII, p. 73; XVI, p.

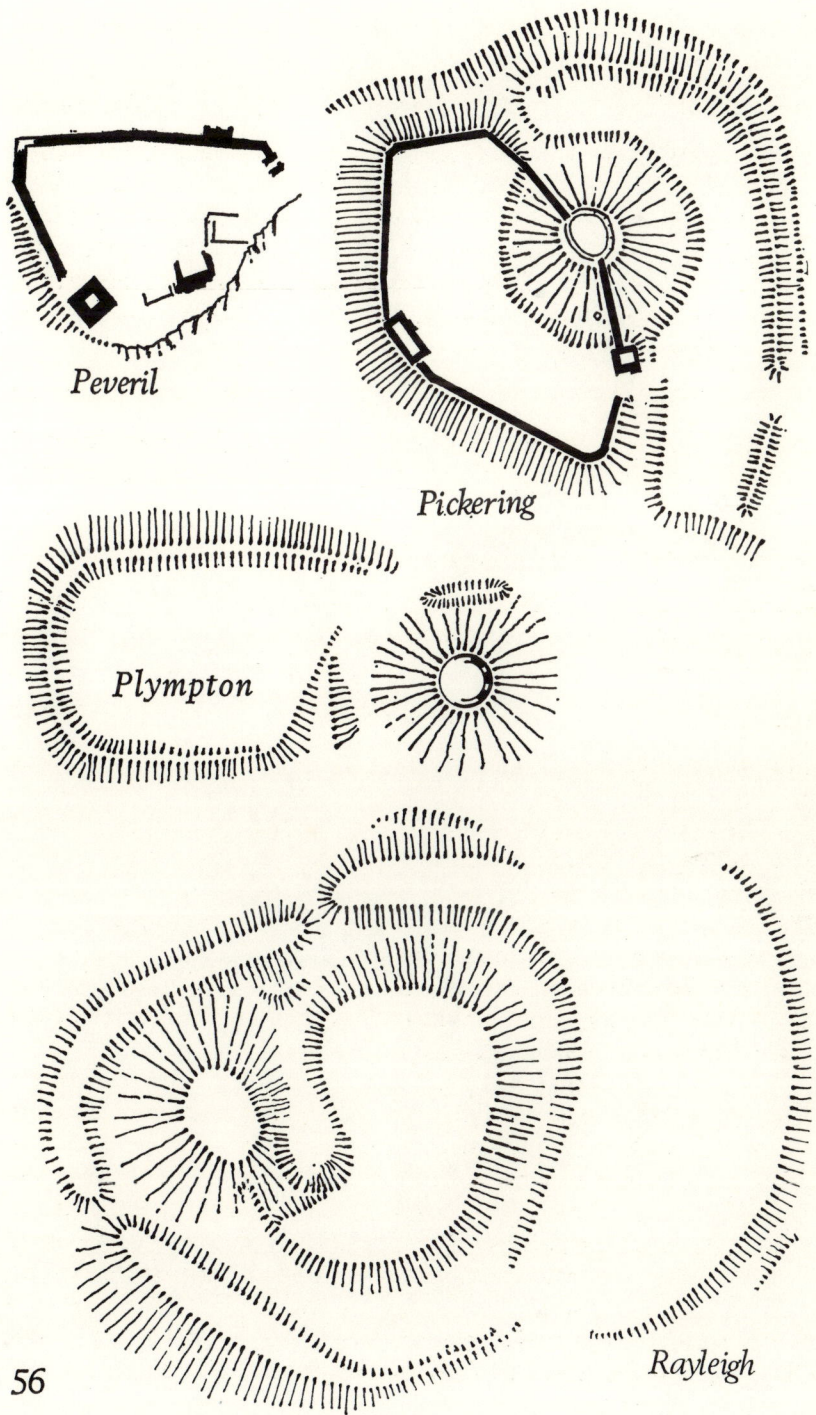

56

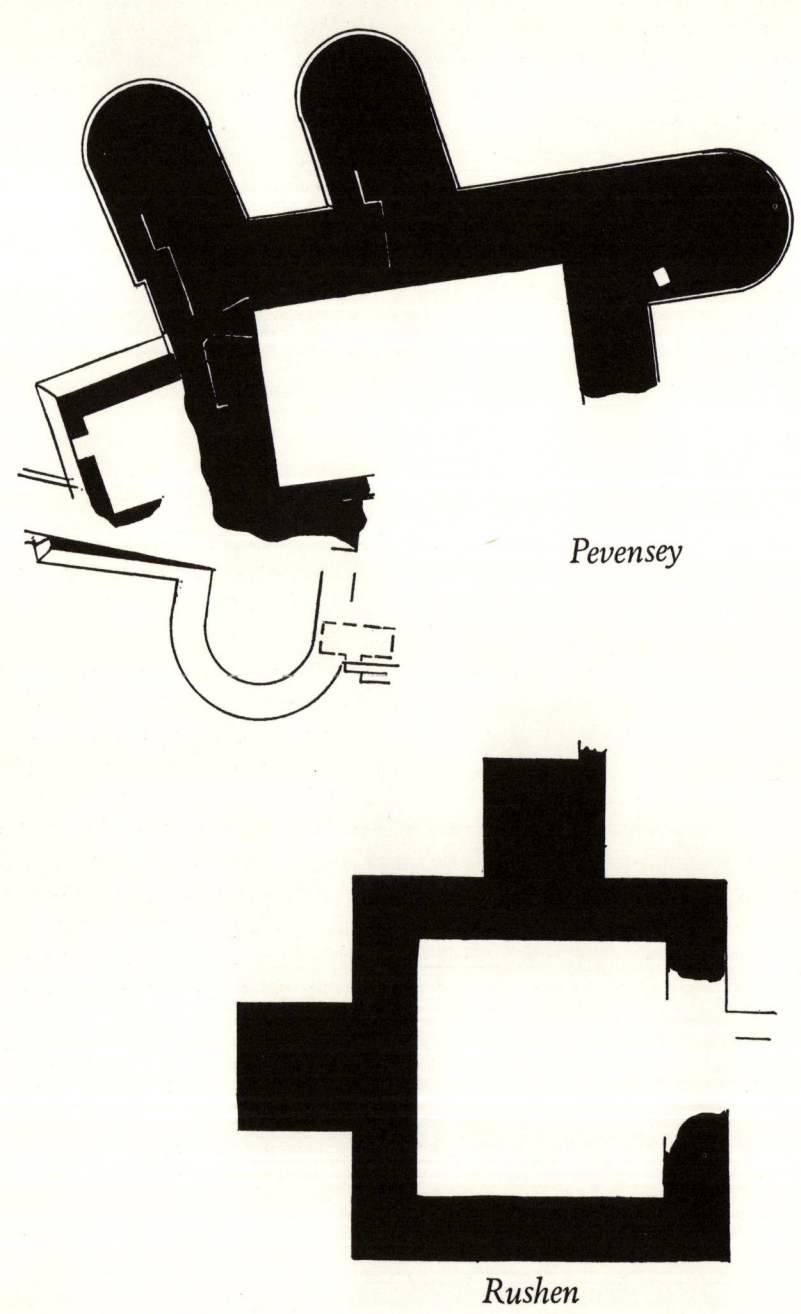
57

413-9) and the clay filling of the interior contained scratch-marked pottery (writer). A square ashlar block was added to the south, with a sloping plinth overriding that of the keep proper. Little remains of the upper floor, except jambs of a doorway and window in the south wall, doorways to Roman bastion and annexe and a projection over the western bastions.

William landed at Pevensey and built a castle with a strong rampart (*William of Jumièges*). The castle was starved into surrender in 1088 and 1147 by royal forces (*Anglo-Saxon Chronicle*); and the *Turris de Pevensel* is mentioned in 1129-30 (*Pipe Roll*). Only small sums were spent later on repairs; the palisade was repaired in 1188 and heckage payments commuted in 1254 (which probably dates the stone curtain). The castle was dismantled in 1216 (*Annales Monastici*, III, 46; *Rot. Litt. Pat.* 184) *Sussex Archaeological Collections*, XLIX, pp. 1-30; LXXIV, pp. 1-15.*

(Fig. 57)

| PEVERIL | SK 148826 | Derbyshire |

Bank and ditch enclosing triangular site. Inner enclosure to east, the north curtain wall in herringbone masonry revetting clay levelling-up. A shallow buttressed turret and round-arched gateway were added later, together with parapet. The north-west angle was rebuilt in the thirteenth century, the western curtain wall with herringbone work was partly destroyed when the keep was erected across the south splayed angle. There are foundations of an early chapel and a (rebuilt) hall (with a plinth like that of the keep).

The ashlar has been robbed from the exposed sides of the keep, which has clasping and central pilaster buttresses, the south and west angles having an inset column with a reeded capital. The keep was entered from the south end of the north-east wall, with an adjacent newel stair to the ground floor lit by round-headed windows in the northern walls, with larger windows on the floor above; windows also light wall-passages in the north and south angles, the latter with a corbelled-out latrine. The gabled roof ran north-west/south-east, with a window in the latter gable and another above the roof in the south-west wall, reached from the newel stair turret by a wall stair.

The castle of Pechefers ('Domesday' I, 276), strengthened and garrisoned in 1173-4 and the keep built in 1175-7 for £184; bridge nearby repaired in 1183-4 and the castle generally repaired from 1194-9; over £100 spent on it during 1205-12 (*Pipe Rolls*) (M.P.B.W. *Official Guide*).*

(Figs. 55; 56)

| PICKERING | SE 800845 | Yorkshire |

Motte and bailey (AC1) north of town; the carotid shape was divided by a cross-ditch to give two boomerang-shaped baileys. The broader bailey to the north has a rubble curtain built in straight lengths and running up the sides of the *motte* to a round shell-keep on top. Early thirteenth century rebuilding (in coursed rubble with a plinth) can be seen in parts of the curtain and the whole of the shell, which has ashlar dressings to the slight internal angles and the long arrowslits. The bailey entrance is flanked by a square tower of rubble (with ashlar quoins) which protects a staircase rising with the wall to the *motte*-top, with a parapet looped for arrows.

Both *motte*-top and north bailey contain foundations of buildings of various dates. On the axial line of the bailey are the narrow foundations of an early hall with entrances at the northern ends of the short walls (see Huttons Ambo). The north-west wall was rebuilt against the curtain, with a central seat recess under a bead-moulded round-headed arch with shafts and scalloped capitals, and a fireplace buttress in the opposite wall.

Some work on the castle was paid for in 1179–80, but the main expenditure was after 1216 (*Pipe Rolls*) (M.P.B.W. *Official Guide*).* (Fig. 56)

PICKHILL   see page 356

PIRTON   TL 146316   Hertfordshire

Partly destroyed *motte*, with bailey enclosing twelfth century church (Be3). Traces of outer village enclosure. Pottery from the *motte* ditch includes inturned-rim bowls of Saxo-Norman type (Hitchin Museum).

PLESHEY   TL 666144   Essex

Terraced *motte* and bailey (IBb4) with traces of second bailey (making a figure of eight plan) inset into carotid village enclosure. A gravel track led to a point opposite a break in the bailey rampart, with an 'island' in the moat for bridging. A late medieval brick bridge gives access to the *motte*-top, on which stood a rectangular building on narrow buttressed flint-rubble foundations (*Transactions of the Essex Archaeological Society* 16, pp. 109–24), probably a hall. Excavations showed that in the late twelfth century timber buildings were built on the tail of the bailey bank (which had a timber revetment) using some reddish-brown sandy bricks 13 × 9 × 1¼ in. (P. A. Rahtz, *Pleshey Castle: First Interim Report* 1960). Two small round foundations (late twelfth/early thirteenth century) underlay the stone chapel in the bailey. (*Medieval Archaeology* VII, pp. 252–3).

Geoffrey de Mandeville's surrender of his castles to Stephen in 1142 (J. H. Round, *Geoffrey de Mandeville*, pp. 88–9, 172, 286) was followed by a general order for their destruction in 1157–8 (*Pipe Roll*) but Pleshey was refortified with Henry II's permission between 1167 and 1180 (*P.R.O. Duchy of Lancaster Misc.* 10/12) (R.C.H.M. *Essex* II, pp. 201–2).* (Fig. 61)

PLYMPTON   SX 546559   Devon

Motte and bailey (Bb4) with fragments of rubble wall 8 ft thick with flat offset, about 50 ft in external diameter around *motte*-top. The castle is said to date from the first year of Henry I (*Transactions of the Plymouth Institution* 1876–8, p. 246). In 1136 the castle surrendered and was levelled to the ground (*Gesta Stephani*, pp. 23–4) but appears to have been rebuilt and then confiscated by the Crown in 1204 (*Rot. Litt. Pat.* 48; *Rot de Oblatis et Finibus*, p. 235). (Fig. 56)

PONTEFRACT   SE 460224   Yorkshire

Motte (later encased in masonry) with oval inner and two rectangular outer baileys (Bbdd3). The tower north of the *motte* has a blocked segmental-headed doorway with round relieving arch flanked by pilaster buttresses, with a barrel-vaulted ashlar passage. From the picture by de Mompers at Hampton Court Palace the curtain wall had similar pilasters on the south side, and square towers, one with a recessed round-headed entrance arch. Within the enclosure are several ashlar-faced cellars with rubble barrel-vaults, reached through a round-headed door from a tunnel, and also an apsidal chapel with scalloped capitals to the arch.

The castle of Ilbert I was built by 1086 ('Domesday Book', I, 373b; *Regesta Regum Anglo-Normannorum* II, 372; and Farrer, *Early Yorkshire Charters* 1, 415), and the chapel founded in the reign of William II (*Monasticon* V, p. 128).

PONTESBURY   SJ 401058   Shropshire

Ring-work with possible traces of bailey (Ca1) and village enclosure. Excavation revealed a V-section ditch and bank (later heightened) surrounding timber buildings on drystone foundations. A robbed wall 14 ft thick with sandstone footings and mortared quartzite rubble core was interpreted as an angle of a tower about 60 ft square. Finds included infolded-rim pottery, a scratched lead disc, and leather sheath (*Transactions of the Shropshire Archaeological Society* LVII, pp. 206–23).

PONTHENDRE   see LONGTOWN

PORTCHESTER   SU 625046   Hampshire

The medieval castle was built by cutting off the north-west angle of a Roman fort with a curtain wall and ditch. The Roman posterns in the north and south walls of the fort were blocked, and square outer gatehouses built in the east and west walls, using the left-hand (as seen from outside) inturn of the recessed Roman gate as the base for one side wall, the other being on the axial line of the earlier entrance. The inner of the two ditches was recut with a wide flat bottom; an eleventh century timber hall has been found west of the priory church (*Antiquaries' Journal* XLIII, pp. 218–27; XLVI, pp. 39–49). The angle of the fort was destroyed when the square keep was built across it; at one time the base of the keep was covered by a

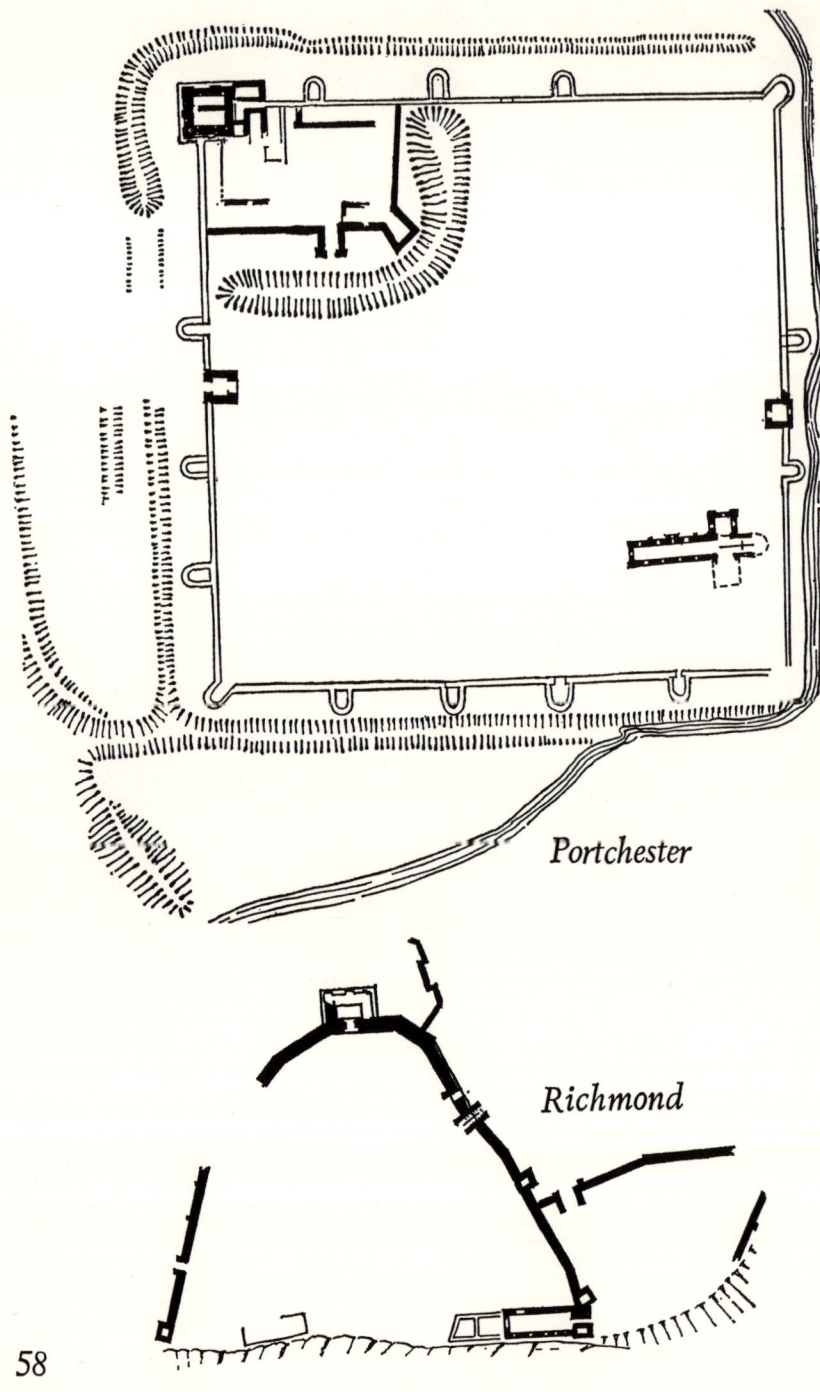

58   Portchester

282   Richmond

mound of earth (see V.C.H. *Hampshire* III, plate facing p. 158) of some antiquity, since the ditch curves outward round its line.

The inner curtain wall is of Caen ashlar, with a square southern gatehouse with plain jambs (later extended and altered) and a timber ceiling. The open-backed south-east angle turret is slightly trapezoidal in plan, with nooked outer angles and beam-holes of an upper floor, lit by a round-headed loop on each face. Within the enclosure, a long building against the north (Roman) wall had a barrel-vaulted basement of three bays, with a pilaster buttress clasping the angle and an upper doorway to the rampart. The later palace ranges south of the keep contain re-used Norman mouldings, with a wall that has a round-headed doorway and blind arcade.

The keep is ashlar-faced with pilaster buttresses clasping the angles and in the centre of the north and west sides where there is a tall stepped plinth, with a moulded string-course on the west wall only. The buttresses die back into the walls at the level of the original parapet, except that at the south-west angle which continues upward, carrying the spiral stair linking all floors. Recent excavations have shown several rebuildings of the forebuilding on the east side of the keep (*Medieval Archaeology* VIII, p. 253). At present a straight stair rises from a doorway beside the north curtain wall and turns left to a landing in front of the narrow round-headed entrance arch. This is flanked by a plain northern room projecting beyond the curtain and a wide round-headed recess at the west end of a chapel (the jamb of one south window survives). Creasings indicate low-pitched roofs replacing a high-pitched one over the chapel.

Internally the keep is divided by an east–west wall, and has latrines in the north angles and a well-pipe in the south-east angle. The basement is lit by two double-splayed round-headed loops in each wall (except the east); the entrance floor windows are similar, but of wider splays, and those in the north and south walls have engaged shafts, with foliated capitals, carried round the rear-arch as a roll-moulding. A round-headed fireplace has a domed shaft with narrow vent-holes in the wall. Above this level are the W-shaped creasings of the original roof, the central gable resting on the spine wall, which has a round-headed doorway. There are traces of eight small loops, one under each gable, and a door to the (Roman) wall-walk. The two added storeys have square-headed windows; two in the west wall of the lower and two in each wall of the upper, those facing into the castle (i.e. south and east) being of two lights recessed under a round head.

The Augustinian priory in the opposite corner of the Roman fort was founded in 1133, being the king's gift, although the endowment was provided by the lord of the manor. Together with a reference to the castle 'when King Henry was alive and dead' (*Add. MS.* 28024, f. 21b, quoted

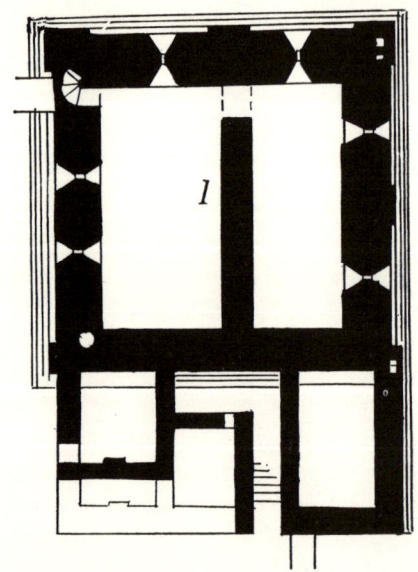
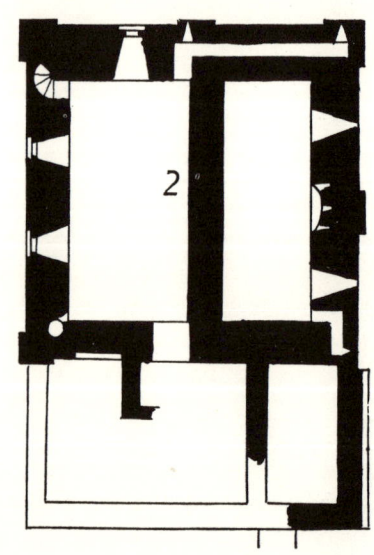

Portchester

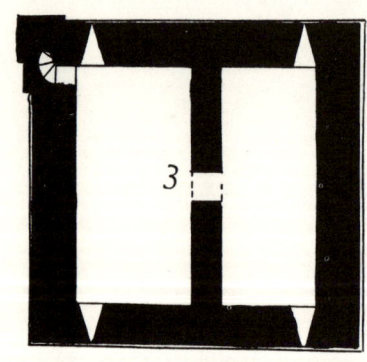
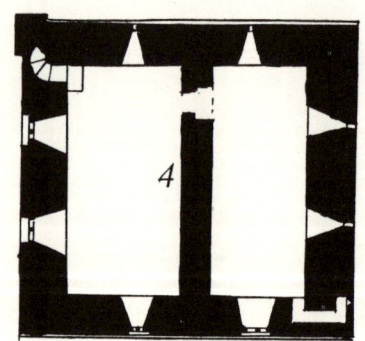

59

by Sayles and Richardson, *The Governance of Medieval England*, p. 434), and its use as a treasure house in 1163 (*Pipe Roll*), this suggests the castle may have been built in Henry I's time. The date of the elevation of the keep is uncertain – only repairs are recorded in 1172–3 (*Pipe Roll*) and it can hardly be as late as the alterations of 1253 (*Cal. Close Rolls*). The castle was to be destroyed – or at least burnt – in 1217 (*Patent Roll*). (M.P.B.W. *Official Guide*; *Studies in Local History: Portchester*; *The Portsmouth Papers* I.)* (Plate XXXVI; Figs. 58, 59)

PORTSMOUTH   Hampshire

The town was founded by Richard I, and the dock for the royal galleys surrounded with a strong wall. The king's house was built at Kingshall Green between 1194–8 and had a defensive ditch. (*Pipe Rolls; Rot. Litt. Claus.* I, p. 117)

POTTO see WHORLTON

POWDERHAM   SU 803469   Hampshire

Small *motte* (IIB) with strong counterscarp bank. Flint foundations about 4 ft 6 in. wide and 40 ft across can be traced on its surface. Norman pottery was found in the ditch in 1922–3. (*Proceedings of the Hampshire Field Club and Archaeological Society* XII, pp. 308–9). A post-hole and timber revetment to the mound were discovered in 1951 (*The Times*, 26 October 1951). See 'LIDELEA'.

POWERSTOCK   SY 521959   Dorset

Motte and bailey (Be3) with triangular outer enclosure much altered by quarrying. Henry of Anjou captured Bridport and its castellan in 1149 (*Gesta Stephani*, p. 147) – since no castle is known within the town, this may refer to Powerstock.

The stone buildings visible until the eighteenth century (Hutchins' *History of Dorset* II, p. 318) were probably the king's houses built in 1206–7 at a cost of £373 (*Pipe Rolls*). A spur, horsehoe and pottery were excavated in 1840 (*Proceedings Dorset N.H.A.S.* LXVI, p. 69) (R.C.H.M. *Dorset* I, pp. 183–4).*

PRESTATYN   SJ 073833   Flintshire

Motte and bailey (Ba3). The excavation of masonry 4 ft thick (probably the large blocks of dark limestone and yellow sandstone still visible) on a cement and gravel foundation is reported in *Archaeologia Cambrensis* sixth series, 13, p. 350, where the castle is attributed to Robert Banastre (1164). Mentioned in 1165–6 (*Pipe Roll*).

PRESTON   SD512302   Lancashire

Motte and bailey (Bb2) in grounds of Tulketh Hall. Site given to monks of

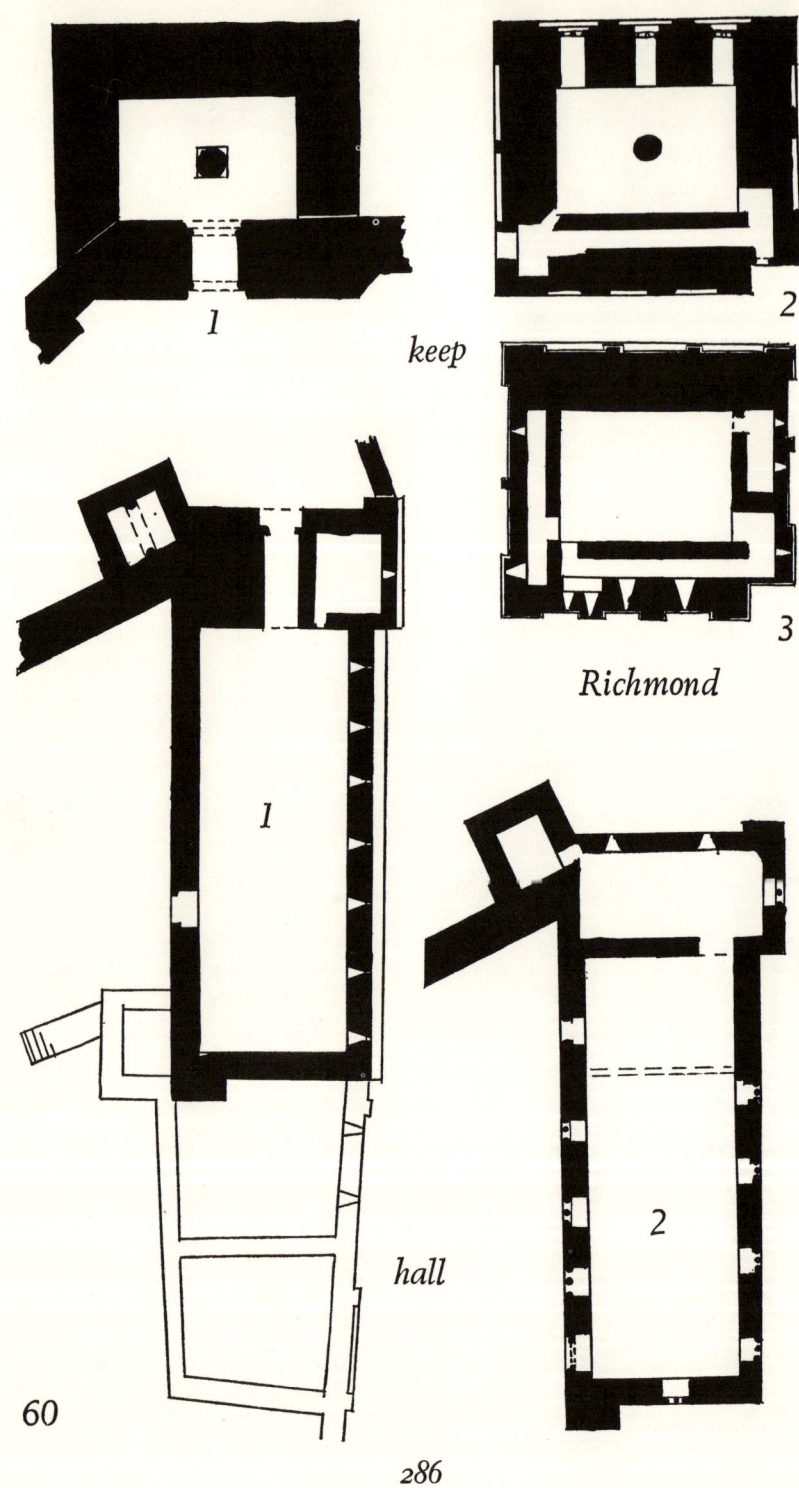

keep

Richmond

hall

60

286

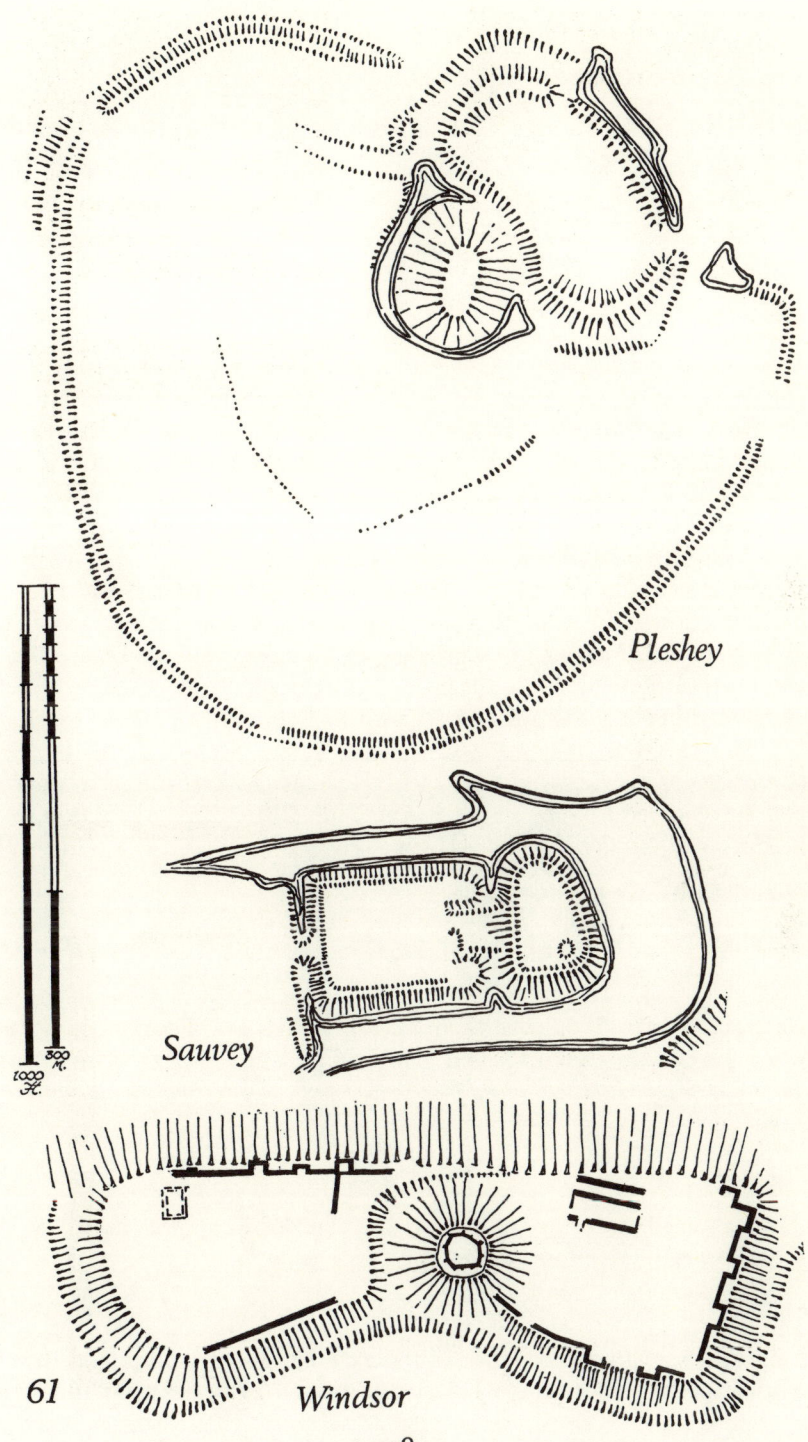

61 Pleshey, Sauvey, Windsor

Furness in 1123 [Baines, *History of Lancashire* IV, p. 304 (1836); II pp., 437, 630 (1868) (the castle could be earlier or later, however).

PRESTON CAPES   SP 576549   Northamptonshire

Ring-work on spur with strong counterscarp bank and another on the natural scarp to the north-east, with traces of scarps beyond farm to the south (Cc2 ?). Daventry Priory was first founded near Hugh de Leycestre's castle at Preston Capes about 1090 (*Monasticon* IV, p. 178).

PRUDHOE   NZ 092634   Northumberland

Oval walled area on natural spur with traces of bailey to south (ICd4). The square gatehouse has round-headed arches of two chamfered orders springing from plain imposts; the tunnel vault has a transverse rib resting on double imposts, the upper with chamfer, roll and hollow moulding, and the lower with a beaded one, resting on two human heads each side. The upper part has been rebuilt above a chamfered string-course.

The square keep has narrow pilasters in the centre of the south and west faces and clasping the angles. Those on the east angles are wider, and there is a forebuilding on this side of two cells, the southern one giving on to a spiral stair rising to a square-headed doorway into the keep. There are traces of altered loops in the north wall at each floor level and an upper spiral stair in the north-west angle, with roof corbels.

The castle was besieged twice in vain by the Scots army in 1173–4 (*Chronicles of the Reigns of Henry II*, III, lines 596ff, 1650ff; *Pipe Rolls*) and surrendered to John in 1212 (*Rot. Litt. Claus.* I, p. 122b) (Dodds, *A History of Northumberland* XII, pp. 111–35).*   (Fig. 54)

PUELLARUM   see EDINBURGH

PULFORD   SJ 375587   Cheshire

Motte and bailey (Bd2) beside River Alyn, mentioned in a document of about 1190–1220 (Tudor copy in Lincoln Archives Office, M.M. 1/3/1) when one Hacon agreed to hold Lincolnshire lands — *et faciet servicium unius militis ad custodiam de Pulford scilicet per quadragesime dies unoquoque anno.*

PULVERBATCH   SO 422022   Shropshire

Motte and bailey on ridge (Ab or f2) mentioned in 1205 (*Rot. Litt. Pat.* I, p. 50) when perhaps derelict.

PURITON   ST 309414   Somerset

Excavations of this site (IIBd4) produced a spouted pitcher and other Norman pottery (*Proceedings of the Somersetshire Arch. Soc.* LV, pp. 162–74), pp. 162–74), possibly the property for which *burgriht* was paid from 1159 (*Pipe Rolls*).

QUATFORD   SO 738907   Shropshire

Motte and bailey (IIAa/2) on cliff beside River Severn. The *motte* ditch was cleared out in 1830–1 and the finds included a horseshoe, spur, and whetstone, together with a silver-gilt ring and penny of Henry I and a quantity of burnt straw. Excavation of the east side of the bailey in 1960 showed a complex of post-sockets and no trace of a ditch.

    The *nova domus et burgus* is mentioned in 'Domesday' (I, 254) and the *oppidum de Quatford* was transferred to Bridgnorth in 1101–2 (*Ordericus Vitalis* IV, 32) (*Transactions of the Shropshire Archaeological Society* LVII, pp. 37–62).*

RADCOT   SU 285995   Oxfordshire

Angular mound near river (IIB) may be the castle 'surrounded by water and marsh' built in 1142 and taken by Stephen (*Gesta Stephani*, p. 91–2).

RADNOR   Radnorshire

The castle mentioned in 1196 and 1215–16 (*Brut y Tywysogion*) may be either the *motte* (A) at SO 246600 or Castle Nimble (Bd3) at SO 248594.

RADSILLAN   see CASTLEMORE, TULLOW

RAMPTON   TL 431680   Cambridgeshire

Incomplete ditched square mound (see p. 50).

RAMSEY   TL 291851   Huntingdonshire

Little remains of the twelfth-century abbey except some re-used stones in the churchyard wall. There are traces of a bank and ditch enclosing an oval precinct around the abbey, on the south part of which is an oval ditch surrounding a mound (Ab3?).

    In December 1142 the Earl of Essex seized the abbey, expelling the disunited monks, and turned it into a fortification. Despite a personal act of heroism by the displaced abbot (who set fire to the fortified outer gate and the troops' tents) it was only with difficulty that the earl's son was made to surrender the abbey after his father's death at Burwell in 1144 (*Monasticon* IV, 142; *Gervase* I, 129; *Chron. Ram.* 331–2; *Gesta Stephani*, p. 109) (R.C.H.M. *Huntingdonshire*, pp. 207–10).*

RATH'   see DUNDRUM

RATHCONRATH   N 2953   Westmeath

Motte (B) near church built in 1191 (*Annals of Loch Cé*; *Song of Dermot*).

RATH CUANARTAIGH   see RATHCONRATH

RATHEINARTHI   see RATHCONRATH

RATHWIRE   N 5343   Meath

Motte and bailey (Bd2). Wine for castle garrison bought 1211-12 (*Irish Pipe Roll*).

RATOATH   O 0351   Meath

Motte (B) near church built by 1215 (*Calendar of Documents* I, 110).

RAVENGER'S   London

The 'little castle that was Ravengers' was granted to Geoffrey de Mandeville in 1141 by the Empress, together with the Tower of London. Stephen's counter-charter refers to the Tower 'with the castle that the belongs to it' (J. H. Round, *Geoffrey de Mandeville*, pp. 89, 141). It may have been one of the fortifications erected after the surrender of London in 1066 (*William of Poitiers*, p. 218).

RAVENSTONE   Leicestershire

The castle was to be destroyed by the Earl of Leicester unless the Earl of Chester allowed it to remain; each was to assist the other to destroy it if it was held against either, according to the treaty of between 1148 and 1153 (see Whitwick). Possibly the earthwork at SK 411131.

RAYLEIGH   TL 805910   Essex

Motte with small bailey (Ad4). Excavations in 1909-10 and 1959-61 showed that part (at least) of the *motte* slopes were revetted with ragstone and flint rubble, with up to 3 ft of mortar in one part of the ditch and stone blocks elsewhere at a similar depth sealing an earlier ditch between *motte* and bailey. There was no trace of any masonry at all on the *motte*-top. A level patch of rubble 20 ft below the top suggests an intermediate stage in its erection. Several rough sloping floors were found in the bailey, with palisade trenches on the east side and the 9-ft wide foundations of part of the curtain wall, with a square turret at the north-east angle. In the north part of the bailey a pit was found filled with tooled clunch blocks (one with a roll-moulding). Near by was an oak gangway in a layer of branches and wood chips, with 10 ft tall squared uprights diagonally braced into reused planks (now in the Prittlewell Priory Museum, Southend on Sea). Small finds included a bronze model dog, Saxon ring-brooch, tubular padlocks and keys, gilt-bronze strip and other small ornamental fragments, with pottery (including a group found 6-7 ft down in the west bailey near seven pennies of Stephen), schist whetstones, worked bone, arrow-heads, knives, horseshoes and a prick-spur.

'In this manor Suene has made his castle' says 'Domesday Book' (II,

43b). His father, Robert fitz Wymarc, had come over with Edward the Confessor and survived the Conquest. The castle passed to the Crown in 1163 and small amounts for repairs are recorded in 1172–3 and 1183–6 (*Pipe Rolls*); there is no mention of the castle in the grant of the manor to Hubert de Burgh in 1215 (*Patent Roll*) (*Transactions of the Essex Archaeological Society* 12, pp. 147–85; L. Helliwell and D. G. Macleod, *Rayleigh Mount Handbook*, 1965).* (Figs. 1, 56)

READING　　　　　　　　SU 718736　　　　　　　　Berkshire

Much-altered mound in the Forbury Gardens may be the castle built by Stephen within the Abbey grounds in 1150 and destroyed by Henry II in 1153 (*Chronicles of the Reigns of Stephen* IV, p. 174; Matthew Paris, *Chron. Maj.* II, 184).

REBAN　　　　　　　　S 5898　　　　　　　　Laoighise (Leix)

Motte and bailey (Bd3) mentioned in a charter of *c.* 1200 (*Cartulary of St. Mary's Abbey, Dublin* I, 99, cited in *English Historical Review* XXII, p. 253).

RED CASTLE see THETFORD

REIGATE　　　　　　　　TQ 252504　　　　　　　　Surrey

Oval ring-work within wide and deep ditch formerly extending over Tunnel Road to form a bailey (Cc/22). Castle mentioned in 1203 (*Curia Regis Rolls* II, 264).

REIGNI see RUMNEY

REMBAUDSTON see RODBASTON

RENFREW　　　　　　　　　　　　　　　　Renfrewshire

The *opidum Reinfrew* is mentioned in 1163–5 (National Library of Scotland, *Advocates' MS.* 34.4.14, f. clii, cited by Barrow, *Regesta Regum Scottorum* I, p. 270).

RENNI see RUMNEY

RESTORMEL　　　　　　　　SX 104614　　　　　　　　Cornwall

Ring-work with faint traces of bailey (Cd?). The earthwork (within a sharp V-sectioned ditch) has a shell-wall of local slate and Pentewan stone as an interior revetment, the buried foundation having a 9-in. offset at ground level; a wide buttress backs a latrine block. The original entrance, a simple square gate-tower, is now largely ruined and rebuilt; its axis is offset from the radius of the shell (which is almost a true circle) and it may predate it. Straight stairs beside the gateway rise to the battlements, which have

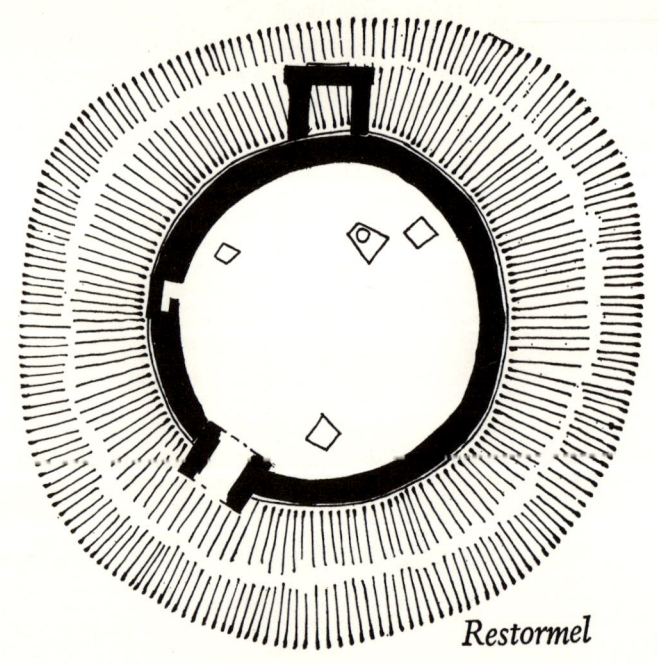
Restormel

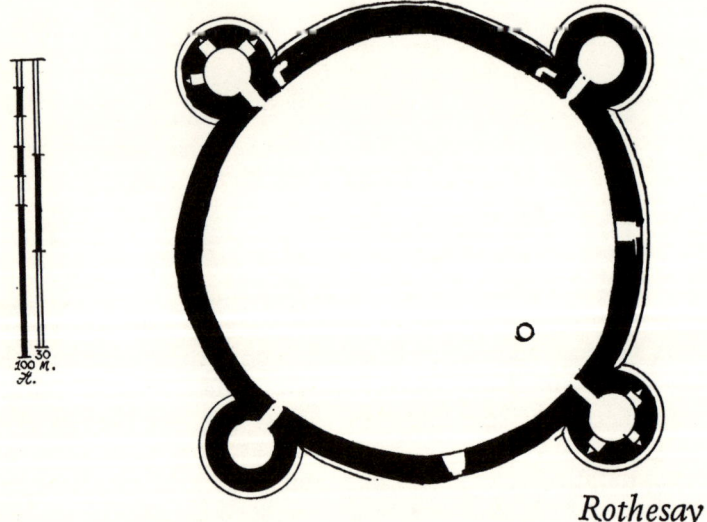
Rothesay

62

narrow crenels (only as wide as the parapet is deep) and an internal corbel-table like those at Trematon (q.v.). A row of beam-holes for an external wooden gallery remain. The inner shell and linking radial walls oversail rock-cut pits (including a well-chamber) and are not bonded into the outer shell, but form a range of annular segmental rooms.

Almost opposite the entrance a square tower with side buttresses projects from the shell-wall into the ditch. It has been much altered at various times, but appears to have been originally designed as a keep — or at least as a flanking tower — but later weakened by the cutting back of the internal wall faces and the whole shell opened up with wide windows.

Traces of stone foundations are reported in the bailey, together with lead pipes from a spring to the west (*Archaeologia* 83, pp. 220–26; M.P.B.W. *Official Guide*).* (Fig. 62)

RHAYADER   SN 968680   Radnorshire

Disturbed site (Bc3?) on ledge beside River Wye, built in 1177 and destroyed in 1194, but possibly the castle in *Gwerthrynion* captured in 1202 (*Brut y Tywysogion*).

RHUDDLAN   SJ 026777   Flintshire

Motte and bailey (Ab3) beside River Clwyd south of Edwardian castle.

Castle attacked in 1075 (*History of Gruffyd ap Cynan*, pp. 116–17) and mentioned in 'Domesday' (I 269d, 1). Rebuilt in 1157, destroyed ten years later (*Brut y Tywysogion; Pipe Roll*) and rebuilt again (M.P.B.W. *Official Guide*).*

RHYMNEY   ST 210789   Monmouthshire

Motte (B), perhaps the *castellum Remmi* of the 1184 *Pipe Roll*.

RIBAN   see REBAN

RICHARD DE LA MARE'S   see LLANIO

RICHARD'S   SO 483703   Herefordshire

Motte and bailey (Ab2) with strong counterscarp bank with an outer bank and ditch around church (and village) to east. The *motte* carried an octagonal keep of sandstone ashlar with a chamfered string, and the curtain wall was butted up against this; there was a square keep-like tower on the wall around the bailey (*Journal of the British Archaeological Association* 3, XXXII, pp. 105–127).

Mentioned in 'Domesday Book' (I, 185–6) and again a century later (1189: *Pipe Roll*).

RICHMOND   NZ 173007   Yorkshire

Triangular enclosure backed against cliff of River Swale. The earliest masonry is the curtain wall on the east and west sides, of shale blocks occasionally laid as herringbone work; the southern part of the west wall has a round-headed archway flanked by pilaster buttresses, with two further pilasters to the north and a plinth running south to a small square angle tower. The east curtain had four projecting square towers (one having largely collapsed). The foundations had been prepared by clearing 9 ft of upper clay and then building on a raft of holly and birch piles driven into the lower clay. The walls themselves were built around a timber framework, notched and overlapped (*Report of the Inspector of Ancient Monuments for 1913*, pp. 24–8). The tower to the north has two original barrel-vaulted storeys (the topmost is later), the lower having a blind arcade of round-headed arches, except in the east wall where a round-headed loop in a similar recess (with square holes in the jambs) was flanked by two round double-splayed openings. An entrance doorway through the curtain just to the north was partly blocked and solid piers added to carry the wallwalk. The southern pair of towers form a latrine block at the north-east corner of the hall, and a solar to the south-east, with traces of a linking timber gallery over the gate-passage leading to the eastern basement, lit by two square-headed windows in the south wall. Another five windows to the west of the cross-wall have a row of beam-holes below them externally. The main floor of the hall was entered by a wooden stair on a rubble base leading to a round-headed doorway of two orders, the outer with shafts and Corinthian capitals, the inner a roll-moulding continued across the sill. There were probably originally five two-light windows in the north and south wall, each with a central shaft under a cubical capital and jamb shafts carried round the soffit of the round heads. There was another two-light window in the west wall, and a spiral stair in a buttress projection at the northern end of this wall. The top of the south wall has an inner corbel-table carrying shallow-arched stones.

In the twelfth century the hall block was extended by service rooms to the west, and the curtain wall continued along the cliff edge; walls were added to form a triangular bailey outside the south-east gate and a round bailey in front of the north gate, which was blocked by an ashlar-faced keep, and a new gate broken through the curtain wall beside it. The original round-headed doorway had two orders on each side of the wall, with voluted capitals to shafted jambs; the straight curtain was used as the south side of the rectangular keep, with a nook at the south-east angle. There were clasping pilaster buttresses with one mid-wall buttress to the east and west and two to north and south (but not in the ground floor south wall). The ground floor was lit by a narrow loop in the east and west walls and both it and the floor above had a central column to support the floor, above. The upper floor was entered from the wall-walk by two square-headed doorways with jamb-shafts and a round arch (the western being later used as a window). The eastern doorway gave on to a wall-stair rising to the next floor. The entrance floor was lit by three round-headed windows in the north wall standing on a billet string-course with jamb-shafts, above a half-bead external string. Both this floor and that above have vaulted mural chambers to east and west, the upper lit by two loops to the east and one to the west above the chambers. The top floor (above the east/west roof ridge) has narrow crenels in the parapet and corner turrets rising above them, reached by round-headed doorways in the wall walk. All the floor levels are marked, both internally and externally, by wall offsets.

The castle was begun by Alan Rufus before 1089 (*Monasticon* V, 574) and the castelry is mentioned in 'Domesday' (I, 381a). The keep is attributed to Earl Conan (1146–71) (*Monasticon* V, 578) and over £100 was spent on the castle, tower and houses between 1171–87 (*Pipe Rolls*) (*Yorkshire Archaeological Journal* IX, pp. 33–54; M.P.B.W. *Official Guide*).*

(Plates XXXVII, XXXVIII; Figs. 58, 60)

RICHMONT   see HARPTREE

RISING   TF 666246   Norfolk

Oval ring-work built across rectangular earthwork which forms two flanking baileys (ICd1). The ring is entered from the east through a square gatehouse of coursed rubble, with ashlar quoins and dressings to the round-headed front and rear arches rising from imposts. There is a pair of round-headed recesses on each side of the passage, and also a spiral stair to an upper floor. Scalloped capitals set at an angle form corbels for a destroyed vault.

The rectangular keep is of ashlar, apart from the coursed flint rubble wall panels between buttresses. The clasping angle buttresses have shafts with cushion capitals below a string course and moulded bases; in addition the north and south have three intermediate pilaster buttresses rising from a sloping plinth. The upper part of the west wall is set back beside a tall central round-arched recess; below this to the north is a pendant double-half-round and to the south two recesses, one above the other, covering the latrine shafts.

The square forebuilding is approached through an enclosed stairway entered through a roll-moulded round arch, springing from imposts, with intermediate and inner arches with cushion capitals and moulded bases. Above the outer arch is a corbelled frieze of quatrefoils with diamonds below a blank arcade of roll-moulded arches springing from moulded

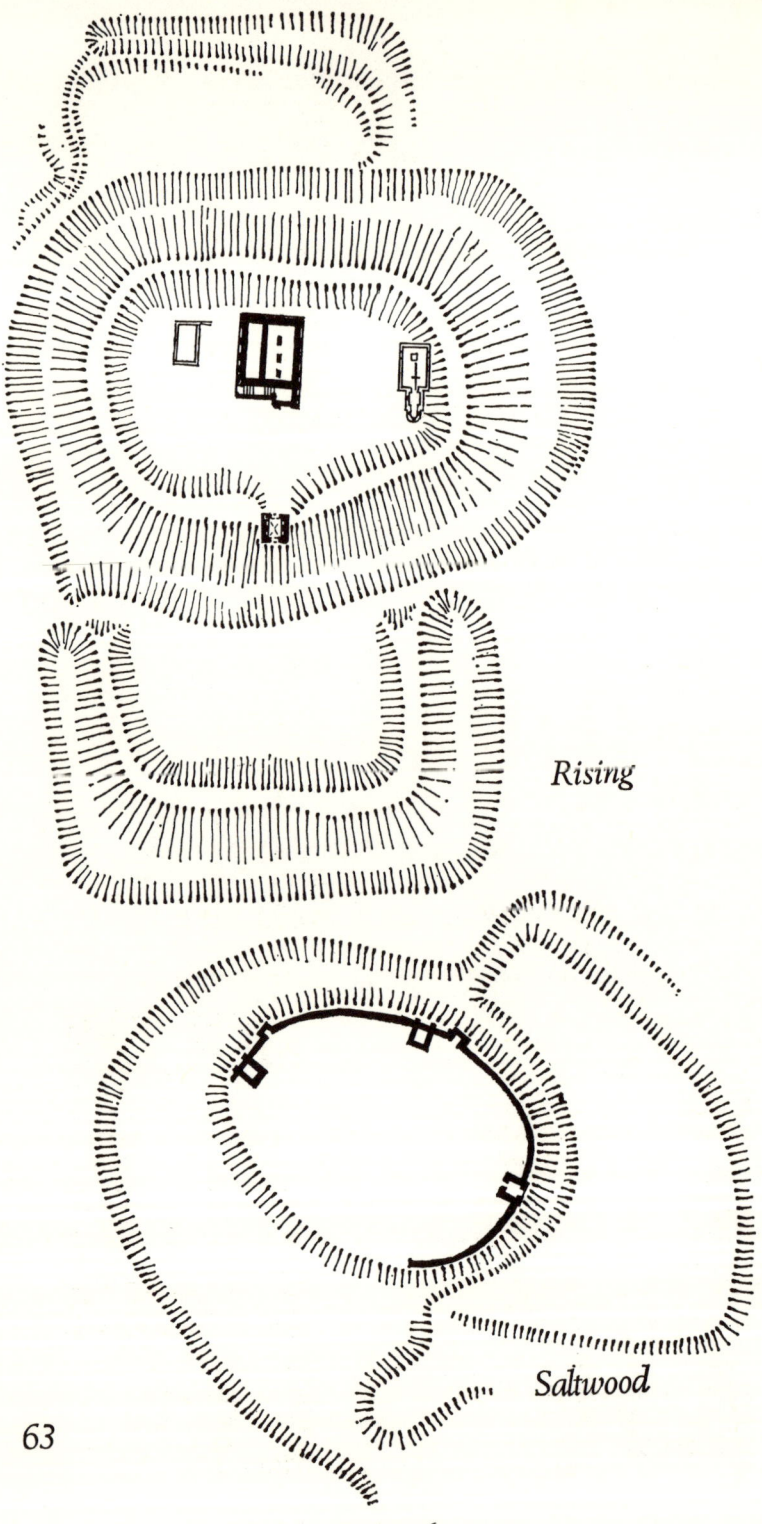

63

Rising

Saltwood

296

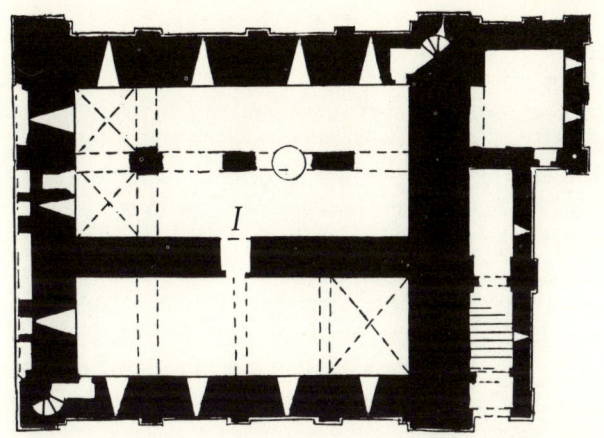

Rising

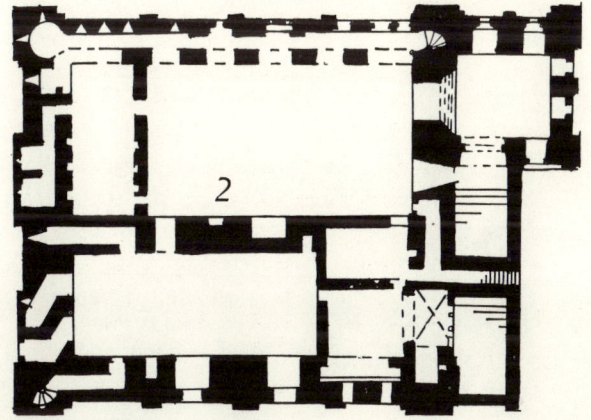

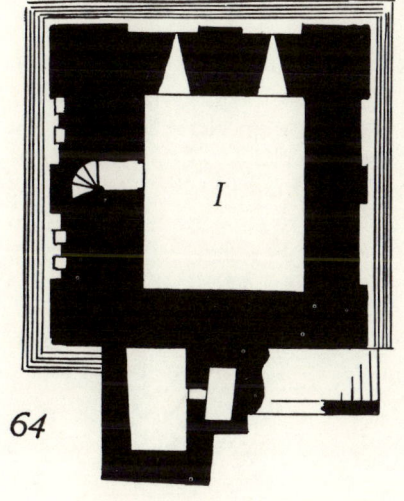

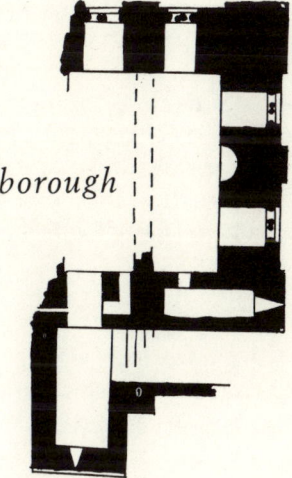

Scarborough

64

capitals, with an axework background and chevron string-course above and below. This arcade continues to a plain pilaster buttress, beyond which the arches are taller and intersecting, finally terminating in a shaft beside a tall arch on the forebuilding proper descending to ground level. (Apart from this pilaster, the angle and mid-wall buttresses to the forebuilding and entrance all have nook shafts ending at a string-course below that on the keep.) Above the single arches on the stairway is a row of circular roll-mouldings containing weathered carving of alternate human and feline heads (there is another carving centrally over the entrance). The forebuilding is lit by five round-headed windows with mullion and flanking shafts; the upper transom is continued as the string-course. The groined vault and upper floor are insertions and the main doorway (of three orders decorated with chevrons between roll-mouldings, supported on shafts with cushion capitals) is blocked. The ground floor has an east-west cross-wall, the central round-headed doorway having a bar-hole. The north part had an east-west arcade of four arches on square piers, with cross-arches for the vaulted east bay; the south part had three transverse arches, the east bay being vaulted. Each part has a rectangular loop in a round-headed embrasure in the west wall, with four similar loops to north and south. Spiral stairs in the north-east and south-west angles link all the floors, and there is a well beneath the arcade. The upper floors were carried on corbels; the first was lit by five round-topped embrasures in the north wall, behind which a gallery was driven to match that in the upper floor, with a domed shaft with recesses and vents in the north-west angle, probably a fireplace. There are two two-light windows at the east end, one with cable and interlace moulding to the mid-shaft. Two other windows, and one in the south wall, have trefoil lobed heads (see *Bull. Soc. Arch. Corrèze* 60, pp. 12–40 for Limousin examples). The latter adjoins a corner room with blind arcading and a roll-moulded dividing arch. There was a three-light east window and the vault keystone was four conjoined crowned heads. A doorway in the central buttress gives on to a minor stair running *across* the entrance stair. In the right hand end of each of the main walls is a two-light window on the top floor; the eastern one may have been one light only. Six pairs of corbels carved with grotesque human heads carried the roof with a chevron string-course. An apsidal chapel with herringbone walling is partly buried in the north part of the ring bank. Castle strengthened in 1216 (*Rot. Litt. Claus.* I, 255). (H. L. Bradfer-Lawrence, *Castle Rising* 1954).* (Plate XXXIX; Figs. 63, 64)

| RISINGHOE | TL 091509 | Bedfordshire |

Type A mound with slight scarps. William, son of Wigain, granted '*quic quid habui al baille veteris castelli apud molendium de Risingeho*' to Warden Abbey, and a contemporary (1180–1200) reference to '*inter motam et*

GAZETTEER

terram' may refer to the same site. (Warden Cartulary — *Bedfordshire Historical Record Society* 13, pp. 125, 131) (Widmore, *Earthworks of Bedfordshire*, pp. 241-3).*

ROCHDALE   SD 892128   Lancashire

Motte and bailey (IIBf2) now built over, disused by the end of the twelfth century; *Whalley Coucher* (Chetham Society II, pp. 599, 608) (Fishwick, *History of Rochdale*, pp. 65-6).*

ROCHESTER   TQ 742686   Kent

The Bishop of Rochester held land at Aylesford in exchange for the land in which the castle (of Rochester) sits ('Domesday Book' I, 26) and built a stone castle at a cost of £66 in exchange for the manor of Haddenham (*Textus Roffensis*, pp. 145-8) in an agreement closely dateable to the period between the accession of William II (Sept. 1087) and the death of Lanfranc (May 1089).

The stone castle was probably a circular enclosure occupying the southern part of the later bailey. A fragment on the west side has narrow crenels (built up when the wall was heightened) and is based on the core of the Roman town wall, above which the ragstone is laid herringbone fashion, facing layers of chalk and ragstone rubble in shelly brown mortar. Part of a similar wall backs on to the far side of the road to the east, laid in rammed gravel, and some reused tufa laid in gravel underlies the southern wall-tower. The 'Domesday' castle has alternatively been identified as the Boley Hill district immediately to the south, a ditched enclosure containing a much-altered mound facing *away* from the city (Bd2?). Despite the suggested analogy of Le Mans (*Archaeologia Cantiana* XLI, pp. 127-41), its use as a siege-work in 1215 may have been its origin also.

The tower-keep, of coursed ragstone rubble with Caen dressings, in the northern enclosure was erected with the consent of Henry I soon after 1126 by the Archbishop of Canterbury (*Regesta Regum Anglo-Normannorum* II, No. 1475: *Gervase of Canterbury* II, p. 382). Robert of Gloucester was imprisoned in it in 1141 (William of Malmesbury, *Historia Novella*, p. 66). It is square, with pilaster buttresses (in the middle and ends of each wall) rising from a flat plinth and carried up as turrets and projecting bays of the parapet, except the rebuilt southern angle (rounded, but square base) and the north-east wall; this has two mid-wall buttresses instead of one, as it carried a rectangular forebuilding at the eastern end. The entrance was reached by a flight of steps on a rubble base rising along the north-west and north-east walls through a square tower at the angle (the springer of an arch remains) to a drawbridge pit in front of the round-headed entrance with chevron moulding and engaged columns with plain

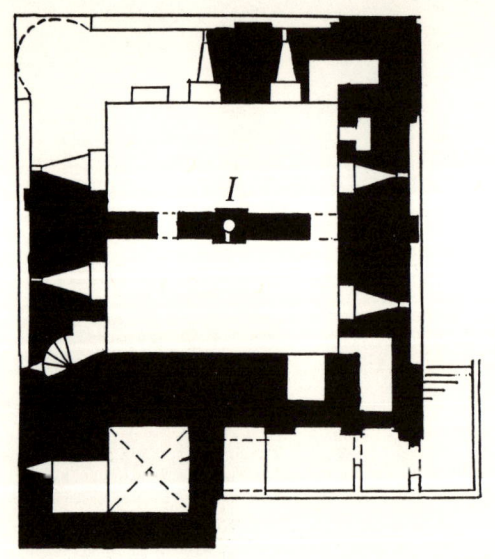

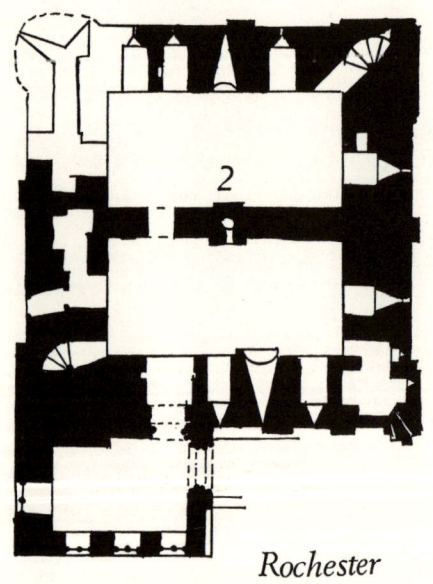

Rochester

Stokesay

65

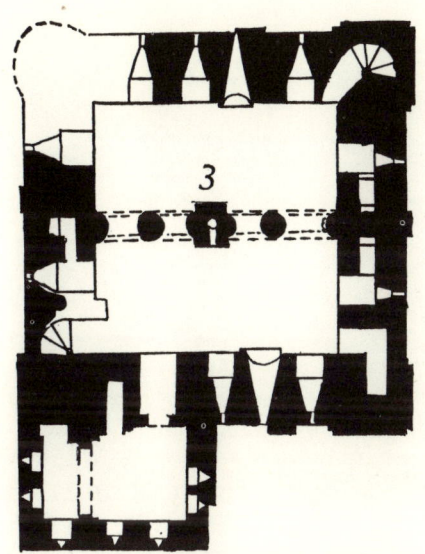

Rochester

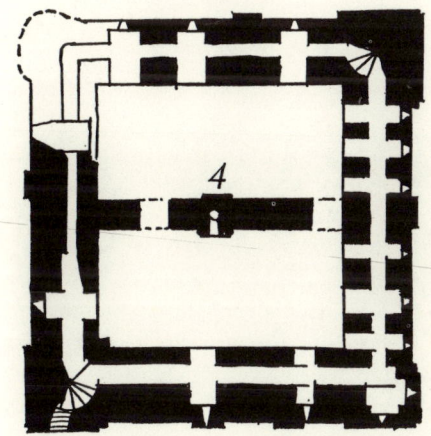

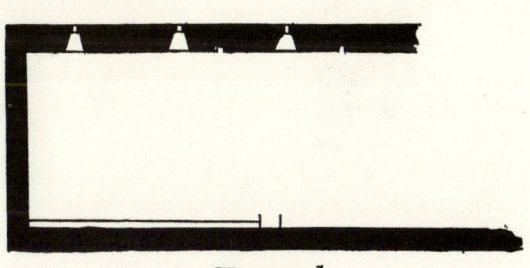

Sutton Valence

Tintagel

66

capitals. The forebuilding had a partial barrel-vault and was lit by round-headed windows, the three to the north-east being of two lights. The timber floor was the ceiling of the upper of two basements (the lower with a groined vault) with air-shafts but no windows, entered from the keep basement by a passage and steps respectively.

The interior of the keep is bisected by a north-west/south-east cross-wall with central pilasters covering an ashlar-cased well-pipe serving all levels through round-headed doorways. During repairs the capitals and wall were found to be spattered with lead from the burnt roof. The basement has mural chambers in the west and north angles and is aired by two round-headed steeply-shelving loops in splayed recesses set into flat-sided inner recesses in each wall except the north-east where only one was possible. The eastern angle carries a spiral stair to all floors. The entrance from the forebuilding is of two orders, the outer decorated with chevrons and jamb-shafts and backed by a portcullis-slot and bar-hole, with round-headed recesses at the sides leading on to a timber floor on joists. There are two square-headed loops in each wall (three to south-west), partly blocked to strengthen the wall with round-headed rear arches. A vaulted chamber in the northern angle has two loops and gave access to the upper part of the entrance tower. This chamber (and the centre of the north-east and south-west walls) each had a fireplace with a conical flue leading to vents in the wall; the former has a hood, the others are round-headed in pilaster buttresses.

An additional spiral stair rises in the western angle to all upper floors. The upper floor, on beams like that below, had windows in similar positions to the floor below, but they are windows with roll-and-hollow-moulded half-shafts and the similarly arranged fireplaces have chevron ornament. Instead of two doorways, as on other floors, the cross-wall has an arcade of columns with scalloped capitals and an arch with roll-and-hollow and chevron decoration, filled in with an inner (and lower) stone screen, not bonded in. There is a door leading into the forebuilding, divided by a round-headed arch with a half-octagonal vault to the eastern part, with a stone floor on the vault below.

Above this level a barrel-vaulted gallery runs right round the keep, with round-headed recesses allowing light from the windows into the interior (the windows here have chevron-decorated half-shafts); there are six windows in the north-west wall, three to south-west and north-east and two to the south-east, with two further windows in a wall-chamber at the north angle. The top floor has short inter-window galleries in the northern half and fireplaces with horizontal flues. There are five windows in the north-west wall, four to the north-east and three each in the other walls. The wall-walk above the low-pitched twin-gabled roof (resting on the cross-wall, with a window in the northern gable) had parapet and parados, between the angle turrets, each of which had two doorways. The parapet had five merlons on each face, above an external row of brattice-holes and and an internal double row of pigeon roosts. Access to the brattices was obtained by opening in the centre of the parapet (now blocked).

The rebuilding of the southern angle preserved half of a round-headed archway of two roll-moulded orders with inner cushion capital and outer sculptured one.

The keep was repaired in 1166 and 1170, and the castle strengthened in 1173–4 and in 1191–1205 (*Pipe Rolls; Rot. Litt. Pat.* 47). The southern angle was undermined by John's sappers in the siege of 1215, but the garrison held out for a time beyond the cross-wall, and repairs in the next reign cost over £500 (*Coggeshall* 175–6; *Wendover* II pp. 148–51; *Walter of Coventry* II, 226–7; *Rot. Litt. Claus.*) (M.P.B.W. *Official Guide*).*

(Plate XL; Figs. 65, 66)

ROCHESTER CATHEDRAL   TQ 743685   Kent

The stump of a square tower, with clasping buttresses at the angles, on the north side of the cathedral is attributed to Gundulph, Bishop of Rochester 1077–1102, and has some resemblance to St Leonard's Tower at Malling (q.v.). However, the masonry includes some re-used twelfth-century ornamented stones and its first reference in 1150 suggests a bell-tower (*Archaeological Journal* 86, pp. 187–212).

ROCKINGHAM   SP 867914   Northamptonshire

Lowered mound south of church between two quadrilateral baileys (Bdd2/3). 'The manor was waste when William (I) ordered the castle to be built' ('Domesday Book', I, 56). £2 was spent on repairs in 1187–8 and nearly £200 in 1206–11, including a new tower (*Pipe Rolls*), perhaps the keep badly cracked by 1250 (*Cal. Inq. Misc.* I, 91).

RODBASTON (PENKRIDGE)   Staffordshire

Castle mentioned in 1215 (*Rot. Litt. Pat.* p. 144).

ROFFT   SJ 357561   Flintshire

Motte and bailey on high bluff (destroyed by quarrying) above River Alyn.

Mentioned in 1161–2 (*Pipe Roll*), this castle may be identical with Bromfield, destroyed in 1140 (*Ann. Cest.* p. 21) (but see Wrexham).

ROKEREL   (Ireland)

Unidentified castle mentioned in 1214 (*Calendar of Documents* I, 81).

ROSCREA   S 1389   Tipperary

The *motte* and bretasche built in 1213 (*Annals of the Four Masters, Calendar of Documents* I, 81) were probably destroyed when the castle was rebuilt.

ROSS see DUNSCATH, ETHERDOUR

ROTHESAY   NS 078648   Bute

Oval curtain wall on square island in pentagonal moat. The curtain was built against an earlier bank, of sandstone ashlar above a (later) plinth. The original parapet with narrow crenels can be traced below a raising of the wall in whinstone rubble. The partly-blocked pointed arch through the north side of the curtain was fronted by another on Romanesque corbels, and there is a postern to the west, the doorway protected by a drawbar hole (*Transactions of the Glasgow Archaeological Society*, new series, IX, pp. 152–83).*   (Fig. 62)

ROXBURGH   NT 713337   Roxburghshire

Long narrow triangular mound on north bank of River Teviot, with cross banks and ditches, possible motte at north point (Bc2?). Mentioned in 1128 (Lawrie, *Early Scottish Charters* LXXXIII) and the tower in 1134 (*Melrose Chronicle*, p. 33). R.C.A.M. *Roxburghshire* II, pp. 407–11.*

ROY   NJ 007219   Inverness

Walled enclosure of rhombic plan within ditch beside River Spey. The acute north-west angle has a projecting square turret, and there is a latrine passage further south in the west wall. Compare KINCARDINE and SWEEN. Macgibbon and Ross, *The Castellated and Domestic Architecture of Scotland*, I, pp. 65–7.*

RUDGWICK   TQ 077345   Surrey

Ring-work (C) in Broomhall copse, 90 ft across. Excavation revealed a metalled causeway across the ditch, Norman green glazed pottery, charcoal, and a fragment of blue fabric (*Surrey Archaeological Collections* XXXVIII, pp. 96–7).

'RUFFIN'

Unidentified site mentioned in 1160–4 and 1212 (*Pipe Rolls*); unlikely to be Ruthin (Denbighshire). See BRYN AMLWG.

RUFUS see BOW AND ARROW

RUG   SJ 056438   Merioneth

Motte thrown up over Bronze Age cist burial, with possible trace of bailey to west, excavated in 1920 (*Journal of the Merioneth Historical Society* IV, pp. 3–6). Six antler discs with dot and circle ornament were found in an upper layer above the cist and are now in the National Museum of Wales

(*Bulletin of the Board of Celtic Studies* 13, pp. 251-2). Possibly the castle of *Edernion* mentioned in 1160 (*Pipe Roll*).

RUGBY   see WAVREI

RUMNEY   see RHYMNEY

RUSHEN   SC 265675   Isle of Man

Square keep of dressed limestone rubble, with modern sloping plinth. Traces of a forebuilding survive, underlying the eastern two-thirds of the fourteenth century gatehouse built against the north side. Square turrets were later added to the west and south faces of the keep, and the former has the stub of a projecting wall. Their basements were solid and the first floor altered internally in the fourteenth century, when a similar turret was added on the east face (*Archaeologia* 94, pp. 1-26).*   (Fig. 57)

RUSHTON   SP 840825   Northampton

Castle captured in 1140 (*Symeon of Durham* II, p. 306) might be the (?) *Motte* (B) in Gaultney Wood, perhaps the Galclint castle of 1148-53 (Stowe MS. 437, f.7, cited in *Early Yorkshire Charters* IV, p. 90).

RYE   see page 356

ST ANDREW'S   NO 513169   Fife

Castle on cliff promontory north-east of city. The inner bay of the Fore Tower on the south side is a refaced square tower lacking its inner wall and with a blocked round-headed entrance arch in the outer face. Castle mentioned in 1197 (*Wyntoun*, VII, c. viii, lines 2155-9).

ST ANN'S HILL   see MIDHURST

ST BRIAVELS   SO 558046   Gloucestershire

Ring-work (C) south of the church, with rubble curtain and fragments of square keep which collapsed in 1752. The castle mentioned in 1129-30 is probably the earthwork a mile to the north (SO 564064), since the present site was then in Lydney Parva. Although in royal possession from 1160, the only payments recorded are £5 in 1197-8 and again in 1202-3, but £291 was spent in 1209-11. The keep was repaired in 1224-5 (*Pipe Rolls*).

ST CLEARS   SN 280154   Carmarthenshire

Motte and bailey (Bd2) beside river. Stone, lime, mortar and ashes were found on top of the *motte*. (Lhuyd, *Parochialia* III, p. 52). The castle was captured in 1153 and 1189 and destroyed in 1215 (*Brut y Tywysogion*).

ST LEONARD'S TOWER   see WEST MALLING

ST MELLONS   ST 227803   Monmouthshire

Excavation of this ring-work (C) in 1965 showed that the marl bank had been heightened; twelfth-century pottery was found (*Medieval Archaeology* X, p. 196).

ST MICHAEL'S MOUNT   SW 515299   Cornwall

Nothing appears to survive of the fortification erected in 1193–4 (*Roger of Hoveden* III, 237; *Pipe Roll*).

ST NICHOLAS   see COED Y CWM

SALTWOOD   TR 161359   Kent

Large oval ring-work with widened ditch to the south and triangular bailey to the east (ICc3). Rubble curtain wall round bailey with open-backed square turrets to west and north adjoining square internal towers whose side walls are extended to form external buttresses. A similar tower to the east forms the inner part of the present gatehouse. The southern wall has been demolished, perhaps in 1175 (*Pipe Roll*), twelve years after the disgrace of Henry of Essex (who held it of the Archbishop of Canterbury) had provided an excuse for its seizure (*Gervase of Canterbury*, 174).

(Fig. 63)

SANDAL   SE 337182   Yorkshire

Motte and bailey (Ba3) with strong counterscarp to west and south. None of the masonry excavated (*Yorkshire Archaeological Journal*, XIII, pp. 154–88) is dated to an early period, although a round-headed window in the lobed tower on the *motte* has a curious roll-moulded impost. The castle was withheld by Henry II in 1157 (*Chronicles of the Reigns of Henry II* IV, pp. 192–3).

SAUKEVILLE   see ARDGLASS

SAUVEY   SK 786052   Leicestershire

Triangular ring-work with bailey (IICd3) near Withcote. Nearly £450 was spent in 1210–11 on the castle of Sauvey (*Pipe Rolls*).   (Fig. 61)

SCARBOROUGH   TA 048892   Yorkshire

Triangular headland with precipitous slopes to all sides except the south-east, where a wide ditch was cut, backed by a curtain of limestone rubble with sandstone facings. The entrance was across a narrow neck to the west, the area within being cut off by an inner ditch and curtain enclosing the keep. The west and south walls have solid rounded bastions, with pilaster buttresses and a chamfered plinth of four offsets, repeated beyond the rebuilt Mosdale Hall to the south-east and again beyond the postern. The east inner curtain makes an awkward junction into a hollow angular bastion.

Between these stretches are two pairs of open-backed semicircular towers, much repaired.

The square keep has a sloping plinth above four chamfered offsets and has clasping angle buttresses with shafted angles and mid-wall pilasters, but not on the south side. Most of the west wall has been destroyed, but a central spiral stair can be seen flanked by pairs of latrine shoots in the plinth. The basement was lit by two stepped round-headed loops in the north wall. An entrance stair rose westward along the south wall under an outer arch (of which the scalloped corbel survives) to a forebuilding with a loop-lit pit below and flat roof above guarding the entrance passage, which has a simple segmental arch externally and round-headed internally. There were pairs of two-light windows in the north and east walls, round-headed internally and externally; the east ones flank a round-headed fireplace, the chimney being carried up in the wall thickness. A cell at the south-east angle has a square-headed loop in the east wall, and there are traces of a wall-passage on to the roof of the forebuilding, and of a north/south cross arch springing from plain pilasters.

The second floor has a door-jamb in the cross-wall, and mural chambers at the angles with round-headed loops pointing east and west, with two wider loops above the forebuilding. A segmental-headed fireplace in the east wall is flanked by two-light windows with a round-headed embrasure and outer arch, the central double-shaft capital being scalloped. The top floor has no trace of a cross-wall, but has pairs of windows in the three surviving walls, each of two separate round-headed lights with a double-splayed inner order.

South-east of the inner bailey are the foundations of a late twelfth-century hall and service block, dated from the mouldings excavated (*The Reliquary*, new series III, pp. 24–30), and further east are the foundations of an eleventh- and twelfth-century chapel on the site of a Roman signal station.

A curtain wall and tower had been built by the third Count of Aumale (1127–79: *Chronicles of the Reigns of Stephen, Henry II*, I, p. 104) and rebuilt by Henry II between 1157–65 and 1167–9, work on the tower being mentioned at both ends of the period, during which over £650 was spent. The great ditch was being cut after 1168 (Egerton MS. 2827 f.91, quoted in *Early Yorkshire Charters* V, p. 142). John spent over £2,000 on the castle during his reign (*Pipe Rolls*) (Rowntree, *The History of Scarborough*, pp. 51–3; 141–59; V.C.H. *North Riding of Yorkshire* II, pp. 541–9; M.P.B.W. *Official Guide*).* (Plate XLI; Figs. 64, 67)

SCILLY see page 356

SEDFELD see SHEFFIELD

SELBY   Yorkshire

Henry de Lacy built a castle here soon after 1143; it was besieged within a week of the commencement of building (*Historia Monasterii Selbiensis* in *Coucher Book of Selby* I, p. 33).

SELKIRK   NT 470281   Selkirkshire

Motte and angular bailey (Bd3) on north shore of Loch Haining, mentioned in 1119 (Lawrie, *Early Scottish Charters* XXXV) (R.C.A.M. *Selkirkshire*, pp. 47–8).*

SENTENCE   see NARBERTH

SHAFTESBURY   ST 858228   Dorset

Triangular bank and ditch enclosing promontory. During excavations in in 1949, a 'cut' halfpenny of Stephen was found in the large pit, and fragments of tripod pitchers nearby (*Proceedings of the Dorset N.H. and Archaeological Society* LXXI, pp. 54–7).

SHANID   R 2448   Limerick

Motte and bailey (Bc3) with strong counterscarp bank. Part of the shell-wall of coursed rubble survives round the *motte*-top, running close to a polygonal keep of similar masonry, of which the north half has vanished. The interior was circular, with a round-headed loop and the jamb of another at ground level, and with beam-holes below narrow crenels, one on each surviving face, and a plunging loop beneath each merlon.

SHEFFIELD   SK 357976   Yorkshire

Rectangular ditched enclosure north of Exchange Street, at confluence of rivers Don and Sheaf. The moat had sloping sides above vertical rock-cut ones to a depth of 30 ft. Excavations at the north-east of the enclosure revealed a buttressed angle of a building with two chamfered offsets overlying made ground with a horizontal beam on oak supports resting on slabs, level with a nine inch clay floor reinforced with wattling. Eleventh century pottery was recovered (*Transactions of the Hunter Archaeological Society* IV, pp. 7–27; *Medieval Archaeology* II, p. 308). £55 was spent on the castle in 1183–4 (*Pipe Roll*).

SHERBORNE   ST 648168   Dorset

The Old Castle consists of a rectangular curtain wall (with the angles canted off) inside a wide ditch with outer rampart. There were simple rectangular towers near the centre of the north side and at each two of the east and west angles. The north tower (the only one not projecting inwards at all) was a gate, leading (by a drawbridge) to a long barrel-vaulted passage

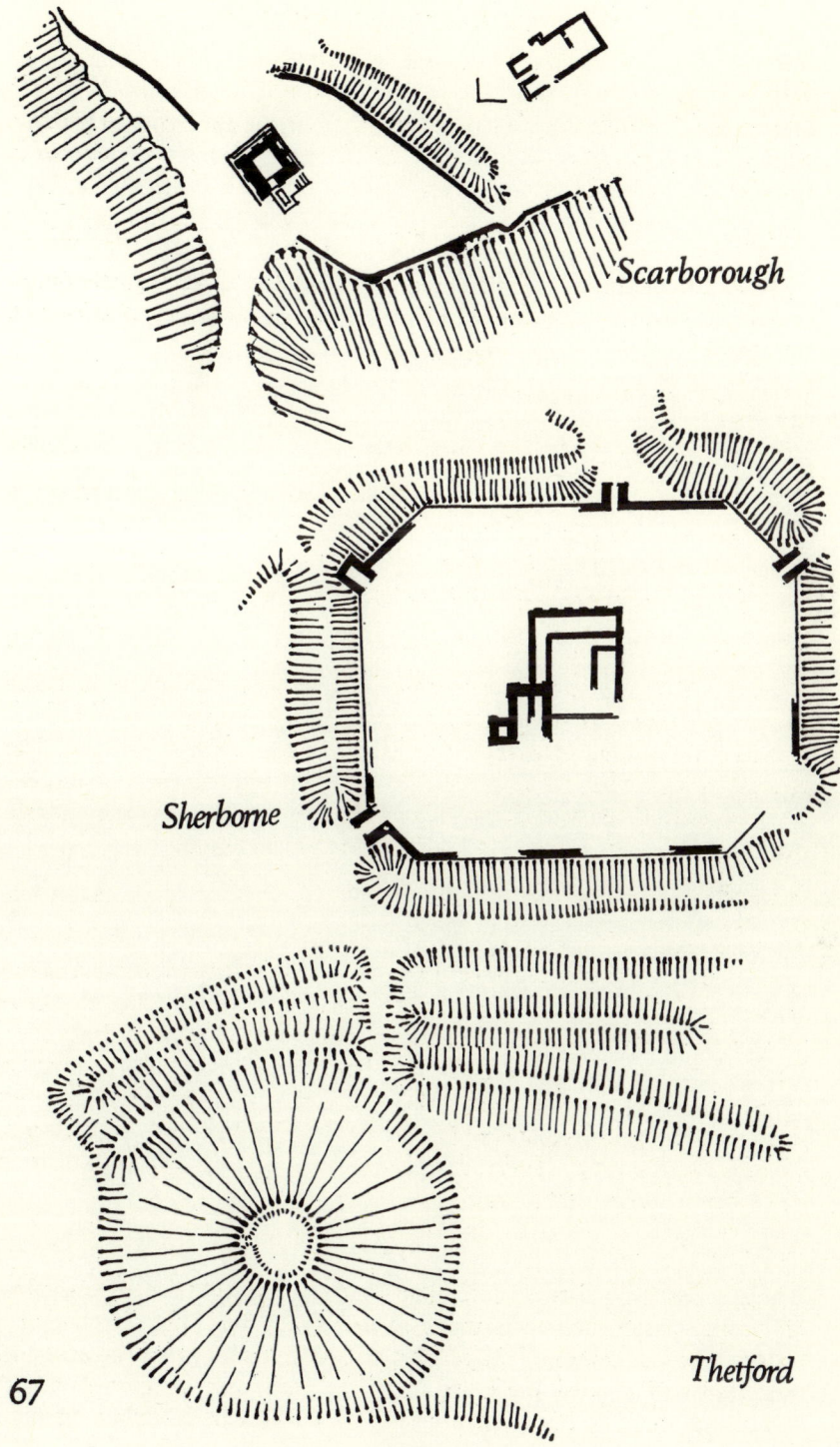
67

through the outer bank. The south-west gatehouse tower is of ashlar with a sloping plinth and clasping buttresses. The entrance retains a lintel socket and the segmental arches of the inner and outer doorways, with traces of a round-headed arch above each, reached by a blocked spiral stair. The two upper floors are much altered. The central pier of the approach across the moat survives, as does one opposite the north-east gatehouse tower, of which only a chamfered plinth and foundations survive.

Within the curtain stands a rectangular keep of rubble with freestone dressings, with a central and clasping buttresses to the west, on which side there is a square extension with clasping buttresses. The internal north/south cross-wall has been altered and the barrel-vaults groined on to a re-used column with scalloped capital standing on the south wall foundation. A barrel-vaulted passage outside the north wall leads to a spiral stair leading to the first floor and the upper part of the latrine block. The keep forms the south-west angle of contemporary ranges of buildings with external pilaster buttresses round a courtyard, the south range has gone (apart from foundations) except for a chevron string-course and beam-holes on the keep, and little remains of the east range apart from round-headed windows in the walls of the barrel-vaulted ground floor. The west range resembles the east, but one upper window has an internal jamb-shaft and string course; the north range was vaulted in four bays (groined, except that within the west round-headed entrance doorway which was barrel-vaulted). The upper floor was reached by a covered passage to a spiral stair (mirroring that of the keep), with an internal and external (to the courtyard) arcade of intersecting round-headed arches, with scalloped capitals and a billetted string course. In the south wall are the fluted jambs and round head of a window, and another with chevron ornament in the east wall of the range; another in the adjoining bay of the north wall has continuous chevron ornament on the inner order, the outer chevron surrounded with a cabled moulding springing from shafts with crocket capitals.

The castle was built by Roger, Bishop of Salisbury, between 1107 and 1139 when it was seized by Stephen (*Gesta Stephani*, pp. 49, 53). Although John spent over £100 on it, his overseer in 1215 claimed to have spent £1,000 (*Pipe Roll* 5 Henry III rot. 6d quoted in *The History of the King's Works*) (R.C.H.M. *Dorset* I, pp. 66–8).*   (Plate XLI; Figs. 67, 68)

SHERIFF HUTTON   SE 658663   Yorkshire.

Square mound (IIB) south of parish church may be the castle of Bertram de Bulmer in 1140 (Camden, *Britannia* (ed. Gough) III, p. 336).

SHOTWICK   SJ 350704   Cheshire

Motte and bailey (Bd2) on old shoreline. Old drawings (especially *B.M.*

Harleian MS. 2073, f.111) show a buttressed rectangular keep surrounded by a towered curtain wall. (*Transactions of the Historic Society of Lancashire and Cheshire* LXIV, pp. 82–142).*

SHRAWARDINE   SJ 400154   Shropshire

Motte and bailey (IBd4) beside River Severn, existing before 1165 (*Liber Niger Scaccarii,* I, p. 148). There are fragments of a shell keep on the *motte,* mainly rubble, apart from an ashlar face with a partly buried relieving arch. Both this and other stonework found on the site (*Transactions of the Shropshire Archaeological Society* 2nd series, VI, pp. 120–41) may be twelfth century. Expenditure on repairs is recorded after 1165 (*Pipe Rolls*), although the castle was rebuilt in 1220 (*Patent Roll*).

SHREWSBURY   SJ 495128   Shropshire

Motte and bailey (IBa3) at neck of loop of River Severn. The curtain wall is much altered, but the short straight lengths of foundation are probably contemporary with the round-headed entrance arch, decorated with a roll-moulding. The foundations of an outer bailey wall with hollow square towers to the south have been excavated on the slope above the High Street (*Transactions of the Shropshire Archaeological Society* VI, opposite p. 257). The castle may have been the *praesidum regis* besieged in 1069 (*Henry of Huntingdon,* p. 205); 51 houses had stood on the site in 1086 ('Domesday Book' I, 252).

The tower of Shrewsbury was mentioned in 1164–6 and small sums spent on building and repairs in 1164–9, 1172–3 and 1181–1215 (*Pipe Rolls*). The tower may have been the great wooden one which collapsed in 1269–71 (*Rot. Hundredorum* II, p. 106).

SILBURY HILL   see page 356

SKELTON   see page 357

SKENFRITH   SO 457203   Monmouthshire

Low *motte* beside River Monnow with bank and ditch of village enclosure to the north (Bc3). The *motte* now carries a round tower (on trench-built foundations) of roughly coursed rubble with a roll-moulding at the top of the sloping plinth. One diagonally-tooled chamfered jamb of the ground-floor entrance survives, slightly offset from the semicircular headed entrance passage above, with the gabled creasing for a porch extending downward to the left to cover the staircase. The entrance floor was lit by two sloping loops, with an unlit basement below. The upper floors were linked by a spiral stair in a semicircular buttress projection. Two round-headed windows in rectangular embrasures survive above the sockets for the first floor beams. The upper floor had a main beam resting on corbels, with a fireplace and three windows, one an oriel opposite the stair buttress.

The tower was enclosed in a coursed sandstone rubble curtain within a stone-revetted moat. The foundations of a gate have been excavated in the centre of the north side, and of an elaborate suite of rooms within the west curtain.

The best preserved part of the curtain is the eastern, with an internal offset, and runnels to drain the wall-walk. The water-gate had a draw-bar hole in the vaulted passage. There is a solid D-shaped tower on the opposite curtain, with a chamber at wall-walk level. The round corner towers were similar to each other with unlit basements, three loops to the lower floor (marked by a sloping face externally) and two intermediate ones above. Narrower doorways beside the south-east tower led to the (destroyed) mill.

Repaired in 1163 and 1183 onwards (*Pipe Rolls*); much of the masonry probably dates from after 1216 (*Archeologia Cambrensis* CXVI, 133–158).

SKIPSEA　　　　　　　TA 162551　　　　　　　Yorkshire

Motte with counterscarp bank, separated by 100 yds of marsh from a long narrow bailey with incurved ends (Bc/24?). Fragments of a wing-wall of mortared pebbles running down the *motte* to the east, and of a causeway on 10-in. piles 9 ft apart leading to the bailey are recorded (*Yorkshire Archaeological Journal* XXI, pp. 188–9; XXIV, pp. 258–62).

The castle was founded by Drogo de Bevrère by 1086 (*Chron. Mon. de Melsa* I, p. 89) and its chapel existed by 1102 (*Early Yorkshire Charters* III, p. 27).

SKIPTON-IN-CRAVEN　　　　SD 995519　　　　　　Yorkshire

A barrel-vaulted passage and a recessed flanking tower are the sole surviving fragments of the castle held in 1178 (*Early Yorkshire Charters* VII, 12). There is a central transverse arch with moulded capitals to the jambs and an inner portcullis slot and outer arch of two square orders, chamfered within.

SKREEN　　　　　　　N 9458　　　　　　　Meath

Altered *motte* and bailey in garden is probably the castle of Adam de Futepoi (1181) (Giraldus Cambrensis, *Opera* V, 356; *Song of Dermot*).

SLANE　　　　　　　N 9674　　　　　　　Meath

Motte and bailey (Ba1) built by Richard the Fleming in 1176 (*Song of Dermot*; *Annals of Ulster*).

SLEAFORD　　　　　　TF 065455　　　　　　Lincolnshire

A plan reproduced in the *Associated Architectural Societies' Reports and Papers* VII, p. 73, shows the castle as enclosing a rectangular courtyard and surrounded on three sides by a rectangular moat which extends to enclose an outer enclosure to south and west.

The Bishop of Lincoln's castle was surrendered to Stephen in 1139 (William of Malmesbury, *Historia Novella*, p. 27).

SLEDE   see LEEDS

SNODHILL   SO 322404   Herefordshire

Motte and bailey (IBd3) with counterscarp bank covering exposed side of *motte* on oval hill-top, with a trapezoidal outer bailey further east below the main site. The southern part of a shell-wall in sandstone rubble remains round the *motte*-top, the plan being an octagon with elongated north and south walls and some remains of a sloping plinth. Solid drum towers have been added to the entrance doorway.

Mentioned in 1194–7 (*Pipe Roll; Roll of Escheats* (Pipe Roll Society) 8 Ric. 1) (R.C.H.M. *Herefordshire* I, pp. 212–3).*

SOMERFORD   ST 965831   Wiltshire

Motte and bailey (Bc3) south-west of church. Excavations of the *motte* revealed a wall with a doorway and two round-headed windows (Britton, *Beauties of Wiltshire* III, p. 111; *Wiltshire Archaeological Magazine* 45, pp. 88–9). Possibly the remains of an earlier church, although the earthworks appear too definite for this to be the entire explanation, and it might be one of the three castles built near Malmesbury in 1144 (*Gesta Stephani*, p. 113 – see TETBURY).

SOMERLED'S   Argyll

Clay-built tower on rock with battlements, described in the *Roman von Guillaume le Clerc c.* 1209 quoted by R. L. G. Ritchie, *The Normans in Scotland*, pp. 307–9.

SOUTHAMPTON   SU 418115   Hampshire

Motte and bailey (Bc3); a coin of Offa was found on the mound which was lowered in 1822 and is now built over. Excavations have shown that the curving northern bailey bank (now largely removed) was thrown up from a V-section ditch over Saxo-Norman huts, and later strengthened with a curtain wall of coursed rubble blocks on foundation arches supported on rubble piers sunk to the original ground level. The straight west curtain incorporated at least two Norman buildings near its southern end (where a heavy square buttress marked a right-angled turn toward the *motte*). The northern vault had ribs springing from water-leaf corbels, lit by loops in the west wall; the southern appears to have had a similar vault, with an upper floor lit by round-headed windows in addition.

The 1153 agreement between King Stephen and Prince Henry provided that the Bishop of Winchester was to give security for the delivery of the *munitio* of Southampton (*Foedera* I, pp. 13–14). Repairs were paid for in 1155–61, and a new stone building erected in 1186–7. Buildings on the *motte* and in the tower were repaired in the following years, and the expenditure of £150 in 1190–3 and £275 in 1204–8 may have been on the stone curtain (*Pipe Rolls*).

Money for walling the town was paid in 1203 (*Pipe Roll*) and the East Gate mentioned by 1217 (*Calendar of Ancient Deeds* II, p. 404; B.M. Add. MS. 15314, f. 35). North-east of the castle, the innermost arch on the north side of the Bargate has a Norman roll-moulding (*Proceedings of the Hampshire Field Club and Archaeological Society* XII, pp. 241–70; *Aspects of Archaeology in Britain and Beyond* (ed. W. F. Grimes) pp. 242–57; L. A. Burgess, *The Origins of Southampton*).*

SOUTH CERNEY   Wiltshire

Captured by Stephen in 1139 (*Gesta Stephani*, p. 62; William of Malmesbury, *Historia Novella*, pp. 36, 42). Possibly the earthwork at Ashton Keynes (q.v.).

SOUTH MORETON   see BRIGHTWELL

SOUTH MYMMS   TL 230026   Hertfordshire
                                                (formerly Middlesex)

Excavations of the *motte* and bailey (Be2) a mile north-east of the church have revealed flint footings, 3 ft wide, of a timber tower 35 ft square on the levelled ground surface, the timbers overlapping at the corners. A timber-lined passage ran south and the whole was covered with a chalk mound retained with a ring of clay and flints. Pinkish-white plaster, lead sheet, and bricks 1¼ in. thick have been recovered besides Saxo-Norman pottery, gilt-bronze strip and brooch, a spoon-bit, and pick-tine.

The building of the castle is tentatively equated with the permission granted to Geoffrey de Mandeville in 1141–2 by Matilda and Stephen successively (J. H. Round, *Geoffrey de Mandeville*, pp. 89, 140, 166 quoting Dugdale MS. Lf. 81; Ashmole MS. 841, f. 3; Duchy of Lancaster, Royal Charters No. 18; Lansdowne MS. 229, f. 109; Dugdale MS. Lf. 19; Dodsworth MS. XXX, 113).

SOUTHOE   Huntingdonshire

Two ring-works south-west of the church were excavated in 1937 and 1942 (*Proceedings of the Cambridge Antiquarian Society* XXXVIII, pp., 158–63; *Transactions of the Cambridgeshire and Huntingdonshire Archaeological Society* VI, pp. 1–6). The first excavation (TL 178638) showed an embanked area with a yard paved with Collyweston slates. A latrine pit produced Saxo-Norman pottery; other finds were a stone mortar and a large shield-shaped buckle with forked pin. The later excavation (TL 184644) produced pottery from the eleventh to the fourteenth century, together with ornamented bronze strip, tweezers, arrow-heads and schist hones.

Odo de Dammartin was granted 'as much land as the site of the castle comprises' at Boughton in Southoe by the Earl of Northampton between 1140–53 (*B.M. Add. Charters* 11233, quoted by F. M. Stenton, *The First Century of English Feudalism*, p. 197).

SOUTH WITHAM   SK 929205   Lincolnshire

Excavation of the preceptory of the Knights Templar revealed a hall-keep with a defended entrance. There is documentary evidence for the preceptory from at least 1182, and perhaps as early as 1164. (*Current Archaeology* 9, p. 232).*

SOWERBY   Cumberland

Robert de Vaux had been in possession for 10 years of the castle of *Sourebi* in 1186–7 (*Pipe Roll*), possibly the hill fort of Castle How (NY 360383).

STAFFORD   SJ 901223   Staffordshire

Motte and bailey (IBc3) south-west of town is probably the castle of *Estafort* built by William in 1070 (*Ordericus Vitalis* II, p. 199) and called *Burton* in 1086 ('Domesday Book' 1, 248). It was rebuilt by 1101 and the documentary evidence for the chapel in the bailey identifies it with the present site (*Salt Archaeological Society's Transactions* VIII, pp. 6–22) (V.C.H. *Staffordshire* V, pp. 82–6).*

STAMFORD   TF 028071   Lincolnshire

In 1932–3 the site of the castle was levelled, and a drybuilt stone wall 60 ft in diameter found, having been partly destroyed by diagonally-tooled walling (*Report of the Congress of Archaeological Societies* 1933). The Saxo-Norman pottery found has been published (*Antiquaries' Journal* XVI, p. 410, figs. 4–6; *Proceedings of the Cambridge Antiquarian Society* LI, pp. 45–8). The ashlar well on the *motte* was excavated in 1962, producing a Stamford-ware vessel and wooden bowl (notes in Stamford Museum). The *turris* was surrendered to Henry II in 1153 (*Gervase of Canterbury* I, 156; *Gesta Stephani*, p. 155). Mentioned in 1086 (*Domesday*).

STANTON HOLGATE   SO 562896   Shropshire

Motte and bailey (Ab3) east of church, with traces of masonry on *motte*-top. Helgot's castle is mentioned in 'Domesday Book' (1, 258) and in documents of 1115 and 1121–6 (*Monasticon* I, p. 482; *Salop Cartulary*, quoted by Eyton, *History of Shropshire* IV, pp. 51–4).

STAPLETON   SO 323656   Herefordshire

Much altered *motte* and bailey (Be2 ?) on quarried hillock with oval outer bailey to the north. Castle mentioned in 1207 (*Rot. Litt. Pat.* I, 73b) R.C.H.M. *Herefordshire* III, pp. xxix, 182.

STEPHEN'S   SN 579482   Cardiganshire

Damaged *motte* (A) in Lampeter College grounds. Probably the Norman castle 'destroyed' in 1136-7 and the castle of Mabwynion destroyed in 1164 (*Brut y Tywysogion*; *Annales Cambriae*).

STIRLING   NS 790940   Stirlingshire

No part of the existing castle is dated before the fourteenth century, but the massive Prince's Tower and the curtain wall are reminiscent of a Norman square gatehouse and towers and may represent an earlier design. The chapel of the castle existed by 1115 (*Registrum de Dunfermerlyn*, 4; Barrow, *Regesta Regum Scottorum* I, p. 163; Lawrie, *Early Scottish Charters* CLXXXII) (R.C.A.M. *Stirlingshire*, pp. 179-223).*

STOCKBRIDGE   see ASHLEY

STOCKPORT   SJ 894903   Cheshire

Site of castle north of church, occupied by circular building (Ormerod, *History of Cheshire* III, p. 796).

    Held against Henry II by Geoffrey de Costentin in 1173 (*Gesta Henrici Secundi* I, p. 48).

STOGURSEY   ST 203426   Somerset

Ring-work and multiple baileys (Cbd3) first mentioned in 1090 (*Ordericus Vitalis* III, pp. 359-77). The castle was held for John in 1215 (*Rot. Litt. Claus.* I, 239) but the prior was ordered to destroy it in the following year (*Rot. Litt. Pat.* p. 190). Part of the rubble shell-wall round the ring-work (with ashlar quoins) may be of twelfth century date.

STOKE COURCY   see STOGURSEY

STOKES

Unidentified house which G. fitz Peter had licence to fortify in 1202 (*Rot. de Liberate*, p. 32). (Stokesay is a possible identification.)

STOKESAY   SO 437817   Shropshire

An earlier tower survives at the end of the thirteenth-century range, of coursed rubble with ashlar quoins. In plan it is an irregular pentagon, having three right angles, one of which is separated from the other two by obtuse angles. The north obtuse angle has a square projecting turret enclosing the well, with loops in north and east walls on the ground floor and narrow windows above. There are two loops adjoining the west angle of the tower. The timber framing above is of later date but may reproduce an earlier gallery, braced out from the north and west sides (see STOKES) (*Arch. Journal* CV Supplement, p. 65, pl. XIV).* (Plate XLII, Fig. 65)

STONE   see page 357

STRATE   see SNODHILL

STURMINSTER   ST 784134   Dorset

A deep ditch cutting off a promontory overlooking the bridge over the Stour into Sturminster Newton is all that now remains of a *motte*, perhaps the site of the king's chamber mentioned in 1207 (*Close Roll*).

STRIGUIL   see CHEPSTOW

STYFORD   see 'TIEFORT'

SULGRAVE   SP 556454   Northamptonshire

The ring-work west of the church (triangular with rounded angles) was preceded by a timber hall, partly on stone footings, which was reconstructed during the eleventh century (*Medieval Archaeology* VI/VII, pp. 333–4). A tower of drystone masonry embedded in the bank was noted at the close of excavation (B. K. Davison, speaking at the Royal Archaeological Institute, 7 April 1965).

SUTTON VALENCE   TQ 815491   Kent

Square keep on south side of rectangular plateau east of church. Most of the facing has gone but the sandstone rubble keep had 8-ft thick walls with clasping buttresses at the angles and traces of mural chambers flanking window recesses in the south and east walls above a line of beam-holes. Excavation in 1956–7 showed that a forebuilding had been added to the western end of the north wall. A new stair had been begun later within the forebuilding, but the new masonry wall was not completed. An inner partition had been burnt down and a new floor laid. Pottery ranging from 1150 to 1300 was found (*Archaeologia Cantiana* XXV, pp. 195–206; LXXI, pp. 227–8).   (Fig. 66)

SWANSCOMBE   see SWEYN'S CAMP

SWANSEA   SS 658930   Glamorgan

Nothing appears to survive of the castle attacked in 1116 (*Brut y Tywysogion*) and mentioned in 1187–94 and 1208 (*Pipe Rolls*).

| SWEEN | NR 714788 | Argyll |

Rectangular keep on south shore of straits of Loch Sween, of coursed rubble with clasping and central pilaster buttresses. That in the south wall is supported on the corbels of the round-headed arch of the barrel-vaulted entrance passage, which is rebated for a door with bar-hole. An altered round-headed first-floor window embrasure remains in the west wall, with recesses for timbers — two floors to the east, but only the upper in the north wall, west wall and west half of the south wall. A straight stair rises over the inner end of the entrance passage to the wall-walk with parapet and parados; there is a small square turret at the north-east angle with lintelled doorways to the wall-walk and splayed loops with stepped lintels to the outside; traces of similar openings remain in the east parapet, and there are blocked crenels in the west part of the south parapet. The south wall has an offset in freestone carried round the buttresses and the upper part is in a darker, more even, stone; the wall is not parallel to the north one, and the buttresses are wider, which may indicate a change of plan. Built by a predecessor of Dugall McSwine (*c.* 1220) (Scottish History Society, *Miscellanea* IV, p. 207) (*Transactions of the Glasgow Archaeological Society*, new series, XV, pp. 1–14; S. Cruden, *The Scottish Castle*, pp. 22–5).* (Plate XLIII; Fig. 70)

| SWERFORD | SP 373312 | Oxfordshire |

Motte and bailey (II Bb2) with strong counterscarp bank north of the church built of piled limestone, with oval enclosure beyond to the north-east. Pottery from the *motte*-top and bailey in 1938 was dated to the mid-twelfth century (*Oxfordshire Archaeological Society Report* No. 84, pp. 85–93).

| SWEYN'S CAMP (SWANSCOMBE) TQ 600741 | Kent |

Ring-work (C) with a sinuous bank and ditch running north from it, on the hill west of Swanscombe church, destroyed in 1928 in clay workings. A number of rectangular pits were found to the east and north of the ring-work, some interrupting the line of the ditch.

The site may be that called Svinescamp in 'Domesday Book' (I, f. 6). *Archaeologia Cantiana* XLI, pp. 13–18.*

| SWINESHEAD | TF 243410 | Lincolnshire |

Oval enclosure largely occupied by *motte* (Bb1) north-west of abbey, mentioned in 1186 (*Pipe Roll*).

SWORDS   see CASTLEKEVIN

TAFOLWERN   see WALWERIN

GAZETTEER

TAHMEHO see TIMAHOE

TAMWORTH	SK 206038	Staffordshire

Large *motte* (B) with traces of bailey on north bank of River Tame. A wing-wall running up the *motte* is of slabs laid herringbone fashion below a parapet. The *motte*-top has a polygonal shell-wall of coursed rubble with a sloping plinth and no quoins, with one projecting square buttress and two straight stairs in the thickness of the wall. A square tower projects slightly from the wall, with external pilaster buttresses at the ends of each wall and an internal round-headed entrance. The shell has been breached by post-medieval buildings and the original entrance destroyed.

Robert le Despencer held the castle (*Rot. Scacc. Normanniae* II, introduction), presumably in the eleventh century since his brother was Urse d'Abitot (see Worcester); the *castellum de Tameword* is mentioned in 1141 (B.M. *Add. MS.* 28024, f. 126b). (Fig. 68)

TAUNTON	ST 227248	Somerset

Pointed oval enclosure on south bank of River Tone, the north point cut off by a further ditch to form a triangular inner enclosure (IICd2). The hall on the north-west side was built over a levelled bank of marl; originally it was shorter and wider, with two barrel-vaults supporting an upper floor, now rebuilt. A cross-wing with a vaulted room runs east from the south end of the hall; a segmental-headed doorway has diagonally tooled dressings. The vault has been altered by thickening the outer wall and blocking a square-headed loop. The lias rubble exterior has clasping and mid-wall pilaster buttresses of Ham stone ashlar, as is the chamfered plinth, carried north-east along the outer wall of the hall.

The curtain was continued along the south side of the inner enclosure with round towers at the angles; it has been largely rebuilt, but there is a late Norman arch in the north-east bastion.

The south and west walls of a rectangular keep about 63 ft by 80 ft have been excavated within the enclosure; the rubble walls were 13 ft thick, and one has an ashlar face with 18 chamfered offsets and a rectangular projection with three alternate offsets carried round it. (*Proceedings of the Somersetshire Archaeological Society* LXVI, p. 38; LXXXVI, pp. 45-79; XCVIII, pp. 55-94). The square well produced a Norman corbel with a moustachioed face, a wooden bucket and pottery; a 'Coronation' spoon and schist hone were found nearby (*Antiquaries' Journal* X, p. 156; XXI, pp. 67-8).

The original hall is attributed to William Giffard (1107-29) and the keep to Henry of Blois (1129-71), although the latter may have begun the castle in 1138 (*Annales Monastici* II, p. 51). Extensive building (including the curtain) was in progress from 1207 (*Winchester Pipe Rolls*). (Fig. 68)

Sherborne

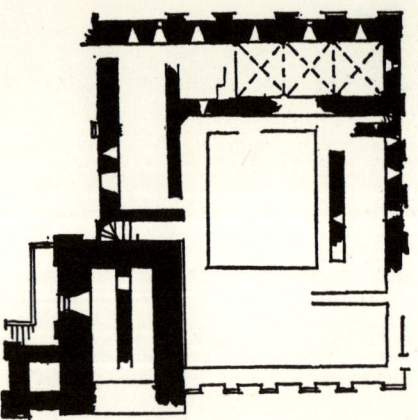

Taunton

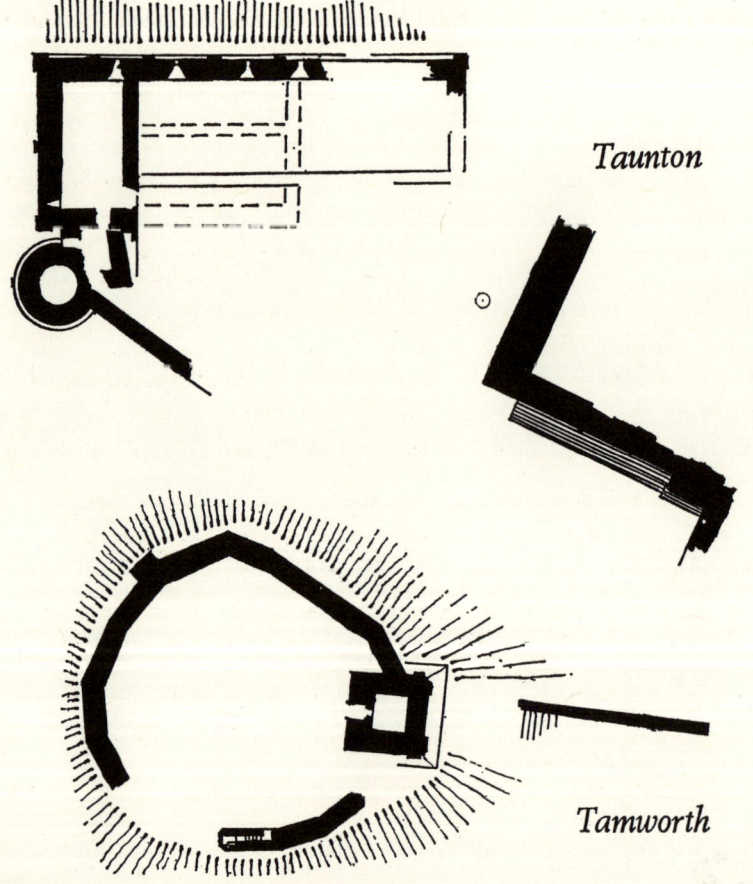

Tamworth

68

GAZETTEER

TENBY   SN 138005   Pembrokeshire

None of the masonry on the headland appears to be as early as the castle of 1153 (*Brut y Tywysogion*).

TERBET   see TURBET

TETBURY   Gloucestershire

The enclosure south of the church (ST 891929) may be part of the castle built by Robert of Gloucester and taken by Stephen in 1144 (*Gesta Stephani*, p. 113).

TEWKESBURY   SO 892325   Gloucestershire

Holme castle, a moated site south-east of the Abbey, largely levelled in 1826, was probably the site of the house of the Earls of Gloucester which was held by King John (1200–14). Brattices are mentioned in the repairs of 1210–11 (*Pipe Roll*). (Moore, *Tewkesbury* pt. III, pp. 37–58).*

THE BERRIES   see BALLAN MOOR

THERFIELD   TL 335373   Hertfordshire

Motte and bailey (Bd1) with traces of a contemporary village enclosure immediately west of parish church. Excavated in 1958; the *motte* appeared to have been unfinished and the bailey bank sealed a gully, slots and post-holes of a domestic site probably of the eleventh century. The clay bank had been revetted with palisades supported by split logs in front and a sleeper-beam to the rear; a deep post-hole might be a gatepost.

The likely date is during the disturbed period of the Anarchy; the later pottery from the site can be paralleled at South Mymms (q.v.) (*Journal of the British Archaeological Association*, 3rd series, XXVII, pp. 53–91).*

THETFORD (CASTLE HILL)   TL 875828   Norfolk

Very large *motte* built within an Iron Age fort with double banks and ditches (Ab3). The houses occupying the south part of the site have diagonally tooled ashlar block reused in their walls. Excavations in 1962 showed that the *motte*-top was of chalk rubble, and the north-east inner ditch had been recut and the bank heightened. Oval chalk foundations were added outside the outer ditch; floors and rubbish-pits in the bailey contained late-eleventh to mid-thirteenth century pottery and an outer bailey on the north side was discovered.

The first Earl Warren (d. 1088) was said to be lord of the town and castle of Thetford (*Norfolk Archaeology* XVI, p. 42) and the castle was destroyed in 1174 (*Pipe Roll*), (*Medieval Archaeology* VIII, p. 257).

(Fig. 67)

THETFORD (RED CASTLE)   TL 864830   Norfolk

Excavations in 1957–8 showed Saxo-Norman pottery in the make-up of the bank of the ring-work (C) enclosing eleventh-century church and burial ground and covering the late Saxon town ditch. The ring-work has an internal perimeter track. (*Norfolk Archaeology* XXXIV, pp. 119–86).

THIRSK   SE 438810   Yorkshire

Remains of oblong bailey (*motte* built over) (Bd3 ?) of castle mentioned in 1130 and destroyed 1174 (*Pipe Rolls; Gesta Henrici Secundi* I, pp. 48, 126).

THORNGATE   Lincolnshire

The *castellum de Tornegat* was pledged to Stephen before 1141, and the pledge was granted to the Bishop of Lincoln (*Registrum Antiquissimum of Lincoln* I, pp. 61–2, 282–9). J. W. F. Hill (*Medieval Lincoln*, pp. 159–60) suggest that this may have been Kyme Hall, north-west of Thorn Bridge.

THORNHAM   see BINBURY and GODARD'S

THORPE   see HANSLOPE

THURLES   S 1259   Tipperary

A *motte* existed in the grounds of the later castle (Lewis, *Top. Hib.* cited by Armitage, *Early Norman Castles*, p. 346) mentioned by 1189 (*Journal of the Royal Society of Antiquaries of Ireland* (1854–6), p. 381).

THURSO   Caithness

The castle destroyed by William the Lion in 1196 (*Hoveden* IV, pp. 10–12) may have been either at ND 107692 or ND 127689.

TIBBERAGHNY   see TIBRAGHNY

TIBRACCIAM   see TIBRAGHNY

TIBRAGHNY   S 5715   Kilkenny

Motte (Ab3) across road from later castle and church; first castle built in 1185 (*Annals of Loch Cé*; Giraldus Cambrensis, *Opera* V, 386; *Calendar of Documents*, I, 19).

TICKHILL   SK 593928   Yorkshire

Motte and bailey (IAb3) with little trace of any ditch between the two, but both have a strong counterscarp bank on the north and east sides. Excavation of the *motte*-top has revealed the foundations of an eleven-sided tower eccentrically placed on a circular plinth, with pilaster buttresses at the angles. Much of the early rubble curtain wall of the bailey survives, entered through a square gatehouse of ashlar with diapered triangular panels above the string-course on the outer side. The round-headed arches are of two square orders carried down the jambs without imposts. A round-headed arch springing from imposts is incorporated in the later house within. The castle had belonged to Roger de Busli before Robert of Belleme surrendered it in 1102 (Ordericus Vitalis, *Historia Ecclesiastica* iv, 33; xi, 3; *Regesta Regum Anglo-Normannorum* II, No. 598) and nearly £30 was spent on the castle in 1129–30 and over £120 on the tower and bridge in 1178–80. Money was spent on repairs in the reigns of Richard I and John (*Pipe Rolls*). (Fig. 71)

TIEFORT   Northumberland (?)

Mentioned in 1216 (*Histoire des Ducs de Normandie*, p. 163) – possibly Styford, Tynemouth or Tweedmouth.

TIMAHOE   S 5390   Laoighis (Leix)

Motte and bailey (Ba3) west of village, probably the castle of 1182 (Giraldus Cambrensis *Opera* V, p. 356). The building beside the round tower seems to have been a chapel upon which a tower house was imposed (*Journal of the Royal Society of Antiquaries of Ireland* LIV, pp. 31 ff.).

TIMBEI   see DENBIGH

TINTAGEL   SX 050890   Cornwall

In the detail-less local slate, it is extremely difficult to demonstrate the sequence of building on this site, particularly in the upper and lower wards on the mainland. The Celtic monastery on the 'island' is partly overlaid by a twelfth-century chapel with billet-moulded cornice fragments and an impost patterned with sunken stars. Near the causeway, the foundations of the hall survive – a long narrow building divided into bays (seating and slots for roof-trusses can be traced), each with a narrow splayed window on the seaward side at least. The legends attached to the site confuse its history; mentioned by two unreliable chroniclers (Geoffrey of Monmouth and Wace) in the middle of the twelfth century, the castle is referred to in the *Mappa Mundi* of Gervase of Canterbury. (Fig. 66)

TOMEN Y FAERDE (IAL)   SJ 192561   Denbighshire

Motte (A) on rock beside river, perhaps that fortified by King John in 1212 (*Pipe Roll*) (since it refers to iron mallets for breaking the rocks in the ditch) rather than Tomen y Rhodwydd (q.v.). (Fig. 73)

TOMEN Y MUR   SH 705386   Merioneth

Motte within rectangular Roman fort earthworks with cross-ditch cutting off part of enclosure (Ad2); loose ashlar lies on the *motte*-top. Built about 1090 (*History of Gruffyd ap Cynan*, pp. 141, 153). (Fig. 69)

TOMEN Y RHODWYDD (BUDDUGRE)   SJ 177516   Denbighshire

Motte and bailey (Be2) at head of valley. Built in 1149, destroyed 1157 (*Brut y Tywysogion*). (Fig. 73)

TONBRIDGE   TQ 589466   Kent

Motte and bailey (Ad3) with River Medway to south, water-meadows to west and town ditch to north and east. There are traces of an outer bailey (e) north of the *motte*. The *motte*-top has an oval shell-wall of sandstone ashlar some 5 ft thick and up to 8 ft high, with large deep buttresses to the south-east. The buttresses have chamfered courses below a sloping plinth. The shell surrounds a polygonal depression some 13 ft across north of the well. The wing-wall descending the *motte* to the Edwardian gatehouse has been rebuilt, and fragments of another run south to link up with the bailey curtain, which also has heavy buttresses and a sloping plinth, a small blocked round-headed doorway near the rounded south-east angle and traces of an angle turret to the south-west.

    The castle was held against William II in 1088 (*Anglo-Saxon Chronicle*; *Florence of Worcester*). (Fig. 69)

TONG   SJ 793080   Shropshire

Mound (IB) beside stream, probably the Tong castle mentioned in a charter (*Monasticon* VI, 263) dated to 1185–90 (Eyton, *Antiquities of Shropshire* II, pp. 211–2, note).

TONGE   TQ 933636   Kent

Earthworks adjoining millpond, which forms two sides of a trapezoidal ditched area. Strong bank on north side; a triangular ditched area on the east side was excavated in 1930 and 1964–5, giving evidence of a timber building replaced by thirteenth-century stone buildings; one had pilastered flint rubble walls not bonded together, with squared jambs to the entrance. Much shelly red pottery was found (*Archaeologia Cantiana* XLIV, pp. 60–66; LXXIX, pp. 207–10; LXXX, pp. 265–9).

TOPCLIFFE   SE 410750   Yorkshire

Motte and bailey (Aa3) by ford at junction of River Swale and Cod beck. The castle was fortified in 1174 (*Hoveden* II, p. 58; *Pipe Roll*).

TORPEL   see page 357

TORRE   see DUNSTER

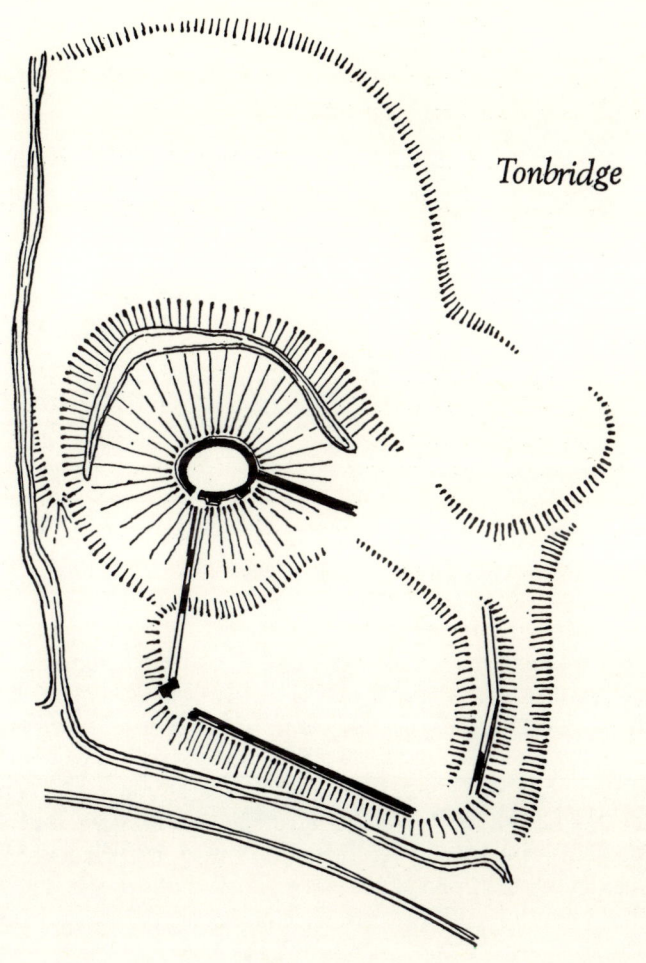

Tonbridge

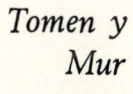

Tomen y Mur

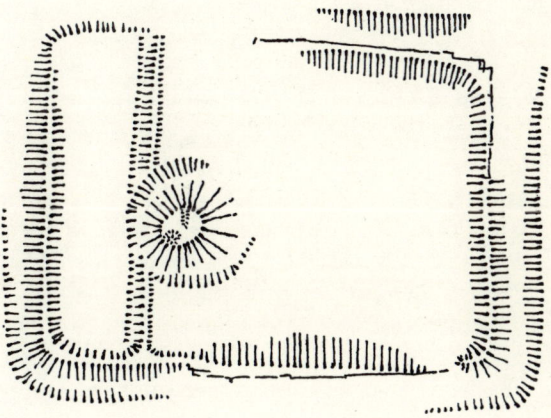

69

325

TORRINGTON   see NETHER STOWEY

TOTINGEHAM   see COTTINGHAM

TOTNES   SX 800605   Devon

Motte and bailey (Ba4) at west end of borough enclosure; round arch in wall near by. A quadrilateral clay-packed rubble foundation (about 16 ft by 13 ft internally) was found going down at least 11 ft into the *motte*, partly faced in clay-set coursed rubble. The walls were only 2 ft 6 in. thick, with a square projection near the east angle and a clay spur retained by a rubble face at the other end of this wall.

The reference to lands *subtus castellum* before 1087 (*Monasticon* IV, 63), may not be original, but there was certainly a castle at Totnes in 1105 (*Regesta Regum Anglo-Normannorum* II, 735). (*Transactions of the Devonshire Association* LXXXVI, pp. 228–56).*   (Fig. 73)

TOTTERNHOE   see page 357

TOWER OF LONDON   TQ 336805   London

Excavations in 1962–63 (*Medieval Archaeology* VIII, pp. 255–6) have shown that the first medieval defence was a bank and ditch running due north from the river across the site of the Wakefield Tower and then turning to run across the parade ground north of the White Tower as far as the Roman city wall, which enclosed the east and south sides. Within this enclosure was built the White Tower, perhaps begun in 1078 (*Textus Roffensis*, p. 212). The White Tower is of Kentish rag with Caen ashlar — Portland stone is used in the early eighteenth-century remodelling. The plan is rectangular with a round stair turret to the north-east and the chapel apse to the south-east. There are wide pilaster buttresses adjoining the western angles and narrower ones making five bays (north/south) and four bays (east/west) rising from a much-altered plinth, now sloping. The angles are carried up above the parapet as square (except north-east, round) turrets. The forebuilding at the western end of the south wall has been completely destroyed, and the entrance doorway altered and blocked. There is an inserted spiral staircase in the next bay. The first floor windows are set back slightly in round-headed recesses with string-courses above and below. The top floor bay above the entrance has two original two-light windows, the western central shaft having a moulded capital and base. Internally there is a north/south cross-wall, with a subsidiary wall cutting off the chapel. The basement is lit by steeply shelving loops in the east and west walls. The sub-crypt of the chapel has an internal offset, with a round-headed doorway in the north wall; the crypt above has a small groined chamber in the north wall. There are round-headed fireplaces in the middle of the east and west walls, and groined recesses in the west end

Sween

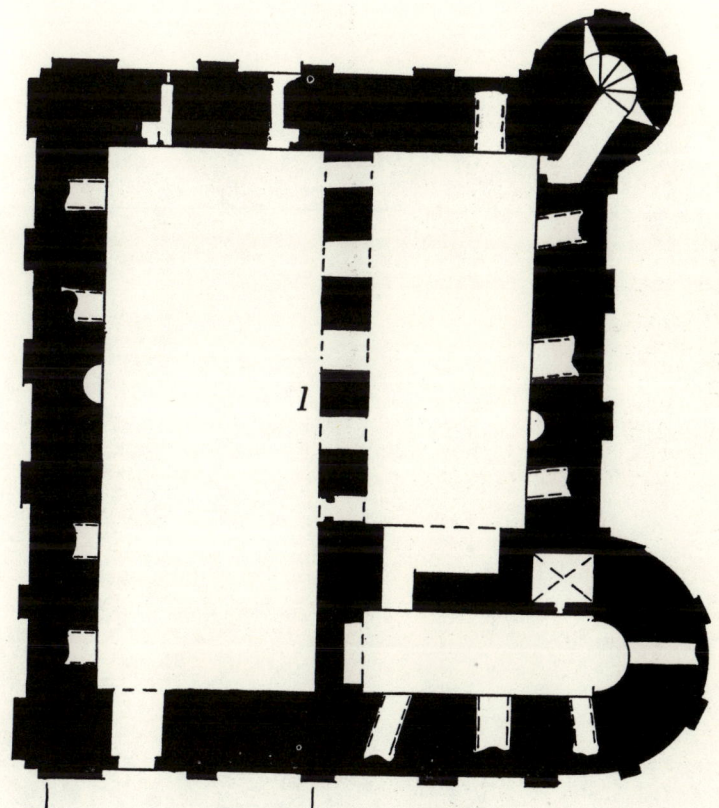

70　Tower of London

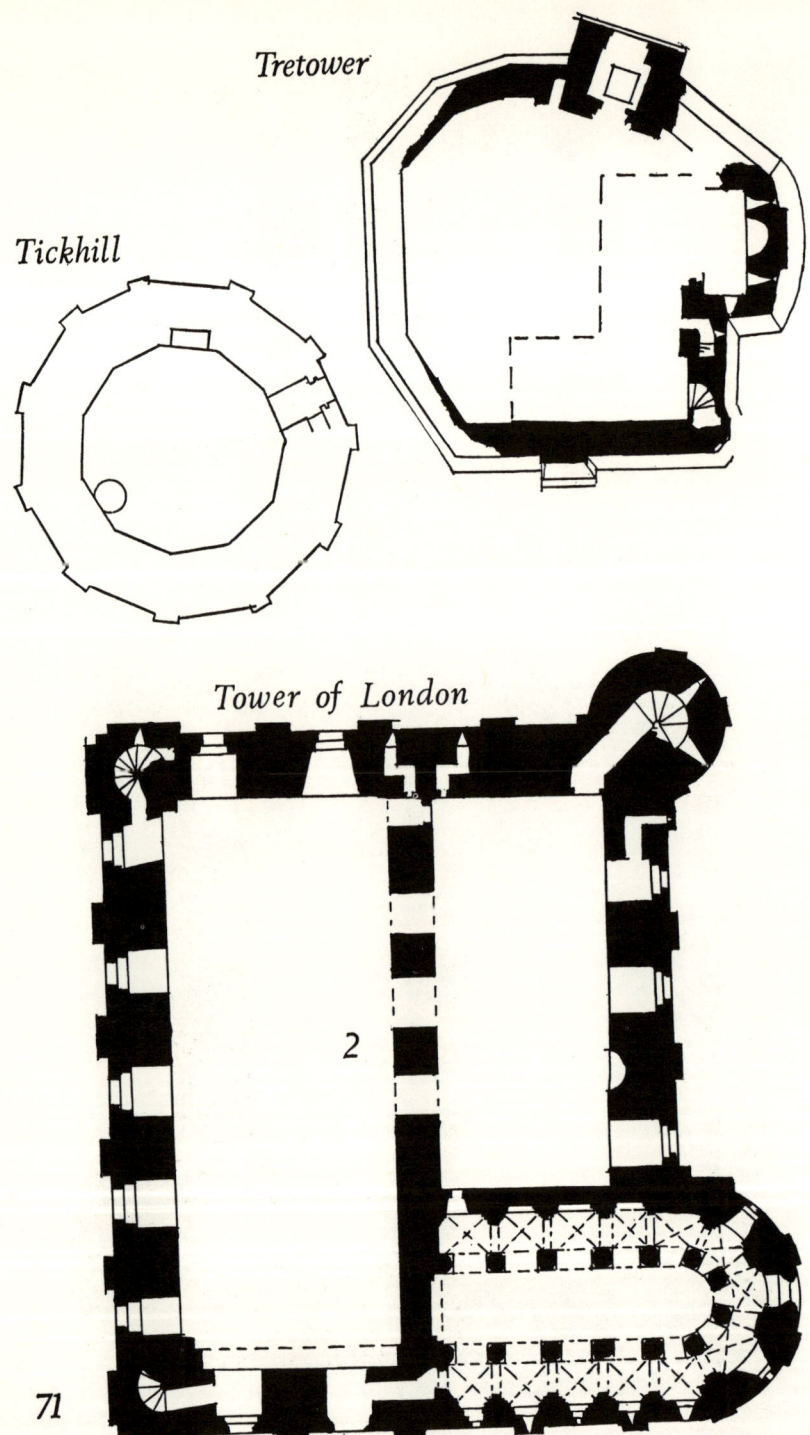

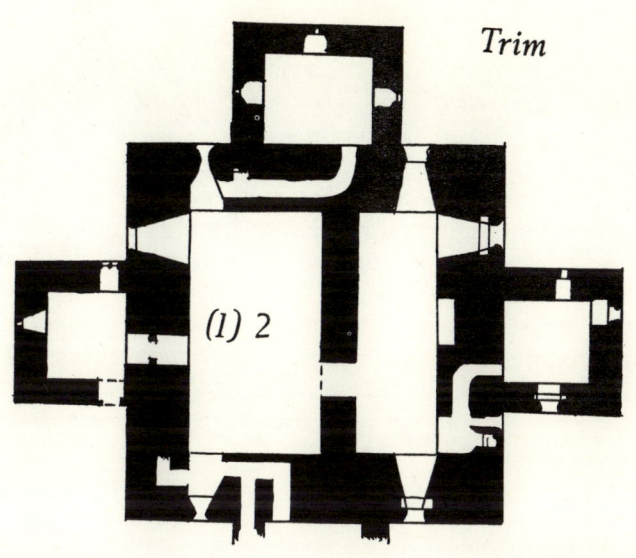

Trim

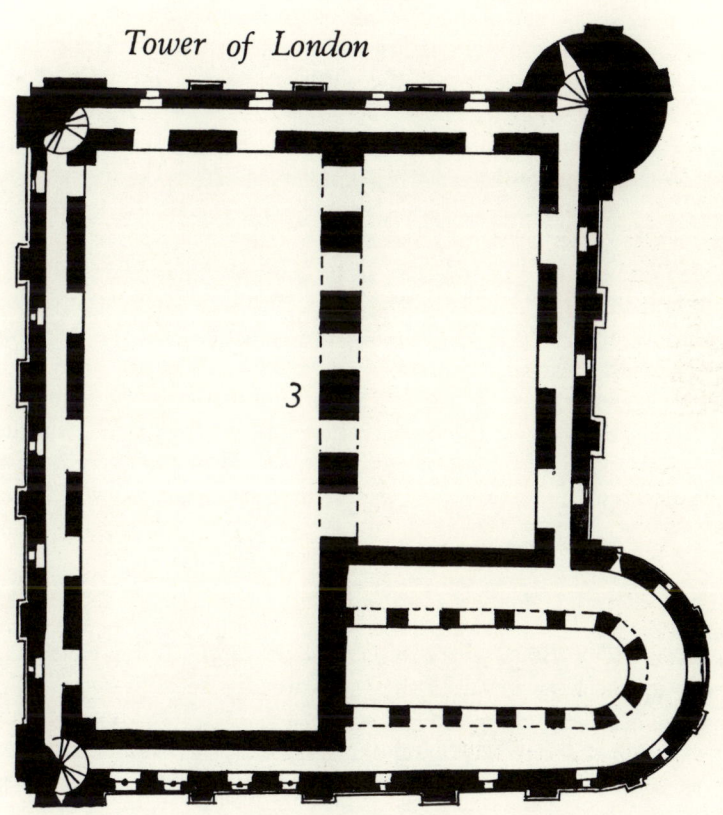

Tower of London

72

329

of the north wall. The cross-wall is pierced with three round-headed arches between two round-headed doorways. The floor above is similar, but the round rear-arches of the windows with flanking recesses are original, and there is no fireplace in the west wall. There are further spiral stairs in the western angles, with latrine passages adjoining the north-east angle. The chapel has an arcade of four bays continued round the apse in stilted versions of the semicircular arches on round columns with moulded bases and cushion capitals with tau-crosses, either scalloped abaci or with a necking row of leaves. These link to similar wall-responds to carry a groined vault, lit by round-headed windows. Above the aisle is a triforium with plain round-headed arches and a barrel-vaulted passage linked to a continuous barrel-vaulted wall-passage round the whole Tower. This floor level is again generally similar to that below; the roof is modern.

The Anglo-Saxon Chronicle records the building of a wall round the Tower in 1097, and expenditure on the castle is recorded in 1129–30 and 1171–2, on the White Tower in 1172–8 (including floor-beams and roof-lead) and other buildings in the 1180s (*Pipe Rolls*). During 1190 the enormous sum of £2,881 was spent, partly on a new bank and ditch (*Hoveden* III, 33), extending the enclosure westward to the line of the later inner west curtain wall, and partly on masonry on the south and east sides. Of this, the Bell Tower at the south-west angle and the curtain wall running east from it remain. The Bell Tower is octagonal in plan, rising from a ragstone rubble foundation with a chamfered plinth to a Purbeck string course – this plinth continues eastward across the gateway of the Bloody Tower (see *The History of the King's Works* plate 46b). The interior of the Bell Tower is pentagonal with a pointed vault springing from moulded corbels to a foliated boss, lit by arrow-loops in wide embrasures, with a latrine in the south-east angle. The upper floor is circular within and without, with traces of two-light windows externally, the round heads turned with thin slabs.

Of the contemporary Wardrobe Tower (immediately east of the apse of the White Tower) the curved south-east wall survives with two pilaster buttresses, based on a bastion of the Roman Wall (R.C.H.M. *London* V, pp. 79–93).* (Plate XLIV; Figs. 70, 71, 72, 73)

TRALLWNG   see WELSHPOOL

TREMATON   SX 410580   Cornwall

Motte and bailey (Bb3), with rubble masonry on the bailey bank running partway up the *motte* toward a shell-wall around the *motte*-top. The gate-house has been entirely rebuilt after the twelfth century, but the remains of the curtain wall have a sloping plinth on the inside and narrow crenels only as wide as the parapet is thick. A postern entrance has a slightly

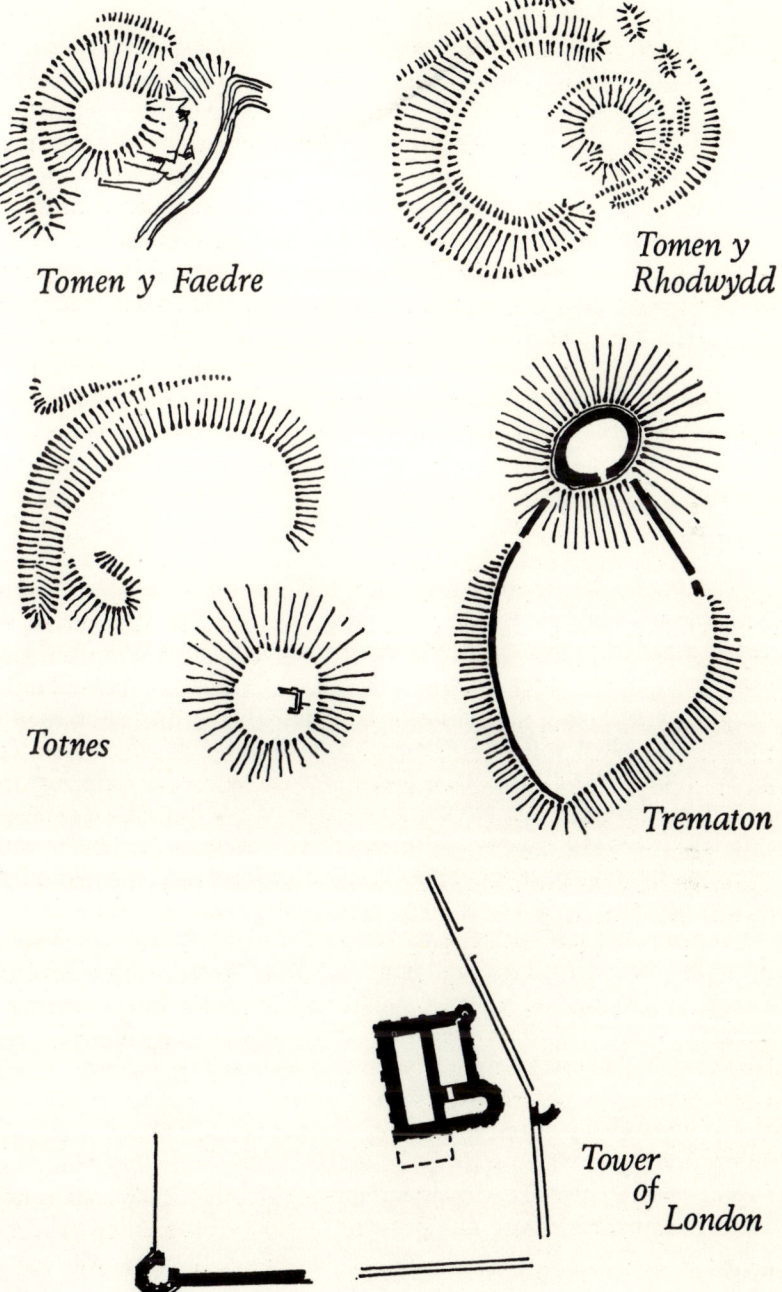

pointed arch backed by a hole for a door-bar, with a higher arch on the inner face of the wall.

The ovoid shell-wall on the *motte*-top has a high sloping plinth; the crenels are wider than those of the curtain wall, and the parapet may be a rebuild, judging by the masonry differences and the solitary cross-loops guarding the bailey. A regular row of corbels survive internally just below the wall walk. The shell is entered by a plain round-headed archway springing from chamfered imposts (like Launceston); the sockets of a timber lintel survive, with a deep draw-bar hole in the jamb.

The castle of *Tremetone* is mentioned in 'Domesday Book' (I, 122) *Archaeologia* 83, pp. 217-9. (Fig. 73)

TRENTHAM   SJ 866409   Staffordshire

The mention of a *castellum de Trentham* in the *Pipe Roll* of 1168 may refer to the predecessor of Newcastle under Lyme, since Mount Field occurs as a place-name (*Journal of the North Staffordshire Field Club* XLVII, pp. 144-50).*

TRETOWER   SO 184212   Brecknockshire

Slight traces of a *motte* and bailey (Bc2) underlie the stone castle. Across the *motte* was built an L-shaped building, the internal walls being destroyed when the great circular tower was built, probably after 1233 (*Close Roll*). To the south is a first floor hall over a basement cut out of the mound; the springing of a chevron bordered arch and the outline of a similarly decorated window remain, adjoining the east solar wing. The first floor solar has a central fireplace, flanked by a wall passage and a blocked window, the flue carried up in an external buttress. The south gable has a blocked window of three orders; chevrons, colonettes with twisted shafts and a plain inner one. A spiral staircase in a polygonal turret links the floors.

The west wall has been heightened but retains traces of the original wall-walk, carried through the gable as a wall passage. Another wall passage leads to the hall basement and thence to the kitchen, contrived in the curve of the rubble revetment of the mound. The semicircular fireplace has a double row of draught vents and no true flue, and is flanked by narrow lighting loops. The roof sloped towards the hall to improve the latter's light. The rest of the mound was surrounded by a curtain wall (largely destroyed) with a stair to the wall-walk adjoining the foundations of a rectangular gatehouse with a central pit. The bailey walling appears to be later in date (*Brycheiniog* VI, pp. 1-50).*   (Plate XLVI; Fig. 71)

TRIM   N 8057   Meath

Triangular bailey enclosing flattened mound (Bc1) on south bank of River

Boyne. The rectangular gatehouse of roughly coursed rubble is approached by a stone causeway and has a round arch of two plain orders. The upper part of the outer angles is chamfered off (like the Colton Tower at Dover) and there is a flanking room to the north-east set back from the line of the curtain wall which runs to a large square tower projecting from the north angle of the bailey. Most of the east (river) front has gone, apart from a rectangular turret on the slope. There is a small round tower at the south-east angle (from which a ditch runs to the river) and the curtain further west has a large round tower astride it of three storeys (the upper rounded octagons) with long arrowslits in segmental embrasures. A long forework (with pointed arches carrying portscullis before and behind a drawbridge pit) projects through the round tower. There are four plain semi-circular towers with open backs further west still.

The square keep of roughly coursed limestone rubble with red sandstone dressings has a square projection from each side (only the toothings remain of that on the north). The basement of the central tower and east projection are filled up, but the others have rooms lit by narrow loops. The segmental-headed entrance with roll-mouldings was at the north side of the east projection hard against the central tower, with a similar arch into the tower. There was a north/south cross-wall with recesses in its west face and a square-headed fireplace opposite. Each projection had a small square window with side recesses in each face, and was flanked by a larger round-arched window embrasure with roll-mouldings (except that overlooking the entrance). The embrasures at the east end of the north and south walls (and the north end of the west wall) had wall passages into the adjoining projection, with a branch wall-stair to the floor below. In addition spiral stairs open off the window embrasures at the east end of the north wall and the west end of the south leading to the two floors above, which are carried on wall offsets.

The cross-wall only rises to the level of the first floor above the entrance and there are the creases of an early roof in the north and south walls at this level, and the exterior masonry of squared blocks changes to flat slabs above a row of putlog (or hourd?) holes. There are traces of a chapel on the upper floor of the east projection and the angles of the central tower are carried up as turrets, the walling between them and the projections being set back.

The *motte* and ditched fortified house were restored after being destroyed in 1174 (*Song of Dermot*; Giraldus Cambrensis, *Opera* V, 313) and considerably rebuilt in 1220 (*Close Roll*; *Annals of Innisfallen*) but the details of the keep and north curtain suggest a slightly earlier date. Expenditure in 1211–12 included a cable for demolishing a tower (*Irish Pipe Roll*).   (Plate XLV; Figs. 72, 74)

TRISTERDERMOT   see KILKEA

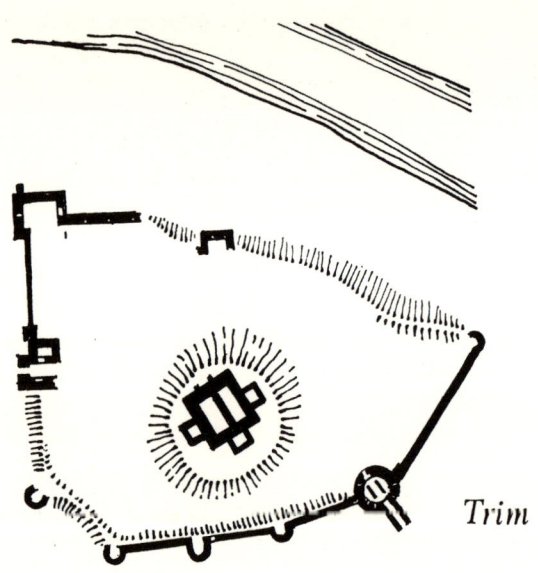
Trim

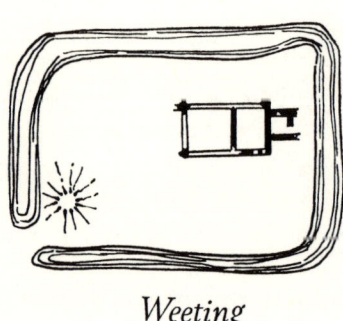
Weeting

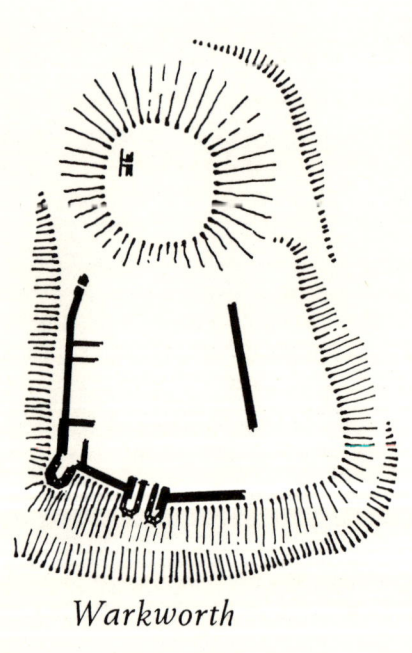
Warkworth

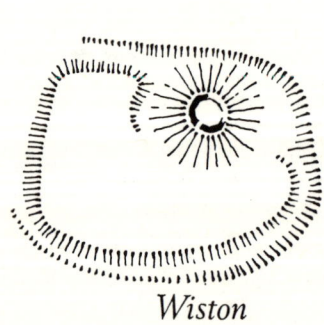
Wiston

74

GAZETTEER

TROWBRIDGE   ST 854579   Wiltshire

Site of ring-work (c/2) between Fore Street and the River Biss; stone foundations have been found. The castle had been built by Henry de Bohun by 1139 (*Gesta Stephani*, p. 61; William of Malmesbury, *Historia Novella*, p. 36) (*Wiltshire Archaeological Magazine* 15, pp. 208–21).*

TRURO   see page 357

TUAM   M 4352   Galway

Romanesque carvings in the later ruined church might be from the stone castle of Rory O'Connor (1166–75; Ware, *de Hibernia* (1658), p. 111).

TULAGH BARI   see TULLABARRY

TULLABARRY   S 4572   Kilkenny

Motte (A) a mile north of Ballyragget, built by 1202 (*Reg. St. Thomas Dublin* cl, cited in *Journal of the Royal Society of Antiquaries of Ireland* XXXIX, pp. 330–1).

TULLOW or TULLACHT   S 8574   Carlow

Church stands on *motte* with bailey to north-west (Bb3 ?) mentioned by Giraldus Cambrensis (*Opera* V, 355) as John of Hereford's castle of 1181 (cp. Castlemore). The *castellum de Tulach* is mentioned in 1185 (*Reg. St. Thomas, Dublin*, p. 113).

TURBET   H 3617   Cavan

Motte and bailey (Ad2) on Turbet Island in river Erne, fortified in 1211–12 (*Irish Pipe Roll*).

TUTBURY   SK 210293   Staffordshire

Motte and bailey (Ac/43) beside steep slope to River Dove. The *motte* has a counterscarp bank to the west, and there are three outer platforms; that to the south of the *motte* is rectangular, those beyond the bailey to the north-east are quadrant-shaped, and there are traces of a village enclosure to the south. The foundations of a twelfth-century chapel lie in the bailey, with shafted doorways to nave and chancel, but the shell-keep on the mound (Shaw, *History of Staffordshire* I, p. 49) is replaced by a later 'folly'.

     William I gave the castle to a newcomer in 1071 (Ordericus Vitalis, *Historia Ecclesiastica* II, p. 222) and it was demolished in 1175 (*Diceto*, I, p. 404) (Duchy of Lancaster, *Official Guide*).*

TWEEDMOUTH   Northumberland

Nothing appears to survive of the castle built by Philip of Poitou by 1208 and destroyed by the Scots King William the Lion in 1209 (*Pipe Roll* 13 John, pp. 38–9; *Chronica de Lanercost* I, 4–7; *Chronica de Mailros*, 108).

TYNEMOUTH   NZ 373694   Northumberland

Promontory cut off by bank and ditch to west (traceable on each side of later gatehouse). The castle withstood a siege in 1095 (*Symeon of Durham* II, p. 225; *Florence of Worcester* II, pp. 38, 52).

TYTHERLEY   see LIDELEA

TYPERMESAN   see KILMESSAN

ULLERSWOOD   SJ 800838   Cheshire

Earthworks beside River Bollin at Castle Mill. Hamo de Masci held the Castle of 'Ullerwada' against Henry II in 1173 (*Gesta Henrici Secundi* I, p. 48; see Ormerod *History of Cheshire* I, p. 133; III, 586 n.).

UPPER SLAUGHTER   SP 157232   Gloucestershire

Motte on end of ridge east of late twelfth-century church, with bailey beyond (Bb2). A chamber was found 30 ft down the stone-lined well in the nineteenth century, and twelfth century pottery in 1963 when the road bisecting the site was widened (*Proceedings of the Cotteswold Naturalists Field Club* XXXIV, pp. 32–6). The church was converted into a castle 1139–48 (*Letters of Gilbert Foliot* No. 5, ed. Morey and Brooke).

URR   NX 816648   Kirkcudbrightshire

Motte and bailey (Bd1) on gravel mound between old and new channels of Urr water. Excavations showed that the *motte* had a central hearth, revetted when the entire surface of the *motte* was coated with rammed clay. A rectangular pit at the edge of the *motte* had central and peripheral post-holes, those on the outer side abutting against large boulders. The V-shaped ditch had post-holes on the counterscarp. (*Archaeological News Letter* II, p. 141; *Discovery and Excavation in Scotland*, 1953; *Transactions of the Dumfriesshire and Galloway Archaeological Society*, third series, XXIX, pp. 167–72).

USK   SO 377010   Monmouthshire

Rectangular keep of roughly coursed rubble with ashlar quoins projecting from later curtain; the only early feature is two round-headed embrasures with inset narrow loops in the upper part of the south wall. The castle is mentioned in 1138 by Ordericus Vitalis (*Historia Ecclesiastica* XIII, c. 26) and in the *Pipe Rolls* of 1174 and 1185. A. J. Taylor (*Archaeologia Cambrensis* 99, pp. 249–55) suggests that the later reference implies that the keep was not then built.   (Plate XLVI)

GAZETTEER

WAKEFIELD   SE 327198   Yorkshire

Eroded *motte* and bailey (Bc2) in Clarence Park. Excavations revealed twelfth-century pottery, particularly around a hearth underlying the bailey bank, with an iron/bronze stud and prickspur. The *motte* ditch was shallow and the earthworks may never have been finished.

The constable of the castle of Wakefield witnessed a document of 1174–8 with his fellow-constable of Conisbrough (q.v.).

B. Hope-Taylor, Report on the Excavations at Lowe Hill (*Wakefield Historical Society* 1953).

WALDEN   TL 538387   Essex

Motte and bailey now practically levelled, but ditches marked by street lines; rubble wall foundations have been found in the bailey. The square keep is of flint rubble with traces of herringbone-work facing. The entrance was by a flight of steps against the outside of the west wall leading to a forebuilding; the other faces had clasping and central pilaster buttresses. Internally there was a central pier base and round-headed recesses in the western half of the walls. The well-shaft lay in the north-west angle and the spiral stair in the opposite one. Traces of a fireplace are recorded in the upper part of the west wall.

Walden was one of Geoffrey de Mandeville's castles (see Ashmole MS. 843, f. 3, quoted by Round, *Geoffrey de Mandeville*, p. 89) surrendered to Stephen in 1142 and destroyed in 1157–8 (see Pleshey) (R.C.H.M. *Essex* I, pp. 233–4).*   (Fig. 75)

'WALELEGE'   Herefordshire

The *domus defensabilis* mentioned in 'Domesday Book' may have been sited at Old Castle Farm, Ailey (SO 340486).

WALLINGFORD   SU 608897   Berkshire

Motte and bailey (Bd1) in north-east corner of village enclosure. Fragments of walling of uncertain date — the *motte* is said to be based on a stone 'saucer' (Hedges, *History of Wallingford* I, p. 139) — perhaps merely a revetment.

The Abbot of Abingdon was imprisoned in the castle in 1071 (*Chron. Mon. de Abingdon* I, p. 486); eight *hagae* had been destroyed for the castle ('Domesday Book' I, 56).

The castle was strengthened in 1173–4 and repaired in 1178–9, 1182–3, 1194–6 and throughout John's reign (*Pipe Rolls*); it was strongly fortified in 1215 and the moats repaired (*Rot. Litt. Pat.*, pp. 135, 142, 186; *Rot. Litt. Claus.* 8, 187, 199).

WALLINGFORD SIEGEWORKS		Berkshire

When Brian fitz Count declared for the Empress in 1139, Stephen built two forts to besiege Wallingford, one made from a church (*Gesta Stephani*, pp. 61-2). One was levelled by Robert of Gloucester in 1140 (William of Malmesbury, *Historia Novella*, p. 42). Stephen's building of two forts and the capture of the bridge are mentioned in 1152 and, in 1153-4 the fort at Crowmarsh was attacked and demolished by agreement between Henry and Stephen (*Gesta Stephani*, pp. 156-7).

The one made from a church may have been the mound beside St Peter's church (SU 609896) and the Crowmarsh fort is the rectangular enclosure on the opposite bank of the Thames from the castle (SU 616906).

WALMER	TR 367504	Kent

Double two-storeyed hall of flint rubble with forebuilding and angle turrets. Pottery of 1150-75 was found at foundation level (*Arch. Jnl.* CXXVI pp. 215-7).

WALTON	TM 322358	Suffolk

Site of Roman fort eroded by sea. A plan (reproduced in the V.C.H. *Suffolk* I, opposite p. 288) shows a narrow rectangular fort with round towers at the angles, with a sketch of a building with a square tower in the north-east corner (which might be ecclesiastical, as suggested in *Journal of the British Archaeological Association*, third series XXIV, pp. 58-9). The castle was surrendered to Henry II in 1157 (*Diceto* I, p. 404; *Torigny*, p. 192) and was garrisoned thereafter (*Pipe Rolls*) but Hugh Bigod seems to have recovered it in 1173-4 (*Diceto* I, p. 377) when the *excelsae turri muris fundatae fortissimis* are mentioned, but it was demolished in 1176, the provisions being taken to Ipswich and sold (*Pipe Roll*).

WALWERN	SH 891026	Montgomeryshire

Motte at junction of streams with enclosure (Ac2) mentioned in 1162 (*Brut y Tywysogion*).

WAREHAM	SY 922872	Dorset

Excavation of the rectangular ramparts enclosing the town in 1952-4, showed that the primary bank and ditch were post-Roman (possibly the *burh* of Alfred's time). Later a stone wall was erected on the crest of the bank, perhaps *c.* A.D. 1000. Finally the wall was robbed to its foundations, the bank heightened and both bank and ditch recut in the twelfth century (*Medieval Archaeology* III, pp. 120-138).

The foundations of the keep were found in 1910 during the building of a house on the mound in the south-west corner of the enclosure, and re-excavated in 1950-1. The keep was built of coursed rubble, with a flat offset a yard wide with a mortared rubble core. There were ashlar buttresses at the end and centre of each face, of alternate courses of brown and white freestone, and the walls had been mortar-covered and buried 5 ft in a gravel mound; above this the walls were of re-used mortared rubble, some of it granite, quartz, and green slate. A foot-wide internal offset marked the earliest floor, fine sand over clay, littered with charred oak timbers. Apart from the usual run of Norman finds, a crossbow 'nut' of antler was recovered, and a baluster shaft (from a two-light window?) is built into a wall near by, and a blocked round-headed arch with polychrome jambs and chevron decoration into another.

Over half the houses in Wareham were derelict or destroyed at the time of 'Domesday Book' (I, 75) — a common situation when land was taken for a castle — but the reference to 'castellum Warham' (I, 78) may relate to Corfe (q.v.).

Robert, Duke of Normandy was imprisoned at Wareham from 1106, so the reference to his being in *arce regia* in 1119 (Ordericus Vitalis, *Historia Ecclesiastica* IV, 402) may be to this keep. At the outbreak of the Anarchy, the Earl of Gloucester strengthened Corfe and Wareham and soon recaptured the latter when it fell to Stephen and again after it fell while he was abroad in 1142 (*Gesta Stephani*, pp. 95–6). The castle was repaired in 1203-4 and 1206-7 (*Pipe Rolls*) and fortified in 1216 (*Wendover* II, 183) (*Medieval Archaeology* IV, pp. 56–68).* (Fig. 75)

WARK ON TWEED   NT 824387   Northumberland

Motte and bailey (Bf3) on south bank of river, with traces of rectangular village enclosure on south and east. Some overgrown rubble remains of a polygonal keep on the mound, and some remains of a plinth have been dated to the early thirteenth century.

The castle was taken in 1136 and destroyed in 1138, and rebuilt at a cost of nearly £400 in 1158-61 (*Pipe Rolls*) so that it withstood the Scots army in 1174-5 (*Chronicles of the reigns of Stephen, Henry II . . . III*, pp. 145, 172, 303–13). (*History of the Berwickshire Naturalists' Club* XXIX, pp. 76–103).*

WARKWORTH   NU 247058   Northumberland

Motte and bailey (Bd4) on hill south of River Coquet. A fragment of a splayed plinth and doorway incorporated in the north part of the west wall of the later medieval tower on the mound may be contemporary with the twelfth century lower part of the central sections of the east and west bailey curtain of sandstone ashlar with an external plinth. A doorway is of two square orders, the inner round-headed arch springing from moulded imposts. The western curtain wall formed the outer wall of the hall, with a Norman fireplace in the south wall. The hall was widened eastward at the beginning of the thirteenth century (the foundations of aisle pillars and a corbel with nailhead ornament carrying an arch survive) with a service block to the north and a cellar to the south with a cross-beam on three pillars to carry the solar over, reached by a stair in the thickness of the curtain wall. This makes an awkward junction with the south-west angle tower, semi-octagonal with a cross-bow loop in each external face, like the south gatehouse towers, which have polygonal buttresses at the angles and other loops facing each other across the gate passage; the towers are entered from within the bailey with flanking stairs rising to the curtain wall, which is also of ashlar with a sloping plinth. The pointed entrance arch of two square orders is set in a recess to take a lifting bridge, and the whole south front was later raised. A rectangular tower at the north-west angle of the curtain has a tall pointed entrance arch, with narrow loop-holes in the portcullis chamber over, reached by an external spiral stair, with the foundations of a curtain wall of similar (early thirteenth century) date on each side.

The castle was in existence by 1158, and perhaps as early as 1138 (*Assize Roll* n. 4, 36; *Cal. Placito de Quo Warranto*, p. 595) but was too weak for defence in 1173–4 (*Chronicles of the reigns of . . . Henry II . . . III*, pp. 251–2) (M.P.B.W. *Official Guide*).* (Figs. 74, 75)

WARRINGTON   SJ 609876   Lancashire

Ring-work and bailey (ICb3) beside Mersey marshes north-east of church. Excavation of the ring in 1832 produced jet chessmen, pottery with tubular spouts and triangular rouletting and a Norman horseshoe, together with a well lined with horizontal oak staves laid against four corner posts. An upper pavement produced a coin of Henry III (*Transactions of the Historic Society of Lancashire and Cheshire* V, pp. 59–68).

WARWICK   SP 283647   Warwickshire

Motte and bailey (Ad4) on north bank of River Avon. Three faces of a polygonal shell-wall on the *motte* may be early, but are now refaced and buttressed. The castle was built in 1068 and given to Henry of Beaumont (Ordericus Vitalis, *Historia Ecclesiastica* II, p. 181); 'Domesday Book' (I, 238) says that four *masuras* were waste for the site of the castle. A royal garrison was put in in 1173–4 and bretasches erected (*Pipe Roll*).

WATERFORD   Waterford

Reginald's Tower is probably a successor to that mentioned in 1171 (Giraldus Cambrensis, *Opera* V, p. 255) and nothing survives of the castle mentioned in 1215 (*Calendar of Documents* I, 89). Fortifications are mentioned in 1211–12 (*Irish Pipe Roll*).

GAZETTEER

WATTLESBOROUGH SJ 354128 Shropshire

Small square keep of sandstone ashlar with pilaster buttresses clasping the angles. A round-headed entrance arch of two chamfered orders above a plain lintel survives in the north-west wall, with a bar-hole in the passage. This floor is joined to that above by a spiral stair in the north angle. In two of the walls there are blocked two-light windows with solid tympana and chamfered heads and jambs, with round-headed embrasures within; the south window has two similar lights roughly cut above it. An engraving of the north wing (reproduced in Eyton, *Antiquities of Shropshire* VII) shows round-headed windows above a similar doorway. (Fig. 75)

'WAVREI' SP 518788 Warwickshire

Mentioned in 1201 (*Rot. Litt. Pat.* p. 3; see *Place Names of Warwickshire*, pp. 103-4).

WAYNARD'S see BWLCH Y DDINAS

WAYTEMORE TL 490215 Hertfordshire

Large *motte* with traces of bailey (I/II Af2 ?). The *motte*-top is surrounded by a mortared flint wall 12 ft thick (in plan like a horseshoe magnet) which abuts awkwardly against a rhomboidal foundation (17 ft by 15 ft internally) and oversails another (18 ft by 15 ft 6 in.). These foundations go down at least 7 ft into the *motte*.

The castle of *Estortford* was given to Maurice, Bishop of London, by William I (*Early Charters of St. Paul's Cathedral*, p. 12), Maurice's predecessor having bought the manor from the king ('Domesday Book' I, 134a), and the castle was seized by the abbot of St Edmund's in 1137 (*Diceto* I, 250) and was specially referred to in the charter of 1142 (Round, *Geoffrey de Mandeville*, pp. 167, 174) (V.C.H. *Hertfordshire* III, pp. 297-8).*

Fig. 76)

WEETING TL 778892 Norfolk

Rectangular moated enclosure with semicircular annex and large mound into which an ice-house has been built, possibly an altered *motte* and bailey (Type Be2). There are remains of a barrel-vaulted hall, rebuilt with a solar at the south end. A rectangular tower lit by round-headed loops with square embrasures is attached to the south-east angle. (Fig. 74)

WELBOURNE SK 968544 Lincolnshire

Robert Rabaz was to make one perch of the wall of the castle of Welbourne in return for a grant of land by Hugh of Bayeux about 1158 (B.M. *Add. Chart.* 6038 quoted by Stenton, *The First Century of English Feudalism* appendix 31). A ring-work (C) survives.

WELSHPOOL Montgomeryshire

The castle captured in 1196 (*Pipe Rolls; Brut y Tywysogion; Annales Cestrienses*, p. 45) may be either the site near the railway (SJ 230074 (IBb4)) or the Lady's Mount in Powis Park (SJ 212063 (Cc4)).

WEOBLEY SO 403513 Herefordshire

Altered site south of the village, apparently a ring-work and bailey (Cb2) with an outer bank and ditch protecting the exposed (south) side of the ring. Stephen captured it in 1138 (*Florence of Worcester* II, 106; *Chronicle of John of Worcester*, p. 49) and it is mentioned in the *Pipe Roll* for 1186–7 (R.C.H.M. *Herefordshire* III, 196, 198).*

WEST DEAN see LIDELEA

WEST DERBY (LIVERPOOL) SJ 397934 Lancashire

Ploughed-out and bailey (Bc4) excavated in 1927 and 1956, producing a square bridge framework and other squared oak timbers. The *motte* ditch had a central 'island' (*Annals of Archaeology and Anthropology* (Liverpool University Institute of Archaeology) XV, pp. 47–55). The pottery found included a diamond-rouletted handle (Plate XIX, c) but most of it appeared to be later than the suggested date (1207–8) of abandonment of the site; it had been repaired in 1196–7 and is mentioned in 1216 (*Pipe Rolls*).

WEST MALLING TQ 675570 Kent

St Leonard's Tower is square, of ragstone rubble (with tufa quoins and window dressings) built on a natural sandstone shelf. Narrow pilaster buttresses rise from a sloping plinth to clasp each angle, and one runs up the centre of the south face to the level of the upper floor. The north-west angle is widened and thickened to take a spiral stair, carried above the wall-head as a turret. The tower has been restored, and there is now no external trace of the blocked entrance mentioned by G. T. Clark (*Medieval Military Architecture* II, p. 292), although the interior recess remains opposite the present entrance passage at the north end of the west and east walls respectively. Like all the openings, this is a plain round-headed arch; the herringbone coursing stops before reaching the present opening, but internally the coursing runs through to Clark's entrance.

The first floor level is marked by an external offset below a blind arcade of round-headed arches on the south and east fronts, with a central round-headed window in each wall except the south. There are larger windows to the floor above, two in the east wall and one in each of the others. The south wall is set back at each level, and the east is set back for the first floor and both north and west for the second.

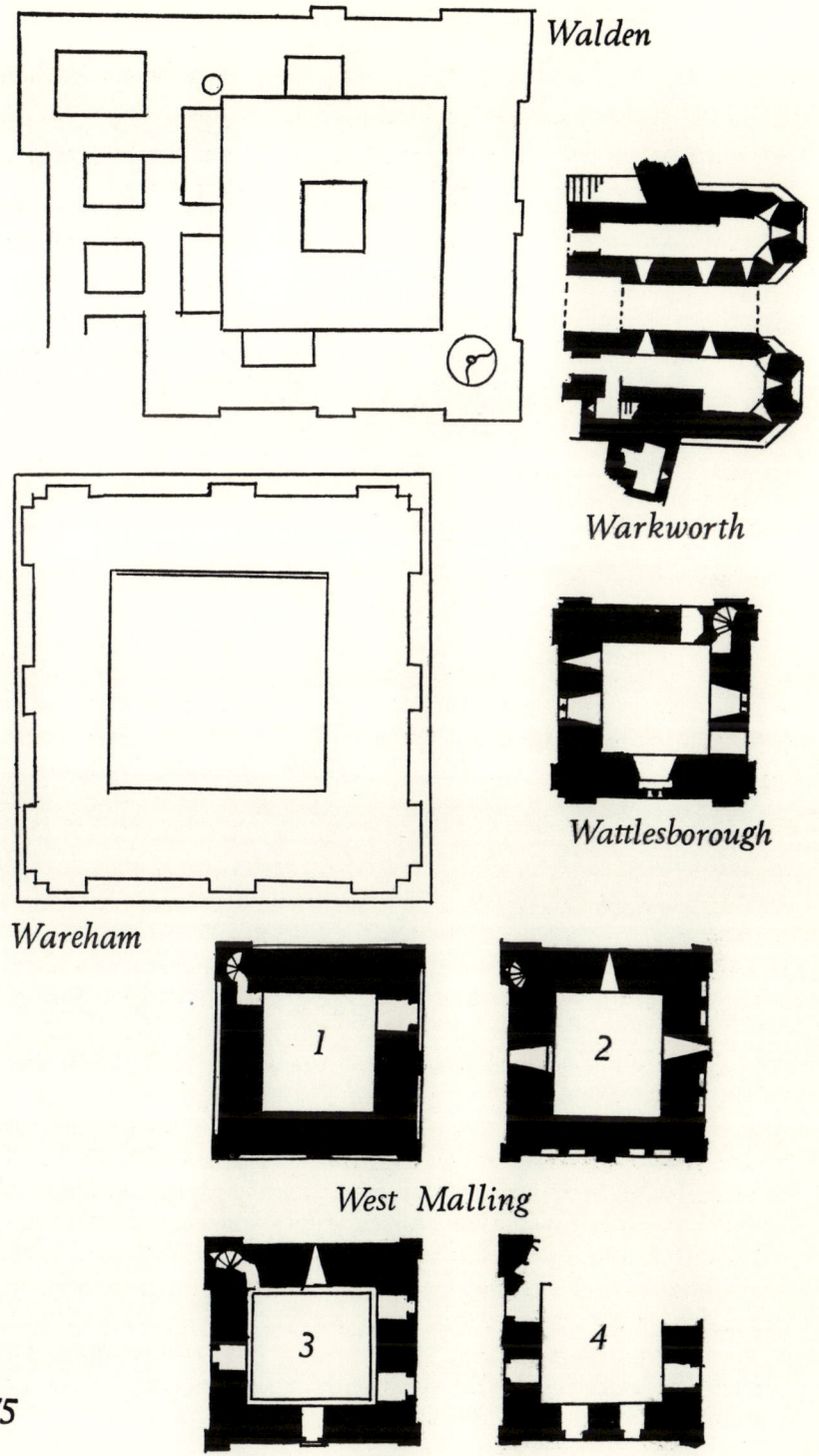

75

The early Romanesque style of the tower supports its traditional attribution to Gundulf (d. 1102). (Plate XLVII; Fig. 75)

WEST WOODHAY   SU 392631   Berkshire

Small low *motte* inside banks and ditches (Bb1 ?) which produced pottery of twelfth century and later date (*Newbury and District Field Club Transactions* 7, pp. 261–73; 10, pp. 65–8).

WESTON TURVILLE   SP 859104   Buckinghamshire

Motte and bailey (Bb3) which produced a fragment of Saxo-Norman pottery (found by the writer and given to Aylesbury Museum) and a Viking finger-ring (British Museum: *Records of Bucks*. V, p. 220).

Castleguard at Weston is mentioned in a grant by Geoffrey de Turville (*fl.* 1127–66): *B.M. Harl. MS.* 3688 f. 59); an allowance to the sheriff of Buckingham *in custodia castelli de Weston 'quod fuit Galfredi de Turevill' antequam prosterneretur* was paid in 1174 (*Pipe Roll*).

WEXFORD   T 0522   Wexford

Built-over mound erected in 1173 (*Gesta Henrici Secundi* I, 30; Giraldus Cambrensis, *Opera* V, p. 298; Hore, *History of Wexford* V, 22; VI, 340).

WHARTON   see HALSTEADS

WHELDRAKE   Yorkshire

The castle was to be destroyed in 1149 (*Symeon of Durham* II, p. 356) but existed between 1178–85 (*B.M. Add. MS.* 18276 f. 184, quoted in *Early Yorkshire Charters* XI, p. 192). A licence to refortify the site in 1199 was revoked before completion. (*Hoveden* IV, p. 117; P.R.O. *Chancery Misc.* 11/1). The moated site at Storwood (SE 712439) may be it.

WHERWELL   SU 392408   Hampshire

An attempt to fortify the abbey in 1140 was prevented (*Gesta Stephani*, p. 87).

WHITCHURCH   SP 800208   Buckinghamshire

Motte and bailey (IBc2) with a tradition of a masonry keep (V.C.H. *Buckingshire* III, p. 443). In 1147, Pope Eugenius mentioned castleworks wrongfully exacted by Hugh de Bolebec (*Chron. Mon. de Abingdon* II, 200) which may refer to this site.

WHITCHURCH   SJ 560425   Shropshire

Motte (B) beside lake, perhaps the castle repaired in 1199 (*Pipe Roll*) unless it was that at Pan (Bd4: SJ 526405).

GAZETTEER

WHITCHURCH (TRE-ODA)　　ST 156804　　　　　　Glamorgan

Early twelfth-century pottery found on top of round barrow before raising into *motte* (*Transactions of the Cardiff Naturalists Society* XCV, pp. 9–23).

WHITE　　　　　　SO 380168　　　　　　Monmouthshire

Large low mound with small crescent-shaped outwork and oval bailey (IBb3). The foundations of a rectangular keep survive, with chamfered quoins at the northern angles and western buttress. Apart from the length over-riding the keep foundations most of the sandstone rubble curtain is of about the same date, having a battlemented parapet.

The castle is mentioned in 1163 (see Grosmont) and 1185–8, the latter perhaps being the erection of the curtain wall; a room in the keep is mentioned in 1186 (*Pipe Rolls*) (M.P.B.W. *Official Guide* and *Medieval Archaeology* V, pp. 169–75).*　　　　　　　　　　　　　　(Fig. 76)

WHITTINGTON　　　　SJ 325311　　　　　　Shropshire

Complex earthworks beside stream, perhaps originally Bb2 site with later subdivision of bailey and multiplication of outer banks to south. Mentioned in 1138 (Ordericus Vitalis, *Historia Ecclesiastica* XIII, cap. 37) and in 1165 and 1195–1206 (*Pipe Rolls*). A small rectangular keep has been found on the *motte* (*Medieval Archaeology* XV, p. 148).

WHITWICK　　　　　SK 436162　　　　　　Leicestershire

Oval natural hill north-east of church with small oval *motte* on top. Castle mentioned in the treaty of 1148–53 (p. 52) but seems to have been repaired thereafter (*Rot. Litt. Pat.* 48; (1205) *Rot. Litt. Claus.* I, 13).

WHORLTON　　　　　NZ 481025　　　　　　Yorkshire

Angular ring-work and bailey (IICb4) on spur west of church, with other ditches further east. Called the castle of Potto in 1216 (*Foedera* I, p. 142).

WICKLOW　　　　　T 3194　　　　　　Wicklow

A stone castle existed by 1173 (Giraldus Cambrensis, *Opera* V, 298) and it may have stood on the headland, a small triangular apex with a rock-cut ditch occupied by the later Black Castle (*Journal of the Royal Society of Antiquaries of Ireland* LXXIV, pp. 1–22).

WIGMORE　　　　　SO 408693　　　　　　Herefordshire

Ring-work and bailey (ICf3) with trapezoidal bailey on end of long spur

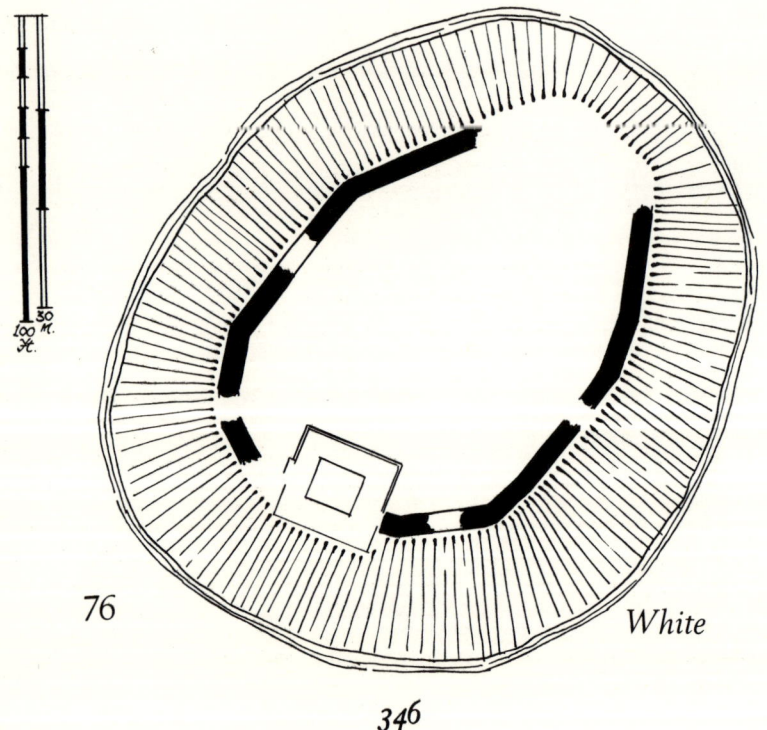

Waytemore

76 White

346

GAZETTEER

west-north-west of church. Two banks with outer ditches running northeast from the site may have been intended for a village enclosure. The lower part of the shell-wall on the north side of the ring-work is of small squared sandstone rubble, unlike the rest of the masonry, and there is no trace of a ditch between the ring-work and the bailey.

The castle is said to have belonged to Edric the Wild (*Monasticon* VI, p. 349) but 'Domesday Book' (I, 183) attributes it to William fitz Osbern (1067-70) (R.C.H.M. *Herefordshire* III, pp. 205-8).*

WILTON   SO 590245   Herefordshire

Traces of an altered *motte* and bailey (Bd3?) underlying the Edwardian masonry. Named in 1188 and 1204-6 (*Pipe Rolls; Rot. Litt. Pat.* p. 46.) R.C.H.M. *Herefordshire* I, pp. 29-31.*

WILTON   SU 100310   Wiltshire

The nunnery west of the site of Wilton House (see V.C.H. *Wiltshire* 6, p. 2) was converted into a castle by Stephen in 1143 (*Gesta Stephani*, p. 96).

WINCHCOMB   SP 023282   Gloucestershire

Castle, captured by the Earl of Gloucester in 1140 and retaken by Stephen in 1144 (William of Malmesbury, *Historia Novella*, p. 42; *Gesta Stephani*, pp. 63, 113).

WINCHESTER   SU 479298   Hampshire

A long oval enclosure with a constricted rounded south end surrounded by a 100-ft wide ditch outside the west gate of the city. A bank of orange clay up to 18 ft high on the east side carried a flint rubble wall (*Antiquaries' Journal* LXIV, pp. 190-2) and some eleventh/twelfth century work can be seen in the basement of the judge's quarters of the hall (*Archaeological Journal* CV Supplement, p. 29, n. 22). Earlier excavations (see the plan reproduced in *Transactions of the Royal Institute of British Architects* 1873-4 before p. 159) show the foundations of a 55-ft square tower north of the hall, with 16 ft thick walls; one angle is thickened internally to protect a shaft. A narrow rectangular building intersects the tower at an angle, with internal abutments dividing it into two compartments; three burials were found within.

It has been argued that William of Poitiers' reference to William I's construction of a castle *within* the walls of *Guenta* refers to Winchester (*Antiquaries' Journal* XLIV, pp. 217-9). Certainly a palace was constructed in 1066-7 north-west of the later cathedral, on the site of the New Minster buildings (destroyed by fire early in 1066) and itself burnt down in 1141 (*Journal of the British Archaeological Association*, third series XXIV, p. 51; *Archaeological Journal* CXIX, pp. 176-9). The massive tower found at the south end of Market Street (Milner, *History of Winchester* II, p. 185) may have belonged to either period. The present castle may therefore be post-1141. Constant expenditure on the castle is mentioned in the *Pipe Rolls* — in particular the castle wall (1169–73) and a chapel (1174–6) and also repairs to the keep (1195–6). Over £250 was spent on castle repairs under John, but the castle fell after a fortnight to Louis in 1216, much of the walls having been demolished. Excavation has shown that the E.I.A. defences had been recut in the twelfth century to fortify the western suburb.

WINDSOR   SU 970770   Berkshire

This *motte* with two baileys (Bb, c3) is on a large scale — the *motte* is 250 ft in diameter at the base and is only *relatively* low. The Round Tower on top has been raised and refaced and the timber buildings inside (surrounding an open courtyard) remodelled more than once. The *motte*-top is surrounded by a wide heathstone wall forming a terrace; this acts as a retaining wall to the tower which is a flattened ovoid in shape with eleven remaining pilaster buttresses. A wall carrying the stairway runs down the *motte* to the site of a rectangular entrance tower.

The Norman stone walls of the upper ward had a rectangular tower at each end and two between them. The corner towers form a re-entrant at the north-east angle — those to the south-east have been replaced by post-medieval work. The north side of the inner ward has been largely rebuilt, but there are thick parallel walls around Horn Court which may be those of twelfth-century houses around a courtyard.

The walls forming a salient north and west of the *motte* appear to be mainly Norman, together with fragments of the eastern half of the north and south walls of the Outer Ward. The foundations of the Great Hall with a chamfered plinth have been excavated north of St George's Chapel.

Land was exchanged for the castle in 1067 (B. M. *Harl. M.S.* 3749, f. 3). The castle is mentioned in 'Domesday Book' (I, 62 b) and a King's house in the castle in 1130. Substantial sums were laid out on the king's houses between 1165 and 1171 and then on the castle, particularly the wall around the houses, in 1173–9. The *motte* was buttressed and its ditch levelled in 1194–5, and the king's cloister and hall were repaired in this and the succeeding year (*Pipe Rolls*). John's work appears to have been confined to repairs, and the castle withstood a three month siege in 1216 W. H. St John Hope, *The Architectural History of Windsor Castle.**

(Plate XLVIII; Fig. 61)

WISBECH   TF 462097   Cambridgeshire

A plan of 1794, before the castle was finally destroyed (Cambridge University Library M.S. plan 581) shows a circular enclosure; an Urnes style brooch was found in the ditch (v.c.h. *Cambs.* I, pl. XI f.).

GAZETTEER

Castle built shortly after 1070 (*Roger of Wendover*; Matthew Paris, *Chronica Majora* II, 7).

WISTON   SN 022181   Pembrokeshire

Motte and bailey (Ba2). The mound carries a polygonal shell-wall of rubble with a sloping plinth. The round-headed doorway has a drawbar hole and socket. The earliest mention of *castellum Wiz* is in 1147 (*Brut y Tywysogion*), although Wizo was dead by 1130 (*Pipe Roll*). (Fig. 74)

WOLVESEY   SU 485291   Hampshire

Foundations and much-restored walls of flint and chalk rubble, now (1968) being excavated and consolidated; until the work is completed it is impossible to analyse the site fully. The original buildings seem to have been arranged around a square courtyard, with a long narrow hall on the east side, beyond which stood a square keep with a sloping plinth and chamfered offset, and ashlar buttresses of Binstead stone in each wall and clasping the angles. A layer of slates was laid as a damp course, and fragments of shafts have been re-used in the east side, and can be seen covering an opening in the north wall; a reversed engaged shaft flanks a wall-opening beside the north-west angle. The hall has a ball-ornamented wall arcade and passage at the north-end with Purbeck marble shafts below round-headed loops. A solid latrine tower has ashlar buttresses like those of the keep but chamfered at the angle with a stepped plinth in rubble between them. There is a vaulted loopholed gallery above; one re-used stone has overlapping scales (like a pier near St Lawrence's church, said to be the Conqueror's palace). A square gatehouse with central passage and flanking ranges were added to the north curtain wall (*Antiquaries' Journal* XLIV, pp. 212-4; XLV, pp. 258-9; XLVI, pp. 326-8 etc.).

Henry of Blois built 'a house like a palace with a very strong tower' here in 1138 (*Annales Monastici* II, 51) which may have been destroyed in 1155 (Matthew Paris, *Chronica Majora* II, 210; *Diceto* I, 301; *Pipe Roll*) and rebuilt between 1158 and 1171 (*Chateau Gaillard* III, pp. 28-36).*

WOOD   see WOOTTON ST LAWRENCE

WOODSTOCK   SP 437165   Oxfordshire

In 1142, the Empress Matilda raised a castle at *Wdestok* 'where King Henry had been wont to live a retired life' (*Gesta Stephani*, p. 91). Landscaping for Blenheim Palace has destroyed the site, but the view in Plot's *Natural History of Oxfordshire* suggests a *motte* beside the raised bailey in which the house stood.

WOOD WALTON   TL 210826   Huntingdonshire

Low ring-work with small enclosure to south-east (Ce3), with outer ditch enclosing natural hill-top. Probably the *castellum quoddam fecerat apud Waltone* by Ernulf de Mandeville before 1144 (*Chron. de Ramesia* I, p. 332) (R.C.H.M. *Huntingdonshire* pp. 298–9).*

WOOLSTASTON   SO 450985   Shropshire

Motte and bailey (Ac2), twelfth and thirteenth century pottery was excavated from the bailey in 1965 (*Medieval Archaeology* X, p. 191).

WOOTTON ST LAWRENCE   SU 584550   Hampshire

Ring-work with traces of bailey (Cb?) at Woodgarston Farm might be the 'castle of the Wood' stormed by Stephen in 1147 (*Gesta Stephani*, p. 138) since the context suggests Hampshire, and the place-name Woodcastle occurs in the fourteenth century (V.C.H.). Professor R. H. C. Davis has suggested Woodchester (Glos.) as an alternative literal translation of *castellum de Silva* (*E.H.R.* 77, 228) but no castle has been identified there.

WORCESTER   SO 849547   Worcestershire

Motte and bailey (Ad3) beside River Severn, now destroyed, built before September 1069 (William of Malmesbury, *Gesta Pontificum*, p. 253). The *motte* was of sand and gravel on a foundation of sandstone (Allies, *Antiquities of Worcester*, p. 15, quoted in V.C.H. *Worcester* IV, 427) and the bailey ditch cut off part of the cathedral cemetery. The wooden castle was burnt in 1113 (*Annales Monastici* IV, 375) and small amounts were spent on the tower, palisade and buildings from 1155 onward, and the wooden gateway was rebuilt in stone in 1204 (*Pipe Rolls*), but the bailey was returned to the monks soon after 1216 (*Transactions of the Worcestershire Naturalists' Club* IV, 225–40; IX, pp. 115–22).*

WREXHAM (ERDDIG)   SJ 327487   Denbigshire

Motte and bailey (Be2) built against Offa's Dyke on river bluff, mentioned in 1161–2 (*Pipe Roll*).

WYCOMBE   SU 867932   Buckinghamshire

Incomplete *motte* (A?) and scarps in the grounds of Castle Hill House. Finds of Saxon date (*Proceedings of the Society of Antiquaries of London*, second series II, p. 361; *British Museum Quarterly* 13, p. 72) from the site cast doubt on its nature, although a charter of Stephen '*apud Wycumbam in obsidione*' (*Cal. Charter Rolls* 1257–1300, p. 132) may refer to the site. The castle at West Wycombe mentioned in 1210–11 (Winchester Pipe Roll) is probably DESBOROUGH (SU 846933).

GAZETTEER

WYRE   see CUBBIE ROO'S

YAFFORTH   SE 347950   Yorkshire

Motte (B) on mound in marshes of River Wiske, disused by 1198 (*Feet of Fines* 9 Ric. I, p. 126–8).

YELDEN   TL 014669   Bedfordshire

Motte and bailey (IBb3) with outworks. Only one chamfered stone was found on the disturbed *motte*-top during excavation, but the inner bailey had a stone curtain with a round tower at one angle. A mound in the southern ditch contained a round tower 30 ft across with 4 ft thick walls — a moulded stone from it was preserved in the church. Mentioned in 1174 (*Pipe Rolls*) (*Associated Architectural Societies Reports and Papers* XVI, pp. 251–63).*

YORK (SE 606515): OLD BAILE (SE 603513)   Yorkshire

Two *motte* and bailey sites on opposite banks of River Ouse (Bd3; Aa3). The latter is that to the west, known as the *vetus ballium* since at least the beginning of the fourteenth century, which may be the same as the *in veteri castello* of Hoveden (iii, p. 34) in apposition to 'The Newarke' of the castle site (Angelo Raine, *York Civic Records* IV, p. 157; *Medieval York*, pp. 23–5). Excavations in 1968 showed timber-revetted layers with a square building on top (*Chateau Gaillard* V, pp. 7–11).

The castle across the river was protected by damming the River Foss ('Domesday Book' I, f.298) which here joined the Ouse. Excavation showed that the *motte* had been thrown up over a cist burial, being based on solid clay overlaid with marl and a layer of gravel 10 ft thick below 2 ft of black soil. A line of timber stakes 6 ft long was found $15\frac{1}{2}$ ft below the *motte*-top, revetting large stones and covered with charred timber; an outer ring of firmer clay had been piled on top and lighter material added to level up. This in turn was covered with 30 in. of black clayey soil and then a platform of oak slabs $5\frac{1}{4}$ in. thick (other $9 \times 1\frac{3}{4}$ in.) with iron nails, resting on forked uprights, roughly dressed trees 7 to 9 in. across and over 8 ft long. Finds included thirteenth century mouldings in magnesian limestone, human and animal bones, bone draughtsmen and combs, arrow-heads and a whetstone. Coins ranged from one of Constantine and another of Aedriled to lead copies of William I pence (*Yorkshire Philosophical Society Report* for 1902, pp. 68–74). Excavations east of the *motte* revealed a mortar-lined post-hole in a steep-sided bank of yellow sand, with a thirteenth-century potsherd in a reinforcement layer, with a stake further south (*Antiquaries' Journal* XIX, pp. 85–9).

A castle was built in 1068 and another early in 1069, both being destroyed and rebuilt in the latter year (Ordericus Vitalis, *Historia Ecclesiastica*

II, pp. 188, 192–5). The keep was repaired in 1172 (*Pipe Roll*) and burnt down in the anti-Jewish riot of 1190, and again rebuilt (*Pipe Roll; Benedict of Peterborough* II, p. 107; *Hoveden* III, p. 34).

The discovery of a Norman town bank and wall in the Micklegate/Walmgate area is mentioned by A. Raine (*Medieval York*, pp. x, 3–4). Micklegate Bar in existence by 1196 (*Pipe Roll*); Walmgate bar existed by 1156 and the King's Ditch nearby by 1170; the *Wirchedic* is mentioned 1161–84, *Lounlelith* 1180–95 (*Early Yorkshire Charters* I, pp. 251, 240, 215–6) and *Mickelith* in 1196 (*Pipe Roll*). See *Archaeologia* XCVII, p. 61, n. 6. (V.C.H. *City of York*, pp. 521–9).*

YSTRAD PEITHYLL   SN 653824   Cardiganshire

Steep *motte* (A) at junction of streams. Castle destroyed in 1116 (*Brut y Tywysogion*).

YSTUFFAN see STEPHEN'S

Addenda for the Second Edition

ABERDEEN   Aberdeenshire

Castle mentioned by 1214 (*Arbroath Liber* I, 367), perhaps the *motte* at Tillydrone (NJ 936089).

ALDINGHAM   SD 278698   Lancashire

Ringwork converted into *motte* (later revetted in timber) and bailey (*Medieval Archaeology* XIII, pp. 258–9).

ALTON   SK 074426   Staffordshire

Diagonally-tooled ashlar wall and rock-cut moat may belong to the castle built by 1176 (*Monasticon* V, 662).

ALVELEY   Shropshire

Castelgrove Wood in Romsley is mentioned in 1209 (*Feet of Fines* cited by Eyton, *History of Shropshire* III, 199).

ALYTH   Perthshire

Castle mentioned by 1199 (Scottish Record Office, GD 28/5).

AULDEARN   NH 917556   Nairnshire

Motte of castle mentioned c.1187–9 (*Inchaffray Charters*, 153–4).

GAZETTEER: ADDENDA

BARDSEY   SE 366434   Yorkshire

Rectangular keep in long mound (*Proceedings of the Thoresby Society*, 49, fig. 39.21a).

BENGEWORTH   SP 041437   Worcestershire

Site of castle destroyed by 1160 (*Chronicle of Evesham*, 100).

BIRMINGHAM   Warwickshire

Grant of market at castle in 1166 (*Cartae Antiquae* 11-20, pp. 190-1) (*Transactions of the Birmingham Archaeological Society* XXXVIII, 24).

BRISTOL (see pages 117-18)

Extensive excavations of the site showed that a wall had been added c.1100 to a clay-revetted bank, subsequently buried in a massive rampart. A simple gateway was later given flanking walls before it was blocked, and the early *motte* demolished when the keep was built. Interim reports in the 1968 and 1970 C.B.A. Groups 12/13 *Archaeological Review*, the third *Bulletin* of the Bristol Archaeological Research Group, and *Medieval Archaeology* XIII, 255.

BROMWICH   SP 158904   Warwickshire

Timber buildings surrounded by bank and ditch with timber-reverted causeway. *Motte* also revetted and later enlarged. (*Archaeological Excavations* 1970, p.83; *Archaeological Journal* CXXVIII, p.214).

BURROW   ST 359305   Somerset

A diagonally-tooled ashlar wall, and pits filled with Norman pottery and ridge-tiles, found underlying the medieval chapel on Burrow Mump may belong to the castle mentioned in the fourteenth century (*Proceedings of the Somersetshire Archaeological Society* LXXXV, pp. 95-133).

BURY ST EDMUNDS   Suffolk

Castle-guard was temporarily transferred here from Norwich in 1139-45 (*RRAN* III, 757) and the town gates are mentioned in 1194 (*Jocelin de Brakelond*, ed. Butler, pp. 55, 103).

CAISTOR   TA 116012   Lincolnshire

Castle hill near church, probably that fortified early in June 1143 (*RRAN* III, 655).

CARHAM   Northumberland

Castle besieged in 1138 (*Chronicles of the reigns of Stephen* ... III, 151).

NORMAN CASTLES IN BRITAIN

CARRICK   Ayrshire

Mentioned by 1199 (Melrose Liber 31).

CARROCK   Cumberland

Place name from c.1165 (*Place Names of Cumberland*, p. 75) probably on the fell-top, as 'fort' near church is natural (*Transactions of the Cumberland and Westmorland Archaeological Society*, n.s. VIII, p. 249).

CASTLEMARTYR   W 9674   Cork

Possible site of FitzStephen's castle of 1177–82 (Exeter City Archives, Misc. Roll 53 published in the *Proceedings of the Royal Irish Academy*, 43C, 347–52). Ballinacurra is the alternative site.

CATTHORPE   Leicestershire (?)

The castle destroyed in 1218 (*Rot. Litt. Claus.* I, 380) may have been one of the *motte* and bailey castles across the river at Lilbourne, Northants.

CLAVERING   TL 470319   Essex

Rectangular moated enclosure with outer mounds and banks. See page 7.

CORNWALL

Baldwin Tyrel fortified a house in the St. Austell/Truro region in 1212 (*Curia Regis Rolls* VI, 94, 168, 257).

CRUTA   Devon (?)

Castle of Baldwin de Redvers (d. 1155) (*Sarum Charters and documents*, 20).

DUN LAGAIDH   NH 143913   Ross and Cromarty

Broch adapted by blocking entrance. Late 12th century coin hoard found in rubble (*Current Archaeology* 12, p. 11).

EDEN   NZ 428385   Durham

Possible mention of castle chapel 1142–53 (*Early Yorkshire Charters* II, 2).

ELDBOTLE   NT 865857   East Lothian

Motte (B) mentioned in 1187 (Dryburgh Liber, 104).

GAITTECASTELLUM   Durham/Yorkshire

Place-name (1½ miles north of Middleton in Teesdale) mentioned in 1161–7 (*Early Yorkshire Charters* I, 441).

GLASBURY   Brecknockshire/Radnorshire

Mentioned between 1180–1211 (Duchy of Lancaster, *Ancient Charters* LS. 27/1).

GAZETTEER: ADDENDA

GLASTONBURY   ST 489387   Somerset

Low mound (B), perhaps the palace-castle of Henry de Blois before 1155 (Adam of Domerham, *Historic Glastonberiensis* I, 309).

GREENAN   Ayrshire

Castle mentioned by 1199 (*Melrose Liber*, 34).

HARTLAND   Devon

A licence to fortify a house here was granted in 1201 (*Rot. Chartarum*, 123).

HOOD   SE 504814   Yorkshire
Built 1215-18 (*Close Rolls* I, 366).

IRVINE   NS 309409   Ayr

Mentioned in 1184 (Benedict of Peterborough, 313): possibly the *motte* (B) at NS 342356.

KILBRIDE   Lanarkshire

Castle mentioned by 1190 (*Glasgow Registrum*, 55).

KNAPWELL   TL 337632   Cambridgeshire

Motte (B) near church producing Saxo-Norman pottery (R.C.H.M. *West Cambridgeshire*, 163).

KNOWTH   N 9974   Meath

V-shaped ditch inside kerb of megalithic burial mound may be conversion into castle of 1175 (*MacCarthaigh's Book*). See SLANE. (*Proceedings of the Royal Irish Academy* 66C, pp. 355, 399).

'LEYLAND'

Castle mentioned in 1160 (P.R.O. c.146/10018, see *Bulletin of the John Rylands Library* XXIV, 168; XXVII, 179) possibly Court Knoll, Nayland, Suffolk (TL 975340).

LLANGENYDD   SS 870810   Glamorgan

Site of castle destroyed 1202-18 (Giraldus Cambrensis, *Opera* IV p. 134). (*Archaeologia Cambrensis* CXVI p. 204.)

LORRHA   M 9204   Tipperary

Motte and bailey (Bd) built in 1207 (Gleeson, *History of Killaloe* I, 180).

LUTON   TL 096211   Bedfordshire

Traces of palisade and ditch found in 1963 (*motte* under bus depot) perhaps the new castle *super Luiam* of 1141 (*Regesta Regum Anglo-Normannorum* III, 275).

MADOC   SO 025370   Brecknockshire

Ringwork producing early medieval pottery (*Brycheiniog* XII p. 131).

MAINCORE   Armagh (?)

Castle near Carlingford mentioned in 1204 (*Stogursey Charters* p. 75)

MILDENHALL   Suffolk

The *antiquum castellum* (*Kalendar of Archbishop Samson*, ed. Davis, charter 106) may be a Roman villa.

MIRFIELD   SE 211204   Yorkshire

Motte (B) probably in existence by 1216 (*Yorkshire Inquisitions* 62 p. 22).

MONTROSE   Angus

Castle by 1214 (*Acts of the Parliaments of Scotland* I, 100).

NEILSTON   Renfrew

Castle mentioned 1182–7 (Glasgow *Registrum* No. 55).

NORTHWICH   Cheshire

Castle derelict by 1199 (*B.M. Harleian M.S.* 2074 f.189).

ONIAHC   Down (?)

Mentioned in 1183–4 (*Stogursey Charters*, 50).

PICKHILL   SE 346836   Yorkshire

Motte and bailey (II Bal) to be dismantled in 1216 (*Rot. Litt. Pat.* I, 143). Pottery and tiles found in ditch (*Yorkshire Archaeological Journal* XXII, p. 372).

RABY   NZ 128220   Durham

Norman gateway, now entrance to stables.

RYE   Sussex

Castle mentioned 1216 (*Histoire des ducs de Normandie*, p. 182).

SCILLY

Possible *motte* beside Hightown to Garrison road on St Mary's may be the castle of 1194 (*Curia Regis Rolls*, I, 86).

GAZETTEER: ADDENDA

SILBURY HILL   SU 100685   Wiltshire

Traces of an early medieval castle were found on top of this prehistoric mound in 1968–69.

SKELTON   NZ 653193   Yorkshire

Site of castle mentioned in 1216 (*Rot. Litt. Pat.* 163, 167) and perhaps earlier (*Monasticon* VI, 267).

STONE   TQ 584742   Kent

Square tower with arrow slits forming south-east angle of later house.

TORPEL   TF 107053   Huntingdonshire

Square keep with pilaster buttresses.

TOTTERNHOE   SP 978222   Bedfordshire

Motte and bailey (Bd2) producing Norman pottery and diagonally-tooled ashlar (Luton Museum).

TRURO   SW 827447   Cornwall

Shell keep with forebuilding found in 1840 (*Notes and Queries, Devon and Cornwall* XIII pp. 40–42).

County Guide to Castles

ENGLAND

Bedfordshire
Bedford   TL 053496
Biggleswade   TL 184445
Chalgrave   TL 009274
Eaton Socon   TL 173588
Luton   TL 096211
Meppershall   TL 132358
Totternhoe   SP 978222
Yelden   TL 014669

Berkshire
Brightwell   SU 578908
Faringdon   SU 297957
Hampstead Marshall
Hinton Waldrist   SU 376991
Newbury   SU 472672
Reading   SU 718736
South Moreton   SU 559880
Wallingford   SU 608897
Wallingford siege-works
West Woodhay   SU 392631
Windsor   SU 970770

Buckinghamshire
Buckingham   SP 695337
Desborough   SU 846933
Hanslope   SP 798446
Lavendon   SP 917543
Newton Longville   SP 842306
Weston Turville   SP 859104
Whitchurch   SP 800208
Wycombe   SU 867932

Cambridgeshire
Alrehede
Bourn   TL 322562
Burwell   TL 588661
Cambridge   TL 446582
Caxton   TL 294587

Cambridgeshire
Ely   TL 540800
Fordham
Knapwell   TL 337632
Rampton   TL 431680
Wisbech   TF 462097

Cheshire
Aldford   SJ 419596
Chester   SJ 404657
Dunham Massey   SJ 734874
Frodsham   SJ 518776
Halton   SJ 539821
Northwich
Pulford   SJ 375587
Shotwick   SJ 350704
Stockport   SJ 894903
Ullerswood   SJ 800838

Cornwall
Cornwall
Launceston   SX 331847
Restormel   SX 104614
St Michael's Mount   SW 515299
Tintagel   SX 050890
Trematon   SX 105580
Truro   SW 827447

Cumberland
Burgh by Sands   NY 314592
Carlisle   NY 396564
Carrock
Dovenby Hall   NY 096334
Egremont   NY 010105
Kirkoswald   NY 560410
Liddell   NY 402742
Sowerby

GUIDE TO CASTLES

Derbyshire
Bakewell   SK 221688
Bolsover   SK 470707
Duffield   SK 343441
Haddon   SK 235664
Horston   SK 373432
Peveril   SK 148826

Devon
Bampton   SS 958226
Barnstaple   SS 556334
Bere Ferrers   SX 458634
Bickleigh   SS 937068
Cruta
Exeter   SX 921929
Hartland
Lundy   SS 137442
Lydford   SX 510848
Okehampton   SX 584943
Plympton   SX 546559
Totnes   SX 800605

Dorset
Bow and Arrow   SY 697711
Corfe   SY 958823
Corfe siege-work
Dorchester   SY 690908
Lulworth   SY 855821
Marshwood   SY 404977
Powerstock   SY 521959
Shaftesbury   ST 858228
Sherborne   ST 648168
Sturminster   ST 784134
Wareham   SY 922872

Durham
Barnard Castle   NZ 049165
Bishopton   NZ 368209
Brancepath   NZ 224378
Durham   NZ 274423
Eden   NZ 428385
Gaittecastellum
Merrington   NZ 263315
Raby   NZ 128220

Essex
Berden
Canfield   TL 594179

Essex
Clavering   TL 470319
Colchester   TL 998252
Easton   TL 608254
Hedingham   TL 787359
Ongar   TL 554031
Pleshey   TL 666144
Rayleigh   TL 805910
Walden   TL 538387

Gloucestershire
Berkeley   ST 684990
Bledisloe   SO 683082
Bristol   ST 594732
Cirencester   SP 022020
Dursley
Dymock   SO 713294
English Bicknor   SO 581157
Gloucester   SO 828185
Hailes
Littledean   SO 677135
Lydney   SO 617025
Miserden   SO 944093
St Briavel's   SO 558046
Tetbury
Tewkesbury   SO 892325
Upper Slaughter   SP 157232
Winchcomb   SP 023282

Hampshire
Ashley   SU 385309
Barley Pound   SU 797468
Basing   SU 663526
Bishops' Waltham   SU 552173
Carisbrooke   SZ 488878
Christchurch   SZ 160926
Lidelea
Merdon   SU 421265
Odiham   SU 726519
Portchester   SU 625046
Portsmouth
Powderham   SU 803469
Southampton   SU 418115
Wherwell   SU 392408
Winchester   SU 479298
Wolvesey   SU 485291
Wootton St. Lawrence   SU 584550

NORMAN CASTLES IN BRITAIN

Herefordshire
Bredwardine   SO 335444
Clifford
Eardisley   SO 311491
Ewyas Harold   SO 384287
Frome   SO 670458
Goodrich   SO 577200
Hereford   SO 512396
Hereford siege-works   SO 508398
Herefordshire Beacon   SO 760400
Kilpeck   SO 444305
Kington   SO 291569
Longtown   SO 321292
Lyonshall   SO 331563
Pembridge   SO 448193
Richard's   SO 483703
Snodhill   SO 322404
Stapleton   SO 323656
Walelege
Weobley   SO 403513
Wigmore   SO 408693
Wilton   SO 590245

Hertfordshire
Anstey   TL 404329
Benington   TL 297236
Berkhamsted   SP 995082
Hertford   TL 325125
Pirton   TL 146316
South Mymms   TL 230026
Therfield   TL 335373
Waytemore   TL 490215

Huntingdonshire
Ellington Thorpe   TL 155704
Huntingdon   TL 241715
Ramsey   TL 291851
Southoe
Torpel   TF 107093
Wood Walton   TL 210826

Kent
Allington   TQ 752579
Binbury (Thornham)   TQ 812602
Canterbury   TR 146575
Chilham   TR 066535
Dover   TR 326417

Kent
Eynsford   TQ 541658
Fairseat   TQ 628614
Folkestone   TR 214379
Godard's (Thornham)   TQ 808582
Leeds   TQ 836533
Minster Court   TR 312643
Rochester   TQ 742686
Rochester Cathedral   TQ 743685
Saltwood   TR 161359
Stone   TQ 584742
Sutton Valence   TQ 815491
Sweyn's camp (Swanscombe)
   TQ 600741
Tonbridge   TQ 589466
Tonge   TQ 933636
Walmer   TR 367504
West Malling   TQ 675570

Lancashire
Aldingham   SD 278698
Clitheroe   SD 742417
Halstead's (Wharton)   SD 516726
Hornby   SD 583698
Lancaster   SD 473619
Manchester
Penwortham   SD 525290
Preston   SD 512032
Warrington   SJ 609876
West Derby (Liverpool)   SJ 397934

Leicestershire
Belvoir   SK 820347
Catthorpe
Donnington   SK 448276
Groby   SK 524076
Hinckley   SP 428935
Leicester   SK 583041
Mountsorrel   SK 581149
Ravenstone
Sauvey   SK 786052
Whitwick   SK 436162

Lincolnshire
Bolingbroke   TF 348654
Bourne   TF 095200
Bytham   SK 990196

GUIDE TO CASTLES

Lincolnshire
Caistor   TA 116012
Carlton   TF 395836
Fleet   TF 385232
Frampton   TA 327391
Gainsborough
Goxhill
Grimsby
Horncastle   TF 260696
Kingerby   TF 056928
Lincoln   SK 975718
Lincoln siege-works
Moulton   TF 314214
Owston Ferry   SE 806002
Partney
Sleaford   TF 065455
South Witham   SK 929205
Stamford   TF 028071
Swineshead   TF 243410
Thorngate
Welbourne   SK 968544

London
Baynard's   TQ 319808
Montfichet   TQ 318811
Ravenger's
Tower of London   TQ 336805

Norfolk
Acre   TF 820152
Buckenham
Mileham   TF 917194
Norwich   TG 232085
Norwich fortified houses
Rising   TF 666246
Thetford (Castle Hill)   TL 875828
Thetford (Red Castle)   TL 864830
Weeting   TL 778892

Northamptonshire
Benefield   SP 987885
Brackley   SP 583367
Earls Barton   SP 852637
Fotheringay   TL 062930
Hymel   SP 973976
Long Buckby   SP 625677

Northamptonshire
Northampton   SP 750604
Peterborough   TL 194987
Preston Capes   SP 576549
Rockingham   SP 867914
Rushton   SP 840825
Sulgrave   SP 556454

Northumberland
Alnwick   NU 187137
Bamburgh   NU 184350
Bamburgh siege-works
Berwick
Carham
Harbottle   NT 933048
Mitford   NZ 170855
Morpeth   NZ 198857
Newcastle upon Tyne   NZ 253639
Norham   NT 906474
Prudhoe   NZ 092634
Tweedmouth
Tynemouth   NZ 373694
Wark on Tweed   NT 824387
Warkworth   NU 247058

Nottinghamshire
Cuckney   SK 566713
Kingshaugh   SK 765735
Newark   SK 796541
Nottingham   SK 569394

Oxfordshire
Ascot Doilly   SP 304191
Ascot Earl   SP 296184
Bampton   SP 310031
Banbury   SP 454404
Deddington   SP 472318
Middleton Stoney   SP 531233
Mixbury   SP 610341
Oxford   SP 510062
Radcot   SU 285995
Swerford   SP 373312
Woodstock   SP 437165

Rutland
Burley   SK 894119
Oakham   SK 863087

361

Shropshire
Alveley
Bishop's   SO 323891
Bridgnorth   SO 717927
Bryn Amlwg   SO 167846
Cans
Caus   SJ 338079
Church Stretton   SO 446925
Cleobury Mortimer   SO 682760
Clun   SO 298809
Clungunford   SO 396788
Ellesmere   SJ 403346
Knockin   SJ 334223
Ludlow   SO 508746
Ludlow siege-works
More   SO 339914
Moreton Corbet   SJ 561231
Oswestry   SJ 290298
Pontesbury   SJ 401058
Pulverbatch   SO 422022
Quatford   SO 738907
Shrawardine   SJ 400154
Shrewsbury   SJ 495128
Stanton Holgate   SO 562896
Stokesay   SO 437817
Tong   SJ 793080
Wattlesborough   SJ 354128
Whitchurch   SJ 560425
Whittington   SJ 325311
Woolstaston   SO 742686

Somerset
Bridgwater   ST 305374
Burrow   ST 359305
Cary   ST 641322
Crewkerne   ST 421107
Dunster   SS 992433
Glastonbury   ST 489387
Harptree   ST 562556
Locking   ST 365609
Montacute   ST 494170
Neroche   ST 271158
Nether Stowey   ST 187396
Puriton   ST 309414
Stogursey   ST 203426
Taunton   ST 227248

Staffordshire
Alton   SK 074426
Chartley   SK 010285
Eccleshall   SJ 828296
Lichfield   SK 118096
Newcastle under Lyme   SJ 850455
Rodbaston (Penkridge)
Stafford   SJ 901223
Tamworth   SK 206038
Trentham   SJ 866409
Tutbury   SK 210293

Suffolk
Bungay   TM 336898
Bury St Edmunds
Burgh Castle   TG 474044
Clare   TL 770452
Eye   TM 147738
Framlingham   TM 286637
Groton   TL 965425
Haughley   TM 024626
Ipswich
Lidgate   TL 722582
Lindsey   TL 980441
Milden   TL 950461
Mildenhall
Offton   TM 064492
Orford   TM 419499
Walton   TM 322358

Surrey
Abinger   TQ 114460
Bletchingley   TQ 322506
Farnham   SU 837473
Guildford   SU 997494
Reigate   TQ 252504
Rudgwick   TQ 077345

Sussex
Aldingbourne   SU 923048
Arundel   TQ 018073
Arundel siege-works
Bramber   TQ 185107
Caburn   TQ 444089
Chichester   SU 862051
Hastings   TQ 820095
Knepp   TQ 163209

GUIDE TO CASTLES

Sussex
Lewes   TQ 415101
Midhurst (St Ann's Hill)   SU 889215
Old Erringham   TQ 205077
Pevensey   TQ 644048
Rye

Warwickshire
Beaudesert   SP 156662
Birmingham
Brandon   SP 408759
Brinklow   SP 439797
Bromwich   SP 158904
Coventry
Hartshill   SP 324944
Kenilworth   SP 279723
Oversley   SP 095554
Warwick   SP 283647
Wavrei   SP 518788

Westmorland
Appleby   NY 685199
Brough   NY 790140
Brougham   NY 532290
Kendal   SD 523924
Pendragon   NY 782026

Wiltshire
Ashton Keynes   SU 049943
Combe   ST 837777
Cricklade   SU 098938
Devizes   SU 003613
Downton   SU 181214
Ludgershall   SU 265513
Malmesbury   ST 933873
Marlborough   SU 184686
Membury   SU 305745
Old Sarum   SU 138327
Silbury   SU 100685
Somerford   ST 965831
South Cerney
Trowbridge   ST 854579
Wilton   SU 100310

Worcestershire
Bengeworth   SP 041437
Dudley   SO 947908

Worcestershire
Elmley   SO 980403
Hanley   SO 838414
Hom(m)e   SO 733618
Inkberrow   SP 017473
Worcester   SO 849547

Yorkshire
Aldborough   SE 407660
Almondbury   SE 152140
Bardsey   SE 366434
Barwick in Elmet   SE 398375
Bowes   NY 991135
Bridlington   TA 176680
Burton in Lonsdale   SD 650722
Buttercrambe   SE 733584
Conisbrough   SK 517989
Cotherstone   NZ 015200
Cottingham   TA 040330
Danby   NZ 691082
Drax   SE 676260
Driffield   TA 035585
Helmsley   SE 611837
Hood   SE 504814
Hunsingore   SE 428532
Huttons Ambo   SE 763674
Hutton Conyers
Kilton   NZ 702177
Kirkby Malzeard   SE 236745
Knaresborough   SE 349569
Malton   SE 792717
Middleham   SE 128877
Mirfield   SE 211204
Mount Ferrant   SE 795639
Mulgrave   NZ 839117
Northallerton   SE 364941
Old Baile   SE 603513
Pickering   SE 800845
Pickhill   SE 346838
Pontefract   SE 460224
Richmond   NZ 173007
Sandal   SE 337182
Scarborough   TA 048892
Selby
Sheffield   SK 357976
Sheriff Hutton   SE 658663

NORMAN CASTLES IN BRITAIN

Yorkshire
Skelton   NZ 653193
Skipsea   TA 162551
Skipton-in-Craven   SD 995519
Thirsk   SE 438810
Tickhill   SK 593928
Topcliffe   SE 410750
Wakefield   SE 327198
Wheldrake
Whorlton   NZ 481025
Yafforth   SE 347950
York   SE 606515

WALES

Anglesey
Aber Lleiniog   SH 617793
Castle of King Olaf (Bon y Dom)

Brecknockshire
Blaen Llynfi   SO 145229
Brecon   SO 043288
Bronllys   SO 149346
Builth   SO 044510
Bwlch y Ddinas   SO 179301
Glasbury
Hay
Madoc   SO 025370
Pencelli   SO 095248
Tretower   SO 184212

Caernarvonshire
Bangor
Caernarvon   SH 497627
Degannwy   SH 781794
Dinas Emrys   SH 606492
Dolbadarn   SH 586598
Dolwyddelan   SH 722523
Garn Fadrun   SH 278352

Cardiganshire
Abereinon   SN 687968
Aberrheidol   SN 585790
Blaenporth   SN 266489
Caerwedros   SN 376557
Cardigan   SN 164464
Castell Gwalter   SN 622868
Dinierth   SN 495624
Humphrey's   SN 440476
Llanio   SN 661579
Llanrhystyd   SN 552696
Meurig
Stephen's   SN 579482
Ystrad Peithyll   SN 653824

Carmarthenshire
Aber Cowyn (Aber Tav)   SN 297136
Carmarthen   SN 413420
Cenarth Fawr   SN 269414
Dinefwr   SN 611217
Kidwelly   SN 409070
Laugharne   SN 302107
Llandovery   SN 767342
Llanegwad
Llanelly   SN 501004
Llanstephan   SN 351101
Llychewin   SN 709276
Pencader   SN 444362
St Clears   SN 280154

Denbighshire
Chirk (Castell y Waun)   SJ 291375
Denbigh   SJ 052660
Llanfair Rhyd Castell
Overton   SJ 356435
Tomen y Faerde (Ial)   SJ 192561
Tomen y Rhodwydd (Buddugre)   SJ 177516
Wrexham (Erddig)   SJ 327487

Flintshire
Basingwerk   SJ 220734
Ewloe   SJ 290673
Hawarden   SJ 319653
Holywell   SJ 186762
Llys Edwin   SJ 235697
Mold   SJ 235644
Prestatyn   SJ 073833
Rhuddlan   SJ 026777
Rofft   SJ 357561

Glamorgan
Aber Afan   SS 768920

Glamorgan
Bishopston SS 582900
Cadwallon ST 137969
Cardiff ST 180767
Coed y Cwm (St Nicholas)
  ST 083736
Coity SS 923816
Dinas Powis
Fonmon ST 048682
Kenfig SS 801827
Llandeilo-Talybont SN 587027
Llangenydd SS 870810
Llantrithyd ST 045727
Loughor SS 564980
Morgraig ST 160843
Neath SS 753977
Newcastle Bridgend SS 902801
Ogmore SS 882769
Oystermouth SS 613883
Penard SS 544885
Penllyn SS 979761
Penmaen SS 534880
Penrice SS 492879
Swansea SS 658930
Whitchurch ST 156804

Merionethshire
Bala SH 928361
Crogen SJ 006370
Cymmer SH 732195
Cynfal SH 615016
Deudrait SH 586371
Rug SJ 056438
Tomen y mur SH 705386

Monmouthshire
Abergavenny SO 299139
Ballan Moor (The Berries)
  ST 488895
Caerleon ST 342905
Caerwent ST 470903
Caldicot ST 487885
Chepstow ST 533941
Dingestow SO 455104
Dixton SO 520135

Monmouthshire
Grosmont SO 405244
Llanhilleth SO 219020
Monmouth SO 507129
Newport ST 312884
Rhymney ST 210789
St Mellons ST 227803
Skenfrith SO 457203
Usk SO 377010
White SO 380168

Montgomeryshire
Caereinion SJ 163055
Carreghofa
Llandinam SO 046905
Mathrafal SJ 131107
Montgomery SO 214980
Walwern SH 891026
Welshpool

Pembrokeshire
Cammeis SN 082401
Carew SN 045037
Cilgerran SN 195431
Haverfordwest SM 953157
Llawhaden SN 073174
Maenclochog SN 083272
Manorbier SS 064978
Narberth
Newport SN 057389
Pembroke SM 982016
Tenby SN 138005
Wiston SN 022181

Radnorshire
Bleddfa SO 209682
Boughrood SO 132391
Colwyn SO 108540
Crug Eryr SO 158593
Cymaron SO 152703
Knighton
Norton SO 303673
Painscastle SO 167461
Radnor
Rhayader SN 968680

SCOTLAND

Aberdeenshire
Aberdeen
Invernochty   NJ 351129
Inverurie   NJ 782206

Angus
Forfar
Invergowrie   NO 395307
Lunan Bay
Montrose

Argyll
Fraoch Eilean   NN 108252
Inchconnell   NM 976119
Somerled's
Sween   NR 714788

Ayrshire
Ayr   NS 333224
Carrick
Craigie   NS 409318
Greenan
Irvine   NS 309409

Berwickshire
Lauder

Bute
Rothesay   NS 078648

Caithness
Thurso

Dumfriesshire
Annan   NY 199666
Caerlaverock   NY 026656
Castlemilk   NY 150775
Dumfries   NX 970764
Lochmaben   NY 089812

East Lothian
Dunbar   NT 678792
Eldbotle   NT 865857
Linlithgow   NT 002773

Fife
Crail   NO 603074
St Andrew's   NO 513169

Inverness
Inverness
Roy   NJ 007219

Kincardineshire
Dunottar   NO 882839
Kincardine   NO 671751

Kirkcudbrightshire
Urr   NX 816648

Lanarkshire
Kilbride

Mid Lothian
Edinburgh   NT 251735

Morayshire
Duffus   NJ 189673
Elgin   NJ 212629
Forres   NJ 034587

Nairnshire
Auldearn   NH 917556
Nairn   NH 885566

Orkney
Cairston   HY 263112
Cubbie Roo's, Wyre   HY 442264
Damsay   HY 390140
Kirkwall   HY 448110

Peeblesshire
Oliver's   NT 099250
Peebles   NT 236405

Perthshire
Alyth
Cargill   NO 157373
Kinclaven   NO 158376
Perth

Renfrewshire
Neilston
Renfrew

Ross and Cromarty
Dun Lagaidh   NH 143913
Dunscath   NH 820694
Ederdover   NH 584495

GUIDE TO CASTLES

Roxburghshire
Hawick   NT 499140
Jedburgh NT 647202
Roxburgh NT 713337

Selkirkshire
Selkirk   NT 470281

Stirlingshire
Stirling NS 790940

West Lothian
Abercorn NT 083794

IRELAND

Antrim
Antrim   J 1586
Carrickfergus J 4287
Doonmore   D 1842

Armagh
Maincore

Carlow
Carlow   S 7177
Castlemore (Tullow) S 8574
Leighlin   S 6465
Tullow   S 8574

Cavan
Cloghoughter H 3405
Kilmore   H 3804
Turbet   H 3617

Clare
Killaloe   R 7074

Cork
Castlemartyr W 9674
Cork   W 6174
Inchiquin   X 0176

Donegal
Assaroe   G 8662
Ballintra G 9068

Down
Ardglass   J 5637
Ardkeen   J 5957
Ballyroney   J 2240
Castleskreen J 4740
Clough   J 4140
Downpatrick J 4845
Dromore   J 2153

Down
Dundonald J 4274
Dundrum   J 4037
Lismahon   J 4339
Oniahc

Dublin
Castlekevin   T 1892
Castleknock   O 0736
Dublin   O 1734
Kildreenan   O 2525
Newcastle Lyons O 0234

Galway
Meelick M 9314
Tuam   M 4352

Kildare
Ardree   S 6698
Balimore Eustace N 9311
Bigarz   S 6698
Kilkea   S 7497
Maynooth   N 9338
Naas   N 8919
Narraghmore   N 7402

Kilkenny
Castlecomer S 5273
Kells   S 4643
Kilkenny   S 5056
Knocktopher S 5337
Tibraghny   S 5715
Tullabarry S 4572

Laoighise (Leix)
Dunamase S 5797
Killeshin S 6777
Lavagh   S 3283

Laoighise (Leix)
Lea   N 5312
Reban   S 5898
Timahoe   S 5390

Limerick
Adare   R 4546
A'qi
Ardpatrick   R 2161
Askeaton   R 3350
Blathatch   R 5858
Caherconlish   R 6750
Carrickittle   R 2626
Carigogunnel   R 4655
Castleconnell   R 6563
Knockainy   R 6738
Limerick   R 5758
Shanid   R 2448

Londonderry
Coleraine   C 8532
Mount Sandel   C 9020

Longford
Granard   N 3382

Louth
Ardee   N 9690
Carlingford   J 1810
Drogheda   O 0976
Dundalk   J 0507
Louth   N 9800
Mount Ash   H 9514

Meath
Athboy   N 7265
Clonard   N 6544
Derver (Loughan)   N 6680
Derrypatrick   N 8272
Duleek   O 0468
Galtrim   N 7949
Kells   N 7476
Killallon   N 6468
Kilmessan   N 8755
Knowth   N 9974
Nobber   N 8286
Rathwire   N 5343

Meath
Ratoath   O 0351
Skreen   N 9458
Slane   N 9674
Trim   N 8057

Monaghan
Clones   H 4926
Donaghmoyne   H 8506

Offaly
Ballyboy   N 2312
Birr   N 0504
Clonmacnoise   N 0130
Drumcullen   N 0007
Durrow   N 3131
Geashill   N 4322
Kinnclare
Kinnitty   N 1508

Roscommon
Boyle   G 7903

Tipperary
Ardfinnan   S 0818
Ardmayle   S 0547
Kilfeakle   R 9939
Kiltinan   S 3728
Knockgraffon   S 0241
Lorrha   M 9204
Nenagh   R 8679
Roscrea   S 1389
Thurles   S 1259

Waterford
Dungarvan   X 2593
Lismore   X 0498
Waterford

Westmeath
Ardnurcher   N 2638
Athlone   N 0341
Castletown Delvin   N 6062
Fore   N 5270
Kilbixie   N 3162
Killare   N 2748
Loxhundy   N 1853
Rathconrath   N 2953

GUIDE TO CASTLES

Wexford
Baginbun S 5412
Carrick T 0023
Ferns
Wexford T 0522

Wicklow
Arklow T 2373
Newcastle Mackynegan O 2903
Wicklow T 3194

ISLE OF MAN

Cronk y Mur SC 204696

Rushen SC 265675

CHANNEL ISLES

Guernsey
Cornet

Jersey
Mont Orgueil

SCILLY ISLES

Scilly